THE WORLD'S GREATEST
RAILWAYS

THE WORLD'S GREATEST
RAILWAYS

CHRISTOPHER CHANT

An illustrated encyclopedia with over 600 photographs

LORENZ BOOKS

This edition published in 2010 by Lorenz Books,
an imprint of Anness Publishing Ltd,
Hermes House, 88–89 Blackfriars Road,
London SE1 8HA, UK; tel. 020 7401 2077;
fax 020 7633 9499; www.lorenzbooks.com;
www.annesspublishing.com

UK agent: The Manning Partnership Ltd;
tel. 01225 478444; fax 01225 478440;
sales@manning-partnership.co.uk
UK distributor: Book Trade Services;
tel. 0116 2759086; fax 0116 2759090;
uksales@booktradeservices.com;
exportsales@booktradeservices.com
North American agent/distributor:
National Book Network; tel. 301 459 3366;
fax 301 429 5746; www.nbnbooks.com
Australian agent/distributor: Pan Macmillan
Australia; tel. 1300 135 113; fax 1300 135 103;
customer.service@macmillan.com.au
New Zealand agent/distributor: David Bateman
Ltd; tel. (09) 415 7664; fax (09) 415 8892

Contents

Chapter One
EARLY PIONEERS

PAGES 6-7: *The Lackawanna Valley, by George Inness.*

RIGHT: *The engine* Firefly *on a new trestle built by the Union Construction Corps on the Orange & Alexandria Railroad during the American Civil War.*

PAGE 9: *Tin mine between Cambourne and Redruth, Cornwall, England. From H. Besley's* Views of Devonshire and Cornwall, *Exeter, circa 1860.*

9

EARLY PIONEERS

The date 27 September 1825 is generally regarded as the beginning of the 'Railway Age', for on this day the word's first public steam line, the Stockton & Darlington Railway, opened for business. It should not be forgotten, however, that the day's run by George Stephenson's *Locomotion No. I* marked only one evolutionary and commercial stage in a process that had begun slowly many years earlier and was destined to proceed with increasing rapidity into the present.

This process may be deemed to have begun with the wooden tracks and wheeled trucks believed to have been used by German mining operators, possibly as early as the 12th century. Such a system, powered by men and/or draft animals, spread slowly to other mining areas of Europe, but became common in Britain only in the 17th century when systems of wooden tracks for wheeled trucks became increasingly common in the coal-mining regions of north-east England. Although workable, as indicated by the fact that it lasted for so long, the system was by no means fully practical, although a move in this direction came in the 18th century, when the wooden rails were replaced by cast iron rails that were considerably better lasting as well as

stronger than their wooden predecessors, and as such also paved the way for the advent of powered traction in the form of the steam locomotive, which became increasingly accepted in the first quarter of the 19th century.

The steam locomotive was a true child of the Industrial Revolution, and also helped to make this revolution the world-shattering force that it soon became. As is often the case with movements that rapidly become huge forces for change in the world, it is difficult to put a precise date on its beginning, but it is fair to say that by about 1760 in Britain the combination of scientific and technological development, the availability of raw materials such as iron and coal, and the entrepreneurial spirit was so stimulated that the process was inevitable. Thus the reign of King George III (1760–1820) may be taken as the beginning of the Industrial Revolution that turned the United Kingdom from a country that relied mainly on agriculture and trade for its livelihood into a country that based its living on the manufacture and export of goods.

In any such country the swift and economical delivery of raw materials to the factories, and the steady shipment of

George Stephenson (1781–1848), a British locomotive and railway pioneer, builder of the Rocket *and engineer for the Stockton & Darlington and Liverpool & Manchester Railways.*

finished goods to major cities and ports are both essential to economic success and continued growth. Canals certainly played their part in the movement of bulk freight such as coal and iron to the factories, but was too slow and roundabout for the outward movement of finished goods, which in any case needed to reach more destinations than could be served by the

geographically limited canal network, even when aided by horse-drawn wagons. Another factor of the Industrial Revolution that helped the invention and development of railways was the change in the pattern and distribution of the British population. Manufacturing industries had to be highly concentrated, leading to the rapid growth of the population of industrial cities: these new urban populations could not of course feed themselves, and their demand for food could only be met by the timely arrival of fresh produce from the surrounding countryside. And as the cities continued to grow as the Industrial Revolution gathered pace, the area from which food had to be shipped increased to the extent that only railways could supply the right quantities in the time before the food began to rot.

The single most important factor that allowed the development of a successful railway network in the United Kingdom was steam power, itself both a child of the early Industrial Revolution and parent of the later one. As suggested above, however, the 'railway concept' was much older than the Industrial Revolution. Certainly by the beginning of the 16th century, for example, German miners had found that it was easier to move their heavy loads of coal if their

BELOW: *An advertisement for the first passenger railway carriage called* The Experiment *to operate on the Stockton & Darlington Railway, whose main purpose was to transport coal. The* Experiment *was a crude version of an omnibus on wheels.*

RIGHT: *George III, 1738–1820 (reigned from 1760), shown in military uniform in a full-length portrait by William Beechey, (1775–1839).*

BELOW: *A railway in a mine. From Sebastian Munster's* Cosmographie, *1550. This is said to be the earliest picture of a railway.*

cart wheels ran on smooth tracks. The solution was to lay parallel tracks of wooden planks over the rough ground and push the carts along them. The inevitable problem was how to prevent the carts from wandering off the tracks on their flat-rimmed wheels: the solution evolved by the middle of the 15th century in places such as Leberthal in Alsace was the railed cart, and by the middle of the 18th century this had been developed into a system of flanged metal wheels running on cast iron rails. This improved the overall capability of the system to the extent that horses could be used to haul the carts, which were soon developed into wagons with yet-heavier loads, on what became known as tramways or wagonways.

By the beginning of the 19th century steam was well established as the fixed power source driving the Industrial Revolution, most notably in the steam engines designed by James Watt in the 1780s, developments on originals by Thomas Newcomen: these were low-pressure beam engines, and were used principally to pump water out of mines. These early steam engines were not notably efficient, and were also very heavy. Even so, far-sighted inventors were already at work trying to develop a steam-powered form of transport. Two of the earliest pioneers were James Watt and William Murdoch, who sought to exploit the possibilities inherent in steam power for the creation of a mechanical road carriage.

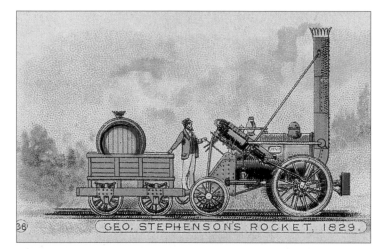

GEO. STEPHENSON'S ROCKET, 1829.

Less far-sighted but eminently more practical was a Cornishman, Richard Trevithick, who appreciated that the best way to harness the power of current steam engines was in a locomotive for use on a wagonway. Starting work in the 1790s, Trevithick embarked on the design of high-pressure steam engines offering a considerably better power/weight ratio than their predecessors. It is to Trevithick that there falls the distinction of having built the world's first practical steam locomotive, which first ran at Coalbrookdale in Shropshire in 1803. Trevithick's next steam locomotive (page 13) was completed in the following year for use on the tramroad of the Pen-y-Darren ironworks in South Wales, and in trials proved itself able to haul wagons carrying 15 tons of iron. The third

TOP LEFT: George Stephenson's Rocket, *winner of the Rainhill Trials in 1829.*

TOP: The Pitman: from George Walker's The Costume of Yorkshire, *Leeds, 1814. Left of the picture is a steam locomotive built by Matthew Murray for John Blenkinsop which was used to haul coal from Middleton Colliery to Leeds.*

LEFT: Barge viaduct over the Irwell on the Bridgewater Canal, England. Engineer: James Brindley.

RIGHT: Bottom of a pit shaft with a train of wagons waiting to be hoisted to the surface. Note the flanged wheels on the coal wagon. Picture first published in 1860.

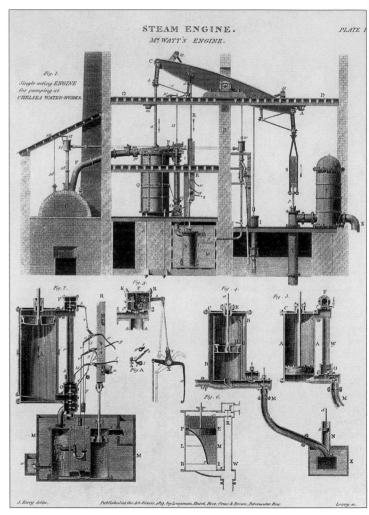

of Trevithick's engines was completed soon after this, and was the *Catch-Me-Who-Can*, a steam locomotive powered by a single vertical cylinder at the rear and which was demonstrated during 1808 near Euston in London (see page 12): behind a sturdy fence, the trials of this pioneering steam locomotive were undertaken on a circular track pulling a single carriage.

Trevithick's steam engines were of the type with a geared drive from a single front- or rear-located cylinder to smooth flanged wheels. The steam locomotives were in themselves moderately successful at the technical level, but their development was

TOP: *Wooden trucks on the wagonway at the head of the Derby Canal at Little Eaton. Coal from the Denby Colliery near Derby, England was loaded into these wagons and hauled by horses to the canal side, where is was loaded by crane, still in the wagon body, into canal boats for on-shipment. The tramway was built following an Act of Parliament of 1793 and operated until 1908.*

RIGHT: *Watt's steam engine, built for the Chelsea waterworks, London. From a print published in London in 1820.*

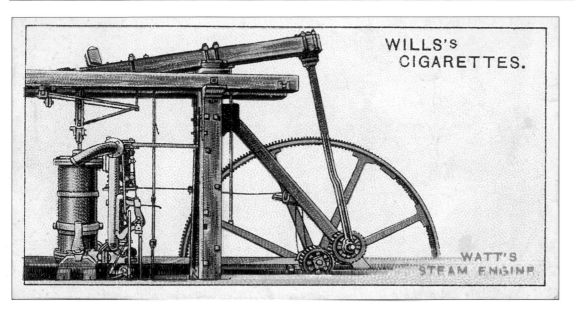

WILL'S
CIGARETTES.

WATT'S
STEAM ENGINE.

to a certain extent a dead end, for there was immense antipathy to the primitive wagonways by ironworkers and others who feared for the loss of their jobs if horses were replaced by steam locomotives. Moreover, the wagonways of the period were in any event insufficiently strong to carry the weight of the locomotive (derived from a stationary steam engine and therefore very heavy) without frequent breakages.

While the South Wales iron industry may have rejected the steam locomotive, the coal-mining industry of north-east England was more perceptive. In 1812 the

Middleton Colliery Railway (established by Act of Parliament in 1758) started to use the world's first commercial steam locomotive, designed by Matthew Murray (page 13). This locomotive had two vertical cylinders and ran on strong cast iron rails, one of which had a rack section engaged by a matching rack on the locomotive's geared driving wheel to ensure maximum traction. By 1820 steam locomotives designed by Timothy Hackworth, George Stephenson and William Hedley were in service on the comparatively steep wagonways of the collieries at which these men were the chief engineers.

ABOVE: A steam engine of James Watt's own design showing sun-and-planet gear converting up-and-down motion of beam to rotary motion for driving machinery. From a cigarette card published in 1915.

ABOVE RIGHT: *Thomas Newcomen's schematic steam engine. A colour print published in London in the early 19th century. Newcomen lived from 1663–1729.*

RIGHT: *James Watt (1736–1819), Scottish engineer and inventor. From a chromolithograph published in London in 1824.*

LEFT and ABOVE: Catch-Me-Who-Can, *a railway locomotive designed by Richard Trevithick in 1808. It was demonstrated on a circular track near to where Euston Station, London now stands.*

OPPOSITE

TOP LEFT: *Portrait of English engineer Richard Trevithick (1771–1833) after the 1816 portrait by John Linnell. Trevithick specialized in the design of high-pressure road and railway locomotives.*

TOP RIGHT: *Trevithick's high-pressure tram engine for Pen-y-Darren ironworks, South Wales (1804).*

BELOW: *Steam locomotive built by Matthew Murray for John Blenkinsop and used to haul coals from Middleton Colliery to Leeds, beginning in August 1912.*

in Northumberland ran on flanged wheels with the driving wheels powered by two vertical cylinders powering a chain drive between the axles.

All of these pioneering efforts were undertaken on private 'railways' designed solely for the movement of coal and some of the collieries' heavy equipment. Considerable design, manufacturing and operating experience had been gained, however, and this proved invaluable when the world's first public steam railway was planned. The spur for this development was the need of local businessmen to move coal as well as goods between the mines in the south of County Durham and the port of Stockton on the River Tees. The local consortium employed the self-taught Stephenson, a young colliery engineer from Northumberland, as the chief engineer of the Stockton & Darlington Railway. Stephenson designed and supervised the construction of the track, and also designed and built the pioneering steam locomotive *Locomotion No. I*, which as noted above initiated the 'Railway Age' in September 1825 by hauling a load of 68 tons along the 21-mile (34-km) track from Shildon to Stockton. There was enormous enthusiasm for the overall concept, but the fact that people did not altogether trust the concept of steam locomotion is demonstrated in its first eight years of operation in that the Stockton & Darlington Railway moved only coal and goods under steam power, people being transported in horse-drawn carriages.

Even so, George Stephenson must be regarded as the 'father of the railway'.

Hedley's *Puffing Billy* (page 14), introduced in 1813, was a notable advance over its predecessors as it was driven by a single crank on one side. As originally completed, the *Puffing Billy* had a 0-4-0 configuration, but was then revised to a 0-8-0 layout in an effort to better cope with the poor track on which it ran, but then reverted to the original configuration. Hedley's next steam locomotive was the *Wylam Dilly*. Stephenson's 0-4-0 steam locomotive of 1815 for the Killingworth Colliery Railway

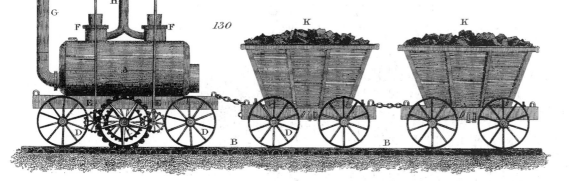

OPPOSITE

TOP LEFT: *William Hedley's* Puffing Billy *(1813). From Amédée Guillemin's* The Applications of Physical Force, *London, 1877.*

TOP RIGHT: *The Baltimore & Ohio* Tom Thumb *locomotive, with additional horse power.*

BELOW LEFT: *An early 1850s Baltimore & Ohio train with stagecoach and covered wagon.*

BELOW RIGHT: *The* Experiment, *the first passenger coach built by George Stephenson for the Stockton & Darlington Railway in 1825.*

Despite the technical success of *Locomotion No. 1*, the Stockton & Darlington Railway did not become the world's first steam-worked 'inter-city' passenger line for, after the inaugural run, passenger services reverted to horse power.

Thus it was not until the inauguration of the Liverpool & Manchester Railway in the course of September 1830 that the world's first genuine passenger-carrying railway came into existence. Designed by Stephenson, the Liverpool & Manchester Railway had to overcome considerable engineering difficulties, including that of crossing Chat Moss Bog, and made use of new and more reliable steam locomotives, such as the *Rocket* designed by Robert

Stephenson, George Stephenson's even more talented son.

This was only the beginning of the story, though, and in the mainland of the European continent the introduction of steam railways followed not long after those in the U.K. The first French railway, extending between St.-Étienne and Andrézieux, started operation with horse power in October 1828. Developments in France were comparatively slow at this

BELOW LEFT: *Blenkinsop's cog railway, 1811. This ran from Middleton to Leeds, a distance of 3½ miles (5.6km), and was used to haul coals.*

BELOW: *George Stephenson's engine* Locomotion. *From Louis Figuier's* Les Nouvelles Conquêtes de la Science, *Paris circa 1890.*

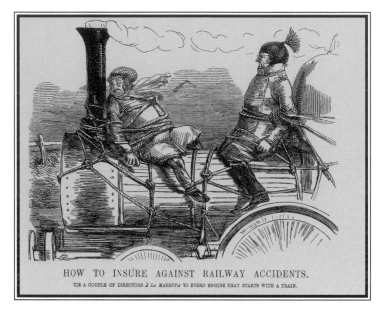

HOW TO INSURE AGAINST RAILWAY ACCIDENTS.
TIE A COUPLE OF DIRECTORS À LA MAZEPPA TO EVERY ENGINE THAT STARTS WITH A TRAIN.

NAVVY IN HEAVY MARCHING ORDER.

STEPHENSON TEACHING THE NAVVIES.

time, however, and by a time as late as 1850 there were a mere 1,927 miles (3100 km) of railway in that country when compared to the British figure of more than 6,600 miles (10620km) in a geographically smaller country. This was an odd time for the development of modern technology in France, and lack of adequate indigenous capabilities (in terms of engineering skills, financial resources and even labourers) meant that the U.K. played a major role in the development of the French railway network in the form of financiers to make the development possible, civil engineers to lay out and build the tracks (often with the aid of 'navvies' imported from the U.K.), and mechanical engineers to design and manufacture the required steam locomotives and rolling stock.

It was not long after the establishment of the first British railways that the concept crossed the Atlantic Ocean to the United States of America. The first U.S. railroad to launch services was the Baltimore & Ohio Railroad, which began with horse-drawn carriages, in April 1827. The first steam locomotives did not arrive in the U.S.A. until 1829 when the distinction of being the first steam locomotive to run on an American railroad, in this instance the Delaware & Hudson Railroad, was secured by the *Stourbridge Lion* (page 20), one of four locomotives bought in the U.K. and shipped across the Atlantic. The locomotive was too heavy for the rails, however, for these rails were of iron-plated wooden construction, therefore the Delaware & Hudson had to return to horse power for several more years.

It was the Baltimore & Ohio that succeeded, on 25 August 1830, in making the first public run of the first American-built steam locomotive, named the *Tom Thumb*. Within a year of this important date, U.S. railroads were becoming increasing well established with steam power, the next two entrants onto this scene being the Camden & Amboy and the Mohawk & Hudson Railroads.

The technical and commercial success of the early railways and railroads spawned a 'vicious circle' in reverse: success spurred the start of more companies, and the continued spread of railway and railroad availability in Europe and the eastern side of the U.S.A. encouraged the growth in passenger and freight traffic, which in turn laid the groundwork for the further expansion of the railway and railroad networks and the launching of new companies.

OPPOSITE

LEFT: A cartoon from Punch *magazine, spring 1853.*

CENTRE: Railway navvies were sent out to the Crimea to build a railway and to help with digging trenches. From Punch *magazine, January 1885.*

RIGHT: George Stephenson instructing the navvies during the construction of the Liverpool & Manchester Railway. From an engraving published circa 1890.

THIS PAGE: Train crossing Chat Moss Bog. From T.T. Bury's Coloured Views on the Liverpool & Manchester Railway, *1831. The engineer was George Stephenson.*

This rapidly overcame the often high levels of suspicion and indeed fear with which steam locomotives had initially been greeted. By the early 1840s, railways and railroads were so popular with the public in general that investors were more than happy to begin pouring capital into existing and also new companies. The result was a huge boom in the financial importance of railways and railroads in a process that was inflated by the general perception that travel behind a steam locomotive was extremely safe and the very epitome of 'modern' peace and prosperity.

This 'railway boom' inevitably led to

failures. Some plans for new railways were realistic, but many others were not, and the period was characterized by the floating of huge numbers of schemes in what became known as 'railway mania'. (*The Times* suggested in 1845 that more than 600 new lines had already been proposed for construction in the U.K., with another 600 likely to be proposed and indeed accepted in the near future.) Lack of financial prudence and the possibility of apparently limitless profits to be made from railway construction and operations persuaded large numbers of investors, small as well as large, to risk their entire capital in railway shares. As is so often the case, however, the 'boom' was followed by a 'bust', in this instance sparked in 1847 when the Bank of England raised its interest rate and investors panicked. Typical of those who eventually lost out was George Hudson (1800–1871), a businessman from York who after receiving a legacy decided to invest in railways and developed the capability of driving down the shares of rival companies so that he could then buy them cheaply and so gain control. Hudson became a member of parliament and by 1846, as the British 'railway king', directly controlled 20 per cent of the British railway system as well as exercising a strong influence over another 30 per cent before his fall as a result of the 'bursting' of the railway bubble and the revelation that he had used illegal methods.

Except in France, the railways of Europe expanded dramatically in extent during a short period, and thus mirrored the corresponding British railway mania. The first steam railway in Bavaria, still an independent kingdom in southern Germany in this period before the unification of 1871, saw the start on 7 December 1835 of its first steam railway, named the Ludwigsbahn in honour of King Ludwig and which extended between Fürth and Nuremburg. This operation used rails and rolling stock manufactured in Germany, but its first steam locomotive was *Der Adler* (The Eagle), an example of the 'Patentee' design built by Robert Stephenson & Company. Other earlier railways completed in Germany included the Saxon State Railway inaugurated in 1837, with a service between Dresden and Leipzig, and a Prussian operation launched in the following year with a line linking Berlin and Potsdam.

European enthusiasm for the railway can be gauged from the fact that initial lines came into existence in Belgium during 1835, in Austria during 1837, the Netherlands during 1839 and in Switzerland during 1844. Progress in Italy was slower, for this region was akin to Germany in that period, being a conglomerate of many small and notionally independent states. Thus the first Italian railway appeared only in October 1839 as a line linking Naples and Portici.

The introduction of railways farther from the U.K. took place slightly later, and the development of railways in these areas was generally slower than in the U.K., Western Europe, the U.S.A. and, to a more limited extent, Canada. In these industrially less advanced regions there was no railway mania. In the Scandinavian area, the first

OPPOSITE

LEFT: The DeWitt Clinton, built for the Mohawk & Hudson Railroad by the West Point Foundry, which made the 17-mile (27-km) trip from Albany to Schenectady in less than an hour.

RIGHT: The David & Gartner locomotive Grasshopper of the Baltimore & Ohio Railroad was built in the 1830s.

THIS PAGE RIGHT: The locomotive Atlantic with a pair of Imlay coaches, built for the Baltimore & Ohio Railroad in 1832.

BELOW RIGHT: Construction crew at work on the Northern Pacific Railroad.

country to introduce a railway was Denmark, where in 1844 the Baltic Line was created to link Altona with Kiel in 1844. As well as having a relative lack of industrial capability, the development of railways in Scandinavia was also made difficult by the harsher climatic and geographical features of the area, and as a result the first Norwegian and Swedish railways did not start business until 1854 and 1856 respectively.

In Russia, the country's first railway was the St. Petersburg and Pavlovsk, which began a mainly horse-drawn service between Tsarskoye Selo and Pavlovsk, using a track gauge of 6ft 0in (1.83m), although the launch of work on the line between Moscow and St. Petersburg in 1851 saw the switch to the 5-ft (1.52-m)

gauge still used in the countries of the former Russian Empire, later to become the Soviet Union and which is now the Commonwealth of Independent States.

Although the advent of the railway had been initially viewed with modest suspicion that later turned to great enthusiasm, there were some who foresaw major catastrophe, fearing that those of nervous disposition (as well as children and animals) would be terrified and that the large-scale ruination of the land was imminent as a result of steam and smoke emissions. Experience soon revealed these fears to be without foundation, and railways soon became accepted in Europe and North America as increasingly 'natural' elements of the landscape in an ever more industrialized age. Simple habituation with the railway

STOURBRIDGE LION.

WILL'S CIGARETTES

⑦

1ST LOCOMOTIVE IN THE U.S.A.

ABOVE: Early U.S. engineers surveying in Cheat River Valley for the Baltimore & Ohio Railroad in the late 1840s.

RIGHT: Laying the first stone of the Baltimore & Ohio Railroad on 4 July 1828.

OPPOSITE
ABOVE LEFT: A view of Euston Station, London in 1837.

ABOVE RIGHT: The opening of the first railway in Canada between La Prairie and St. Johns on 21 July 1836.

BELOW LEFT and RIGHT: Two depictions of the Stourbridge Lion. *It was built in England under the direction of Horatio Allen and was the first locomotive to be used in America, where it was bought to work the Delaware & Hudson Railroad in 1829.*

was one of the reasons for its rapid acceptance, but another was the enormously improved levels of comfort and speed that railway services were able to provide. Opened for service in 1841, for instance, the Great Western Railway offered a journey time between London and Bristol of a mere five hours in comparison to at least 24 and often 48 hours required by the horse-drawn coach services on a road that was very poor despite the fact that it linked two of England's major cities.

Travel by rail was, in its early days, very much something of an adventure, and it was only from 1890 that the standard of overall comfort improved dramatically. In the early days of rail travel, passengers travelling on a first-class ticket had good seats in compartments with glass windows, but there was neither heating nor any corridor linking the various compartments or carriages. Passengers in second-class accommodation had a reduced level of comfort in carriages that were roofed, like those of the first-class passengers, but there was no glass in the windows. Worst off were those travelling third-class in open carriages without roofs, where they were exposed to smoke and sparks pouring from the locomotive's stack.

The profit made from third-class passengers was so small that many companies provided no such accommodation, or ran trains for third-class passengers at wholly inconvenient times and slow speeds. In 1844, however, a third-class passenger froze to death in an

open carriage of the Great Western Railway near Reading in Berkshire, and as a result of the ensuing public outcry, an Act of Parliament was passed ordaining that each railway line should provide at least one covered carriage per day for third-class passengers, who were to be charged no more than 1 penny per mile.

Early trains also lacked the facilities to offer passengers refreshment, and it was not until the later part of the 19th century that restaurant cars became common. Up to that time, passengers were wholly reliant on food they provided for themselves, or had to

take what could be bought at stations, which varied enormously in quality and price.

Another factor that helped rail travel to acquire a measure of common acceptance, especially among the middle classes, was the royal approval of the new transport system provided by Queen Victoria's 1842 journey from Slough, near Windsor in Berkshire, to Paddington in west London. The availability of rail travel now started to change the nature of British society with increasing speed from this time forward, and though most rail travel was the province of the affluent, who could afford first- and second-class accommodation, the poor were still able to travel by rail in the specially arranged excursions, generally between cities and nearby rural beauty spots or coastal resorts that became increasingly popular as the rail network expanded.

On the other side of the Atlantic, the period between the arrival of rail travel and the outbreak of the Civil War in 1861 was marked by a rail mania not unlike that which had swept the U.K. Increasing numbers of railroad companies were established in the states along America's eastern seaboard, most of these producing lines which stretched parallel to the coast; but increasingly, these north/south lines were connected by lateral east/west ones that were swiftly extended westward to the more heavily populated states of the hinterland and also to points on the great rivers and lakes (typically the Mississippi, Missouri and Ohio rivers and Lake Erie) that were the jumping-off points for the increasing numbers of people heading west in wagons in search of new land. Among the 'classic' lines of this period were those connecting Baltimore in Maryland with St. Louis in Missouri, Richmond in Virginia to Memphis in Tennessee, and New York to Lake Erie.

The rapidly developing railroad network therefore allowed the possibility for settlers to move west in larger numbers and begin the process of opening up new territories that the U.S. Government rightly judged to be the practical way of extending the size of the U.S.A. It was within the

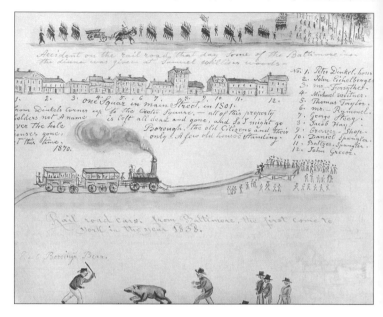

ABOVE: Images of the Baltimore & Ohio Railroad locomotives showing early and late steam examples.

ABOVE RIGHT: Train and coaches, the first to come from Baltimore to York in 1838.

RIGHT: Nickel's Atmospheric Railway carriage of 1845.

OPPOSITE
ABOVE and BELOW: Prosser's Wood Guide-Wheel Railway with engine, tender and carriage, operating on Wimbledon Common, London in 1845.

In 1862, therefore, Congress passed the Pacific Railroad Bill into law, although it was not until the end of the Civil War that work was initiated by two companies. In the east was the Union Pacific Railroad, and in the west the Central Pacific Railroad. The two organizations were given enormous incentives to complete the railroad link as quickly as possible, which included a grant of land to a distance of 10 miles (16km) in alternating strips on each side of the track they laid, and loans of up to $48,000 per mile to help finance construction. There was an inadequate pool of cheap labour for the task within the U.S.A. and as a result large numbers of labourers were shipped in from China. Even so, the railroad link was an enormous and daunting task that was at times hampered by extremes of climate and geography as the two halves of the railroad forged from west and east.

Even so, the transcontinental railroad link across the United States was completed in just four years (rather than the 10 years that had originally been

context of this notion of 'manifest destiny' (a U.S.A. spanning the continent from the Atlantic to the Pacific oceans) that the idea of creating a transcontinental railroad line was first introduced during the Civil War (1861–1865). California, northward to Oregon and Washington, was already part of the United States, but President Abraham Lincoln had realized that if these areas were not to become isolated by the plains and deserts to the east of the Rocky Mountains, a transcontinental railroad link was essential.

ABOVE: *The Conestogo covered wagon and the classic American 4-4-0 locomotive did more than any other types of transport to open up the West.*

LEFT: *Opening of the Leipzig–Althen line in Germany in 1837.*

ABOVE: *A Currier & Ives lithograph of the Niagara Suspension Bridge between the U.S.A. and Canada, 1856.*

ABOVE RIGHT: *An American railroad scene: clearing the snow from the track.*

LEFT: *Navvies at work at Roseby's Rock on the Baltimore & Ohio Railroad, December 1852.*

estimated) and tracks from west and east met on 10 May 1869 at Promontory Point in Utah to create a railroad line some 1,780 miles (2865km) long. A valuable off-spin was the establishment of a transcontinental telegraph service which was developed in parallel to the railroad.

Although the transcontinental railroad link was vitally important for the continued development of America into a single nation in the aftermath of the Civil War, it was by no means the only development of its type. In order to open up additional parts of the western United States, other railroad companies also received comparable land grant aid. The Chicago & North Western, the Burlington, and the Rock Island Railroad companies were only

some of the organizations that received significant incentives to provide profit as they forced the expansion of their lines. By 1890, other railroads had been completed to expand the connection across the U.S.A. These were the Southern Pacific, the Northern Pacific and the Atchison, Topeka & Santa Fe Railroads.

The extraordinary extent and pace of railroad expansion is illustrated most tellingly by a simple statistic: in 1845 there had been slightly more than 9,000 miles (14485km) of railroad line, but by 1890 this had increased to a figure of more than 163,500 miles (263120km).

The development of railroads in Central and South America was a lengthy and complicated matter. The railroad in Mexico

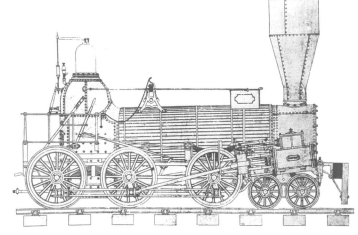

is somewhat atypical, for this substantial network was created between 1880 and 1900, largely with U.S. engineering skills and financing. The Panama Railroad, opened in 1855 long before the excavation of the Panama Canal that made its largely redundant from 1905, was constructed for the important task of moving passengers and, more importantly, freight across this narrowest point of the Central American isthmus, thereby allowing ships to avoid making the long and dangerous passage around Cape Horn and thus providing greater ease of travel, especially for journeys between the U.S.A.'s eastern coast and the Far East.

The development of railroads in South America began somewhat later than in the U.S.A., and was again made possible largely by external finance, although in this instance the capital was provided by European nations rather than the U.S.A. The task of creating an effective railroad network over so vast an area was difficult enough in itself, but was also exacerbated by extremes of climate and geography as well as by frequent instability in the realms of national and international politics.

The development of railroad networks in Africa generally reflected the nature of the various regions and the ambitions of their colonial masters, most notably Belgium, France, Germany and the U.K. In general, each colony was served by a

slowly expanding network of services linking the main port or ports with the hinterland that might produce export cargoes and need the input of European equipment; but the single most ambitious scheme was Cecil Rhodes's 'Cape to Cairo'

line extending through British territory to link Cape Town in South Africa with Cairo (or more importantly Alexandria) in Egypt and thus provide a magnificent north-south route linking most of the British possessions in South, Central and North Africa. This far-sighted, even visionary scheme was terminated by the outbreak of World War I (1914–1918) after which no further progress was made and the line unfortunately came to an end in Rhodesia (now Zimbabwe).

Rhodes played an important part in the race between British and Dutch commercial interests to create a railroad link between South African ports and the gold-mining region of the Witwatersrand. In the event, Rhodes's driving force was largely responsible for the success of the British

31

Cape Government Railway in reaching Johannesburg in September 1892.

The first stage in the development of the world's initial flush of railroad building can be said to have ended in March 1899 when the Great Central Railway, which was the final large-scale railway programme of the age of Queen Victoria, began operation and in the process ended a period of just under three-quarters of a century of almost frantic railway development since the opening of the Stockton & Darlington Railway in 1825. This period had witnessed

revenues), and a measure of internal consolidation as a number of less successful companies were taken over or merged with more successful ones, resulting in the loss of once-celebrated names such as the Liverpool & Manchester and the London & Birmingham. In overall terms, the network of railway lines in the U.K. had reached its definitive goal that was only marginally altered by a small number of later additions.

Just as significantly, the cost of a journey had been vastly reduced in real terms, and rail was now very much the

developments that had made the train considerably faster as well as safer and also more comfortable. By about 1850, the standard design for a steam locomotive was virtually standardized as a 2-2-2 layout, but 50 years later the 4-4-0 layout was mostly standard on the longer British services. Hand-in-hand with improvements in the technology of train movement proper were important advances in other aspects of railway operation, including features such as the Westinghouse braking system, more effective signalling, and the interlinking of

OPPOSITE
ABOVE LEFT and BELOW: *Pope Pius IX and the papal train in Italy in the 1860s.*

ABOVE RIGHT: *Locomotive pulling a train towards the Mont Cenis Tunnel which linked France with Italy. This was the first of the great alpine tunnels to be completed. From* The Illustrated London News, *1869.*

BELOW RIGHT: *The station at Campobasso, Italy, 1883.*

LEFT: *An early mixed passenger-freight train on the Belgian State Railway.*

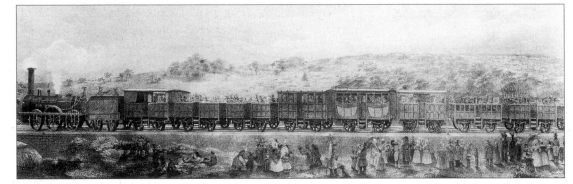

enormous developments in bringing a measure of sophistication to the railroad, both in steam locomotive technology and such ancillary services as signalling, the construction of a vast rail network linking virtually every populated region of the U.K. (often by two different companies, each with its own station, as a result of rivalry between companies to secure the maximum possible numbers of passengers and their

standard means of travel for all classes of society in the absence of rivals such as internal combustion-engined road vehicles although, for any with eyes to see, the writing was on the wall as the first primitive cars made an appearance.

Part of the pre-eminence of the train, hauled by a steam locomotive, stemmed from the absence of any realistic rival, but also from the rapid pace of technical

signals and points, which had done wonders to improve public confidence in the train, not only as a means of getting from one place to another in comfort at a moderately high speed, but also for travelling from one place to another in safety without the possibility of collision or failure to stop when required.

Also worthy of note in this area of British railway development was the

LEFT: *An early track inspection car and crew, circa 1890.*

OPPOSITE
LEFT: *The highly spectacular steel Lethbridge Viaduct under construction, Alberta, Canada.*

RIGHT: *S.S.* Slocan *at the wharf at Rosebery, British Columbia with the Canadian Pacific passenger train coming in from Nakusp 30 miles (48km) to the north. The train discharged passengers at Rosebery destined for points south on Slocan Lake, the remaining passengers going east to Sandon or Kaslo on Lake Kootenay.*

solution of the 'Gauge Question', which made standard a single track gauge for British railway lines and thereby made it eventually possible for any combination of steam locomotive and rolling stock to travel virtually the whole extent of the British network. After considerable deliberation and argument, in 1850 a royal commission ruled that the British national track gauge should be 4ft 8½in (1.432m) rather than the figure of 7ft 0in (2.436m) that had been adopted by the Great Western Railway at the instigation of the great engineer Isambard Kingdom Brunel. The Great Western Railway began to modify its track network in the early part of the 1870s, but completed the task only in 1892 with the conversion of the final stretch in the line extending between Paddington in London and Penzance in Cornwall.

This development of the railway networks, and the consolidation of the companies operating trains over them, was mirrored in Europe over much the same period, and at much the same time the separate railway networks of each country were gradually linked together to create a greater system of lines covering most of industrialized Europe and many lesser regions. Germany, however, made the slowest progress in this direction where efforts at rationalization were effectively stymied by the fact that until 1871, and the creation of a unified Germany after the

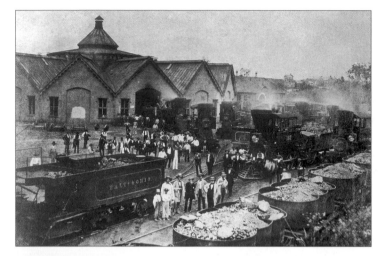

Franco-Prussian War of that year, Germany was a hotchpotch of large and smaller states, all of which guarded their 'individualities' with enormous zeal.

One of the main beneficiaries of this creation of a pan-European railway network was the Compagnie des Wagons-Lits established by Georges Nagelmackers, a Belgian, to provide services of the highest quality for the rich in the form of extremely comfortable accommodation (including sleeper berths for the night sections of these long-distance routes), excellent facilities and the best of food and wine. The most celebrated of the Wagons-Lits' services was the *Orient Express* from Paris in France to Constantinople (now Istanbul) in Turkey, but other notable services were the *Calais–Nice–Rome Express* and the *Sud*

RIGHT: *Poster advertising train tickets at Hornellsville for the Erie Railway.*

OPPOSITE

TOP LEFT: *Baltimore & Ohio Railroad 'Camelbacks' at Martinsburg, Virginia with, in the foreground, a coal train bound for Baltimore in 1858.*

TOP RIGHT: *The original Stoney Creek Bridge, British Columbia.*

BELOW: *The Bridge at Canyon Diablo in Arizona on the Atchison, Topeka & Santa Fe Railroad.*

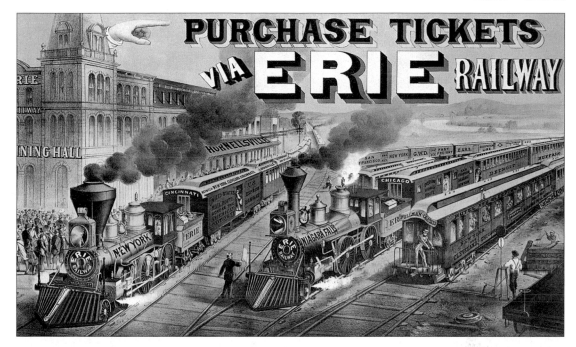

Express linking Paris with the Portuguese capital of Lisbon via Madrid.

The railway network grew only slowly in Russia, where a mere 108 miles (174km) in 1850 was extended in the following 20 years to just 5,000 miles (8050km). During the next 30 years, however, there was a major surge in Russian railway-building with the result that by the turn of the century its network totalled more than 27,000 miles (43450km), including the justly celebrated

Trans-Siberian Railway connecting Moscow in western Russia with Vladivostok on the Pacific Ocean and by extension Port Arthur. Work on the Trans-Siberian Railway began in 1891 and was completed just under 10 years later after prodigious efforts under extraordinarily difficult conditions.

Farther to the east, Japan inaugurated its first railway in 1872. This was relatively late in comparison with many other countries as a result of the country's

essential medievalism in the period leading up to the Meiji restoration and the decision to turn Japan into a modern industrial nation; but Japan then made rapid strides and by 1890 possessed some 1,500 miles (2400km) or more of track.

By 1900, therefore, the impact of the railway and railroad as a force for economic and social change was fully evident, not least for its part in the creation and exploitation of the mass transportation market. Scrutiny of revenues

reveals that it was the transport of goods that yielded the greater part of the profits even though this was the more unglamorous aspect of the business, the imagination of the public having been caught more fully by passenger operations in general, and express passenger services in particular. The glamour attached to express passenger services should not be decried, moreover, for it was this aspect of the rail business, with its higher passenger revenues, that introduced restaurant

37

carriages as well as ones for passengers that were smoother-running and therefore more comfortable, and also pioneered innovatory features such as corridors linking compartments, toilet facilities and effective heating. The increasing levels of comfort evident from 1890 in longer-distance express services marked a major change in the concept of passenger travel, and the features soon became so standardized that they began to be extended further down the ladder, becoming available to ordinary passengers travelling shorter distances.

The need to cater for the creature comforts of the larger numbers of passengers paying lower fares was also spurred by the competition between rail companies, especially when two of these

were serving the same area and the competition between them was at its most direct. Another facet of this competition was speed of service, for it soon came to be appreciated that, in general, passengers preferred the faster service even if this meant travelling in slightly less comfortable surroundings.

OPPOSITE

TOP: *Baltimore & Ohio 4-4-0 Locomotive No. 232, built by William Mason at Taunton, Massachusetts in 1875 and seen here along the Potomac river near Cumberland, Maryland.*

BELOW LEFT: *The four-tiered 780-ft (238-m) long trestle built by Union engineers at Whiteside, Tennessee. 1864.*

BELOW RIGHT: *A train ticket of 1858 for the Canadian Grand Trunk Railway from Toronto to Grafton.*

THIS PAGE TOP: *Canadian Pacific Railway construction workers.*

BELOW LEFT: *1868. Construction work on cut No 1 west of the Narrows, Weber Canyon. The Narrows are situated 4 miles (6km) west of Echo and 995 miles (1600km) west of Omaha and presented some of the most difficult grading in the building of the Union Pacific Railroad. Successive shelves were hacked into the rock, then pickaxed and blasted down to grade. Rough, temporary tracks were laid to haul away rubble, while two-wheeled mule carts and wheelbarrows did the job on higher levels.*

FAR RIGHT: *Section gangs, like this Chicago, Burlington & Quincy crew, rode the rails on handcars to replace rotted ties, tamp loose spikes and tighten bolts. As a memento of their shared sense of responsibility, they struck this pose in the 1870s, their foreman's solemn little daughter in a place of honour.*

As noted above, in the U.K. many towns (many of them comparatively small) had at least two railways serving them. For instance, the Great Western Railway and the London & North Western Railway companies each operated on the route linking London and Birmingham and, in the period around the turn of the century, there was intense rivalry between the two to secure the lion's share of the market by providing a two-hour service between the British capital and its main manufacturing centre in the Midlands.

The distances covered by many railroad companies in the U.S.A. were generally considerably greater than their counterparts in the U.K., due to the U.S.A.'s generally lower population density and far larger geographical extent. This in no way lessened the rivalry between operators, however, for the same factor of directly competing services was often present. For instance, the route linking New York and Chicago in Illinois, both of them major centres of population, financial services and industry, pitted the New York Central Railroad and the Pennsylvania Railroad companies against one another and by 1902 the Pennsylvania Railroad had trimmed the time of its *Pennsylvania Special* express service to 20 hours.

Railways and railroads also played a not inconsiderable part in creating the nature and extent of the modern cities and conurbations through the inauguration of train services for commuters. This is inevitably a chicken-and-egg situation in which the question of which came first

OPPOSITE: The arrival of the first train into Vancouver, British Columbia on 23 May 1887.

RIGHT: The first passenger trains over the newly-built Canadian Pacific mainline north of Lake Superior were troop trains, carrying soldiers from the east to the scene of the Northwest Rebellion on the prairies.

BELOW: C.P.R 285, the first locomotive built by Canadian Pacific Railways.

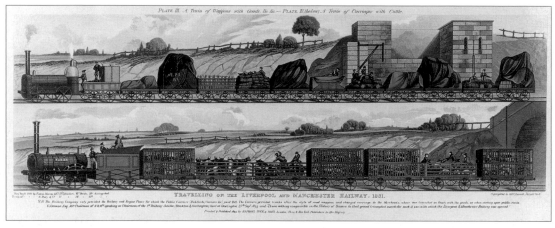

ABOVE: *Travelling on the Liverpool & Manchester Railway, 1831. Top: Goods train drawn by* Liverpool. *Bottom: Cattle train pulled by* Fury.

BELOW: *Top: 1st-class carriages hauled by* Jupiter. *Bottom: 2nd- and 3rd-class carriages drawn by* North Star.

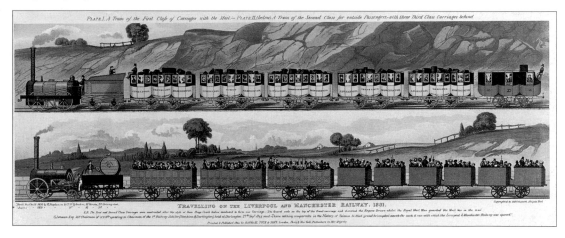

should perhaps be replaced by an appreciation that each is essential to the other. The spread of short-distance rail services from stations located strategically in the central areas of a metropolis to serve as termini for services to and from outlying areas allowed the development of the metropolis as a commercial and administrative centre serviced by workers for whom working rather than living space had to be found. Workers were eventually able to commute on a daily basis to and from their places of work in the metropolis and their homes in the suburbs whose rapid growth turned them into conurbations of the metropolis with the core surrounded by a ring of self-contained towns linked to the metropolis by commuter rail services.

This situation first developed in the areas around major cities, typically London and New York, but the process then acquired an almost inevitable momentum of its own, and as the complexity of modern life gradually approached the point of choking other increasingly important cities with traffic and a high level of pollution, large parts of their growing populations opted to move to suburbs linked to the city proper by rail services. This tendency was first apparent in other European and North American cities, but the development of important centres of government, commerce and industry in other regions has seen the development of basically the same concept in countries as widely separated as Australia, Brazil, India and Japan, whose major cities have gradually become conurbations as their cores are surrounded

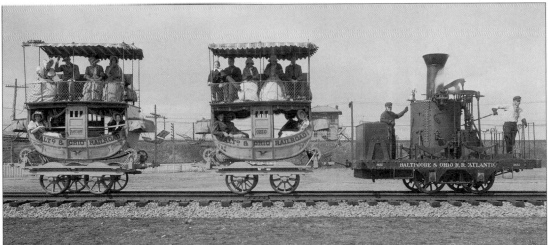

ABOVE LEFT: *In its eagerness to push towards Utah in its race with the westward-building Union Pacific, Central Pacific bridged many of the High Sierra chasms with timber trestles. When the railroad was completed, they came back and the Chinese labourers that built the railroad filled them in with solid earth and embankments.*

ABOVE: *The Union locomotive* Fred Leach *after escaping from the Confederates. The holes in the smokestack show where the shots struck while she was working on the Orange & Alexandria Railroad near Inion Mills. 1 August 1863.*

LEFT: *Replica Baltimore & Ohio Railroad* Atlantic *heads a train at the Fair of the Iron Horse, Seattle, 1927.*

by belts of suburbs and growing commuter networks still based largely on the train even though road transport has eroded its previously predominant position. In this instance it is worthy of note that the improvements in the creature comforts enjoyed by long-distance passengers were generally not mirrored in the trains built for the commuter; rather it was believed that the monopoly in this short-distance trade could be made most profitable by packing in the maximum numbers of passengers who, in realistic terms, had no other means of travelling between their places of work and their homes.

In overall terms, therefore, it can be seen that the commuter services not only provided an essential service for suburban areas, but also helped to create and fashion

OPPOSITE. A refurbished 4-4-0 representing Jupiter *at Promontory Point, Utah, from Cecil B. DeMille's movie* Union Pacific.

ABOVE: A still of the Golden Spike ceremony at Promontory Point, Utah, from Cecil B. DeMille's movie Union Pacific.

ABOVE RIGHT: Driving in the golden rivet (spike) in the ceremony connecting the Atlantic and Pacific by railroad. Promontary, Utah, 10 May 1869.

RIGHT: Union Pacific construction train, 1868.

ABOVE LEFT: *Ruins of the Confederate engine-house at Atlanta, Georgia showing the engines* Telegraph *and* O.A. Bull *in September 1864.*

ABOVE RIGHT: *A construction crew of the 1850s.*

LEFT: *A scene on the Union Pacific Railroad in 1868 showing a construction train from General Casement's outfit near the railhead at Bear River City. Such trains included flat cars for tools, a forge for blacksmithing, coaches for sleeping and other cars for cooking, eating and storage.*

OPPOSITE
ABOVE LEFT: *Construction of the Northern Pacific Railroad at Big Rock, one mile above Cabinet.*

ABOVE RIGHT: *An historic occasion when Great Northern officials drove the final spike into a roughly hewn cross tie to complete a continuous track from Minnesota's twin cities to Puget Sound, Cascade Mountains on 6 January 1893.*

BELOW: *Crew of the first train west of the Big Savage Tunnel near Deal, Maryland on the Western Maryland Railroad, 29 October 1911.*

them as additional suburbs were generally built close to suburban commuter rail lines.

In the areas removed from the major conurbations, the railway and railroad companies operated slower branch services to cater for the needs of these smaller and less bustling towns. In concept, this type of service was different from that designed for the commuter, which had to make frequent stops at closely-spaced stations. Branch services, on the other hand, largely connected rural towns that were more widely separated, possessed smaller populations, and were in no real way wholly dependent on the train services. These branch services generally linked their mainline services to a town of modest size, but were generally created by local interests as a convenience rather than a total necessity. As a result, the profit margins of such operations were small if not absent, and the speed of their services was low. The importance of such branch services should not be underestimated, however, for they were of considerable importance in allowing the relatively rapid transport of farm produce from the country to the metropolis in the period before the useful life of such produce could be economically extended by refrigeration.

Given the fact that it was in the U.K. that the railway began life as a commercial proposition, it was inevitable that it should be the British experience, at the practical as well as the theoretical level, that was widely responsible for stimulating the creation of fledgling railways and railroads in many other parts of the world. This naturally

included the export of the hardware required for these developments, for the U.K. was the world's leading manufacturing and exporting nation of the period. British companies did export relatively simple items such as rails, but these were soon manufactured in most of the countries in which they were used, so of greater long-term importance was the export of key features of the rolling stock (axles, wheels etc.), as well as complete steam locomotives, of which the first 'best seller' was the Stephenson 'Patentee', a 2-2-2 type that was extensively used on pioneering rail networks all over the world. This technical lead and export skill combined with the

ABOVE LEFT: *On 31 December 1886 the city council of Fort Madison, Iowa passed an ordinance granting the Chicago, Santa Fe and California Railroad the right to construct in Iowa. On 1 January 1887, construction work began on the Fort Madison embankment.*

ABOVE: *Inspection Locomotive No. 1370, built at Beardstown in 1886. It was later renumbered twice, and was retired in June, 1924.*

LEFT: *The first Northern Pacific passenger train into Minnewaukon. The engine was called* Dakota, *the fireman was William Buckley and the engineer George Kingsley.*

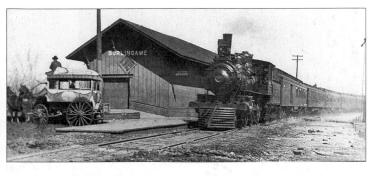

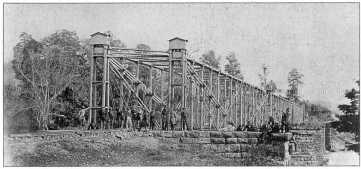

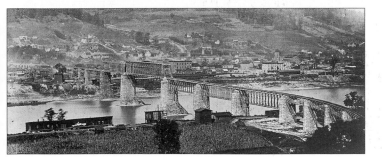

ABOVE: *An 1882 poster by Swaim & Lewis advertising the Illinois Central Railroad.*

LEFT TOP: *An early 4-6-0 locomotive on the Santa Fe Railway at Burlingame.*

CENTRE: *A Wendell Bollman truss bridge crossing the Monorgahela River near Fairmont, West Virginia. Originally a single track, it was later doubled and carried traffic between 1852 and the 1930s.*

BOTTOM: *Baltimore & Ohio Railroad bridge over the Ohio river between Benwood, West Virginia and Bellaire, Ohio, built in 1871.*

nature of the U.K. in the Victorian age as the world's most significant financial and colonial power, made it inevitable that British railway expertise would extend far and wide.

Railway networks were of signal importance to the British as they extended and consolidated their empire in the second half of the 19th century, and the spread of rail transport was instrumental in helping them to open up large areas of hitherto undeveloped territory. To this extent, therefore, burgeoning rail networks in the empire had very considerable economic and social impact. However, most of them were also of strategic importance, and many

ABOVE: *The suspension bridge over the Niagara, 1859.*

ABOVE RIGHT: *Construction of the chemin de fer in Guinea, Africa.*

RIGHT: *The locomotive* Minnetonka *of the Northern Pacific Railroad, purchased in 1870 for use in construction work in northern Minnesota.*

OPPOSITE: *A train crosses Stockport Viaduct on the London & North Western Railway. Note pollution of river banks, smoking chimneys, and complete domination of the scene by the railway viaduct. (Coloured lithograph circa 1845.)*

came complete with a large measure of military input in their location and design so that troops and their equipment could be moved rapidly and surely from main base areas to potential trouble spots. This latter was useful in terms of cost effectiveness, for it allowed the British to garrison their colonial possessions with far fewer troops than would otherwise have been the case: instead of maintaining a small but potentially vulnerable and highly costly garrison in every small region, the British were able to use the strategic mobility provided by the railways to move troops as and when needed.

Some of the earliest colonial railways

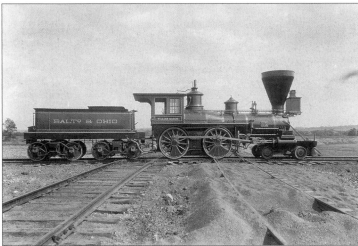

appeared in India, a large, highly populated and very rich country with only a small industrial base. The first railway in India was inaugurated between Bombay and Thana as early as 1853, but in the short term the size of the country and its distance from the U.K. meant that development of a comprehensive railway network was slow. However, as a result of the efforts of one of the country's most far-sighted and effective governors general, Lord Dalhousie, India then developed a very well planned network of railway services that grew steadily in overall size and concept. By 1870 there were lines, each more than 1,000 miles (1600km) long, linking major centres such as Delhi and Calcutta on the one hand and Bombay and Calcutta on the other, and a mere 10 years later the network totalled 9,000 miles (14500km). This length of track may seem, and indeed is small in a country the size of India, which at the time included

LEFT: The Hercules, *built by Garret & Eastwich of Philadelphia in 1837 for the Beaver Meadow Railroad. The locomotive weighed 15 tons, an exceptionally large engine for the period.*

BELOW LEFT: The 1856 Baltimore & Ohio 4-4-0 locomotive William Mason, *posed at the Fair of the Iron Horse, Baltimore. 1927.*

BELOW RIGHT: Chicago & North Western Railroad's The Pioneer *4-2-0.*

OPPOSITE
ABOVE LEFT: A train on the Takanawa Railroad, Japan, circa 1880.

ABOVE RIGHT:
The Express Train, *a print published by Currier & Ives, New York 1870.*

BELOW RIGHT: A Pullman carriage of 1876.

what are now Bangladesh and Pakistan. But the effect of the network was augmented by its careful planning and execution.

The most radical aspect of British railway planning in Africa may have been the 'Cape to Cairo' line planned and partially completed by Cecil Rhodes, as noted above, but it was far from being the only British development on the continent, where there was an enormous surge of railway construction in the period between 1880 and 1920. As in India, there was always an element of strategic thinking in the developments of these lines, which generally reached inland from the main ports to areas of major population and/or economic importance, and typical of the process was the line, more than 500 miles (800km) long, constructed between the Gold Coast (now Ghana) and the deep interior of the country to allow the development of important exports such as manganese, cocoa and timber. The construction of the line, in a gauge of 3ft 6in (1.067m), was completed in the face of a host of obstacles (man-made such as tribal uprisings and natural hazards such as huge ravines and apparently numberless diseases) before the line could start useful work.

Another part of the British empire that secured a major advantage from the local construction of railways was Australia. Here the evolution of the system was fragmented, for it was developed largely for and around the very widely separated centres of population rather than as a means of linking these centres, and a number of different gauges were used, the most popular being a gauge of 3ft 6in (1.067m), but there were also tracks with gauges of 5ft 3in (1.60m) and 4ft 8½in (1.432m).

OPPOSITE: Three lines converged in western South Dakota in the 1880s. On top is a local mine railroad, in the centre the Fremont, Elkhorn & Missouri Valley (a Chicago and North Western subsidiary), while below is a predecessor of today's Burlington Northern.

RIGHT: Plush coach accommodation before the turn of the century.

FAR RIGHT: Interior of the Northern Pacific Railroad's North Coast Limited *in April 1900, the first train lit by electricity to cross the north-west.*

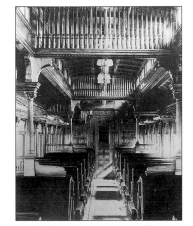

RIGHT: A Union Pacific 4-4-0 of 1870, with its smoke-arresting smokestack, cow-catcher and simple rugged construction that made this locomotive type so suitable for 'frontier' country.

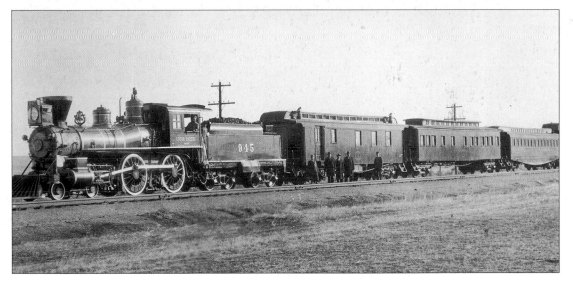

ABOVE: North American Indians who have left their reservation and are attacking a train on the Southern Pacific Railroad, Arizona. The picture was taken from a weekly journal published in Paris in February 1906.

RIGHT: An advertisement for the Chicago & North Western Railroad's Short Line.

LEFT: *Metropolitan Railway Electric Locomotive No.1, with a train of Ashkney coaches bound for Harrow, Middlesex, England in 1904.*

BELOW: *The first suburban train arriving at Park Ridge in 1874. The Chicago & North Western still carries close to 50,000 commuters daily on lines to the west, north and north-west.*

Although much of the pioneering British experience in railway planning and construction was initially exported to the British Empire, it was also spread to other countries, both independent and the colonies of other European powers. It was the growth of this export trade that turned several middle-sized British companies into large operators, and typical of this process were the Vulcan Foundry of Newton-le-Willows in Lancashire, Beyer Peacock of Manchester, Hunslet of Leeds, and North British of Scotland. Thus the British railway influence in parts of the world outside Europe stretched far wider than its imperial

context: the development of South American railways involved the activity of many British railway companies, who constructed lines all over the continent and included the privately British-owned Buenos Aires Great Southern Railway, which had over 5,000 miles (8000km) of track in Argentina, and the British-owned Buenos Aires Great Western Railway that had 1,000 miles (1600km) of track in Argentina. The two most important Chilean railway operators were the Antofagasta Railway and the Nitrate Railway Company, and both of these were British-owned. Inevitably, many of the steam locomotives and much of the rolling

LEFT: *The North-West railway station, Vienna in a painting by Karl Karger, circa 1890.*

ABOVE: *A group of Toronto, Hamilton & Buffalo Railway employees in their office.*

ABOVE: *Front and back covers of a Canadian Pacific Railway (Western Division) pocket time card. This issue came into effect on 3 July 1886.*

LEFT: The Station, *a painting by Frith from 1862.*

RIGHT: *Harrisburg, Pennsylvania, the station in the 1860s just after the American Civil War. Shown here are trains operated by four railroads: Pennsylvania, Northern Central, Cumberland Valley and the Philadelphia & Reading. The first three are now included in the Pennsylvania Railroad system.*

BELOW RIGHT: *An old Grand Trunk railway station at St. Williams, Ontario, Canada.*

stock for these lines was manufactured by British companies.

As the 19th century progressed, however, the British share of the export market was eroded by the increasing success of rival companies, especially those of the U.S.A. This increasing level of export success resulted in part from the increasing size and skill of the American industrial machine, whose rapid growth had been kick-started in the north of the country by the requirements of the Civil War, but also in part by the technical success of American steam locomotives, which were becoming increasingly different from their British counterparts in features such as bar-frame rather than plate-frame construction, 'haystack' fireboxes and, perhaps most

importantly of all, great ruggedness and reliability. This last factor stemmed from the size of the American railroad network and in combination with the relative paucity of towns in which major repairs or even routine maintenance could be undertaken. Thus steam locomotives of American design and manufacture were seldom as attractive in external shape as their European counterparts, but on the other hand were very reliable, easy to maintain and powerful. This last was of singular importance in many parts of South America, for instance, where it was the norm for heavy trains to be operated over lines with frequent gradients of a severity seldom encountered in the U.K. and Europe.

OPPOSITE
ABOVE LEFT and RIGHT: *Steam-coaches on the Pilatus rack railway in Switzerland. These vehicles were characteristic of the Pilatus, the passenger coach and locomotive being built in one to save weight. The driver and stoker rode in the cab at the valley end, while passengers and conductor travelled on the upper platforms.*

BELOW: *Japanese during the Russo-Japanese War, firing on a Russian Red Cross train on the Trans-Siberian Railway carrying wounded to Port Arthur. From a weekly newspaper published in Paris on 15 May 1904.*

ABOVE LEFT: *A passenger train pauses in front of the Toronto, Hamilton & Buffalo Railway station and offices.*

ABOVE: *La Gare du Midi, Brussels, 1902.*

LEFT: *Russian cavalry during the Russo-Japanese War on their way to the Manchurian Front, crossing a river on a raft after disembarking from the Trans-Siberian Railway. (Illustration from a weekly paper published in Paris in 1904.)*

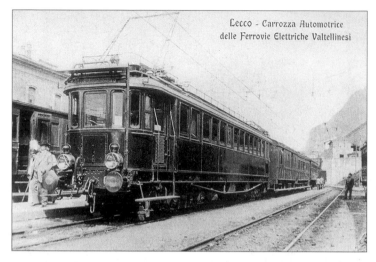

Lecco - Carrozza Automotrice
delle Ferrovie Elettriche Valtellinesi

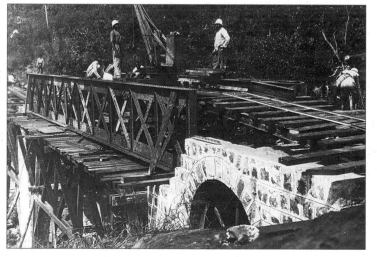

CLOCKWISE FROM TOP LEFT: *Type El electric unit on the Società Adriatica's Valtellinesi line at Lecco, waiting to leave for Colico, 1904.*

Union troops at City Point, Virginia await train transport to the front in 1864.

Belgian State Railway's 2-4-0 Vienna Express *leaving Ostend.*

Construction of the Pont de la Samakousse on the chemin de fer, *Guinea, Africa 1902.*

A Belgian saddle-tank moves freight in the late 1940s.

A Belgian railway steam train.

OPPOSITE
ABOVE: *View of Bombay Churchgate Station built in 1893, in a photograph taken in the 1920s.*

BELOW LEFT: *U.S. Military Railroad's engine* General Haupt, *named after General Hermann Haupt, Chief of Construction and Transportation for the Union armies. The locomotive was built in 1863.*

BELOW RIGHT: *Construction of the Pont de la Douona on the* chemin de fer, *Guinea, Africa.*

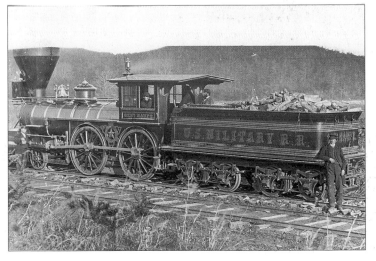

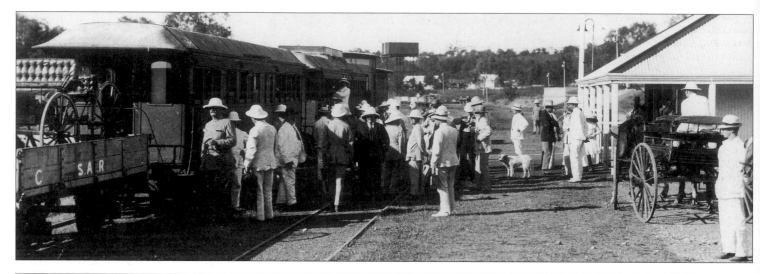

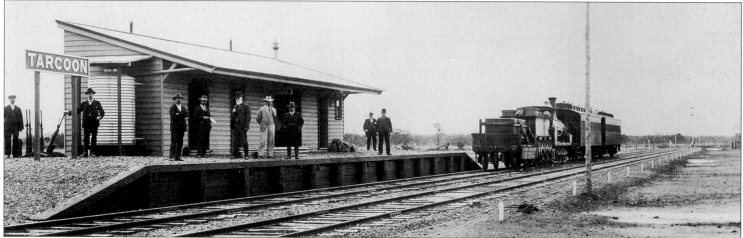

American steam locomotives for the export market differed enormously in size, from small tank locomotives to large articulated ones to cater for the full range of operating requirements, and the most common wheel arrangements were the 2-6-0, 2-8-0, 2-8-2 and 2-10-2 layouts. The first U.S. exports of steam locomotives were made, naturally enough, to neighbouring countries (Canada and Mexico), but their geographical extent later spread to South America, and then to markets that had hitherto been dominated by the British: these last included Australia, India, New Zealand and South Africa. American companies also managed to secure sales of their steam locomotives to Russia

OPPOSITE
ABOVE: *Darwin railway station, Australia, circa 1900.*

BELOW: *Tarcoon railway station, New South Wales, circa 1900.*

RIGHT: *The 125th anniversary Victorian Government Railways 4-6-0.*

Chapter Two
LOCOMOTIVES

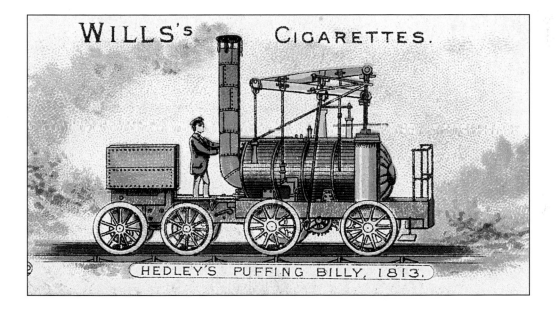

PAGE 68: Replicas of Stephenson's Rocket and Cooper's Tom Thumb.

PAGE 69: Puffing Billy, *William Hedley's locomotive patented in 1813. It began work in that year and continued in use until 1872. From a set of cigarette cards published in 1901.*

RIGHT: Replica Planet crossing Swithland viaduct on the Great Central Railway, England.

LOCOMOTIVES

The working of a steam locomotive is based on the use of the physical principle that water heated to a temperature above boiling point tries to become steam, in the process expanding in volume about 1,000 times. Kept inside the boiler, the steam is confined in volume and its pressure therefore increases, but once moved to a piston-fitted cylinder it drives the piston down the cylinder. This movement of the piston is transferred to the wheels by a system of connecting rods, the pressure of the steam thus being translated into the rotation of the wheels.

In essence, therefore, the steam locomotive comprises the two separate but indispensable elements of the boiler and the engine. The former is a closed unit that, in the majority of steam locomotives, also comprises a rear-located firebox and tubes to lead the fire's hot gases through the boiler proper (braced internally by large numbers of stays to resist the steam pressure) to a front-mounted smokebox. A valve, known as the regulator (in fact the throttle), controls the movement of steam along the steam pipe to the engine from which, after the majority of its useful energy has been extracted, it is removed by means of the blast-pipe into the smokebox and thence up the chimney. The

steam emerging from the blast-pipe creates a partial vacuum in the smokebox and thus helps significantly in 'drawing' the fire in the firebox in a fashion directly proportional to the amount of steam being used in a neat arrangement which ensures that the more steam is used (and therefore needed), the more steam is made.

The fires of most steam locomotives are of the coal-burning type with the fire burning on a grate of iron firebars through which the ashes fall into an ashpan. Other elements of the boiler include a method for filling the boiler with water (and then of replacing the water that has been turned to steam and used before being exhausted) from a water tank that is fitted on the locomotive itself or on a towed tender: a steam locomotive with onboard tank(s) is a tank locomotive, while that with a towed tender is a tender locomotive.

The structural core of the engine proper is a number of frames fabricated from iron (later steel) plates or bars, or alternatively produced as a single casting. In this unit are the slots for the axle-boxes carrying the wheel sets, each comprising a pair of wheels on a single axle: the axle-boxes are attached to the frames by springs to provide shock absorption. Each containing a single piston,

OPPOSITE: *A commemorative medal of Scottish engineer and inventor James Watt, the inventor of the first condensing steam engine.*

BELOW: *An interesting painting illustrating progress in the 19th century, showing telegraph, printing press, steam ship and railway.*

BOTTOM LEFT: *Guyot's Steam Carriage of 1769, an example of a steam locomotive.*

BOTTOM RIGHT: *Timothy Hackworth's* Royal George *locomotive of 1826.*

BELOW: *Trevithick's* Coalbrookdale *locomotive, 1803. Museum drawing based on an original contemporary sketch. A single horizontal cylinder, 4.75 x 36in (121 x 914mm), enclosed in a cast-iron return-flue boiler and provided with a flywheel, drove the wheels on one side only through spur gears. Steam was distributed* *through valve plugs worked by tappets. The cylinder was placed at the same end of the boiler as the furnace door and boiler pressure was around 50lb/sq in (3.5kg/cm²). There were cast-iron plate rails, and axles were mounted directly on the boiler, without a separate frame. There were no flanges on the wheels.*

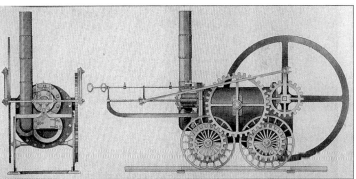

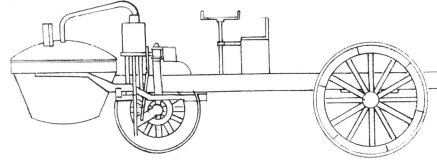

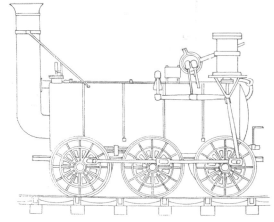

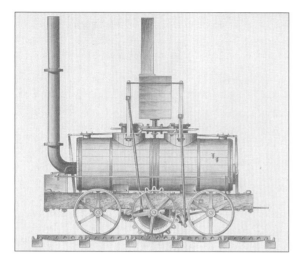

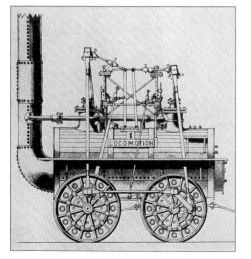

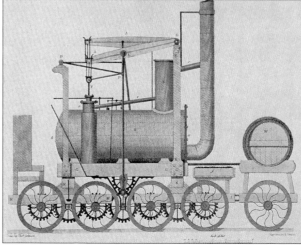

ABOVE LEFT: *Blenkinsop's rack locomotive, 1812.*

ABOVE: *Braithwaite and Erricsson's 0-2-2* Novelty *well-tank locomotive of 1829.*

FAR LEFT: *Stephenson's 0-4-0* Locomotion *of 1825 for the Stockton & Darlington Railway.*

LEFT: *Hedley's 0-8-0 locomotive for Wylam, 1813–14.*

OPPOSITE: *Trevithick's 0-4-0 Newcastle locomotive of 1805, probably the first railway locomotive with flanged wheels. The rails would have been made from wood and too weak, so the track was later made of iron.*

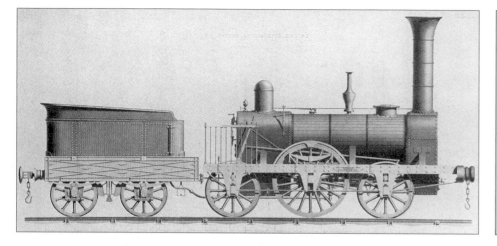

the cylinders are attached to the frames, and the driving force of the pistons as each is driven by the admission of steam to its cylinder (alternately at each end) is communicated to the wheels by a rod-and-guide system, this comprising a cross head and one or more guide bars. A circular-section piston rod connects the piston to the cross head by means of a steam-tight gland in the end of the cylinder, and a connecting-rod attaches the cross head to the driving wheels, with drive to other pairs of wheels possible by the addition of coupling rods.

A valve or valves are used to duct the steam into or out of the end of the cylinder when and (according to the direction and speed of movement) where it is required. These valves are linked with the wheels by means of valve gear. There have been

many types of valves and associated valve gears, but all work on the concept that admission of steam into one end of a piston-fitted cylinder will result in movement of the piston with a force based on the steam's pressure and the piston head's area.

The development of the boiler and steam engine in terms of efficiency and power is, inevitably, the driving force behind the design and manufacture of the great steam locomotives in the 'golden age' of steam, the period between the success of the *Rocket* in the Rainhill Trials of October 1829 and the outbreak of World War II (1939–45).

Although it was the Stephenson *Rocket* that secured victory over four other contenders (*Novelty*, *Sans Pareil*, *Cycloped* and *Perseverance*) in the Rainhill Trials to

select the locomotive for the passenger service soon to be inaugurated by the Liverpool & Manchester Railway, the steam locomotive actually used for this first inter-city service on 15 September 1830 was the *Northumbrian*. This was superior in several important respects to the *Rocket*, having a smokebox for the accumulation of ashes drawn through the boiler tubes and the integration of the boiler with the water jacket round the firebox, in effect creating for the first time the locomotive type of boiler that was to become wholly standard. Another improvement was the location of the cylinders with their axes in an almost horizontal position rather than the ungainly angle of some 35° used in the *Rocket* and causing the locomotive to rock. In addition, the cylinders of the

Northumbrian were installed in a readily accessible position outside the wheels. The *Northumbrian* massed 16,465lb (7469kg) without its tender, a weight nearly twice that of the *Rocket*, and the locomotive's potential for causing damage was reflected in the installation of a front buffer beam carrying horsehair-filled leather buffers. Finally, a proper tender rather than merely a barrel on wheels was used.

The features that made the *Rocket* a success at the Rainhill Trials were continued in the *Northumbrian*, albeit in forms that were stronger and larger. The multi-tube type of boiler (one with many tubes rather than one substantial pipe to conduct the hot gases through the water in the boiler) was again used as it was now clear that the greater area of multiple small tubes provided superior heating capability,

OPPOSITE LEFT: Stephenson's 2-2-2 standard passenger engine. Cylinders were 12 x 18in (305 x 457mm), the boiler was under pressure to the extent of 50lb/sq in (3.5kg/cm²), and the wheelbase was 9ft 2in (2.75m). It had four eccentric valve gears.

RIGHT: Timothy Hackworth's locomotive Sans Pareil. From Luke Herbert's Engineer's and Mechanic's Encyclopedia, London, 1836.

THIS PAGE: A replica of the Northumbrian at the Derby works circa 1930, built by Stephenson for the Liverpool & Manchester Railway in 1830. After the Rainhill Trials in 1829, locomotive development was very rapid.

and so too was the other highly significant feature of the *Rocket*, namely the blast-pipe to ensure the exhaust of the spent steam up the smokestack to create a partial vacuum at the forward end of the whole boiler arrangement to create greater draw in the firebox at the rear of the boiler. The *Northumbrian* possessed just two cylinders outside the frames and directly connected to the driving wheels in the pattern that rapidly became and remained the norm for all but articulated steam locomotives.

The positive features of the *Northumbrian* should not be construed as meaning that this pioneering steam locomotive lacked poorer features. The two large driving wheels were located toward the front, so the positioning of the heavy firebox and the heavy cylinders at the rear, over the two small carrying wheels, where their weight was offset only by the relatively light smokebox forward

of the driving wheels, meant that tractive effort was reduced, a process exacerbated by the action of the drawbar, which tended to lift the front end of the locomotive.

Another problem resulted from the combination of outside cylinders and a short wheelbase, which caused the locomotive to sway directionally until it was revised with a longer wheelbase and the cylinders shifted to the front.

Another failing in the *Northumbrian*

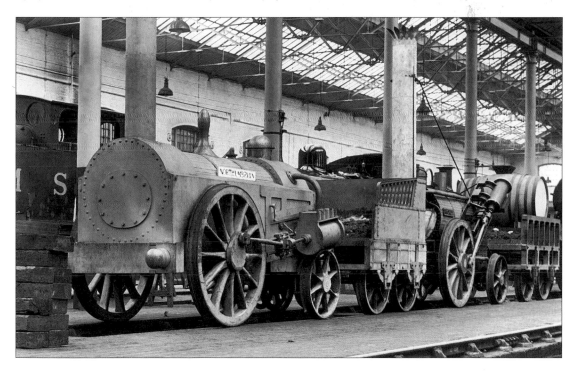

was the lack of any effective means to reverse the drive while the locomotive was in motion, and this feature proved disastrous when William Huskisson, MP, stepped in front of the *Rocket* and was severely injured as the driver had no means of stopping quickly. Huskisson was rushed to medical aid by the *Northumbrian*, but died of his injuries.

The *Northumbrian* is usually listed as a member of the 'Rocket' class, of which seven had been delivered to the Liverpool & Manchester Railway in 1829 and 1830. Those immediately following the *Rocket* were the *Meteor*, the *Comet*, the *Dart* and the *Arrow* with their cylinders almost horizontal, and the *Rocket* was rapidly altered to the same condition. The *Phoenix* and the *North Star* each possessed a smokebox, while the *Majestic*, which followed the *Northumbrian*, possessed all the new features.

The specification for the *Northumbrian* included a 0-2-2 layout, a tractive effort of 1,580lb (717kg), two 11 x 16-in (280 x 406-mm) cylinders, driving wheels with a diameter of 4ft 4in (1.321m), a steam pressure of about 50lb/sq in (3.5kg/cm^2), about 2,200lb (998kg) of coke fuel, about 480 U.S. gal (400 Imp gal; 1818 litres) of water, total weight of 25,500lb (11567kg), and overall length of 24ft 0in (7.315m).

The successor class introduced on the Liverpool & Manchester Railway from October 1830 was the 'Planet' class of 2-2-0 steam locomotives. The new type reflected the rapidly developing design concepts of the two Stephensons, and as such had two

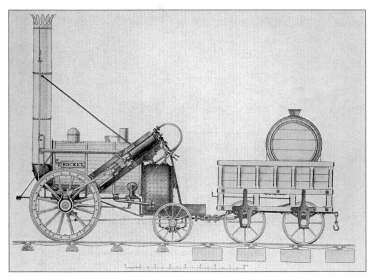

forward-mounted horizontal cylinders, which enhanced the locomotive's weight distribution, as well as the driving wheels at the rear under the firebox, whose weight now improved the locomotive's adherence to the rails. Another significant improvement, introduced to eliminate the tendency of earlier locomotives to sway as the drive power switched from one wheel to the other, was the relocation of the cylinders inside the wheels to drive the axle by means of a double-crank.

The Planet class was relatively successful and many of these engines, some of them with four coupled wheels, were manufactured by the Stephensons and also by others including, perhaps most importantly, Matthias Baldwin of Philadelphia in the U.S.A. who in 1832 produced the *Old Ironsides*. This was the first full-size steam locomotive from a company that became the world's most prolific manufacturer of such engines, totalling some 60,000 over a period of 130 years.

In historical terms it was the Planet class that may rightly be seen as the steam locomotive that proved beyond doubt that the age of mechanical transport was safe and not just feasible but commercially viable. It was the success of the Planet class that in reality lifted the Stephensons into the 'millionaire' bracket and led to their acceptance as the true originators of rail transport.

The other data for the Planet class included a tractive effort of about 1,450lb (658kg), two 11.5 x 16-in (292 x 406-mm)

OPPOSITE ABOVE: Robert Stephenson's locomotive Planet, *1830.*

BELOW: Stephenson's Rocket *0-2-2 locomotive for the Liverpool & Manchester Railway, 1829. A museum drawing based on remains and contemporary illustrations and descriptions.*

THIS PAGE

ABOVE: The Best Friend of Charleston, *built in 1830 by the West Point Foundry for use on the South Carolina Canal & Railroad Company.*

BELOW: A selection of locomotives with, from left to right, the Batavia *built by the Baldwin Locomotive Works for Tonawanda Railroad, the locomotive* America, *Baldwin's* Old Ironsides, *built for the Philadelphia, Germantown & Norristown Railroad, 1832, and one of the first 4-2-0 locomotives built by Baldwin for the Utica & Schenectady Railroad, 1837.*

cylinders, driving wheels with a diameter of 5ft 2in (1.575m), steam pressure of about 50lb/sq in (3.5kg/cm^2), about 2,200lb (998kg) of coke fuel, about 480 U.S. gal (400 Imp gal; 1818 litres) of water, total weight of 29,500lb (13381kg) and overall length of 24ft 4in (7.42m).

It was on 15 January 1831 that the first full size steam locomotive manufactured in the U.S.A. entered service. This was the *Best Friend of Charleston*, an odd 0-4-0 locomotive operating on America's first commercial steam railroad, the South Carolina Canal & Railroad. Made by the West Point Foundry in New York late in 1830 to the design of E. L. Miller, the *Best Friend of Charleston* had a vertical boiler, a well tank manufactured integral with the locomotive, four coupled wheels and two modestly inclined cylinders. None of the locomotive's features except the coupled wheels became standard, but the *Best Friend of Charleston* was nonetheless successful at the technical level and could pull five carriages, carrying 50 or more passengers, at 20mph (32km/h). The explosion of the locomotive's boiler in 1831, after the

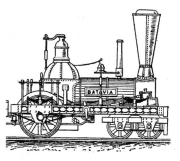

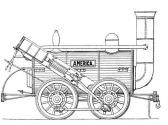

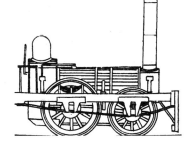

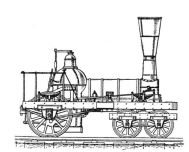

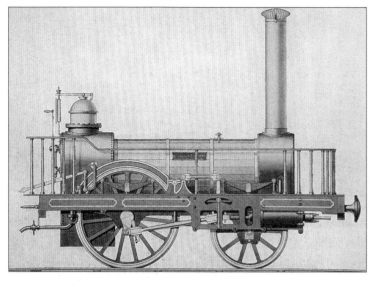

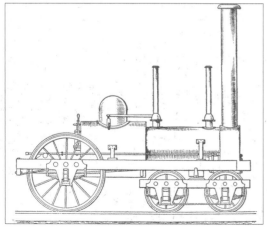

ABOVE LEFT: *Forrester's 2-2-0* Vauxhall *locomotive of the Dublin & Kingstown Railway, 1834. It had horizontal outside cylinders of 11 x 18in (279 x 457mm), with vibrating pillar parallel motion and was said to have had four eccentric gab valve gear.*

LEFT: *The 4-2-0 locomotive* Experiment *built by John B. Jervis at the West Point Foundry, U.S.A. in 1832.*

ABOVE: *Gooch's 2-2-2 Prince-class* Queen *locomotive of the Great Western Railway of 1847, from a watercolour by E.T. Lane dated 3 July 1849. It had a broad-gauge engine with inside sandwich frame and cylinders of 18 x 24in (457 x 610mm). Boiler pressure was around 100lb/sq in (7kg/cm^2) and the heating surface was 1081sq ft (100m^2). Weight was around 26.2 tons and the locomotive had a wheelbase of 14ft 10in (4.5m).*

OPPOSITE: *Stephenson's 0-2-2 locomotive* Northumbrian, *Liverpool & Manchester Railway, 1830. From an engraving by I. Shaw, 1831. It was generally similar to the* Rocket, *but the cylinders were nearly horizontal and the boiler had an internal firebox and smokebox. The main frames were formed of vertical plates to which the axle-box horns were bolted.*

fireman had tied down the lever controlling the safety valves to prevent the noise of escaping steam, led finally to the universal adoption of tamper-proof safety valves to prevent any recurrence of this fatal incident. The locomotive was rebuilt with a new boiler and the revised name *Phoenix*.

Of more overall importance than the *Best Friend of Charleston* was the *Brother Jonathan*, a 4-2-0 steam locomotive designed in 1832 by John B. Jervis for another American operator, the Mohawk & Hudson Railroad. This pioneering locomotive introduced the pivoted leading truck (otherwise known as the bogie), which was derived from a notion that Robert Stephenson suggested to Jervis during a

visit to England. Originally known as the *Experiment*, the *Brother Jonathan* was manufactured at the West Point Foundry. Among its features was a comparatively small boiler, space for the connecting rods between the firebox and the main frames, which were outside the driving wheels, which was fitted to the rear of the firebox. Of these features, it was only the four-wheel truck that became standard as a means of improving guidance round curves, where the outer fore-and-aft pair of truck wheels pressed against the outer rail tangentially, giving all three outer wheels a correct angle of contact on the outer rail of the curve.

The *Brother Jonathan* had a relatively long and distinguished career in which it

was later transformed into a 4-4-0 layout, and among its details were a tractive effort of about 1,023lb (464kg), two 9.5 x 16-in (241 x 406-mm) cylinders, driving wheels with a diameter of 5ft 0in (1.52m), boiler pressure of about 50lb/sq in (3.5kg/cm²), weight of 14,999lb (6804kg) without tender, and length of 16ft 5.5in (5.017m) without tender.

The 'Vauxhall'-class locomotive, designed and built for the Dublin & Kingstown Railway of Ireland in 1834 by George Forrester, introduced two important features to the concept of the steam locomotive. The first of these was the installation of the cylinders outside the driving wheels in a horizontal position at the front of the locomotive in a position in which they were effective and also readily accessible; here the pistons and connecting rods powered the driving wheels by means of separate cranks on the outside of the wheels. Of greater importance was the provision for the first time of an effective mechanism to reverse the drive, although the locomotive had first to be halted before the reverse system could be engaged.

By 1836 most of these steam locomotives, also sold to other railways in the United Kingdom, had been altered from their original 2-2-0 configuration to a 2-2-2 layout in an effort to improve their running. The data for the Vauxhall-class locomotive, which could pull a useful load at more than 30mph (48km/h), include a tractive effort of about 1,550lb (703kg), two 11 x 18-in (280 x 457-mm) cylinders, driving wheels with a diameter of 5ft 0in (1.524m), steam

pressure of about 50lb/sq in (3.5kg/cm²), and overall length of about 24ft 0in (7.315m).

The first steam locomotives made in Germany during 1816 and 1817 were both unsuccessful and as a result it was December 1835 before the first successful steam railway began operation. This was the Ludwigsbahn of Bavaria, linking Nuremberg and Fürth. Approval for the railway had been given by King Ludwig I in the preceding year, and the railway's promoter initially considered the purchase of equipment from Robert Stephenson, but then changed his mind as a result of Stephenson's 'high' price and instead contracted with two citizens of Württemberg for the supply of equipment that they warranted the equal of any British items. The two men then moved to Austria-Hungary and more than doubled the price they wanted so, with the announced date of the railway's opening fast approaching, Herr Scharrer turned to Stephenson for a 2-2-2 locomotive known as *Der Adler* (The Eagle) and possessing a number of features of the 'Patentee' delivered to the Liverpool & Manchester Railway in 1834. The Patentee was a development of the 'Planet' class with improved axles and wheels.

The success of the *Adler* is attested by the fact that the Ludwigsbahn operation bought further steam locomotives of the same type, and that the original locomotive was used up to 1857. Details of the *Adler* are both scarce and in some cases inconsistent, but the most salient data include a tractive effort of 1,220lb (553kg),

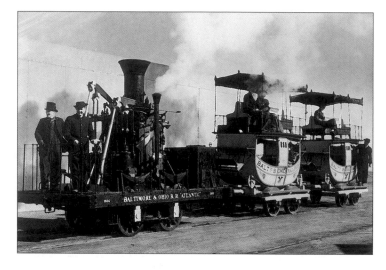

ABOVE LEFT: *The locomotive* Atlantic, *with train built for the Baltimore & Ohio Railroad in 1832.*

ABOVE RIGHT: *The locomotive* Tom Thumb, *built by Peter Cooper for the Baltimore & Ohio Railroad in 1829.*

LEFT: *The locomotive* Hercules *built by Garret & Eastwich of Philadelphia for the Beaver Meadow Railroad, 1837. The locomotive weighed 15 tons.*

OPPOSITE PAGE
LEFT: *Norris' 4-2-0 locomotive, probably of the Birmingham & Gloucester Railway, 1839–42. It was an American-designed* engine, with front bogie and bar frame. The B&G had 40 of these, made between 1838 and 1840 by Nasmyth in England. Cylinders were around 11½ x 20in (292 x 508mm), boiler pressure circa 55lb/sq in (3.85kg/cm^2) and it had four eccentric valve gear.

RIGHT: *Gooch's 0-6-0* Pyracmon *locomotive, Great Western Railway, 1847, from an early watercolour. It was a broad-gauge design with 16 x 24-in (406 x 607-mm) cylinders and an inside sandwich frame. Weight was 27½ tons, wheelbase 15ft 5in (4.72m), boiler pressure 115lb/sq in (8kg/cm^2) and heating surface 1,373sq ft (127.6m^2).*

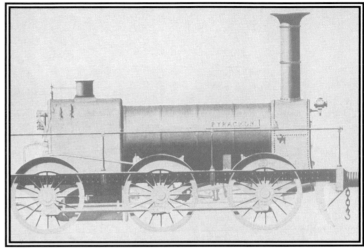

two 9 x 16-in (229 x 406-mm) cylinders, driving wheels with a diameter of 4ft 6in (1.371m), weight of 31,500lb (14288kg) without tender, and overall length of 25ft 0in (7.62m).

In the U.S.A., Henry Campbell, the engineer of the Philadelphia, Germantown & Norristown Railroad, decided that benefits could accrue from the combination of coupled wheels as pioneered on the *Best Friend of Charleston* and the leading truck of the *Brother Jonathan* to secure a considerable increase in adhesive weight in a steam locomotive that would be able to ride smoothly round curves on tracks that were often very irregularly laid.

The result was the world's first 4-4-0 steam locomotive, which was manufactured

in May 1837 by James Brooks and, though in itself designed for coal movement, introduced the most celebrated of all passenger locomotive wheel layouts. The Campbell 4-4-0 locomotive was not in itself successful, being distinctly poor in coping with vertical irregularities in the track. The details for this locomotive include a tractive effort of 4,373lb (1984kg), two 14 x15.75-in (356 x 400-mm) cylinders, driving wheels with a diameter of 4ft 6in (1.37m), the notably high steam pressure for the period of 90lb/sq in (6.3kg/cm^2), and length of 16ft 5.5in (5.017m).

During 1836, Garret & Eastwich of Philadelphia received an order from the Beaver Meadow Railroad for a 4-4-0 steam locomotive. The company's foreman, Joseph

Harrison, knew of the problems of the Campbell 4-4-0 but also remembered the success of the *Brother Jonathan* 4-2-0 locomotive that provided far greater stability through its combination on each side of two driving wheels and the pivot of the leading truck, which provided a type of 'three-legged' stability. Harrison now determined that improved stability could be derived from making the two pairs of driving wheels into a non-swivelling truck through the connection of the axle bearings on each side by a large cast-iron beam that was pivoted at its centre and connected to the main frame of the locomotive by a large leaf spring.

The net effect of this concept was to create a three-point suspension system for an eight-wheel locomotive, a system that fully

solved the problem of running on rough tracks and, indeed, was so effective that it was used in steadily more sophisticated form for locomotives up to much later 4-12-2 units. The resulting locomotive was the *Hercules*, and its success led to the sale of many basically similar locomotives to several railroads and the elevation of Harrison to a partnership in a firm that became Eastwick & Harrison as Garret left it at this time. The details for the *Hercules* included a tractive effort of 4,507lb (2044kg), two 12 x 18-in (305 x 457-mm) cylinders, driving wheels with a diameter of 3ft 8in (1.117m), steam pressure of 90lb/sq in (6.3kg/cm^2), weight of 30,000lb (13608kg) without tender, and length of 18ft 11in (5.766m) without tender.

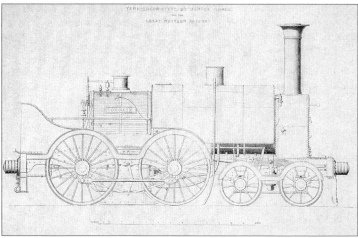

ABOVE: *Daniel Gooch's* Iron Duke *locomotive, Great Western Railway, 1847. From an engraving in Tredgold's* The Steam Engine. *It had a broad-gauge engine with outside sandwich frame. Cylinders were 18 x 24in (457 x 610mm), boiler pressure was originally 100lbsq in (7kg/cm^2), later increased to 115lb/sq in.*

LEFT: *Gooch's 4-4-0* Corsair *saddle-tank locomotive, Great Western Railway, 1849. From D.K. Clark's* Railway Machinery, *1855. It had a broad-gauge engine, cylinders of 17 x 24in (432 x 610mm), wheelbase of 18ft 2in (2.44m) and a weight of 35³/4 tons. It had inside frames, Gooch's link motion, bogie-class engine and skid-rail brake.*

OPPOSITE ABOVE: *Model of the locomotive* Dorchester *of the Champlain & St. Lawrence Railway, Canada.*

BELOW LEFT: *Bristol station, Great Western Railway, England.*

BELOW RIGHT: *Race between Peter Cooper's locomotive* Tom Thumb *and a horse-drawn railway carriage, Baltimore & Ohio Railroad, 1829.*

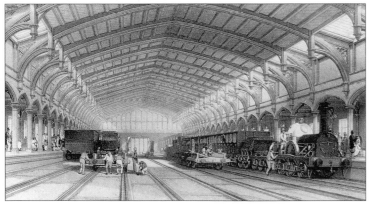

With the 'Lafayette' class of 4-2-0 steam locomotives by William Norris, originally for the Baltimore & Ohio Railroad in 1837, the locomotive took a major step toward its definitive form. Originally a draper by trade, Norris had started to build steam locomotives in Philadelphia during 1831 in partnership with Colonel Stephen Long, but then started up on his own and in 1836 produced for the Philadelphia & Columbia Railroad a 4-2-0 locomotive called the *Washington County Farmer*. This was akin to the *Brother Jonathan* in its use of a leading truck, but differed in its use of cylinders outside the wheels and frames, in the nature and arrangement of the valves, and in the location of the driving wheels ahead of rather than behind the firebox to boost the proportion of the engine's weight carried on them.

The success of the *Washington County Farmer* caught the attention of the Baltimore & Ohio Railroad, which by this time had expanded its network to the extent that could no longer be usefully operated by its first-generation 'Grasshopper'-class steam locomotives, and the railroad therefore commissioned a class of eight

locomotives from Norris. The first of these, delivered in 1837, was the *Lafayette,* that was the railroad's first locomotive with a horizontal rather than vertical boiler, although this was used in combination with a circular-section firebox with a notably domed top. The class was very successful, offering higher performance and lower fuel consumption than earlier locomotives, in common with enhanced reliability and simpler maintenance.

In 1837 Norris also completed a similar unit for the Champlain & St. Lawrence Railway in Canada, and this was the first 'modern' locomotive to be exported from the United States, the well proven capabilities of the type then combining with excellent gradient-climbing capability to secure a significant number of other export sales, including a number to Europe, where the first customer was the Vienna-Raab railway, whose *Philadelphia* was shipped late in 1837. Other Norris locomotives went to railways in Brunswick, Prussia and the U.K. Such was the demand for Norris locomotives that the company found it commercially sensible to offer its type in four sizes and therefore weights, differentiated by cylinder bores and grates

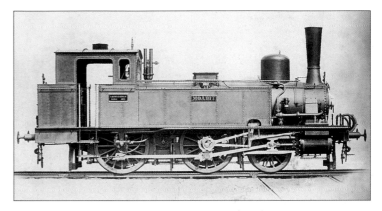

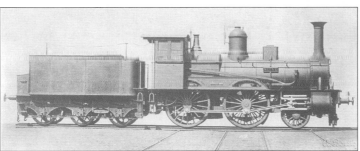

OPPOSITE

CLOCKWISE FROM TOP LEFT: *Central Pacific locomotive No. 82 built by Rogers in 1868. The cordwood piled in the tender is ready for use as fuel. Four-wheeled 15-ft (4.8-m) 'dinky' cabooses like the one shown here were in operation on the Central and Southern Pacific lines.*

There follows a selection of locomotives built by Borsig, including the C locomotive Isar *for the Warra Railway 1865, the 1B* Gotha *for the Berlin-Stettin Railway 1854, and the 1A1* Beuth *for the Berlin Anhalter Railway, 1844.*

THIS PAGE, CLOCKWISE FROM TOP LEFT: *More locomotive designs by Borsig which include* Wannsee *for the Berlin-Potsdam-Magdeburg Railway, 1877, the 1B* Moabit *of 1882 and the 1B* Seeve *for the Berlin-Hamburg Railway, 1872–1879.*

of different sizes: the 'A' class had an 11.5in (292mm) bore, the 'A Extra' 12.5in (318mm), the 'B' class 10.5in (268mm) and the 'C' class 9in (229mm).

Locomotives of the Norris type were also widely manufactured in Europe, often without any form of licence. The details for the Lafayette class included a tractive effort of 2,162lb (981kg), two 10.5 x 18-in (268 x 457-mm) cylinders, driving wheels with a diameter of 4ft 0in (1.219m), steam pressure of 60lb/sq in (4.2kg/cm²), 2,200lb (998kg) of coke fuel, 540 U.S. gal (450 Imp gal; 2044 litres) of water, total weight of 44,000lb (19958kg), and overall length of 30ft 4.25in (9.25m).

Meanwhile, on the other side of the North Atlantic, momentous events in railway history had begun to unfold with the appointment in 1833 of Isambard Kingdom Brunel as engineer of the planned Great Western Railway linking the west of England with London. Brunel was not a man to be impressed with current achievements, and one of his earliest decisions was that the gauge of the new railway was to be 7ft 0.25in (2.14m), which was the largest ever adopted for any railway, rather than the figure of 4ft 8.5in (1.432m) selected by the Stephensons and virtually standard in the United Kingdom: in Brunel's opinion, this was the 'coal-wagon gauge'.

Despite the grandiose nature of his plans and his manifest engineering genius, Brunel decided to take no close part in the ordering and design of the locomotives to pull the trains of the Great Western Railway, delegating these tasks to subordinates within the instruction that no six-wheeled locomotive was to exceed 23,520lb (10669kg) in weight with a piston speed of no more than 280ft (85m) per minute. These limits were impossible to attain within a locomotive of practical value, and there is no doubt that its locomotives were the worst features of the Great Western Railway in its earlier days.

Supervising the locomotive fleet was Daniel Gooch, an erstwhile collaborator of the Stephensons, and it was only after a strenuous struggle with Brunel that Gooch was able to persuade the directors of the Great Western Railway to set in hand orders for more than 100 modern six-wheeled locomotives based broadly on the Stephenson Patentee type with layouts such as 2-2-2 for the 62 locomotives required for passenger services and 2-4-0 or 0-6-0 for the other locomotives that were used for freight services.

Unlike the situation which had prevailed previously, in which the manufacturers were given enormous latitude within the sketchiest of guidelines, the situation now controlled by Gooch was far more structured, and the boilers, tenders, moving parts and many other components were common to all the locomotives in an example of standardization on a hitherto unknown scale. Manufacturers received not only drawings but also templates, and were also made financially responsible for all repairs required within the first 1,000 miles (1609km) of any locomotive's operation with its planned full load.

The first of the new passenger locomotives, delivered in March 1840, was the *Fire Fly*, manufactured by Jones, Turner & Evans of Newton-le-Willows in Lancashire. Later units of the same basic

class from the same manufacturer were the *Spit Fire*, *Wild Fire*, *Fire Ball*, *Fire King* and *Fire Brand*. The capabilities of the new class were revealed on 17 March 1840, when the *Fire Fly* pulled a special train over a 30.75-mile (49.5-km) distance at an average of just under 50mph (80.5km/h) and reached a maximum speed of 58mph (93km/h). By the end of 1840, for the opening to Wootton Bassett beyond Swindon, a further 25 of these locomotives were available and a timetable worthy of the name could be issued at last.

By December 1842 another 56 of the

locomotives had been delivered by another six manufacturers, and the last of the series was not withdrawn from service until 1879. The details of the 'Fire Fly' class included a tractive effort of 2,049lb (929kg), two 15 x 18-in (381 x 457-mm) cylinders, driving wheels with a diameter of 7ft 0in (2.134m), steam pressure of 50lb/sq in (3.5kg/cm²), 3,400lb (1542kg) of coke fuel, 2,160 U.S. gal (1,800 Imp gal; 8183 litres) of water, total weight of 92,500lb (41958kg), and overall length of 39ft 4in (11.989m).

In 1841 the locomotive-building industry began to come of age in Germany

Here, circa 1895, Boston & Maine's American Standard-class locomotive (No. 150) has just moved out of the Danvers, Massachusetts engine house.

as three manufacturers each delivered their first offerings: these manufacturers were Borsig of Berlin, Maffei of Munich and Emil Kessler of Karlsruhe. At the time of Borsig's expansion from several other enterprises into locomotive manufacture, the Norris 4-2-0 locomotives were very popular in European circles, and Borsig's first

ABOVE LEFT: *Central Pacific Railroad's locomotive* Jupiter *with bandsmen of the 21st Infantry, stationed at Fort Douglas, Utah, at the completion of the transcontinental railway at Promontory, Utah on 10 May 1869.*

ABOVE RIGHT: *Train on one of the Bollman truss bridges on the Maryland North Branch of the Baltimore & Ohio Railroad. The train ran between Baltimore and Wheeling and back, carrying 40 photographers and artists making frequent stops so that they could photograph and paint. 1858.*

LEFT: *A one-car Northern Pacific train, with wood-burning balloon stack locomotive is shown at the end of the bridge over the Missouri between Bismarck and Mandan, Dakota Territory, in 1882.*

locomotives were 15 similar units delivered to the Berlin-Anhalter railway company. Though modelled closely on the American original, the German locomotive had several Borsig improvements. The type was very successful and soon attracted additional orders.

Within a period of two years Borsig had added further improvements, some of its own design and others derived from British ideas. The blend of an American core design with German and British improvements was highly attractive, and was fully evident in the *Beuth*, a 2-2-2 locomotive delivered to the Berlin-Anhalter railway in 1843. The equal spacing of the three axles offered a better distribution of weight than in the Norris 4-2-0 type, and the new valves (based on a type developed by William Howe of the Stephenson company) were so good that they became virtually standard for all steam locomotives over the next 60 years.

The *Beuth* was the 24th locomotive manufactured by Borsig, and its success attracted a relative flood of orders to the extent that by 1846 Borsig had completed no fewer than 120 locomotives. The details of the *Beuth* included a tractive effort of 4,123lb (1870kg), two 13.1 x 22.3-in (333 x 566-mm) cylinders, driving wheels with a diameter of 5ft 0.75in (1.543m), steam pressure of 78lb/sq in (5.5kg/cm²), weight of 40,785lb (18500kg) without tender, and length of 20ft 2in (6.143m) without tender.

An exact French contemporary of the *Beuth* was the 'Buddicom' class of 2-2-2 steam locomotives designed for the Paris-Rouen railway by W. B. Buddicom, one of many British engineers who took the ideas of the Stephensons round the world and, in this instance, improved upon them. The Buddicom class of 2-2-2 locomotives was a further step (rivalled by the 'Crew' class designed in the U.K. by Alexander Allan) in the development of European locomotives from the *Northumbrian* toward what became established as the norm with two outside cylinders.

The spur to the creation of the new design was the tendency of the cranked axles of inside-cylinder locomotives to breakage and, as well as adopting outside cylinders, the Buddicom-class design also had the new type of Stephenson link motion and a deep firebox between the two rear wheels. The Buddicom class was very effective, and was built in moderately large

numbers including 22 that were later converted to 2-2-2 tank locomotive standard. The details of the Buddicom class included a tractive effort of 3,219lb (1460kg), two 12.5 x 21-in (318 x 533-mm) cylinders, driving wheels with a diameter of 5ft 3in (1.60m), and steam pressure of 70lb/sq in (5kg/cm²).

During 1836 John Haswell, a Scotsman, travelled to Austria-Hungary to supervise the entry into service of some locomotives bought from the U.K. With this task satisfactorily completed, Haswell was invited to remain in the country as the head of the locomotive element of the short line linking Vienna and Gloggnitz. Haswell

remained in Austria-Hungary to the time of his death in 1897, and among his steam locomotive designs was the 'Gloggnitzer' class of 4-4-0 units based on the Norris type and used mainly on the extension of the Gloggnitz line to Laibach (now Ljubljana) over the Semmering Pass.

The Gloggnitzer class had a number of unusual features, including the ability of the leading truck to move radially rather than just pivot round its centre as on the original Norris design, a change made desirable by the location of the coupled driving wheels close to the truck, which exercised a measure of constraint on the locomotive's axis and therefore made it important that the

truck should possess a measure of lateral displacement capability. The details of the Gloggnitzer-class locomotive included a tractive effort of 5,754lb (2610kg), two 14.5 x 23-in (368 x 584-mm) cylinders, driving wheels with a diameter of 4ft 7.75in (1.42m), steam pressure of 78lb/sq in (5.5kg/cm²), 4,409lb (2000kg) of fuel, 1,796 U.S. gal (1,496 Imp gal; 6800 litres) of water, total weight of 70,547lb (32000kg), and overall length of 42ft 2in (12.853m).

Manufactured by Thomas Rogers of Paterson, New Jersey, during 1855, the *General* remains a classic example of the 'American Standard' class of 4-4-0 steam locomotives, which was arguably the most

OPPOSITE: *Golden Spike National Monument replicas of Central Pacific 4-4-0* Jupiter *and Union Pacific No. 119 at Promontory Point, Utah.*

RIGHT: *Steam locomotives, run on a variety of gauges, have a long and proud tradition in India.*

numerous and successful locomotive design ever created. It was Rogers who was largely responsible for introducing to American practice most of the features which made the true American Standard class. The most important of these was the Stephenson link motion, which permitted the expansive use of steam, and was used in place of the 'gab' or 'hook' reversing gears used up to that time and provided only 'full forward' and 'full backward' positions. Rogers otherwise concentrated on good proportions and excellence of detail rather than innovation as such.

To provide a measure of flexibility on tighter curves, early American Standard locomotives had the same type of flangeless forward driving wheels as their predecessors, but by the late 1850s the leading truck instead had provision for lateral movement to yield the same effect. The use of wood rather than coal was extremely common in the first part of the career of the American Standard locomotives, and as a result there were a wide assortment of spark-catching smokestacks in an effort to reduce the possibility of a spark flying off to the side of the track and setting fire to woods or crops.

By the late 1850s, generally similar locomotives were being made by other manufacturers including Baldwin, Brooks Mason, Danforth, Grant, and Hinkley began offering similar locomotives, which generally operated on the roughly laid tracks of the period at an average speed of about 25mph (40km/h). The American Standard had a relatively long life, the need to pull longer and heavier loads meant that by the 1880s the original type had often been supplemented if not supplanted by larger steam locomotives using the same 4-4-0 configuration or alternatively the 4-6-0 layout. About 25,000 of these classic locomotives were built to a standard that was notable for its general uniformity in all but detail. The American Standard was the first and possibly the only 'universal locomotive', and the main difference between the units built to pull passenger trains and those intended for the freight market was the large diameter of the former's driving wheels, 5ft 6in (1.676m) as compared with 5ft 0in (1.524m).

Some of the locomotives survived in useful American service into the 1950s, and the details of the *General* include a tractive effort of 6,885lb (3123kg), two 15 x 24-in (381 x 610-mm) cylinders, driving wheels with a diameter of 5ft 0in (1.524m), steam pressure of 90lb/sq in (6.35kg/cm²), 2,000 U.S. gal (1,665 Imp gal, 7571 litres) of water, total weight of 90,000lb (40824kg) and overall length of 52ft 3in (15.926m).

The 'Problem' or 'Lady of the Lake' class of 2-2-2 steam locomotives, designed by John Ramsbottom and introduced to British service by the London & North Western Railway during 1859, remained in useful 'first-line' service for nearly 50 years, which was a considerable achievement in its own right and all the more so for a class introduced at a time that locomotive technology was still developing relatively quickly.

The primary advantage enjoyed by the Problem class, as indeed with all of the great steam locomotives right up to the present, was a total avoidance of complexity: the class had no trucks, for example, the leading axle being carried in the frames like the others, the valve arrangement for the outside cylinders was simplicity itself, and after the first ten a simple injector system was used in place of pumps to top up the boiler.

The General Lowell, *an American Standard-type 4-4-0 locomotive, photographed at Burlington, Iowa during the late Civil War period. The engine was named for Brigadier-General Charles Lowell, Jnr., killed at the battle of Cedar Creek on 19 October 1864. Lowell had been assistant treasurer and land agent of the fledgling Burlington & Missouri River Railroad from its earliest days until he resigned on 25 October 1860 to become an ironmaker at Mt. Savage, Maryland. He was replaced by his assistant, 19-year-old Charles E. Perkins, who later became president of the Chicago, Burlington & Quincy Railroad.*

One of the most notable tasks undertaken by the locomotives of the Problem class was the haulage of the *Irish Mail* between Euston in London and Holyhead on Anglesey, the locomotive being changed at Stafford. A retrograde step occurred in 1871 when Ramsbottom was succeeded by Francis Webb, who unfortunately believed in complexity. This gave rise to a number of complex and highly unreliable compound locomotives. The compound locomotives that resulted were not as reliable as they should have been, and this led to a renewed demand for the services of the now-elderly Problem-class locomotives, which were largely rebuilt in the 1890s with greater weight in addition to the crew cabs that had been added during an

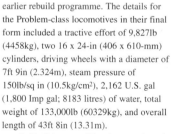

earlier rebuild programme. The details for the Problem-class locomotives in their final form included a tractive effort of 9,827lb (4458kg), two 16 x 24-in (406 x 610-mm) cylinders, driving wheels with a diameter of 7ft 9in (2.324m), steam pressure of 150lb/sq in (10.5kg/cm²), 2,162 U.S. gal (1,800 Imp gal; 8183 litres) of water, total weight of 133,000lb (60329kg), and overall length of 43ft 8in (13.31m).

Gallic flair was evident in a number of French steam locomotive designs, but in none more so than the '121' class that entered service in 1876 on the *Route Impériale* of the Paris, Lyons & Mediterranean railway. Needing locomotives of greater power than the Crampton 4-2-0 units it was currently

operating, the railway initially produced from 1868 some 50 long-boiler 2-4-0 locomotives and then searched for still more power for this prestigious but arduous service between the French capital and the Mediterranean coast. This led to the 121 class of an initial 60 (but ultimately 400 by 1883) locomotives with a 2-4-2 layout, and all of the earlier long-boiler locomotives were then rebuilt to this standard for increased stability.

Further improvement was introduced in 1888, when work was started on another batch of 2-4-2 locomotives, which must be regarded as one of the high points in French steam locomotive design. Only 10 per cent heavier than the originals, these final units introduced three definitive features in the

form of the Walschaert valve gear (later standard all over the world), a boiler designed for a pressure of 214lb/sq in (15kg/cm²) that was a 65 per cent increase over the boiler pressure of the parent design, and a switch from simple to compound operation for much enhanced thermal efficiency to increase the ratio between the power produced and the fuel burned.

The details for the middle tranche of 121-class locomotives included a tractive effort of 12,224lb (5545kg), two 19.7 x 23.7-in (500 x 650-mm) cylinders, driving wheels with a diameter of 6ft 10.75in (2.10m), steam pressure of 129lb/sq in (9kg/cm²), weight of 109,568lb (49700kg) with tender, and length of 56ft 5.75in (17.215m) without tender.

LEFT: Union Pacific's locomotive No. 574 (4-4-0) heading a passenger train at Genoa, Nebraska. The engineer is H.A. Riley, fireman E.P. Rogers, conductor Harry Schaffer and breakman W.F. McFadden.

BELOW: Three switch engines and their crews pose in front of the former station at Pacific Junction, Iowa, in 1905. This is where the Kansas City-Council Bluffs line crosses the main line to Lincoln and where trains for Council Bluffs and Omaha can turn north and follow the Missouri. The one on the left is an E-class, No. 1390 is in the centre and No. 1423 on the right is a G-class engine.

It had been a matter of faith since the Patentee class of 2-2-2 locomotives that 'high-speed' rail travel demanded that the locomotive needed smaller guide wheels ahead of the larger driving wheels, but in 1882 the London, Brighton & South Coast Railway introduced the 'Gladstone' class of 0-4-2 locomotives that were initially regarded with more than a touch of suspicion by the 'experts' of the time. Experience soon revealed, however, that William Stroudley was right to dispense with the guiding wheels, as the Gladstone-class locomotives behaved impeccably and were, moreover, extremely attractive and economical to run. As a result, Stroudley is one of the comparative handful of designers whose locomotives have

enjoyed a career of 70 years or more.

Production of the Gladstone class amounted to 36 locomotives, the last of them completed in 1890, and the success of the type can be attributed mostly to its basically simple design, which resulted in good working and considerable reliability, and the careful arrangement of the suspension arrangements with leaf springs on the leading axle and more 'giving' coil springs on the centre axle. Stroudley was not a believer in too great an emphasis on simplicity when a measure of complexity could provide dividends, however, and as a result the Gladstone-class locomotives included a system to condense the exhaust steam into the feed water, in the process recovering some of the heat that would

otherwise have been wasted, and the use of air-driven assistance (using air from the Westinghouse air-brake supply) for the screw reversing gear. The details of the Gladstone-class locomotive included a tractive effort of 13,211lb (5993kg), two 18.25 x 26-in (464 x 660-mm) cylinders, driving wheels with a diameter of 6ft 6in (1.981m), steam pressure of 140lb/sq in (9.8kg/cm²), 9,000lb (4082kg) of fuel, 2,690 U.S. gal (2,240 Imp gal; 10183 litres) of water, total weight of 153,000lb (69401kg), and overall length of 51ft 10in (15.80m).

Designed by Daniel Gooch and introduced in 1888 on the wide-gauge lines of the Great Western Railway, the 'Rover' class of 4-2-2 steam locomotives were the successors of the Fire Fly class of 2-2-2 locomotives. The prototype for the class, which resulted from a process of continuous refinement, was the *Great Western* that

appeared in 1846 as what was in effect a stretched version of the Fire Fly class with greater grate area and tractive power at the expense of a weight increase of one-fifth. This was too much for the 2-2-2 layout, and after it had suffered a broken front axle soon after completion, the *Great Western* was revised to a 4-2-2 layout with the leading pair of wheels supported by the frames rather than attached to a pivoted truck. In this form the design was good, and there followed a series of steadily improved subclasses that provided the backbone of the Great Western Railway's fleet of locomotives.

The final subclass was the 'Rover' class, of which 54 were built with details that included a tractive effort of 9,640lb (4373kg), two 18 x 24-in (457 x 610-mm) cylinders, driving wheels with a diameter of 8ft 0in (2.438m), steam pressure 140lb/sq in (9.8kg/cm²), 7,000lb (3175kg) of fuel, 3,603

U.S. gal (3,000 Imp gal; 13638 litres) of water, total weight of 160,000lb (72576kg), and overall length of 47ft 6in (14.478m).

With the 'S3' class of 4-4-0 steam locomotives built for the Royal Prussian Union railway from 1893, a thoroughly modern look reached Germany's rail network, which was fast approaching its definitive primary form. The predecessors of the S3-class locomotives in the 1880s were a series of 2-4-0 locomotives with outside cylinders, but at this time there were passenger demands for higher levels of comfort and greater speeds, and the implementation of these constraints demanded the introduction of larger locomotives to provide the power required for what must inevitably be heavier trains. The superintendent of locomotives at Hanover was at the time August von Berries, who was despatched on a tour of

ABOVE LEFT: *Locomotive No. 999 4-4-0 of the New York Central Railroad's Empire State Express.*

ABOVE: *Locomotive No. 810 4-6-0 of the Boston & Maine Railroad poses at Boston's Old North Station shortly after the B&M had leased the Concorde & Montreal Railroad, 1895.*

OPPOSITE
ABOVE: *LNWR Ramsbottom Problem 2-2-2 Prince Alfred at Bletchley Station, Buckinghamshire, England, circa 1900.*

BELOW LEFT: *The first passenger station in Minneapolis, photographed in 1873. The St. Paul & Pacific Railroad was the first in the north-west, and ran from St. Paul to Minneapolis.*

BELOW RIGHT: *Depot of the U.S. Military Railroad at City Point, Virginia.*

the U.K. and the U.S.A. with the brief of assessing the latest locomotive thinking in these countries. The result was the decision that the larger boiler required for the generation of the desired power would require the introduction of another axle to create the 4-4-0 arrangement that was so successful in the U.S.A.

During 1890 the Henschel company manufactured two 4-4-0 locomotives with a two-cylinder compound-propulsion arrangement to a design by von Berries, and in the succeeding year Henschel constructed another four 4-4-0 locomotives (two each with compound- and simple-expansion propulsion) to the design of Lochner, the superintendent of locomotives at Erfurt. Lochner's simple-expansion system was deemed most effective, and there followed 150 locomotives before a reconsideration of the matter led to the decision that the von

LEFT: LNWR Ramsbottom Problem-class 2-2-2 Tornado *at Carlisle, England in 1899.*

OPPOSITE
ABOVE LEFT: *Locomotive No. 101* Central Vermont, *Burlington Northern Railroad.*

ABOVE RIGHT: *Western Railway's* Dragon *locomotive.*

BELOW LEFT: *Great Northern Railway Stirling 8-ft single No. 547, built in 1878. (Photographed circa 1905.)*

BELOW RIGHT: *Boston & Maine's 4-4-0 locomotive No. 53 on the turntable at the Charleston, Massachusetts engine house, circa 1910.*

Berries type of compound propulsion offered advantages. During 1892 August von Berries therefore designed an improved version of his original concept as the S3 design in which the letter stood for *schnellzuglokomotiv* (express locomotive). The type was extremely effective, and 1,073 such locomotives were therefore manufactured between 1892 and 1904 as 1,027 for the Prussian and 46 for other German state railways. Another 424 locomotives with smaller driving wheels

were also constructed as 'P4'-class units.

The S3 class was notable not only for its considerable size, but also for the fact that it was the first locomotive class to make use of steam superheating. The attraction of superheating results from the fact that water evaporates to steam at a specific temperature dependent on the ambient pressure: at the 171-lb/sq in (12-kg/cm²) working pressure of the S3 class, this temperature is 376°F (191°C) and when there is water in the boiler the steam

temperature cannot rise above that of the water. As the steam leaves the boiler it takes particles of water with it, and coming into contact with the cooler metal of the steam pipes, valves, cylinders and pistons it starts to lose its heat, part of it condensing into water to supplement the water droplets already being precipitated from the steam. Most of the work effected on the piston results from the expansion of the steam after the closure of the valve, but as water has no capacity for expansion, its presence in the

cylinder is a waste, and so too therefore is the energy used to heat it in the boiler.

However, the further heating of the steam after its departure from the boiler, and therefore no longer in contact with the temperature-limiting volume of water still in the boiler, allows the particles of water in the steam to be evaporated, in the process drying the steam and further increasing its volume. Additional heat raises the temperature of the dry steam, making it superheated. The slight cooling of

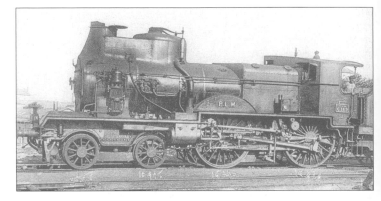

TOP: Paris, Lyons & Mediterranean LM 2-4-2 locomotive No. 85, of which 400 were built.

TOP RIGHT: *Locomotive No. C 169 built 1898–1901 for the famous* Route Impériale *of the Paris, Lyons & Mediterranean railway.*

ABOVE: *LNWR Webb Teutonic-compound 2-2-2-0 1304 Jeanie Deans.*

superheated steam as it touches the walls of the cylinder etc. does not cause condensation until all the superheat has been removed. Superheating therefore removes the possibility of condensation in the cylinder, thereby allowing better use to be made of the energy locked into the steam's heat.

The advantages of superheating had been appreciated for some time, but it was only in the 1890s that there appeared the first workable superheater designs, of which the most significant was that of Dr. Wilhelm Schmidt of Kassel. This was based on the ducting of the steam (between the boiler and the header that distributed the steam to the two cylinders) into a number of small tubes enclosed in a large-diameter tube through which flames from the firebox were ducted to create the superheating effect.

The Schmidt superheater was evaluated in single S3- and P4-class locomotives adapted in 1898 and proved generally successful except for the distortion of the superheater's outside cylinder as a result of the heat of the flames inside it. Schmidt therefore revised his concept to use the cooler but still high temperature of the smokebox, and this proved wholly successful. In 1899 two S3-class locomotives were completed with the definitive Schmidt smokebox type of superheater, and the success of the system was attested by a 12 per cent reduction in fuel consumption. The system soon became standard for all new locomotives of the larger, high-speed type, further refinement of the concept resulting in fuel economies of up to 20 per cent.

So successful were the superheated S3-class locomotives that 34 were still in service when the unified German rail network was created in 1924. The details of the S3 class included one 18.9 x 23.6-in (480 x 600-mm) high-pressure cylinder and one 26.6 x 23.6-in (680 x 600-mm) low-pressure cylinder, driving wheels with a

RIGHT: Class D16/3 No.62618 resplendent in fully lined apple green, with the first British Rail symbol (a very rare combination), heads a Cambridge train out of Colchester, England in the summer of 1950/51.One of the last series of the Claud Hamilton class built by the LNER in 1923, it retained the decorative valancing when converted to a D16/3 in 1944.

BELOW: A line-up of Santa Fe history from left to right: locomotive Cyrus K. Holliday, No. 3767, No. 3460 Blue Goose, diesel freight and diesel passenger locomotives.

diameter of 6ft 6in (1.98m), steam pressure of 171lb/sq in (12kg/cm^2), 11,023lb (5000kg) of fuel, 5,680 U.S. gal (4,729 Imp gal; 21500 litres) of water, weight of 111,993lb (50800kg) without tender, and overall length of 57ft 7in (17.56m).

Although the American Standard class of 4-4-0 steam locomotives performed notably as the main passenger-hauling locomotive of the U.S. railroad networks from the 1850s, by the 1880s it had become clear that the movement of heavier trains at higher speeds on the technically more sophisticated railroads of the states of the U.S.A.'s eastern seaboard required larger and more powerful locomotives, generally of

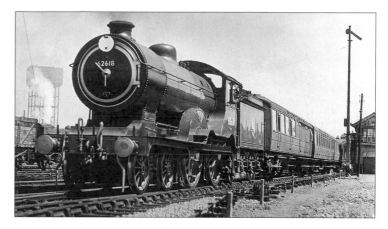

the 4-6-0 configuration created by the simple expedient of adding a third coupled axle to the rear of the axles for the two current pairs of driving wheels and 'streamlining' the whole unit both internally and externally. These alterations were not without their problems, but even so some 16,000 such locomotives were manufactured in the period between 1880 and 1910.

Typical of this impressive breed was the 'I-1' class made by the Brooks Locomotive Works of Dunkirk in New York during 1900 for the Lake Shore & Michigan Southern Railroad, which needed a type to pull the prestige trains on the western section of the rail line (linking New York on the U.S.A.'s eastern coast and Chicago in Illinois on the south coast of Lake Michigan) of what was soon the New York Central Railroad. The locomotives performed well, pulling heavy five-coach trains at moderately high speeds with a smooth ride, including the classic *Twentieth Century Limited* de-luxe service introduced in June 1902, but fell out of favour when the increase in passenger loads from the beginning of the 20th century required more power than could sensibly be delivered by a derivative of the American Standard class. The details of the I-1 class included a tractive effort of 23,800lb (10796kg), two 20 x 28-in (508 x 711-mm) cylinders, driving wheels with a diameter of 6ft 10in (2.032m), steam pressure of 200lb/sq in (14.1kg/cm^2), 17,500lb (7938kg) of fuel, 7,200 U.S. gal (5,995 Imp gal; 27255 litres) of water, total weight of 300,000lb (136080kg), and overall length of 62ft 3in (18.914m).

One of the first in overall terms and one of the most important operators in the U.S.A., the Pennsylvania Railroad had by the end of the 19th century become widely known for its large and powerful locomotives, most of them manufactured in the company's own facilities at Altoona. Typical of this breed were the 4-4-0 steam locomotives produced in several classes on which the most important and successful was the 'D16' class that first appeared in 1895 and was later recognized as one of the high points in the design and manufacture of American steam locomotives.

The class was typified by large cylinders and a boiler that operated at a high pressure by the standards of the period, and it was also notable in purely visual terms for the considerable height of its boiler, which resulted from the installation of the firebox above rather than between the frames.

The class was initially manufactured in two variants, namely the 'D16a' class with driving wheels of 6ft 10in (2.032m) diameter for operation on the railroad's flatter routes, and the D16 proper with driving wheels of 5ft 8in (1.727m) diameter for operation on the railroad's less flat routes. The D16a class was soon known for its high speed, and operated on the 58-mile (93-km) 'racetrack' between Camden and Atlantic City on which the Pennsylvania Railroad vied directly with the Atlantic City Railroad.

The D16 class was built to the extent of 426 locomotives in five subclasses in the period between 1895 and 1910. In the first years of the 20th century the locomotives of the D16 classes were generally outdone by

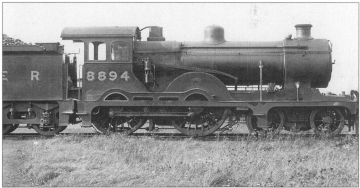

OPPOSITE

ABOVE: *The K4-class 4-6-2 locomotives were the mainstay of steam operations for the Pennsylvania Railroad until after World War II.*

BELOW: *Great Eastern Railway Claud Hamilton-class 4-4-0.*

ABOVE: *Class L Mallet-articulated. Great Northern's L-class 2-6-6-2 locomotives, built by Baldwin in 1906–07, were true Mallets. No.1810, shown here, was an L-2 of 1907 vintage.*

ABOVE RIGHT: *Pennsylvania Railroad 4-4-2 with slide valves, crossing the Skilkill river bridge.*

RIGHT: *The Great Eastern Railway Claud Hamilton-class 4-4-0 locomotive was named for the chairman of the company and came into being at the turn of the century.*

the newer 'Atlantic'- and 'Pacific'-class locomotives in terms of power and therefore performance, but from 1914 just under half of the D16-class locomotives were considerably updated to the 'D16sb' class standard with a number of improvements including cylinders enlarged from the original 18.5 x 26-in (470 x 660-mm) type, and a Schmidt superheating system. In this form the locomotives became important on branch lines, some of them remaining in service until the early 1940s. The details for the D16sb-class locomotive included a tractive effort of 23,900lb (10841kg), two 20.5 x 26-in (521 x 660-mm) driving wheels with a diameter of 5ft 8in (1.727m), steam pressure of 175lb/sq in (12.3kg/cm^2), 26,000lb (11794kg) of fuel, 5,600 U.S. gal (4,663 Imp gal; 21198 litres) of water, total weight of 281,000lb (127462kg), and overall length of 67ft 0in (20.422m).

As noted above, there was intense rivalry between the Pennsylvania Railroad and the Atlantic City Railroad in those regions near Atlantic City in New Jersey where the two operators' networks overlapped, and each tried to secure the lion's share of the traffic between the heavily populated inland cities round Philadelphia and the coastal resorts of New Jersey. This rivalry consisted not of the provision of additional capacity at peak periods, mainly July and August of each year, but in the provision of the fastest services with as much time as possible trimmed from the scheduled journey through regular running at speeds in excess of 90mph (145km/h) for an average journey speed of 70mph (113km/h) or more.

One of the key instruments in the effort by the Atlantic City Railroad from the last years of the 19th century into the first years of the 20th century was the 'Camelback' class of 4-4-2 locomotives, which had an unusual appearance in that they seemed to be squashed longitudinally, but introduced a number of important features. These last included a firebox that was both wide and deep, allowing the effective burning of anthracite coal and, as it was later found, bituminous coal and then oil. Other features that made the class notable were pairs of compound cylinders on each side with drive by means of a common cross head, and the 'camelback' cab for the driver, who was thus carried over the boiler, while the fireman was provided with only the most rudimentary protection in the normal location at the rear of the locomotive. The arrangement certainly gave the driver a good field of vision, but made communication between the driver and fireman extremely difficult.

At the technical level the Camelback class was successful, and was therefore built in moderately large numbers for the Atlantic City Railroad (soon the Philadelphia & Reading Railroad). Several

OPPOSITE: An early passenger train of the late 1880s or 1890s, probably taken between Great Falls and Butte on the line of the Montana Central Railway. The Montana Central became part of the Great Northern Railway.

THIS PAGE
ABOVE: Winans' Camel locomotive No. 65, built by Ross Winans in Baltimore in 1850.

RIGHT: The Italian locomotive Dante Alighieri, built by Henschel and Son in 1873.

other railroads on the east coast of the U.S.A. also built locomotives of the same basic concept. The details of the Camelback class included a tractive effort of 22,906lb (10390kg), two 13 x 26-in (330 x 660-mm) high-pressure cylinders and two 22 x 26-in (559 x 660-mm) low-pressure cylinders, driving wheels with a diameter of 7ft 0in (2.134m), steam pressure of 200lb/sq in (14kg/cm²), 4,000 U.S. gal (3,331 Imp gal; 15142 litres) of water, and total weight of 218,000lb (98885kg),

By the end of the 19th century the 'standard' American steam locomotive for use on passenger services was of the 4-4-0 configuration, but by this time it was clear that further progress in terms of hauling ability and speed demanded a configuration with more than eight wheels. As a result, there emerged a number of 10-wheel designs divided neatly into the 4-6-0 and 4-4-2 layouts. The former type offered greater adhesive weight (the weight on the driving wheels) but was limited by the area of the grate that could be installed between the rear pair of driving wheels, while the latter (later known as the 'Atlantic' type) had lesser adhesive weight but could be fitted with a larger grate between the undriven rear wheels.

The Pennsylvania Railroad almost inevitably adopted the Atlantic type of locomotive as it already possessed the network of heavier track capable of accepting this type's heavy axle loads, and at the technical level wanted to be able to burn large quantities of modest-quality coal rather than smaller quantities of a higher grade.

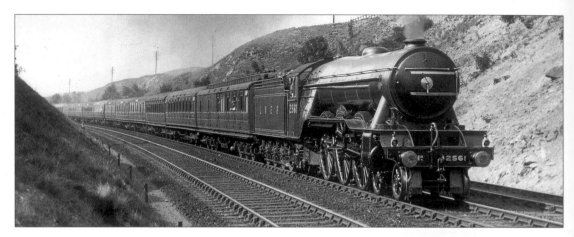

First manufactured in the railroad's Altoona facility in 1899, the first two Atlantic-type locomotives had a grate area of 68sq ft (6.32m²), which was more than twice the figure for any of the railroad's 4-4-0 locomotives. A third locomotive had the smaller grate area of 55.5sq ft (5.16m²), and it was this size that became standard for all later Atlantic-type locomotives, which totalled 576 in a number of subclasses. The 'E2' class had cylinders with a diameter of 20.5in (521mm) while the cylinders of the 'E3' class, intended mainly for heavier work, had a diameter of 22in (559mm).

By 1913, manufacture of the Atlantic type had reached 493 units, and it seemed that the type had reached the limit of its development in the face of competition from the more modern 'Pacific' type with its three pairs of coupled driving wheels. It was just before this stage, though, that Axel Vogt, the

ABOVE: *No. 2561* Minoru *on an East Coast express, England in August 1932.*

RIGHT: *The former New Zealand Railway's A-class 0-4-0 tank locomotive of 1873 departs with a 1st Plains Branch Railway train.*

OPPOSITE
ABOVE LEFT: *A typical mixed train headed by an old J-class dating from the 1870s at Dunsandel station near Canterbury, New Zealand, early 1900s.*

ABOVE RIGHT: *Manchester Locomotive Works 4-4-0 locomotive No. 31 on the Fitchburg Railroad. It was leased by Boston & Maine from 1 July 1900.*

BELOW: *In their day, Claud Hamilton-class 4-4-0 locomotives were the expresses of the Great Eastern Railway.*

railroad's chief engineer, had decided that the driving-wheel arrangement of the Pacific type was unnecessarily complex and planned a further-improved version of the Atlantic type with a boiler increased in maximum diameter from 5ft 5.5in (1.664m) to 6ft 4.75in (1.949m) and with a combustion chamber at the front.

The prototype of this 'E6' class of locomotives first appeared in 1910 and revealed greater power than the Pacific type at higher speeds. Two more locomotives were then made with a superheating system, allowing a further increase in cylinder diameter of 23.5in (597mm), and these locomotives revealed excellent performance. There followed production of 80 E6-class locomotives, all completed between February and August 1914 to become the mainstays of the Pennsylvania Railroad's express services on flatter parts of its route network. After the advent of the definitive 'K4' class of Pacific-type locomotives after the end of World War I in 1918, the E6-class locomotives were gradually relegated to

lesser services. Many of the earlier locomotives were upgraded over the years with features such as superheating, five of them lasting in service to 1947. The details for the 'E3sd' subclass included a tractive effort of 27,400lb (12429kg), two 22 x 26-in (559 x 660-mm) cylinders, driving wheels with a diameter of 6ft 8in (2.032m), steam pressure of 205lb/sq in (14.4kg/cm^2), 34,200lb (15513kg) of fuel, 6,800 U.S. gal (5,662 Imp gal; 25741 litres) of water, total weight of 363,500lb (164884kg), and overall length of 71ft 6in (21.640m).

Back on the eastern side of the North Atlantic Ocean, January 1900 saw the appearance of the first of the 'Claud Hamilton' class of 4-4-0 locomotives named for the chairman of the company that built it, the Great Eastern Railway. Though its inside-cylinder layout was typical of the previous century, the way ahead was presaged in features such as the large cab with four big side windows, the power-operated reversing gear, water scoop, and provision for the burning of waste oil products (a by-product of the company's oil-gas operation) rather than coal. Good features that were not quite as advanced included an exhaust steam injector and a variable-nozzle blast pipe.

The history of the Claud Hamilton class was complex, and eventually extended to cover a total of 121 such locomotives built in the period between 1900 and 1923 in a number of subclasses characterized by the introduction of features such as larger boilers, a superheating system, and piston rather than slide valves. All these features were built into the definitive 'Super Claud' class of which 10 were completed. As new-build locomotives introduced improved features, most of the older units were rebuilt to the improved standard, most of them by the London & North Eastern Railway that introduced its own designation system. In overall terms, therefore, there were 41 of the original Claud Hamilton (LNER 'D14') class locomotives that served up to 1931 and underwent no rebuilds, 66 of what later became the 'D15' class (nine rebuilt) that served between 1903 and 1933 and introduced the Belpaire firebox, four of what later became the 'D15/1' (70 rebuilt) class that served between 1911 and 1935 and introduced the superheating system, none of what became the 'D15/2' class (80 rebuilt) that served between 1914 and 1952 and introduced a lengthened smokebox, 10 of the 'Super Claud' or later 'D16/1' class (five rebuilt) that served between 1923 and 1934 and introduced a larger boiler, none of the 'D16/2' class (40 rebuilt) that served between 1926 and 1952 and were basically

OPPOSITE

ABOVE LEFT: The 232 Nord railway Baltic-class locomotive, No. 1102.

ABOVE RIGHT: Locomotive No. 8 with F15 Pacific No. 434 charges along with four cars of train, east of Russell, Kentucky in June 1947.

BELOW: An Auckland-Wellington express headed by a 'K'-class 4-8-4 locomotive No. 905 between Taupiri and Ngaruawahia in the Waikato district, 7 March 1952.

THIS PAGE

ABOVE: Nord 4-4-2 de Glehn compound.

RIGHT: New Zealand Railways Q-class 4-6-2 locomotive No. 346 at the Oamaru locomotive depot when it was used for hauling passenger trains over the steeply-graded section of line between Oamaru and Dunedin, South Island, New Zealand.

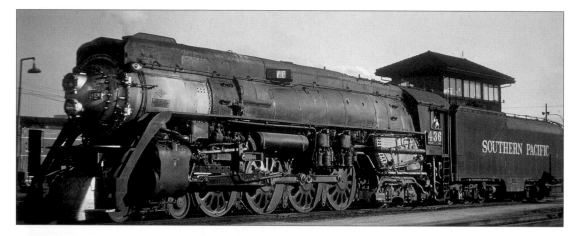

LEFT: *Southern Pacific Railroad 4-8-4 No. 4436 at San Francisco, July 1952.*

BELOW LEFT:
Union Pacific 4-8-4 on a northbound evening passenger service at Denver, Colorado, July 1952.

BELOW: *LNER Gresley Pacific No. 4479 Robert the Devil at Doncaster, England in 1935.*

OPPOSITE: *Norfolk & Western Railroad 'J'-class 4-8-4 No. 609 on a westbound passenger train.*

similar to the 'D16/1' class units, and none of the 'D16/3' class (104 rebuilt) that served between 1033 and 1958 and saw the removal of the coupling rod splashers and the reintroduction of round-topped boilers.

The details of the Claud Hamilton class, of which all (13, 16 and 88 examples of the D15/2, D16/2 and D16/3 classes respectively) were still in service at the time of the nationalization of the British rail system on the first day of 1948, included a tractive effort of 17,100lb (7757kg), two 19 x 26-in (483 x 660-mm) cylinders, driving wheels with a diameter of 7ft 0in (2.134m), steam pressure of 180lb/sq in (12.7kg/cm²), 859 U.S. gal (715 Imp gal; 3250 litres) of oil fuel, 4,143 U.S. gal (3,450 Imp gal; 15864 litres) of water, total weight of 213,000lb (96617kg), and

overall length of 53ft 4.75in (16.276m).

Alfred de Glehn was English but became the chief engineer of the Société Alsacienne de Constructions Mécaniques during the 1870s before he reached the age of 30, and with Gaston du Bousquet of the Nord railway was responsible for the development of one of the classic compound expansion systems for steam locomotives. indeed, most of the 20th-century express passenger locomotives were of the de Glehn compound type.

De Glehn and Bousquet initially collaborated on a number of highly successful compound 4-4-0 locomotives introduced in the 1890s, but their best claim to fame was the 'Atlantic'-type 4-4-2 class first revealed in 1900 as the initial unit of 32 such locomotives for the Nord railway. The locomotives had highly pleasing lines, although some considered it odd that there were outside bearings on the two axles of the leading truck and inside bearings on the single trailing axle. The inside low-pressure cylinders were located in line with the forward axle of the leading truck and powered the leading coupled axle, while the outside high-pressure cylinders were installed in the standard position above the rear axle of the leading truck and powered the rear pair of coupled wheels.

The de Glehn Atlantic-type locomotives were used for services such as the boat trains between Paris and Calais on some of the hardest schedules in the world, but the long-term performance of the locomotives was remarkable. The type

offered very low specific fuel consumption. This gave useful operating economics, but it was also important as the power of steam locomotives was becoming limited by the ability of the fireman to shovel coal onto the grate and a relatively miserly rate of fuel consumption was a considerable bonus in this respect.

The success of the de Glehn Atlantic type was such that orders were placed for an additional 152 locomotives, including 59 for four other French operators, 79 for the Royal Prussian Union railway in Germany, and the other 14 for single operators in Egypt (10), the U.K. (3) and the U.S.A. (1). Some of these later locomotives were completed to slightly different standards, notable mainly for their greater sizes, and the technical success of the de Glehn and Bousquet compound-expansion system led the French railways to keep the system for many later classes of 4-6-0, 2-8-2, 4-6-2 and 4-8-2 locomotives. The details for the de Glehn Atlantic-type 4-4-2 locomotive included two 13.5 x 25.25-in (340 x 640-mm) high-pressure cylinders and two 22 x 25.25-in (560 x 640-mm) low-pressure cylinders, driving wheels with a diameter of 6ft 8.25in (2.04m), steam pressure of 228lb/sq in (16kg/cm²), 15,432lb (7000kg) of fuel, 6,089 U.S. gal (5,070 Imp gal; 23050 litres) of water, total weight of 78,483lb (35600kg), and overall length of 59ft 10.5in (18.247m).

During 1901 there appeared the first example of possibly the single most celebrated class of express passenger

locomotive ever constructed, a type that was built right to the end of the steam locomotive era. Oddly enough, this locomotive was not planned by one of the great locomotive-designing nations, but rather the small country of New Zealand. Here A.W. Beattie, the chief engineer of the Government Railway, felt that the country's railway system needed a locomotive with a big firebox able to burn the poor lignite coal produced at Otago on South Island.

Although Baldwin, the selected American manufacturer, recommended a Camelback 4-6-0 locomotive with a substantial firebox above the rear wheels, Beattie opted instead for a 4-6-0 development with the firebox carried by a two-wheel pony truck to create a 4-6-2. The 13 engines were quickly completed and despatched across the Pacific ocean in a process that created the generic name of the 'Pacific'-type locomotive that was to be built in very large numbers in the years to come.

The Pacific-type locomotives of the 'Q' class also had the classic type of valve gear designed during 1844 by the Belgian engineer Egide Walschaert, and lacked only two features that were added in later locomotives to create the fully definitive Pacific-type steam locomotive: these features were a superheating system and inside admission piston valves in place of outside valves.

After the implementation of some minor modifications, the locomotives of the Q class gave long service, the last of the locomotives not being retired until 1957.

The details of the Q-class locomotive included a tractive effort of 19,540lb (8863kg), two 16 x 22-in (406 x 559-mm) cylinders, driving wheels with a diameter of 4ft 1in (1.245m), steam pressure of 200lb/sq in (14kg/cm^2), 11,000lb (4990kg) of fuel, 2,042 U.S. gal (1,700 Imp gal; 7728 litres) of water, total weight of 165,000lb (74844kg), and overall length of 55ft 4.5in (16.872m).

In 1902 the Chesapeake & Ohio Railroad (chartered in 1785 but beginning operations only in 1836 with the inauguration of the Louisa Railroad in Virginia) took delivery of its first Pacific-type 4-6-2 steam locomotive, the initial unit of the 'F15'-class, and in the process gained the distinction of introducing the truly definitive type of steam locomotive to American passenger services. The locomotive still possessed strong affinities with the past and had no superheating system, but was marked as something notably different from earlier types by its size and power.

The first F15-class locomotive was followed by another 26 units in the period up to 1911, and the overall success of the type is attested by the fact that virtually all of the locomotives survived in useful service until the Chesapeake & Ohio Railroad switched to diesel locomotives in the 1950s. In the later stages of their career of 50 or so years, the F15-class locomotives were gradually relegated to less important services or to lines whose bridges could not support the weight of later locomotives, and a number of upgrades were effected to

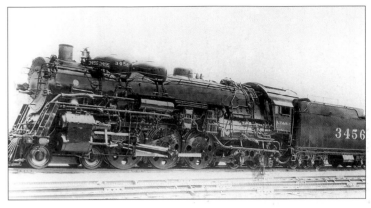

OPPOSITE: Union Pacific No. 9000 Union Pacific-type 4-12-2 three-cylinder locomotive built by the American Locomotive company in April 1926. This was the longest non-articulated locomotive ever built and had a tender capacity of 15,000 gallons (6819 litres) of water.

ABOVE LEFT: Santa Fe's Class 3460 locomotive No. 3461 Pacific-type 4-6-4. It was built by the Baldwin Locomotive Works in 1937 with 84-in (2134-mm) diameter driving wheels and a tender capacity of 20,000 gallons (90920 litres).

ABOVE RIGHT: Santa Fe's Class 3450 locomotive No. 3456 Pacific-type 4-6-4. It was built by the Baldwin Locomotive Works in 1923 with 79-in (2007-mm) diameter driving wheels.

incorporate features such as Walschaert valve gear, superheating and mechanical stoking systems as well as improved cabs and, in some cases, new cylinders and even new frames.

The success of the Pacific type of steam locomotive in service with American railroads was reflected in the subsequent manufacture of some 7,000 units of the same basic type for a host of operators, and the spawning of a number of derived versions for service with the Chesapeake & Ohio Railroad. These derivatives included the 'F16' class of 1913 with a larger grate area and a boost in tractive effort of almost 35 per cent, the 'F17' class of the following year with still further increases in grate area and tractive effort, and then in the period after the end of World War I the 'F18' and 'F19' classes with large 12-wheel tenders carrying increased volumes of water. The details of the F15-class locomotive in its

original form included the tractive effort of 32,400lb (14697kg), two 23.5 x 28-in (597 x 711-mm) cylinders, driving wheels with a diameter of 6ft 0in (1.829m), steam pressure of 180lb/sq in (12.7kg/cm²), 30,000lb (13608kg) of fuel, 9,000 U.S. gal (7,494 Imp gal; 34069 litres) of water, total weight of 408,000lb (185069kg), and overall length of 74ft 0in (22.555m).

Responsible for the introduction to the U.K. of the large boiler with a wide firebox, the 'Large Atlantic' class of 4-4-2 steam locomotives was designed by Henry Ivatt and built to the extent of 94 units (delivered between 1902 and 1910) for the Great Northern Railway at its own facility in Doncaster, south Yorkshire. The class reigned supreme on the southern portion of the service between London and Edinburgh up to 1921, when it was supplanted by 4-6-2 locomotives. Thereafter, the type was still used for a number of celebrated but lighter

services, and finally disappeared from service only in 1950.

In common with most of the world's truly great steam locomotives, the Large Atlantic class was essentially simple in mechanical terms but wholly modern in the features that truly counted. The cylinders were outside, the valves and valve gear were inside, and while the first 81 locomotives of the class lacked a superheating system and possessed balanced slide valves, the final 10 had a superheating system and piston valves: superheating was later retrofitted to the earlier locomotives, most of which were also adapted to piston valves. The details of the Large Atlantic-class locomotive in its superheated form included a tractive effort of 17,340lb (7865kg), two 20 x 24-in (508 x 610-mm) cylinders, driving wheels with a diameter of 6ft 8in (2.032m), steam pressure of 170lb/sq in (12.0kg/cm²), 14,500lb (6577kg) of fuel, 4,203 U.S. gal (3,500 Imp

ABOVE LEFT: *Boston & Maine's Class P-1-6 Pacific (No. 3602) prepares to leave North Station, Boston. Built in 1910, she was extensively modernized.*

ABOVE RIGHT: *Missouri Pacific locomotive No. 6509 Pacific-type 4-6-2, built in 1903 by Alco for passenger services.*

FAR LEFT: *Locomotive No. 3461 of the Santa Fe Railroad. Built by the Baldwin Works in 1937, she is a 3460-class Pacific-type 4-6-4.*

LEFT: *Boston & Maine's classic P-4-a Pacific No. 3712 about to depart Boston's North Station for Portland, Maine. 24 June 1939.*

ABOVE: Prussian S1-class locomotive.

ABOVE RIGHT: Engine 3460, class leader of the Pacific-type 4-6-4 built at the Baldwin Locomotive Works in 1937.

RIGHT: Locomotive No. 2926, Saint Nicholas, a member of the Saint class of locomotives built for the Great Western Railway between 1902 and 1911.

gal; 15911 litres) of water, total weight of 252,500lb (114534kg), and overall length of 57ft 10.25in (17.634m).

By the end of the 19th century George Jackson Churchward saw that he was likely to succeed William Dean as the chief engineer of the Great Western Railway, and also that the time was more than ripe for a virtually total renewal of the Great Western's highly diverse locomotive stock to provide a combination of greater homogeneity and superior performance. As Dean's deputy at the railway's main manufacturing plant at Swindon in Wiltshire, Churchward had been able to have many of his ideas, some of them fairly outlandish, realized in concrete form, but by the turn of the century Churchward had

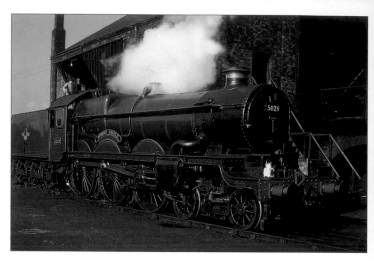

come to focus on more orthodox ideas for locomotives that nevertheless embodied significant improvements over their predecessors.

This fact was reflected in the appearance during 1902 of the *Dean* (later *William Dean*) 4-6-0 steam locomotive. This seemed somewhat apart from the main stream of British locomotive thinking, but this was hardly remarkable given the close working relationship of Churchward and A.W. Gibbs, a senior engineer of the Pennsylvania Railroad in the U.S.A. The new locomotive should thus be seen as a blend of American 10-wheel design thinking and British engineering practices. In overall terms, therefore, the American 10-wheel configuration was combined with cylinders and valve chests located outside

the frames for maximum accessibility, and Stephenson valve gear inside the frames to drive the inside admission valves. Other American features were the cylinders and the smokebox, but most of the rest was of orthodox British concept. With steady refinement incorporated, this combination of American and British features became standard for the 2,000 or so locomotives of the classes designed under the supervision of Churchward and his immediate successors.

Churchward's ideas were far from fixed, however, and it should be noted that it took him a considerable time to decide whether the advantage lay with the two-cylinder 'Saint' class of 4-6-0 locomotives derived from the Dean prototype or with the four-cylinder 'Star' class of 4-6-0 locomotives.

Some 77 and 60 of these two classes were built, and it was not long before his retirement in 1921 that Churchward finally preferred the latter.

The designation Saint class was in fact applied to the two-cylinder Churchward 4-6-0 locomotives only after the completion of 32 units including three prototype locomotives. The 19 locomotives of the first production batch were delivered in 1905, and some of them operated for a short time in a 4-4-2 configuration. The second batch of 10 locomotives was delivered from 1906, and the first of this batch was also the first British locomotive with a thoroughly modern superheating system of the Schmidt type, and such a system was later retrofitted to the earlier locomotives.

From 1907 there followed 20 examples

of the genuine Saint class with a number of improved features, and finally from 1911 25 examples of the derived 'Court' subclass with a superheating system installed from the beginning together with a number of further improved features including a 0.5-in (12.7-mm) increase in cylinder diameter. One of the most important keys to the success of the Churchward locomotives was the designer's super Boiler No.1, which was used not only in the 77 units of the Saint class but also in 74 'Star' 4-6-0, three 'Frenchman' 4-4-2, 330 'Hall' 4-6-0, 80 'Grange' 4-6-0, and 150 '28XX' 2-8-0 class locomotives. A primary feature of the Boiler No.1 was the system to clean and warm the water before it reached the boiler.

Over the years, all of the Saint-class locomotives but the prototype were

OPPOSITE
LEFT: *No. 4079* Pendennis Castle, *photographed in 1967.*

RIGHT: *No. 5029* Nunney Castle.

THIS PAGE
RIGHT: *Great Northern Railway's C2 4-4-2 No. 990* Henry Oakley *pilots C1 4-4-4 No. 251* Planet Centenarian, *celebrating 100 years of the Doncaster locomotive works in England.*

FAR RIGHT: *A BESA-class 2-8-0 hauling freight in India.*

upgraded to the definitive standard typical of the last units to be completed. It is also worth noting that another 330 locomotives were built to a standard described as the Hall class, which differed from the Saint class mainly in having driving wheels with a diameter of 6ft 0in (1.828m) for greater tractive effort with little reduction in maximum speed. The details of the Saint-class locomotive in its later guise with a superheating system included a tractive effort of 24,395lb (11066kg), two 18.5 x 30-in (470 x 762-mm) cylinders, driving wheels with a diameter of 6ft 8in (2.045m), steam pressure of 225lb/sq in (15.8kg/cm^2), 13,500lb (6124kg) of fuel, 4,203 U.S. gal (3,500 Imp gal; 15911 litres) of water, total weight of 251,000lb (113854kg), and overall length of 63ft 0.25in (19.209m).

Wholly British in concept but designed and manufactured for service hauling main trains in India, the 'BESA' class of 4-6-0 locomotives entered service in 1905 and later production examples of the type are still in effective service on the Indian railway system.

The Indian rail network at the beginning of the 20th century represented a combination of private enterprise under a concessionary system that gave the government of India some control in return for a guaranteed return on the operators' investments. This was a highly beneficial system for all concerned and, after the relative fiasco of the first stages of Indian railway development, in which a proliferation of gauges was permitted through lack of adequate overall controls,

the beginning of a more organized nationwide rail system appeared. This process involved the establishment of a number of standard locomotive designs which reflected the appreciation of British locomotive manufacturers that greater profitability resulted from the mass-production of a few standard types than the 'penny packet' production of a larger number.

As far as the Indian rail network was concerned, therefore, there were 'Standard Passenger' 4-4-0, 'Standard Goods' 0-6-0, 'Heavy Goods' 2-8-0 and 'Heavy Passenger' 4-6-0 types of locomotives for the broad-gauge part of the system, which had a gauge of 5ft 6in (1.68m). All of these standard designs remained in service virtually to the present, and the BESA

class was of the Heavy Passenger type.

The first BESA-class locomotives were very substantially engineered, and when introduced were larger and more powerful than virtually any other locomotives in India (now divided into India, Pakistan and Bangladesh). The design was in essence a derivative of the 4-6-0 locomotives produced from 1903 for the South Western Railway by the North British Locomotive Company of Glasgow, which manufactured the first BESA-class locomotives for the Indian market. The size of this market meant that such locomotives were also built by Vulcan Foundry, Robert Stephenson & Company, Kitson, and William Beardmore in the United Kingdom, while numbers were also produced in India as that country's industrial base became capable of the task.

The first examples had no superheating system, outside cylinders, inside slide valves and Stephenson valve gear, but this initial standard was soon upgraded to an improved pattern with outside Walschaert valve gear, outside piston valves and a superheating system. The details of the BESA-class locomotive in its definitive form included a tractive effort of 22,590lb (10247kg), two 20.5 x 26-in (521 x 660-mm) cylinders, driving wheels with a diameter of 6ft 2in (1.88m), steam pressure of 180lb/sq in (12.7kg/cm^2), 16,800lb (7620kg) of fuel, 4,804 U.S. gal (4,000 Imp gal; 18184 litres) of water, total weight of 273,000lb (123833kg), and overall length of 62ft 3.25in (18.980m).

At the start of the 20th century the Prussian state railway system had to decide whether or not the superheating system was an alternative to the compound-expansion system or just an add-on element. The railway had built both simple- and compound-expansion locomotives since 1884, the former being used mainly for secondary routes and services, and the latter for primary routes and express services. The railway in fact continued with the manufacture of non-superheated compound-expansion locomotives right up to 1911, but during this period also brought into service a number of simple-expansion locomotives with a superheating system, typical of the type being the 'P6'class of 2-6-0 locomotives, some 272 of which were manufactured in the period between 1903 and 1910. The two main problems with the P6 class were the small diameter of the driving wheels (only 5ft 3in/1.60m) that were too small for the speeds envisaged, and poor weight distribution.

In 1906 a class of 4-6-0 locomotives with a driving-wheel diameter of 5ft 9in (1.750m) made its appearance with the object of allowing a speed of 68mph (110km/h). The early locomotives were unreliable, however, and their tendency to suffer mechanical failures made them very unpopular. A cure of the class's main difficulties was found in a reduction of cylinder diameter and modification of the weight distribution, but at the same time the railway authorities came to the conclusion that as the motion and valve gear were unsuitable for speeds of 62mph (100km/h) or more, these engines should be used for secondary passenger and mixed-traffic services. This revised type was the 'P8' class, which had initially been schemed for express passenger work on a limited part of the Prussian system but now became history's most widely used and popular mixed-traffic steam locomotive.

In common with most other successful steam locomotives, the P8 class was essentially simple in its basic concept and possessed a pleasing appearance with a round-topped boiler with a narrow but lengthy firebox. At later dates, at least two other boilers were installed, but these did not change the locomotive's pleasant lines. The locomotive had a Schmidt superheating system, and the combination of this and piston valves with Walschaert valve gear provided the locomotives with one of the very highest levels of efficiency

OPPOSITE

ABOVE: BESA-design SP 138 (KS 1921) at Jam Sahib, the Borridge Special *from Mirpur Khas to Nawabshah.*

BELOW: Pakistan PAK 2-15a BESA 0-6-0.

THIS PAGE
ABOVE and RIGHT: Pakistan Railway BESA-class 4-4-0.

achieved in a simple-expansion engine.

Almost inevitably there were a small number of teething problems with the P8-class locomotive, but once these problems had been eliminated the P8 was manufactured in very substantial numbers as its modest axle load allowed the operation of the type over most of the Prussian rail network. The P8-class locomotive was also constructed in small numbers for the railways of Baden, Mecklenburg and Oldenburg states in Germany, and also for export. Though supposedly a locomotive for secondary passenger services, the P8-class locomotive was in fact used for primary passenger services in which there was no requirement for a speed of more than 62mph (100km/h).

By the end of World War I, some 2,350 P8-class locomotives had been manufactured for the Prussian rail network, but 628 of these had then to be handed over to other countries as part of Germany's war reparation: Belgium, for instance, received some 2,000 locomotives including 168 P8s which then remained in service up to 1966, when Belgium retired its last steam locomotives. In Germany, the loss of so many P8-class locomotives as war reparation was offset in part by the construction of more locomotives of the same type, the last of which was delivered in 1928. With the creation of the German state railway organization, the P8 class became the '38' class. Most of these

locomotives were later fitted with new boilers, and their appearance was changed by the addition of feed water heaters, full-depth smoke deflectors and other outside features.

In World War II the operating region of the P8-class steam locomotives soon spread to the east as the Germans seized much of Poland in September 1939 and then from June 1941 sought to extend their empire into the U.S.S.R., and also to the south as Germany took Czechoslovakia in 1939 and then captured Yugoslavia and Greece from April 1941. This wartime exigency resulted in the use of the P8-class locomotive over a considerably larger area than before, and the type was to be seen in Czechoslovakia,

Greece, Poland, Romania, U.S.S.R. and Yugoslavia, where many of the locomotives remained as the Germans were driven back in the later stages of the war. In some of the countries, the surviving locomotives of the P8 class were subjected to a modification process to bring them into line with national systems, but seldom was the successful basic design changed in any significant fashion. German production of the P8 class eventually totalled 3,438 units, and about 500 more basically identical engines were constructed in other countries, including Poland, which also created 190 examples of a derived type with a larger boiler and wider firebox on the chassis of the P8 class.

Some 2,803 example of the P8 class

ABOVE LEFT: A P8 working in Romania. German-built locomotives were exported throughout the eastern bloc.

ABOVE: After World War I, of the 2,350 P8-class locomotives built for the Prussian state railway system, 628 were handed to other countries as war reparation. However, more locomotives of the same class were constructed.

OPPOSITE: German 03-2098 4-6-2.

survived to the end of World War II in Germany, although many of these were unserviceable to greater or lesser extents. The creation of different rail networks in the western and eastern parts of Germany, which later became West Germany and East Germany, meant that the available P8-class locomotives were, like other surviving engines, divided between the two networks. Both organizations generally replaced the full-depth smoke deflectors with a more modern type, and some of the East German locomotives were fitted with revised exhausts of the Giesl type. The P8 class did not survive very long in West German service, for the adoption of diesel locomotives was implemented with some

speed, and by 1968 there were only 73 P8-class steam locomotives, most of them working in the south of the country, where the last of them survived to 1973 as a result of the slowing of the replacement programme. This meant that the P8 class survived longer in West than East Germany, where the final units of the class were withdrawn from service in 1972.

This was not the end of the line for the P8-class locomotive, however, for several units remained in useful service into the late 1970s in Poland and Romania. The details for the P8-class locomotive included a tractive effort of 26,764lb (12140kg), two 22.6 x 24.8-in (575 x 630-mm) cylinders, driving wheels with a diameter of 5ft 8.9in

(1.75m), steam pressure of 170.6lb/sq in (12kg/cm²), 11,023lb (5000kg) of fuel, 5,460 U.S. gal (4,696 Imp gal; 21350 litres) of water, total weight of 173,060lb (78500kg), and overall length of 61ft 0in (18.592m).

Almost certainly the type that should be regarded as the finest example of the elegance associated with the 'golden age' of steam locomotion, the 'Cardean' class and related 4-6-0 type locomotives of the Caledonian Railway marked a genuine high point in the creation and operation of the steam locomotive, not only as a means of pulling trains but also as objects of beauty in themselves and therefore worthy of lavish attention in terms of their spotless appearance (paint and brightwork) and high-

quality running as a result of excellent maintenance and servicing. Evidence of this tendency is provided by the *Cardean* itself, which was the only named locomotive of its class. The engine was the responsibility of only a single driver at any one time, and was used on only one service in any single period. The driver between 1911 and 1916, for example, was David Gibson, who drove the locomotive every weekday on the *Corridor*, the service that departed from Glasgow for Euston at 2 p.m.: the *Cardean* hauled the service as far south as Carlisle, and there turned and waited to pull the reciprocal service from Euston for an evening arrival in Glasgow. The drivers of the *Cardean*, of whom the most celebrated were James Currie and Gibson in that order, certainly believed that the locomotive was their 'property', and ensured the very highest level of maintenance for an almost legendary reliability not really affected by the occasional but inevitable breakdown resulting from mechanical failure. Even then, the *Cardean* seemed to enjoy a charmed life, for on the occasion of potentially the most dangerous of these incidents there were no casualties. The incident happened in 1909, when Currie was the driver: a crank axle broke when the train was travelling at speed, allowing one of the driving wheels to fall away down an embankment, as the train became detached from the engine. It came off the rails and was halted by its automatic Westinghouse brake system, *Cardean* remaining on the rails as Currie brought it carefully to a stop.

Designed by John Farquharson McIntosh, the five Cardean-class locomotives were constructed at the Caledonian Railway's own St. Rollox

OPPOSITE: Sir William Stanier *at Crewe North, England, 8 April 1962.*

RIGHT: A P8 in Leipzig. After World War II, when Germany was divided into East and West, the available P8s were split between the two rail networks. In West Germany, diesel locomotives soon supplanted most of them.

facility and entered service in 1906. The design was wholly conservative, and reflected the belief of McIntosh that the improved ride and lines resulting from the installation of the cylinders and motion inside the frames offset the disadvantages of this arrangement's poorer levels of accessibility and the higher cost of crank axles. A superheating system was added to the locomotives in 1911 and 1912, and at a later time the Caledonian Railway, itself an air-brake operator, ordered the addition of a vacuum brake so that other companies' vacuum-braked trains could be hauled. Other features of the design were a

steam servo-mechanism for the reversing gear, and a large bogie tender for longer non-stop journeys.

One of the locomotives was destroyed in the worst British rail catastrophe, which took place on 22 May 1915 at Quintinshill near Carlisle, but the other four locomotives remained in service to became part of the London Midland & Scottish Railway's fleet in the consolidation of 1923. The last of the class was *Cardean* itself, which was retired in 1930. The details of the Cardean-class locomotive included a tractive effort of 22,667lb (10282kg), two 20.75 x 26-in (527 x 660-mm) cylinders, driving wheels

with a diameter of 6ft 6in (1.981m), steam pressure of 200lb/sq in (14.1kg/cm2), 11,000lb (4990kg) of fuel, 6,005 U.S. gal (5,000 Imp gal; 22730 litres) of water, total weight of 294,000lb (133358kg), and overall length of 65ft 6in (19.964m).

By any of several different types of criteria, the '4500' class of 4-6-2 locomotives created for the Paris-Orléans railway in 1907 could well be regarded as not just one of the classic types of steam locomotive, but possibly as 'the single' most classic locomotive intended for the hauling of express trains. The 4500-class locomotive was the first Pacific-type engine to serve in

Europe (some engines of this type having been made in the U.K. earlier in the same year but intended for service in Malaya), and in its definitive period was the most powerful and also the most efficient Pacific-type locomotive of European origin. Added to this, the 4500 was also extremely attractive and, if it can be criticized at all, its only failing was a comparatively high level of mechanical complexity.

Production of the 4500-class locomotives between 1907 and 1910 totalled 100 including 30 manufactured in the United States; but there were also 90 examples of the '3500'-class locomotive

LEFT: *Krauss-Maffei-class 03 streamline 3-cylinder express locomotive, built for the Deutsche Reichsbahn in 1940.*

BELOW LEFT: *The legendary Maffei-built locomotives steamed all over Germany, finally to be overtaken by progressive electrification of routes.*

OPPOSITE: *SNCF Class 9100.*

manufactured between 1909 and 1918 to a standard that differed from that of the 4500 class only in having a driving wheel diameter reduced by 4in (100mm).

All 190 examples of these two closely-related classes were of the four-cylinder de Glehn compound-expansion type, and with an unusual grate wide at the back but tapering to a narrow front between the frames. Later units were completed with a superheating system, and such a system was then retrofitted to a number of the earlier locomotives. Another feature was the use of piston valves in the high-pressure cylinders but there were balanced slide valves in the low-pressure cylinders.

The limitations of the 4500 class began to become apparent in the period after the end of World War I, when the rebuilding of France's infrastructure saw the replacement of the pre-war type of wooden carriage by a stronger and more durable type of steel construction. During this period, France was also beginning the electrification of its railway network, however, so there was little in the way of financial resources for the replacement of the 4500-class locomotives. However, a development engineer on the Paris-Orléans railway, André Chapelon, successfully suggested in 1926 that the locomotives should be cycled through a relatively major reconstruction programme, which in fact began only in 1929.

The rebuilding of the 4500-class locomotives resulted in the creation of one of the definitive steam locomotive classes. Power production per unit of steam was

increased by 25 per cent, while boiler improvements allowed the generation of more steam and thereby made feasible an increase in possible cylinder horse power from 2,000hp to 3,700hp, which represented an 85 per cent increase over that of the original locomotives. Chapelon produced this transformation after a close examination of the original design to locate the features he felt were limiting overall capabilities. In this process Chapelon analyzed the whole cycle of operations between cold water and exhaust steam, and decided that the features most needed to modernize the cycle were pre-heating of the cold feed water using waste heat from the exhaust; extra heating area in the firebox through the use of 'thermic syphons' (flattened vertical ducts); a 24 per cent increase in the size of the superheater that was also more efficient but additionally complex; enlarged steam pipes for better steam flow; use of poppet valves in place of piston valves and slide valves to provide larger and more quickly operating openings to steam and exhaust; and a double chimney for more draught and reduced back-pressure.

The improved 4500-class locomotive was so successful that the Paris-Orléans railway ordered the conversion of 31 3500-class locomotives in a similar fashion. The continuing electrification of the French railway network, especially in this core region around Paris, meant that some of the original engines became redundant to the requirements of the Paris-Orléans railway, however, but these machines were snapped up by other companies. Some 20 older locomotives were reconstructed to the Chapelon pattern for the Nord and 23 for the Ouest railways, and so successful were the locomotives in these regional operators' services that Nord ordered 20 new-build engines.

In 1932 some 16 3500-class locomotives were rebuilt to a somewhat less ambitious pattern with piston heads carrying two rather than one valve to double the area of port opened in a set distance of movement. In the same year one of the remaining 4500-class locomotives without a superheating system was rebuilt into a 4-8-0 configuration to validate the notion of creating an engine with one-third more adhesive weight and therefore better suited to the gradients typical of the line to Toulouse. The change required the use of a different boiler with a narrow firebox to fit between the rear driving wheels, but in other respects the rebuilding followed the Chapelon pattern even though the introduction of further refinement boosted the cylinder horse power to 4,000hp. The success of the prototype conversion is attested by the fact that 11 more engines were rebuilt to the same standard during 1934, and that in 1940 some 25 more 4500- class locomotives were converted to a standard that was otherwise similar except for the addition of a mechanical stoking system.

By the 1960s the last of these Pacific-type locomotives were based at Calais to haul heavy boat trains arriving from the U.K. The locomotives were very effective in this role, being capable of hauling heavy trains up relatively steep gradients; but there could be no denial of the fact that the locomotives were heavy consumers of coal and were generally costlier to operate than simpler 2-8-2 locomotives of the '141R' class that had been delivered from the U.S. after the end of World War II to boost the reconstruction of France. The details of the 4500-class locomotive, in its form with a superheating system but before rebuilding by Chapelon, included a tractive 38,580lb (17500kg), two 16.5 x 25.6-in (420 x 650-mm) high-pressure cylinders and two 25.2 x 25.6-in (640 x 650-mm) low-pressure cylinders, driving wheels with a diameter of 6ft 2.75in (1.90m), steam pressure of 232lb/sq in ($16kg/cm^2$), 13,228lb (6000kg) of fuel, 5,283 U.S. gal (4,399 Imp gal; 20000 litres) of water, total weight of 300,926lb (136500kg), and overall length of 68ft 2.5in (20.79m).

Dating from much the same time as the

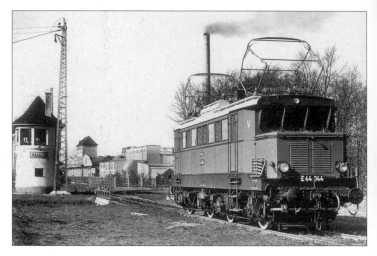

4500-class locomotives in France, the 'S3/6' class of Pacific-type 4-6-2 locomotives, introduced to the railway network of the Royal Bavarian state railway in 1909, reflected both the geographic and climatic differences of Bavaria from Prussia. The keys to this difference were the nature of Bavaria, which is considerably hillier or indeed mountainous than generally flat Prussia, and the greater flair of Heinrich Leppla, the chief designer of Maffei, the primary manufacturer of Bavarian locomotives. This flair reached it apogee in a series of Pacific-type 4-6-2 locomotives delivered for 23 years to the railways of Bavaria and Baden as well as to the German state railway that absorbed both of these operators in the 1920s.

Since 1895 the passenger locomotives of the Bavarian railway had all been of the four-cylinder compound-expansion type, including two Atlantic-type locomotives bought during 1901 from Baldwin of the U.S.A. and, it appears, a major influence on Maffei as this company became the first European company to built locomotives of the bar frame type and also the first to cast the cylinders in substantial blocks including the smokebox saddle. All four of these cylinders powered the same axle, which in the Pacific type of locomotive was the central axle.

The first engines of this type were completed during 1908 for the railway of the state of Baden, the first locomotives for the Bavarian railway following in the next year. Production of 23 such locomotives, with a driving-wheel diameter of 6ft 1.6in

(1.87m) and a steam pressure of 212lb/sq in (15kg/cm^2), had been completed by 1911, and these were followed by 18 locomotives with a driving-wheel diameter of 6ft 6.7in (2.00m), while another 78 locomotives were manufactured between 1913 and 1924 with the original size of driving wheel. This was far from the end of the story, however, for there were a number of other batches with more limited changes such as the addition of feed-water heaters, increased axle load, and steam pressure boosted to 228lb/sq in (16kg/cm^2). The overall designation for the locomotives was S3/6 class, which detailed an express locomotive (*schnellzuglokomotiv*) with six axles of which three were powered. Germany's reparations after the end of World War I included 19 of these locomotives in the form of 16 and three for

France and Belgium respectively.

During 1925 the newly created German state railway took delivery of the first of its standard Pacific-type locomotives, but the axle load of these prevented their employment on all but the most strongly constructed lines. A class of smaller and therefore lighter Pacific types was planned for use on the rest of the German rail network, but while this was being designed and built, the national rail operator needed a Pacific-type locomotive with an axle load of no more than 18 tonnes rather than the heavier type's 20 tonnes. The obvious solution was further production of the excellent Maffei design, of which 40 were completed between 1927 and 1931. These locomotives were soon steaming all over Germany until the advent of the definitive

OPPOSITE

LEFT: *King George V-class No. 6000.*

RIGHT: *Krauss-Maffei-class E44 electric locomotive, built in 1936/37 for the Deutsche Reichsbahn.*

THIS PAGE

ABOVE: *Russian designers created practical locomotives for everyday service in which standardization, reliability and simplicity of operation were of critical importance.*

ABOVE RIGHT: *A Belgian 4-4-0, No. 1805, at Ostend in 1967. Belgian locomotives built in the early 20th century bore a strong conceptual resemblance to the McIntosh locomotives of the Caledonian Railway.*

'03'-class locomotive. Even then the Maffei locomotives had a special niche, operating on the Rhine valley main line for services that included the classic *Rheingold* express before and after World War II. So successful were the locomotives in the Rhine valley that between 1953 and 1956 some 30 of the locomotives were fitted with new welded boilers. Electrification of the line finally saw the disappearance of the Maffei steam locomotives from the Rhine valley, but even so they saw a final period of useful service in Bavaria, where they handled the express services between Munich and Lake Constance, where the last of these classic locomotives was retired in 1966. The details of the S3/6-class locomotive included two 16.7 x 24-in (425 x 610-mm) high-pressure cylinders and two 25.6 x 26.4-in

(650 x 670-mm) low-pressure cylinders, driving wheels with a diameter of 6ft 1.6in (1.870m), steam pressure of 228lb/sq in (16kg/cm²), 18,739lb (8500kg) of fuel, 7,238 U.S. gal (6,027 Imp gal; 27400 litres) of water, total weight of 328,483lb (149000kg), and overall length of 69ft 1in (21.317m).

Early in the 20th century the Belgian national railway built several classes of inside-cylinder locomotives bearing a strong conceptual relationship to the McIntosh locomotives of the Caledonian Railway. During 1904, however, there began a new era in the hands of J. B. Flamme, who was interested in the French type of compound-expansion locomotive and secured the loan of such an engine for evaluation. This French locomotive was clearly so much

better than existing Belgian engines that Flamme ordered 12 similar locomotives, and then 57 of a compound-expansion 4-6-0 design. Flamme's next step was the manufacture of four 4-6-0 locomotives to a new design, and in these he was also to undertake an investigation of the superheating system in simple- and compound-expansion locomotives. This process permitted Flamme to opt for the simplicity and lower cost of the non-compound locomotive, although he appreciated that for the largest classes there were advantages in the use of four cylinders to give the improved level of balance revealed by the four-cylinder compound-expansion locomotives.

The result was two classes of very large locomotives, namely a Pacific-type 4-6-2 for

employment on express services and a 2-10-0 type for employment on freight services. The boilers of the two classes were basically similar except for a few small differences in the size of their fireboxes, and the limiting factor for length was the upper weight figure for the 2-10-0 type. The boiler would have appeared short on any Pacific-type locomotive, but this fact was accentuated by a number of other features, and by the European concepts of the period the boiler was odd as it possessed a very large grate for the burning of low-grade coal. Walschaert valve gear was used for the valves of the two outside cylinders, and rocking shafts were employed to operate the valves of the two inside cylinders that powered the leading axle.

Between 1910 and 1928, 28 of these engines were manufactured, with 30 more following in 1929 and 1930 with a grate of smaller size and shortened rear end, changes that knocked 5 tonnes off the weight. Known as the '10' class under a later classification, these locomotives worked the express routes connecting Brussels with Liège and Luxembourg, and were highly effective.

The Belgian national railway started a major refurbishment of its stock after World War I, and within the context of this programme fitted larger superheating systems, double chimneys for improved draught, strengthened the frames at the

front, and there were a number of detail enhancements. The programme continued with the addition of smoke deflectors and feed-water heaters, and bogie tenders from German war-reparation engines replaced the original six-wheeled tenders. Spurred by the success of Chapelon's efforts in France, the Belgians launched another improvement effort in 1938 with features such as enlarged steam pipes, greater superheating area, and the replacement of the Legein double-chimney exhaust by the Kylchap pattern. These changes did little for the appearance of the locomotives, but did produce the increase in performance and tractive effort that had been demanded. It was 1959 before the last of these locomotives, in fact one of

the first-series machines, was finally retired. The details of the 10 class included a tractive effort of 43,651lb (19800kg), four 19.7 x 26-in (500 x 660-mm) cylinders, driving wheels with a diameter of 6ft 6in (1.98m), steam pressure of 199lb/sq in (14kg/cm²), 15,432lb (7000kg) of fuel, 6,340 U.S. gal (5,279 Imp gal; 24000 litres) of water, total weight of 352,734lb (160000kg), and overall length of 70ft 3in (21.404m).

With the retirement of Francis Webb as its chief locomotive engineer during 1903, the London & North Western Railway was able to start the process of replacing the compound-expansion and other obsolescent locomotives whose retention the autocratic

OPPOSITE

ABOVE: *Chelyabinsk railway station in what is now the Russian Federation.*

BELOW: *About 2,400 Russian Su-class locomotives were built over 15 years and they became the definitive standard Russian locomotives to haul passenger trains.*

THIS PAGE

ABOVE: *The* Caledonian, *resplendent in the livery of the London, Midland & Scottish Railway (LMS), leaves Crewe for Carlisle.*

RIGHT: *LMS Duchess-class 4-6-2 locomotive at Bury, England. This class of locomotive was the most powerful ever to run in that country.*

Webb had demanded. Under the supervision of George Whale and W. T. Bowen-Cooke, Webb's immediate successors, over a period of 10 years the company acquired 336 4-4-0 and 4-6-0 express locomotives, engines manufactured at the company's Crewe plant, which undertook the whole process between the receipt of raw materials and the delivery of complete locomotives, a process for which Webb must take a good deal of the credit.

Four types of express locomotive were constructed at Crewe in this period, and while three of them were useful if not wholly inspired types, the fourth was truly outstanding. This was the later of the two 4-4-0 types, the great 'George V' class of locomotives of which the first was delivered during 1910. The design was in essence a much improved development of the 'Precursor' class of 1903 with more modern features such as piston valves and a superheating system. Some 90 George V-class locomotives were built, to which must be added a further 64 conversions from the Precursor class as well as another 10 from the 'Queen Mary' class of 4-4-0 locomotives without a superheating system.

Despite their limited 4-4-0 configuration, these locomotives hauled much of the prestige passenger traffic between Euston and stations to the north. In the George V class everything was consciously made as simple as possible. The outer firebox wrapper was of the round top rather than the more complicated Belpaire type, and while the cylinders were of the inside type, the use of the Joy-type valve gear, with rods and slides in the same vertical plane as the connecting rods, created a situation in which all the inside motion was readily reached for lubrication and maintenance. The Joy-type valve gear was not quite as efficient as it could have been, possibly because it had been 'improved' for this application and thereby made more complex, while the Schmidt piston valves were also prone to wear: both these features led to high coal and steam consumption, but careful maintenance alleviated the problem.

During 1923 the virtual multitude of British railway companies was consolidated into four large organizations, the George V-class locomotives thereby coming into the ownership of the London Midland & Scottish Railway, a company controlled largely by ex-Midland Railway men who had a low regard for all locomotives originating outside this company. It was hardly surprising, therefore, that the retirement of these effective locomotives started as early as 1935, ending with the retirement of the last unit in 1948. The details of the George V-class locomotive included a tractive effort of 20,066lb (9102kg), two 20.5 x 26-in (521 x 660-mm) cylinders, driving wheels with a diameter of

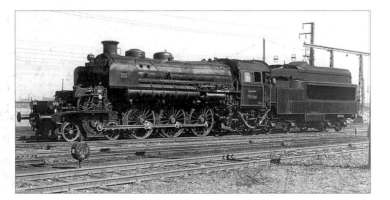

6ft 9in (2.057m), steam pressure of 175lb/sq in (12.3kg/cm²), 13,440lb (6096kg) of fuel, 3,603 U.S. gal (3,000 Imp gal; 13638 litres) of water, total weight of 212,800lb (96526kg), and overall length of 57ft 2.75in (17.445m).

The 'S' class of massive 2-6-2 steam locomotives introduced in 1911 for the Russian Ministry of Ways of Communication may have been the most prolific of all steam locomotives as its manufacture lasted for 40 years and its usage for more than 60 years. Despite the fact that steam-locomotive design in Russia was generally entrusted to academics, who often exploited the chance to create extraordinary prototype machines more notable for their theory than their practice, but were nonetheless able to create truly practical locomotives for everyday service, in which simplicity of concept and operation was all important for reliable use in Russia's vast and diverse geography.

Despite the many aspersions cast on it by large numbers of the ill-informed, both at the time and later, the tsarist government of pre-revolutionary Russia was in fact far ahead of its time in matters of standardization, and this process continued after the Soviet Revolution of 1917 and the tumult of the years that followed.

The S class of 2-6-2 locomotives was a standard design for general use among Russia's many independent railways. The 'S' stood for the Soromovo works at Nizhnii Novgorod (later Gorkiy) where the class was built, and about 900 such excellent locomotives were manufactured before the

revolution. The design was an early example of what was in effect the standard definitive form of steam locomotive with two cylinders, Walschaert valve gear, a wide firebox, a superheating system, and compensated springing.

The 'Su' class of larger, improved locomotives was first manufactured during 1926 at the Kolomna plant near Moscow in 1926. This subclass, of which about 2,400 were completed over a 15-year period, may be regarded as the definitive standard, and the 'u' in the designation stood for *usilennyi* (strengthened). The wheel base, boiler and cylinders were all enlarged but there was no increase in the boiler pressure over the modest figure inherited from the baseline S class, reflecting the fact that the cost-conscious Soviets, with a non-competitive system, felt that a higher boiler pressure would add unnecessary production and maintenance costs.

After the end of World War II in 1945, manufacture was resumed at the Soromovo plant and continued until 1951, by which time some 3,750 S-class locomotives had been built. Variants comprised some 'Sv'-class locomotives built in 1915 for the standard-gauge line from Warsaw south toward Vienna, and some 'Sum'-class units with a system for pre-heating the combustion air. Many of the S-class locomotives burned not coal but oil, a fuel that had been introduced into Russia as early as 1880 and soon became relatively common. The details of the S-class locomotive included a tractive effort of 30,092lb (13650kg), two 22.5 x 27.5-in

(575 x 700-mm) cylinders, driving wheels with a diameter of 6ft 0.75in (1.85m), steam pressure of 185lb/sq in (13kg/cm²), 39,683lb (18000kg) of fuel, 6,010 U.S. gal (5,004 Imp gal; 22750 litres) of water, total weight of 370,370lb (168000kg), and overall length of 77ft 10.5in (23.738m).

OPPOSITE
ABOVE: *Krauss-Maffei Class 50 heavy locomotive, built in 1939 for the Deutsche Reichsbahn (German Railway). This engine was withdrawn in 1965.*

BELOW: *Maffei-Zoelly Class T18 turbine locomotive, built for the Deutsche Bundesbahn between 1925 and 1928.*

THIS PAGE
ABOVE: *A Class A4 streamline 4-6-2, the famous A4 Pacific, which still holds the world's speed record for a steam locomotive. It is probably the favourite locomotive of British rail enthusiasts.*

BELOW: *A unique line-up of A4s at the National Railway Museum, York, England. Nearest the camera is the* Mallard.

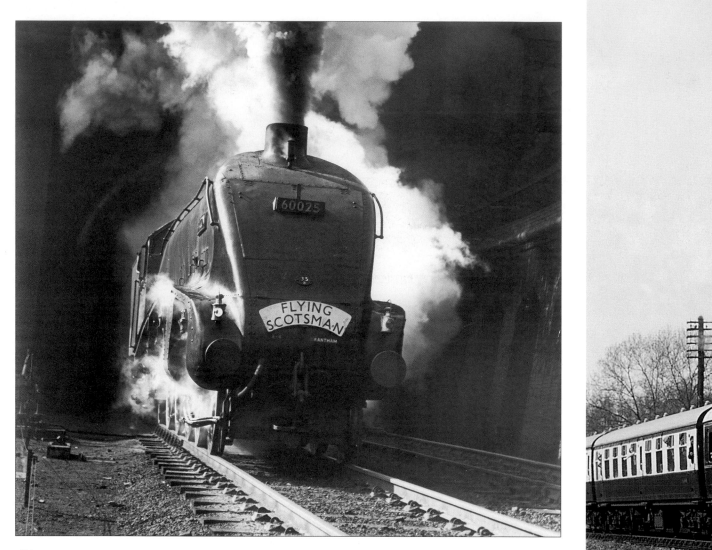

Chapter Three
PASSENGER TRAINS

PAGE 130: *The legendary* Flying Scotsman, *emerging from the King's Cross tunnels, London.*

PAGE 131: *The graceful lines, sparkling paintwork and polished brass make this preserved Stirling 8-foot single-class locomotive a splendid sight.*

RIGHT: *York station in England, and the green and yellow livery of the North Eastern Railway company, which ran fast trains from York to Edinburgh.*

PASSENGER TRAINS

The function of the railroad is to deliver passengers or freight between different towns and cities or, in the case of the latter, between various points in the conurbation. It stands to reason, therefore, that the passenger's initial interface with the railroad system is the railway station or railroad depot, at which the passenger can buy a ticket and board the train when it makes its scheduled stop or, if the railroad depot is the terminus of the line, board the service right at its beginning.

In the period before the Industrial Revolution, land traffic was wholly restricted to the space it occupied in the overall landscape through which it was moving, and this factor continued to be true right through to the particular land transport's destination, which was a town or city. Thus the relationships of the stagecoach to the country and to the city were essentially identical, for this type of conveyance was an integral part of the rural and urban landscapes through which it travelled, and therefore had little impact on them in the fashion that would become so typical of an external factor such as the railroad and the trains that ran on it. This situation prevailed just as much at the stagecoach's terminus as to the rural and urban roads along which it had moved, for while the stagecoach's terminus was located as close to the centre of the city as was practical, generally close to an inn at which alighting or waiting passengers could satisfy their hunger and thirst as well as secure temporary accommodation, it was for all practical purposes little distinguishable from the building around it except for a yard and double gate, a combination that was also typical of larger urban houses with provision for a coach and the horses to pull it.

In general terms, therefore, land transport in the period before the full advent of the Industrial Revolution was fully integrated into the day-to-day situation of the regions through which it passed, and therefore possessed no aspect of intrusiveness. The advent of the railroad changed all that, for the railroad was and still is so basically different from the areas through which it runs and into which it operates that there is little commonality between the railroad and the populated areas it serves: the railroad's tracks are used only by the trains that run on them, in both the country and the city, and the railway station or railroad depot are so radically different in function and architecture from the areas in which they are located that they stand out as totally individual establishments.

Arriving as it did after the time that most towns and cities were established and underwent their first periods of growth, the station or depot cannot in general be an integral part of the town or city, although exceptions can be found in the case of cities such as Brasilia, which are to an extent 'artificial' creations in that they were schemed as a unit with the railroad built into it as an organic feature. In general, however, the station had to be constructed outside the traditional limits of the city, meaning that for a considerable period the station was in effect an extrusion of the city, and only started to become a true part of its organic structure as growth expanded the city round and past the station. In the circumstances, it was perhaps inevitable that the region which first grew up round the station was intimately connected with the railroad in both social and economic terms, and therefore came to be both industrial and working class. In many countries this resulted in the area round the station becoming condemned as the rough

ABOVE: *Railway companies quickly learned to provide refreshments for the train journey.*

OPPOSITE: *The early railway station or depot was built after the city had developed, and often stood apart from the city it served, both geographically as well as architecturally.*

and ready 'railroad district' whose population and businesses were located 'on the wrong side of the tracks', and were therefore regarded as inferior by those who lived in other regions of the city.

Given the fact that the railroad is a genuine child of the Industrial Revolution, with its urban environs a natural home for the type of industrial activity that developed as a major force at about the same time as the railroad and for the same reasons, the station is naturally an industrial artefact, and in general the first stations were built from the middle of the 19th century, and indeed generally remain as classic examples of the 19th century's industrial architecture. As a consequence,

most of the world's great stations are largely of steel and glass construction on a base of brick. The particular nature of the station, with its long platforms that had to be covered and lighted by a structure requiring only the most limited of vertical supports, led to the creation of some of the world's most classic industrial architecture, characterized by glass roofs carried in superb cast-iron frames, themselves supported by cast-iron pillars.

A particular feature of the railroad station, by comparison with most other types of commercial buildings of the same period, was its unashamed functionality: the railway station was designed to facilitate movement, by both the trains and the

traffic, whereas most of the other buildings were designed for what might be described as a far more stationary function as the people and goods using the building were essentially unmoving (goods in storage or on display, or workers standing or seated at their tasks) or only locally moving (shoppers) between their times of arrival and departure on foot. In the case of the railroad station, on the other hand, the trains themselves moved through the structure, in the case of terminus stations in and out of the structure, and the goods and people using the train services flowed through the building in a genuinely active fashion.

To this extent, therefore, the station is a classic example of what has inevitably

and in fact unashamedly been designated as a 'traffic building', and the task of the railroad in the movement of goods and passengers was reflected naturally, and without any attempt at concealment, in its basic design and construction.

Notwithstanding the above, its industrial character is but one of the station's several particular characteristics, especially in regard to the urban passenger terminals that constitute the railway station at its apogee. For example, the station was not created as a unitary building designed solely to facilitate the movement of trains: this was certainly one requirement, resulting in the cast iron and glass coverings of the platform areas, but another

OPPOSITE

LEFT: *In the early days, passengers often had to walk across a number of lines to get to their trains.*

RIGHT: *Finland in the 1920s.*

THIS PAGE

ABOVE LEFT: *A local station in Finland, 1910.*

ABOVE RIGHT: *The first trans-Canadian train on its journey. Arrival at Port Arthur was on 30 June 1886.*

RIGHT: *Buffalo-bone pickers and Red River carts at the Northern Pacific Railroad yard in Minnewaukan, 1886.*

was the movement of passengers in and out of the building as they arrived to use the train services or departed after using them. This led to the design and construction of the station as a double entity in which the cast iron and glass section concerned primarily with the trains was complemented by what might be termed a reception area, generally of a more 'solid' stone or brick construction, whose primary task was to allow the smooth flow of large numbers of passengers between the outside world and the trains they wished to use, and in the process provide the facilities in which they could buy their tickets, refresh themselves, and buy small items (food, beverages, newspapers and periodicals) for the train journey.

An invariable characteristic of such a station was its alignment with the open-fronted train 'half' facing out of the city toward the country and the more enclosed passenger 'half' facing into the city toward roads and buildings. As such, the station fell into two categories with its train half essentially industrial and it passenger half primarily urban. This two-aspect feature of the railroad station in its definitive urban form did not appear overnight, but was rather the result of two decades of initially slow but soon very rapidly accelerating railroad development. The train half of the station did not reach it definitive cast iron and glass form until the 1850s, and was clearly inspired strongly by the technical success and phenomenal popularity in London of the Crystal Palace of 1851, which was responsible for a rapid development of these materials as important architectural features. More important still,

however, was the success of the railroads during their first 20 years of existence, when traffic grew at an unprecedented rate and the railroad operators foresaw no reason that this rate of growth would not continue into the foreseeable future. This growth in traffic called for the creation and implementation of novel technical solutions to problems such as the enclosure of large numbers of parallel platforms and the rapid movement of great numbers of passengers. During the railroad's first days in the 1830s, railway operations were limited to single-line connections between cities, and stations of very modest dimensions and ambitions were more than adequate. Most stations therefore comprised just one platform, separate buildings for arrivals and departures, and a roof that was often of wood.

During the 1840s the network of

ABOVE LEFT: Train concourse, Penne station, Northern Pacific Railroad, 1909, a classic of cast iron and glass construction.

ABOVE: Three Cocks Junction, England, 1962.

OPPOSITE: Bassenthwaite Lake station, Cumbria, England.

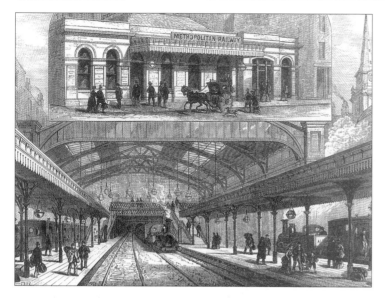

railroads both expanded in overall dimensions and grew denser in its original areas to cater for the demands of more traffic, and this placed an increasing burden on existing stations. More railroad tracks now headed toward them, and this meant that the number of platforms had to be increased and their length extended to cater for trains that had a larger number of carriages now that more potent locomotives were available to pull them. The longer and more numerous platforms had to be interconnected so that passengers could transfer from one train to another, and as the railroads were now emerging from their pioneering period, in which passengers had

ABOVE LEFT: *Engraving of the Metropolitan Railway's Aldgate terminus in the City of London, 1876.*

ABOVE: *South-Eastern Railway's City of London terminus at Cannon Street, 1866. The cast iron and glass construction of early railway stations was inspired by the Crystal Palace, built in 1851.*

LEFT: *A view of the city of Leeds from Holbeck Junction, Yorkshire, England.*

OPPOSITE: *The first British monarch to travel by train was Queen Victoria who, in a train such as this, made her first rail journey from Slough to London in 1842.*

140

been prepared to 'rough it', the larger area of platforms had to be roofed more efficiently, primarily with a transparent or translucent material, to the demands of now more blasé passengers for a higher level of creature comforts such as protection against rain and wind. The answer was a larger station of a new type with a large glass-roofed 'train hall' linked to the 'passenger hall' by an intermediate structure providing access not only to and from the platforms but also between the different platforms.

From the middle of the 19th century, therefore, this definitive type of station becomes a primary feature of urban development, first in Europe and then, at a slightly later date, the eastern part of the U.S.A. Located on the edge of the original, now increasingly the inner, part of the city, such stations were the access to the conduits through which passengers travelled to and from the outlying suburbs and country, and between one city and another. Increasingly from the middle of the 19th century, the city grew very rapidly as the commercial, financial and administrative centre of the region in which it lay, and this spurred the growth of traffic as suburban regions came into existence to provide homes for the increasing number of workers of all types that were now needed by the city. In the morning, trains from the suburban regions converged on the single or multiple terminal stations in the city, the passengers then alighting at what could easily have become a bottleneck before dispersing again by foot or local transport to their places of work. At the end of the

day, this process was reversed as the workers made their way home.

To a great extent the terminal station should thus be regarded as a gateway to and from the city, its architecture accurately reflecting its two-faced nature looking both inward to the city and outward to the suburbs and the country. It might indeed be argued, in over-simplified terms, that the outward-bound passenger's arrival from the city via the passenger hall to the train hall prepared him for the opening of his horizons as his train departed the city for the country, while the converse was true for the inward-bound passenger, whose horizons were steadily contracted as he approached and passed through the station, neatly preparing him for the more enclosed nature of the city with its narrow roads and increasingly tall buildings. To this extent, therefore, the station can be regarded as much as a psychological as a physical gateway in much the same way that the train itself provides an interface between the industrial and non-industrial worlds.

Oddly enough, given the essentially industrial nature of the railroad and all connected with it, and also the unashamedly industrial interior of stations, those who commissioned and designed large stations from the middle of the 19th century were at considerable pains to disavow the industrial connection on the outside of these large buildings. As a result, the great stations of the second half of the 19th century are notable for their neo-classical façades, which were created as an ornamental attempt to disguise the industrial nature of

the buildings' interiors at a time when many urban dwellers were coming to feel that industrialization might have its rightful place, but that this was not in their cities where it might impinge on them directly. This might seem a specious factor, but the neo-classical façades of these essentially industrial buildings did in fact serve a real purpose, for they were aesthetic as well as psychological gateways between an everyday aspect of what was starting to become an increasingly polarized division between the industrial and non-industrial worlds, reflected in the modernity of the railroad station and its environs on the one hand and, on the other hand, the older world of the city on whose edge industry had sprouted.

As noted above, the station thus became a psychological as well as physical gateway between different worlds, allowing easy access between them without undue mental strain. Providing a means of transition between the open nature of the country and the more closed aspect of the city, the railroad and its stations fulfilled a complex role in a fashion that became increasingly complex as time progressed and the size of cities and their suburbs expanded, demanding additional railroad facilities not only for passengers but also for the goods they created or bought, including large volumes of foodstuffs. This increasingly complex physical aspect of railroad operations was reflected strongly in the development of the station from about 1860. Up to that date, there was no means of direct access between the reception area and the station's platforms, the intermediate stage being represented by the waiting room in which the passengers had to assemble and wait for the door to the

OPPOSITE: Grand Central terminal, New York, in the 1930s. As the 19th century progressed, stations were often built with neo-classical façades to disguise their industrial function.

ABOVE: The Baltimore & Ohio Railroad's station at Camden, 1869.

RIGHT: New Street Station, Birmingham, England, 1946. Earlier features of metal and glass construction and a concourse to enable passengers to cross railway lines in safety are still very much in use.

intervening area to open shortly before the train's advertised time of departure. This arrangement was created specifically to prevent the passengers from reaching their trains in an uncontrolled mass as, particularly in the continent of Europe that was as yet only partially industrialized, the authorities doubted the ability of the travelling public to cope with industrial machinery in an unregulated environment. The situation began to change from about 1860, and a direct connection between the reception building and the train hall become increasingly common, in the process

allowing the development of the concourse in which retail outlets soon sprang up. The passenger's progression through a three-chamber arrangement (waiting room, concourse and train hall) was soon modified to provide a waiting room through which no traffic flowed, and the combination of the concourse and train hall through which all the moving traffic passed.

It is this last arrangement that has continued, with developments and modifications to facilitate the rapid transit of an ever larger number of passengers in the peak periods, right up to the present,

OPPOSITE: Waterloo, London, an example of a modern, functional railway station.

BELOW: Two diesel multiple units await departure at York station, England in 1978, surrounded by classic Industrial Revolution railway architecture.

and looks set to remain the norm into the foreseeable future.

Once he had passed the 'obstacle' of the station with its various arrangements, the passenger arrives at his means of transport, which in Europe is generally termed the carriage or wagon, but in North America is known as the car. In the very first stages of railroad travel, the wagon for freight was merely an enlarged version of the chaldron, or mine vehicle of the middle ages, while all but the very earliest passenger coaches were mere developments of the current generation of stagecoaches and private coaches with flanged wheels to keep them on the tracks. Despite the all-too-frequent and invariably unsuccessful experimental variants that emerged constantly, the better type of passenger coach developed for use in western Europe was for some time a flange-wheeled frame (flatbed unit) built up with a wooden structure to provide passenger accommodation in compartments with side-doors: this type of stagecoach body combined three, four or even more compartments on a single railway frame, and first appeared with the opening of the Liverpool & Manchester Railway. The type was probably created by Nathaniel Worsdell, the well-known coachbuilder who had made the tender for the *Rocket*. Each compartment, otherwise known as a 'body', held six passengers on well padded but uncomfortably upright seats. For those with fewer financial resources, cheaper fares were charged for accommodation in an open-sided *char-à-banc* carriage. Both

types are revealed in some detail in the
celebrated Ackermann 'Long Prints' of the
Liverpool & Manchester Railway. On this
railway passengers could pay an additional
charge to travel in compartments belonging
to the mail carriage, which provided only
corner seats. The cheapest fares of all were
charged to those passengers who were
prepared to travel in box-like wagons which
were often without seats and known in
England as 'stanhopes'.

In overall terms, the compartmented
side-door coach served faithfully and well
over a moderately long period, and before
long the rising expectations of passenger
comfort meant that this type of carriage was
being used, albeit with shortened
compartments and harder seating, for the
accommodation of second- and third-class
passengers. More than 100 years later,
basically the same type of carriage was still
being produced in the U.K. for use on
suburban commuter services around the
country's larger cities, its primary attraction
for the railway operators being its relatively
higher capacity on a frame of a given size,
and the ease of entry and exit it provided: it
must be noted, though, that these later
compartment carriages were considerably
larger than their predecessors of the first
half of the 19th century.

Another option, and one that was
favoured by wealthier families not wishing
to travel in a 'promiscuous' proximity to
other travellers, was to remain in their own
private coaches loaded onto and then
chained down to flat wagons. The attraction
of this mode of travel was its exclusivity,

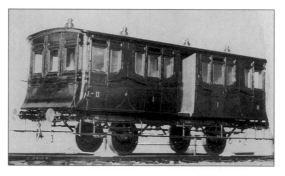

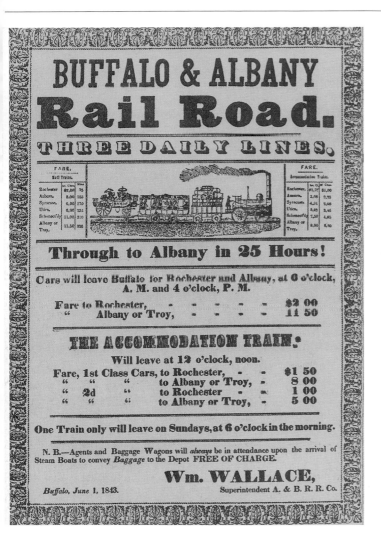

ABOVE LEFT: *A Belgian railway carriage. The compartmental side-door carriage was favoured in Europe.*

ABOVE RIGHT: *A very early open-topped passenger carriage, which would have provided an extremely uncomfortable journey.*

BELOW: *Special car-carrying unit on a passenger train of the Finnish state railways.*

LEFT: *Poster advertising the first through trains between Buffalo and Albany on the Buffalo & Albany Rail Road, 1843.*

BELOW: *Engraving depicting the interior of a 'colonist' car on the Canadian Pacific Railway, 1888.*

which meant that ladies and gentlemen need not worry about the possibility of dirtying their clothes on seats that had previously been occupied by a possibly unwashed member of the public; but its disadvantages became all too obvious in the summer, when the occupants of any type of open carriage would be assailed by dust, fumes and cinders. As improvements to first-class carriages were made and the 'better' classes of person became more accustomed to the concept of railway travel, the practice of loading coaches onto flatbeds gradually disappeared, and it is believed that the last person to make use of the system was an English lady of the 1880s.

It is worth noting, though, that in more recent times there has been a partial

ABOVE: A Belgian 19th-century carriage which favoured the 'central corridor' of American cars rather than the European compartmentalized side-door arrangement.

OPPOSITE
LEFT: 'Old Number 9', the first Pullman sleeper car of 1859. There had been several previous attempts to create a useful sleeping car, but cabinet-maker George Mortimer Pullman achieved the first real success.

RIGHT: The 'Pioneer' car of 1865, which was completely successful in technical terms and proved immensely popular with passengers.

resurgence of the practice in the form of motor cars loaded onto trains for long-distance or specialized routes, the latter including travel through long tunnels such as those under the English Channel or through the Alps. In this instance, however, the social reasons are different and the occupants of the cars generally ride not in their vehicles but in conventional railway carriages.

What is undeniable about the first generations of rail travellers is that those paying only a third-class fare had a decidedly uncomfortable journey. This was as true of the European as the British rail networks, and a French cartoon highlights the discomfort of the cheaper accommodations by showing porters lifting out passengers frozen stiff by the winter weather.

It was standard throughout Europe during this first period of railway expansion to consider all things American as totally backward or, at best, lacking in an element of finesse. Yet the world owes to the American development of its railroad system a number of important features which improved the lot of the passenger. Thus it was the Americans who introduced, at various times, passenger cars that were both more practical and at times more comfortable, especially for longer journeys. As in Europe, it was the stagecoach which provided the model for the first American railroad cars, but even at this stage differences of practice were readily discernible. As a starting point, the American stagecoach was longer and more

sturdy than the British version while remaining lighter than the French equivalent. This permitted the stagecoach to operate effectively on the U.S.A.'s roads, which were generally inferior to those in the more advanced areas of Europe. It was a comparatively simple task to develop the stagecoach as the accommodation of a railroad car, although a distinctly odd appearance was given to many of these early examples by the practice of adding open seating above the enclosed part of the car. This was typical of the cars designed by Imlay for the Baltimore & Ohio Railroad. Other types of car possessed a body that was almost boat-shaped.

The British carriages and American cars of the early period of railroad development both suffered from their possession of only a short wheelbase, which led to an unpleasant pitching motion in the fore-and-aft plane to the extent that children often described them as sick-making. This led to the rapid redesign of the carriage and car with eight wheels in a pair of two-axle trucks or bogies, rather than the original arrangement of four wheels on just two axles, and this alteration significantly reduced the pitching tendency of the carriages and cars.

Another improvement, coincident with the switch from two to four axles, resulted from the adoption for railroad cars of the pivoted truck or bogie, which allowed a far smoother entry into and exit from a curve. Among the first such carriages was a type built in the early 1830s for the St.-Etienne-Lyons railway in

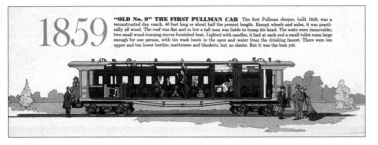

1859 "OLD No. 9" THE FIRST PULLMAN CAR The first Pullman sleeper, built 1859, was a reconstructed day coach, 40 feet long or about half the present length. Except wheels and axles, it was practically all wood. The roof was flat and so low a tall man was liable to bump his head. The seats were immovable; two small wood-burning stoves furnished heat. Lighted with candles, it had at each end a small toilet room large enough for one person, with tin wash basin in the open and water from the drinking faucet. There were ten upper and ten lower berths; mattresses and blankets, but no sheets. But it was the best yet.

1865 THE FIRST REAL PULLMAN SLEEPING CAR First modern sleeper, built 1865, THE PIONEER; much longer, higher, wider, than predecessors; railroad bridges and platforms were changed to permit its passage. Here first came the raised upper deck and folding upper berth. Heated from hot air furnace under floor; lighted with candles, ventilated through deck windows. Two compartments at each end; eight sections; roomy washroom; black walnut woodwork, much inlay and many mirrors. Fully carpeted; French plush upholstery; good beds, ample bedding. Note the 16 wheels: an experiment tried at this period but later abandoned in favor of 12.

France, but perhaps the best known is an American car, the 'Victory', manufactured during 1834 by Imlay for the Philadelphia & Columbia Railroad. Between the pair of two-axle trucks was a body of Imlay's typical boat-shaped configuration, and what appeared as a raised clerestory decking was probably a truss-like structure to prevent the main part of the car from sagging in the middle between the two trucks. The section of each truck was enclosed, leading to suggestions, probably fanciful rather than realistic, that one accommodated a bar and the other a lavatory.

Such eight-wheeled cars were clearly the right technical approach to the further development of the car, and during the 1840s they became common on American railroads under the driving influence of far-sighted men such as John Stevens, of the Camden & Amboy Railroad, and Ross Winans of the Baltimore & Ohio Railroad. By the early 1840s these American cars were no longer based so strongly on stagecoach practice, with a number of separate compartments in a fore-and-aft arrangement, but rather on the omnibuses that were becoming common on

the streets of American cities, with a long, single compartment, wide side doors and a central aisle.

By this time the first sleeping cars, though this might be construed as too grand a name, had made their first appearances. Typical of these comparatively primitive early examples of their genre, which appeared in 1836, were the bunk cars of the Cumberland Valley Railroad: the tiered arrangement of bunks allowed passengers at least to lie down at night, though it is probable that few of these passengers actually managed to sleep! A mere two years later, in the United Kingdom, there appeared the bed-carriage on the night train from London to the north-west of England. This bed-carriage was laid out in the standard compartmented arrangement but possessed, at one end, a boot such as the roadbound stagecoaches had for the carriage of the mail. In the case of the bed-carriage, the relevant partition at the end of the adjacent passenger compartment was hinged, and padded boards could be used to fill in the space between the seats so that a first-class passenger willing to pay the

required supplement could lie down with his feet in the space provided by the boot.

The designations first-, second- and third-class were early arrivals on the European railroad scene, and provided an indication of the relative superiority or inferiority of the accommodation provided by purchase of the relevant and differently priced tickets. In the United States, then as now, there was an antipathy to the use of the word 'class' to denote anything that might smack of social difference (and therefore social division), so American railroad advertisements informed would-be passengers that the fare was a certain number of dollars in what were termed the best cars and fewer dollars in what were called the accommodation cars.

It cannot be denied that during this first period of railroad development the passenger was generally faced with a journey that may be described as uncomfortable to greater or less extents, although it is also undeniable that the American passenger soon came to enjoy a higher level of comfort than his European counterpart. Passenger carriages and cars

were not generally notable for the imaginative way in which they were designed or constructed, but it should also be realized that first-class travel in Europe quickly became comfortable if not actually luxurious in the context of what was feasible within the constraints of an increasingly formal Victorian society. This was particularly the case on the services of English operators such as the Great Western Railway, whose broad gauge track allowed the introduction of wide carriages including comfortable first-class compartments for up to eight passengers on well stuffed leather seats. Even so, there can be no disguising the fact that these early passenger carriages and cars lacked any form of heating during the winter months, had no lavatory facilities for the whole year, or any form of lighting until the later 1830s, when the company introduced dim lanterns that burned vegetable oil.

By the 1860s there had started to appear generally improved passenger carriages and cars, one of the primary driving forces being the desire of the

FAR LEFT: The 'Frontier Shack', the dormitory tap car on the City of Denver, *Union Pacific Railroad.*

LEFT: 'Old Number 9', a day coach remodelled by Leonard Seibert and George Pullman into the first Pullman sleeper. The lavish accommodation included ten sleeping-car sections, a washstand, box-stove heater, oil lamps and plush seats.

travelling public for greater comfort with improved facilities on board the train. While the European railway companies opted to retain the stagecoach concept as the basis on which their improved carriages were developed with a steady flow of modifications, and other nations with genuinely long-distance services opted for the omnibus concept as the starting point for their improved carriages, the Americans took the idea a step further and decided to base their cars for long-distance routes on the canal boats that had started the main phase of the American migration west from the eastern seaboard states by means of the Erie Canal and the like.

This was in fact a second step, the first being represented by further improvement of the omnibus type of car with a central aisle that was once disparaged as a long spittoon. The central aisle did at least allow passengers to move up and down the cars, and among the several other positive aspects of this type of car were comparatively comfortable daytime seating in a side-by-side fashion, the provision of a pot-bellied stove for warmth in what could be extremely cold North American winters, a separate but Spartan lavatory compartment, and lighting in the form of candle-burning lanterns that were replaced from the mid-1860s by notably more effective kerosene lamps hung for the raised clerestory roof along the centre of the car's ceiling. This arrangement, replacing the original type of essentially flat roof, kept the lamps well above the passengers' heads, and the clerestory feature also served to provide better light by day and superior ventilation at all times. A feature made possible by the passenger car's evolution from the omnibus was the omission of hinged doors on the side of the car, passenger access and egress being made by means of forward and rear platforms (reached by steps from the ground-level platforms of American stations) with doors opening onto the central aisle. Although the dustiness of contemporary railroad travel meant that serious consideration was the order of the day before a window was opened, even in the middle of summer, the American cars possessed upward-sliding windows, whereas their passenger-carriage counterparts in Europe had downward-sliding windows in their side-opening doors.

Despite its improvements over the first generation of American passenger car, the car of the 1860s was still not very user-friendly. Daytime travel, especially in the moderate conditions of spring and fall, was generally acceptable, but travel by night was decidedly uncomfortable even by the standards of a period more used to adversity without undue complaint. The reason for this was the absence of any real sleeping accommodation, which meant that passengers who were already tired were faced with the prospect of snoozing in their seats. There had been several efforts to create a useful sleeping car, but the first real success was achieved by an American

cabinet maker, George Mortimer Pullman. Pullman's idea was to install folding berths above the daytime seats, which would be modified to pull out flat so that they met in the foot space between the seats, and this would create two levels of berths that could be made up as proper beds. In the course of 1858–59 Pullman modified three day passenger cars of the Chicago & Alton Railroad for a validation of his idea. The Pullman notion proved most successful, but then the American Civil War intervened and it was only after the end of this four-year conflict in 1865 that Pullman returned to the project and produced the 'Pioneer', which must rightly be regarded as the first real sleeping car.

The Pioneer's roof was raised, together with the large clerestory along its centreline, and sliding boards were introduced between the curtained berths on each level so that no passenger would inadvertently kick the head of another. The Pioneer was completely successful in technical terms and proved immensely popular with passengers on long-distance services, and became what was in effect the prototype for all future American development of what instantly became the Pullman sleeping car and provided a level of comfort and privacy that was adequate for mixed-sex accommodation even on transcontinental journeys lasting several days. For those prepared to pay a supplement, there was a pair of private two-berth compartments at one end of the car.

The European approach to the development of the sleeping carriage was

ABOVE: A Canadian railway sleeping car of 1859. Passengers were grateful for the comfort and privacy of such carriages.

OPPOSITE: The central aisle allowed passengers to move freely and lighting was improved from the 1860s when kerosene lamps replaced candle-burning lanterns.

FAR LEFT: *Advertising poster for the* Blue Bird *Pullman train operating between Anvers, Brussels and Paris, 1927.*

LEFT: *The interior of a second-class Pullman salon (1928-type) operated by the Compagnie Internationale des Wagons-Lits on the* Étoile du Nord *express.*

different, for it retained the compartment arrangement of the standard daytime passenger carriage. Perhaps the best of these European efforts, as befitting the immensely long journeys that might be undertaken in that country, Russia during the 1860s introduced four-berth compartments accessed by a side corridor, and these were ideal for family groups. Some of these sleeper compartments were luxuriously appointed, a factor facilitated by the considerable width of Russian carriages, and a Russian sleeping carriage of the late 1860s could provide five compartments, each with four berths, a central saloon, and above this arrangement an extensively glazed observation compartment accessed by a short stairway. It is worth noting that the Russians were thus the true pioneers of the observation compartment, which next appeared on trains of the Canadian Pacific

Railway in the first decade of the 20th century, and reached its definitive form as the 'Vista Dome' of American railroads in the 1950s.

Another comparatively early European success in the sleeping carriage 'stakes' was Austria-Hungary, a nation of considerable size in its own right and also needing to link its services into an international network providing services from Vienna to destinations such as Berlin. The 'Hernalser' sleeping carriage was essentially a hybrid of European and American features, the former the type of compartmented arrangement favoured by Georges Nagelmackers, the Belgian who became the leading light in European sleeping carriage development, and the latter the Pullman arrangement of seats and berths. Heating was provided by stoves under a floor fitted with gratings, and the central clerestory structure was

American in basic concept but European in features such as its windows and ventilators, which were derived ultimately from stagecoach experience. This type of sleeping car was popular in Austria-Hungary, and also spread to other parts of Europe including Prussia and, to a limited extent, to the Great Western Railway in the U.K.

The definitive form of the European sleeping carriage was created by Nagelmackers, whose success resulted in the establishment of the celebrated Compagnie Internationale des Wagons-Lits (International Sleeping Car Company), which was also known for a time as Mann's Railway Sleeping Carriage Company, Colonel

William D'Alton Mann being a dubious American who injected some capital into the project. The Nagelmackers concept for the sleeping carriage was an arrangement of compartments (with transverse rather than longitudinal berths) opening onto a side corridor providing access to the lavatories.

While sleeping carriages or cars became

increasingly important for long-distance journeys, the type of intermediate-distance journey typical of many central and eastern European regions led to the limited introduction of carriages outfitted with *chaises longues* as well as a primitive underfloor heater and a small lavatory compartment.

ABOVE LEFT: The interior of the first-class Pullman salon on the Étoile du Nord express, the epitome of luxury travel of the period.

ABOVE: A 56-seat restaurant car, built in 1928 and operated by the Compagnie Internationale des Wagons-Lits.

LEFT: Three 2-8-0 locomotives with a wedge snow-plough and accommodation coach used in the Grand Rapids & Indiana Railroad, 1905.

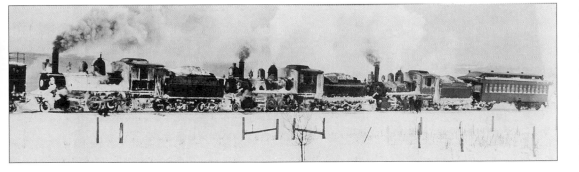

LEFT: *Medlow Bath, New South Wales, the station platform. Australia tended to follow British railway traditions.*

BELOW: *Workers rushing to catch the workman's 'penny' train at Victoria Station, London 1865.*

shipped across the Atlantic in kit form for final assembly in the U.K. and Italy. In overall terms, however, the Pullman type of sleeping car failed to displace the Nagelmackers sleeping carriage on European railways.

With comparatively few exceptions, such as sleeping carriages and special ones for VIPs, western Europe preferred to retain the definitive side-doored compartmented passenger carriage rather than switch to the American style with a platform at each end. Among the British possessions all over the world, Canada favoured the American concept, but Australia and other colonies remained true to the British.

The driving force in the further development of the railways and railroads was the steady increase in the number of passengers. By the 1860s, what is now termed commuter traffic was already considerable, for the increasing urbanization that followed the Industrial Revolution meant that there was more demand for major elements of the workforce to move in and out of towns and cities on a daily basis, manual labourers

The French initially adopted a system in which each berth was created by tipping forward a high-backed seat so that the seat was hidden under the now-horizontal back which became the basis of the berth, and the same concept was adopted for the first British sleeping berths, which were produced in 1873 by the Scotland-based North British Railway for use on its services linking Glasgow with London. The idea had only a short career in the U.K., but lasted into the first quarter of the 20th century in France where such a carriage was called a *wagon-lit* (berth carriage).

Typical of many American entrepreneurs of the period, Pullman soon turned his attention from the U.S.A. to Europe, where his starting point was the U.K. The first British operator of the Pullman type of sleeping carriage was the Midland Railway, which adopted the type in 1874 in a form that was essentially American but scaled down to suit the British operator, and most luxuriously appointed. Several other British railways followed suit, and a good market was also found in Italy for the Pullman carriage which was manufactured in the U.S.A. and often being able to travel at a cheaper rate than office staff. The increasing demand for daily travel was met initially by the use of longer trains with more carriages, but soon the demand exceeded the length of the platforms at which such trains would have to halt, and in some instances passengers were accommodated on two decks to keep the overall length of the train manageable. A pioneer in this process was France, which from the earliest days of its railroad system had allowed a number of operating companies to fit seats on the open tops of many of its carriages. A similar arrangement was also permitted in the United States and was also typical of other countries, such as Austria-Hungary, where the full impact of industrialization came comparatively late at a time when railroads and their stations had already been introduced and platform lengths were severely limited. In the early 1870s, therefore, there appeared in Austria Hungary a double-deck carriage for third-class passengers who were accommodated in a fairly high level of comfort: the carriage had only modest length, but could carry 90 passengers as 50 on the lower deck and 40 on the clerestoried upper deck, which was accessed by a pair of stairways rising from the forward and rear external platforms. The success of this Austro-Hungarian type of mass transport carriage was attested by its production in moderately large numbers in its country of origin, and also by the fact that its concept was copied, with only limited changes, in Denmark, France, Germany and, at a later date, Spain. France also developed its own double-deck carriage

with an open-sided upper deck, but this type was both uncomfortable (especially in the winter) and dangerous as it was not wholly uncommon for weary or careless upper-deck passengers to fall over the side.

Unfortunately for the British, whose need at the time was greater than that of any other country in the world, such double-deck carriages could not be adopted as a result of the low roofs of the tunnels through which any such train would almost inevitably have to pass to reach a major town or city.

At the other end of the social divide were altogether more beautiful carriages, always better made and more luxuriously appointed than the carriages for the ordinary travelling public. These were the carriages specially made and maintained for the royal families of Europe and the highest-ranking politicians and statesman of the world. The first British monarch to travel by train had been Queen Victoria, who made her first rail journey in 1842 between Slough and London when returning to the capital after a sojourn at Windsor Castle. Soon the Austro-Hungarian, British, German and Russian monarchs, occasionally joined by a French emperor, could call on the services of magnificent carriages, indeed trains, for greater comfort and security on longer journeys. A notable feature of these carriages, many of which survive as museum exhibits after their retirement in favour of more utilitarian but nonetheless beautifully appointed versions of standard carriages, is the superb exterior decoration to match the sumptuousness of their interiors.

A classic example of the royal carriage that survives as a museum exhibit is that made for the Romanov dynasty in Russia and used mainly on the line between Moscow and Kursk. The carriage had a large and relatively uncluttered interior, but the need for the carriage to convey the Tsar and members of his immediate family in the worst of Russian winter conditions is reflected in its flat rather than clerestoried roof, which reduced internal volume even though it also trimmed the available headroom, the thick upholstering of the furniture and the depth of the pile on the carpet, the careful fit of the windows and doors to minimize draughts, the extensive and effective insulation, and the enclosed rather than open receivers in the lavatory so that there was no problem of icing up or the admission of super cold external air.

The increase in the weight and speed of trains during the later parts of the 19th century was reflected in the passenger carriages and cars hauled by the more powerful locomotives of the period. The first aspect of these changes was the size of the carriage or car, especially in the U.S.A. By the end of the 19th century the Pullman car of the original American type had become a very much larger item, still manufactured largely of wood but notably roomy, and characterized by its considerable length and weight. Key features of the design, by Pullman employee the great Henry Sessions, included the covered vestibule at each end, the closely engaging gangways with

friction-plate contact for movement between cars, and the large clerestory structure that remained a constant in American passenger-car design for many years to come, as was the arrangement of a central aisle flanked by curtained sleeping berths. Private four-berth compartments, accessed by a side corridor, were available in a variant of the car with a different layout, but the use of such a compartment invariably cost more.

It is likely that the first standard-passenger sleeping carriages with single-berth cabins appeared in the U.K. during 1895 on the east coast express trains operated between London and Edinburgh. Designed by David Bain of the North Eastern Railway, these carriages also offered double-berth compartments for couples. A strong American influence was discernible in the overall nature of the design, which included a large vestibule (with no connection to the neighbouring carriage), and the type proved so popular that it was soon copied throughout Europe, where the Wagons-Lits company later adopted the carriage for its highest-quality international express services.

While in Russia, sleeping carriages and cars were usually of the first-class type only, the western part of the U.S.A. and Canada were providing austere folding berths for impoverished migrants: in Canada these essentially third-class sleeping cars were known as 'colonist' cars.

Another feature that improved considerably in the later part of the 19th century was the heating of passenger

carriages and cars. The U.K. retained a predilection for the metal foot-warmer (heated and then brought to the passenger) on the carriage floor, but elsewhere the stove (sometimes safe and effective and sometimes not) became increasingly standard. Many parts of the U.S.A. can suffer from winter conditions of extreme harshness, and here the standard heater was the Baker heating system, which was a stove-fired hot pipe of the closed-circuit type using water or, in areas of extreme cold, a saturated saline solution that would not freeze when the stove was not lit. Hot-water heating was first introduced in France during 1874, but the most advanced example of this type of heating system was used for a short time by the Great Central Railway in Belgium: developed by M.E. Belleroche as a train-long arrangement using water from the tender heated by an especially developed injector, the system suffered problems with the hose connections, but in overall terms was effective in its primary task of generating heat in the passenger carriages, where copper plates in the floor were heated by the system. A not dissimilar hot-water heating system was used in the Netherlands.

The hot-water concept was quite soon replaced by low-pressure steam heating from a reducing valve on the locomotive, and the first such system to appear in the U.K. was that designed under the auspices of W.S. Laycock in the early 1890s, based on the use of steam piped to storage heaters under the carriage seats.

OPPOSITE: A passenger train of the Northern Pacific Railway at Taylors Falls, Minnesota in the 1880s.

LEFT: Part of Baltimore & Ohio's massive port facilities at Locust Point, Baltimore, Maryland in 1880. Immigrants who had arrived at pier 8 or 9, and been processed in the Immigrant Center (left), prepare to board trains for the West.

BELOW: The first train, a mixed passenger and goods train, crossed over the Missouri river on tracks laid on the ice in 1879.

Another feature that was improved dramatically during this period was lighting. The use of gas for passenger carriage lighting had been pioneered in the U.K. as early as 1863, but the coal gas used in this and similar systems was later replaced by compressed oil gas which superseded coal gas. In the U.S.A. kerosene lamps were still standard, and in Russia candles were still employed. The lighting medium of the future was clearly electricity, and the first use of this to light a passenger carriage was in 1881, when a single Pullman carriage on the route between London and Brighton was first tested. The batteries required for this system were very heavy and required frequent recharging, and it was not until the invention of the J.C. Stone self-generating and self-regulating system at the end of the 19th century that oil and gas lamps were finally replaced by electrical lights.

Throughout the last quarter of the 19th century there was considerable debate as to the relative merits of the two basic types of passenger carriage, namely the European type with separate compartments and the American with a central aisle. The American type was in fact adopted by most countries outside Europe, but even here found favour in the eastern part of the continent and Scandinavia. The prototype for the definitive type of western European compartmented passenger carriage can by found in the so-called D-Wagen introduced to service with the Royal Prussian state railway in the 1890s. This was in effect a hybrid type, for it had vestibules and

gangways like a Pullman carriage, but over most of its length had compartments opening on one side onto the platform, and on the other side onto a side corridor.

The other element that went into the make-up of the typical passenger train in the later part of the 19th century and has remained a standard up to the present is the dining car, which provides waiter service of food cooked on the train. It is probable that the first such car was the convertible diner-sleeper or 'hotel car' of the Great Western Railway of Canada during 1867, but there is a contender in a dining car that was introduced in southern Russia at about the same time. Pullman introduced a dining car on the Chicago & Alton Railroad during 1868, and the first dining car to appear in western Europe was a converted Pullman carriage operated between London and Leeds by the Great Northern Railway during 1879.

A type of organization that was swift to appreciate the value of a railway network to its own operations was the mail service, which saw the train as an ideal transport to replace stagecoaches and riders for the distribution of mail. The first to start such operations, hardly surprisingly as it was the leader among the world's post offices, was that of the British General Post Office. The result was the Travelling Post Office (not only with mail-carrying carriages but also with the facilities to gather and sort the mail while the train was in transit) which was inaugurated during January 1838 in the English Midlands. Within four months of the service's start, further capability had

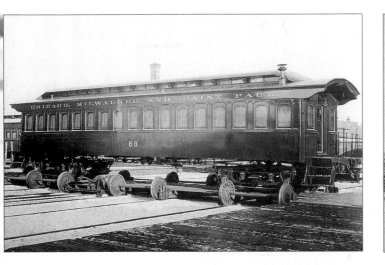

OPPOSITE: New York Central's Empire State Express *No. 999 hauls a single passenger car.*

ABOVE: Chicago, Milwaukee & St. Paul early day coach. American cars had a central aisle and exit doors at each end.

ABOVE RIGHT: Atchison, Topeka & Santa Fe Railroad locomotive hauls a single passenger car in 1880.

RIGHT: Female travellers enjoying a sing-song aboard a Santa Fe Railroad Pullman in the early 1900s.

FAR RIGHT: The compartment-observation car of the Burlington Northern Oriental Limited, *circa 1910.*

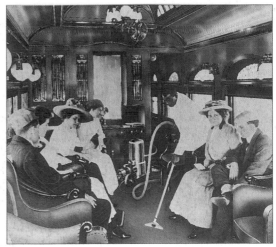

been added to the original transport and sorting of the mail by the development, under the supervision of John Ramsay, of a system allowing the main train to pick up sacks of mail while the train was still moving, and within 10 years John Dicker had improved the situation to the extent that mail trains could both pick up and drop sacks of mail while still steaming at maximum speed.

A similar arrangement was used, albeit on a smaller scale, in Prussia and France. The French travelling post office system was first employed on the route linking Paris and Rouen during 1844. Mail sorting cars were introduced to American postal practice during the American Civil War of the first half of the 1860s, first appearing on the Hannibal & St. Joseph Railroad after the system had been suggested by W. A. Davis. Named the Railway Post Office and rapidly extended as and when the demand justified it, the U.S. postal train held its own on overnight services between cities no more than 600 miles (965km) apart mainly through the advantage it offered, at least until the advent of specialized freight aircraft, of being able to sort as well as transport the mail.

The justification for including a discussion on postal trains when we are concerned primarily with passenger trains rather than freight is the fact that the mail trains are based on passenger carriages and cars adapted for the purpose, rather than on the wagons generally used for freight transport.

The passenger-moving practices of the

late 19th century continued into the first quarter of the 20th century with little significant alteration except in the numbers of passengers carried and the more advanced carriages and cars developed, manufactured and employed for the task. At its lowest level, the movement of passengers was and is one of rail transport's least exciting yet most important aspects, especially when it is concerned with rail-borne commuter traffic. This is the term that has generally been adopted to signify the daily movement of office workers, shop personnel and other workers into the urban area in the morning at the start of the

working day and then out of the urban area in the late afternoon at the day's end. In this context it is worth noting that the commuter is, in the pure sense of the word, a person who, in having to make regular journeys by public transport, has gained the benefit of having his fare commuted to a much reduced sum paid in regular instalments, generally weekly, monthly, quarterly or annually: to the British such a person is a season ticket holder, while in the U.S.A. he is a commuter. But though first adopted in the U.S.A., the concept of the commuter is now universal.

In the U.S.A. the commuter car on the

railroad was at first generally the same as an ordinary day passenger car, and presented difficulties of rapid boarding and alighting at railroad terminals. As a result, in the first part of the 20th century, a number of American passenger-car designers added, in the middle of the car, double sliding doors so that commuters could leave the car at this point as an alternative to the car's ends. So successful was the new type of car that the one used in Boston was adopted in the U.K. by the District Railway when this latter was electrified during 1905. However, the District Railway tried to go one better than the Americans by giving the doors an automatic opening and closing capability, and immediately discovered the dangers of such a system in its ability, indeed propensity, to catch people's clothes, goods and even limbs with decidedly dangerous consequences. After six weeks the system was discontinued.

In overall terms, however, the specialized commuter carriage and car came generally to be accepted as a minimally compartmented or wholly uncompartmented unit generally accessed by a large number of side doors that were either manually- or power-operated.

This division between open and compartmented carriages and cars was not restricted to the trains used only for commuter services, however, but has remained still more important for the carriages and cars used for longer-distance services throughout the world. In the technologically most advanced parts of the

OPPOSITE: *The luxurious interior of Union Pacific's* Little Nugget, *1940.*

RIGHT: *A cook prepares meals for hungry Amtrak superliner passengers. The kitchen, which is air-conditioned and fluorescent-lit, is located on the lower level of the bi-level dining car. Electric convection and microwave ovens afford much more pleasant working conditions for kitchen employees.*

BELOW RIGHT: *Self-service French-style on SNCF (Société Nationale des Chemins de Fer).*

BELOW: *The Baltimore & Ohio's* Colonial *dining car, 1924.*

world, the open type of carriage and car has found steady appreciation mainly in North America, Russia, south-west Germany, Scandinavia and much of eastern Europe, while the compartmented type has been generally preferred by most of western Europe and the countries that once formed the British empire and commonwealth. The exception among the countries once under British influence is New Zealand, which has long favoured American railway concepts.

Until a time in the relatively recent past, the most important medium for the construction of railroad cars and railway carriages was wood, at least for the parts above the frame and trucks or bogies. The use of wood was conducive to comfort as a result of its good qualities as an insulator, but presented distinct flammability problems, when lit by gas or kerosene, in the event of any accident. As the travelling public became wholly at home with the concept of rail transport, and began to turn its attentions away from the wonders of speedy travel toward the type of fate that could befall it, there began the development in the last part of the 19th century of a demand for 'safer' carriages and cars. Railroad companies saw in this an opportunity to steal a commercial advantage over competitors who might still be operating wooden carriages and cars. In the U.S.A. in particular, the railroad companies who could afford it and possessed locomotives of adequate power to haul trains of heavier cars, took the opportunity to undertake the rapid design and

manufacture of Pullman-type cars in steel. The railroad operators with smaller coffers had recourse to the expedient of covering their wooden cars with thin sheet steel, the use of large rivets suggesting that the cars were in fact new and made entirely of steel. The fact that the public believed that it was safer in steel cars is indicated by the advertising material put out by the railroad operators: the Chicago, Milwaukee & St. Paul Railroad, for instance, ran an express named *The Columbian* and the railroad's publicity department emphasized the adoption of the new and safer type of car by calling the express 'The All-Steel Columbian'.

Made up of steel cars and pulled by mighty steam locomotives, most of the American transcontinental trains were the epitome of luxury travel: all included bars, dining cars, sleeping cars and a high level of service, and many of them added to this 'standard' level of luxury a barber's shop and, at the rear, an observation car. This latter offered the choice between very comfortable seating inside the car or, alternatively, seating on the open but railed platform at the extreme rear, which provided superb views of the countryside through which the train was travelling.

In overall terms, the standard of passenger accommodation was extremely varied, and depended largely on the ethos and wealth of the country in which the service was being operated. The most comfortable arrangement for an ordinary daytime traveller in North America was the so-called parlor car, which was either a

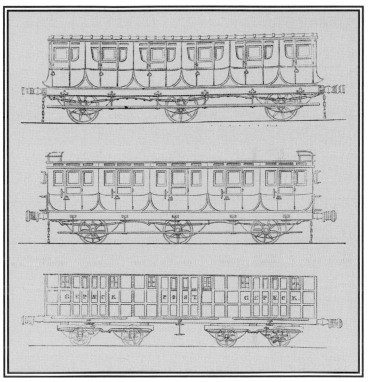

Pullman or a Pullman-type car with well-stuffed chairs on fixed pivots, installed as singleton units on each side of the central aisle. A similar arrangement had been used in the U.K. by several operators, mainly in the south of England, since they had started to import Pullman cars in the mid-1870s. The first British-built Pullman carriage was completed in 1908, and differed from its American counterpart mainly in having single and genuinely massive seats that were movable on legs. Another type of American car was the so-called chair car, which was laid out in a fashion basically similar to that of the day car except for the use of adjustable seats offering greater back support.

The above applies basically to what was known in Europe as the first-class passenger, and the accommodation for second- and third-class passengers was proportionally inferior, in accordance with the reduced fares paid by such passengers. However, in Asia and sub-Saharan Africa the very considerable cheapness of third-class fares was and still is mirrored in the total austerity of the third-class accommodation.

As far as sleeping carriages and cars were concerned, the need for third-class accommodation was met by the adoption of a superimposed trio of berths in each compartment in the carriages introduced in Sweden during 1910: this type of accommodation later spread to Germany,

OPPOSITE: *The Royal Mail van arriving at the Great Western Railway, Churston, England in 1959. Mail services in a number of countries were quick to appreciate the value of the railway network.*

ABOVE LEFT: *Royal Mail sorting van 80375 at Crewe, England. The Travelling Post Office has facilities to gather and sort mail while the train is on the move.*

ABOVE: *German and Danish railway carriages circa 1845 show the influence of the stagecoach on early carriage design.*

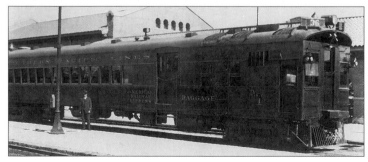

LEFT: *Richmond interurban car, 1909, otherwise known as the 'Car'.*

BELOW LEFT: *Mack model AR 72-seater gasoline-engined railcar of the Southern Pacific Railroad, 1930s.*

BELOW RIGHT: *Union Pacific's 'The Challenger' coffee-shop diner car No. 393 in the Omaha yards, 1940s.*

OPPOSITE
ABOVE: *This compartment-observation car entered service in 1922 on the Great Northern Railway's transcontinental Oriental Limited. It had four compartments, glassed-in card-playing and smoking quarters, a buffet and observation-lounge room.*

BELOW: *The first General Electric locomotive, built in 1895, shown pulling a passenger train out of the Baltimore & Ohio tunnel in Baltimore. This was the first use of electric power on main-line trackage in America.*

and after that to France. The U.K. adopted third-class sleeper accommodation only in 1928, in the form of four-berth compartments with two berths on each side. The French had a similar arrangement in their *compartiments à couchettes*, which were in effect second-class accommodations for first-class passengers unwilling to pay the full supplement for the more luxurious full first-class sleeping cars. The Pullman sleeping cars used by the American railroads, which had become mainly of the side corridor type during the first part of the 20th century, had many gradations: the so-called bedroom was similar in standard to the European Wagons-Lits accommodation, while the

two still more comfortable and well-appointed levels were the roomier drawing room and the genuinely luxurious master suite.

A factor too infrequently understood is that the advent of steel carriage and car construction allowed, and indeed almost demanded, a considerable stride toward standardization of basic design, if not the finishing details. It was only in this way that the manufacturers could keep unit costs down to an acceptable level, given the higher cost of their raw materials and investment that they had to make in machinery to press metal panels and complete the construction of the steel car. As the U.S.A. was the main supplier of rolling stock in all its forms to Canada, as well as the countries of Central and South America, the same situation soon came to prevail in these regions.

It was not the same in Europe, where a measure of national and indeed company individuality was more highly prized, and the carriages of the various private and later state railways therefore differed not only in the detail of their finishes and in the paintwork which the Americans generally eschewed, but also in the basic design of the carriages.

Third-class accommodation on railways of the East has generally been of the poorest type, with emphasis placed on the number of passengers that could be carried hanging onto the outside of the carriage as well as standing or sitting in the interior. The third-class carriages of the Indian railway system each comprised a long compartment with

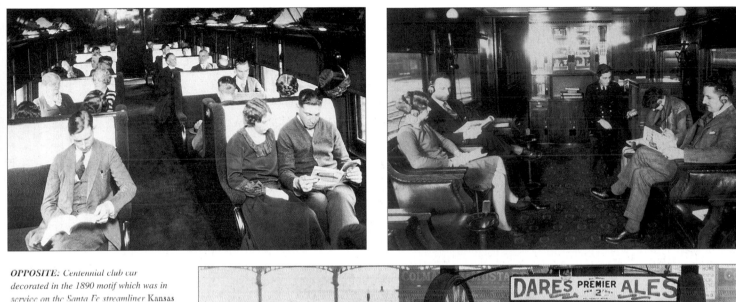

OPPOSITE: *Centennial club car decorated in the 1890 motif which was in service on the Santa Fe streamliner* Kansas City Chief.

ABOVE: *Interior of a Santa Fe Railroad Pullman coach used in the 1930s.*

ABOVE RIGHT: *Passengers listen to radio and phonograph in the observation car of a transcontinental train.*

RIGHT: *The footbridge at New Street Station, Birmingham, England taken around 1910. The concept of the rail 'commuter', ferried by train to work in the morning and home again in the evening, was first adopted in the U.S.A., but is now universal.*

LEFT: *Interurban car No. 1309 at Chilliwack, British Columbia, 6 April 1914. The white flag was to mark the special debut run of this, the last B.C.E.R. car built.*

BELOW LEFT: *Passenger car built in 1873 by Jackson & Sharpe, predecessor of the American Car and Foundry Company.*

BELOW: *A lengthy passenger train of the Illinois Central Railroad.*

OPPOSITE LEFT: *Amtrak's San Diego–Los Angeles San Diegan. Amtrak's standard passenger locomotive from the late 1970s was the F40 PH 'Cowl' Bo-Bo unit.*

RIGHT: *Sleeper on a Santa Fe streamliner.*

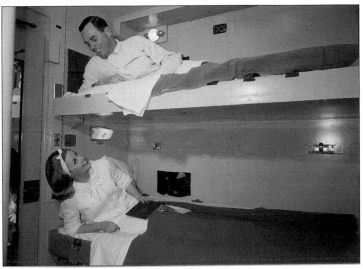

four wooden benches, the middle pair installed back-to-back, and there is only the most primitive of sanitary facilities in the form of a latrine. The same generally applies to the railways of Bangladesh, Burma and Pakistan, although the accommodation in the third-class carriages of the railways in Thailand, the Malay peninsula and Indonesia are somewhat better.

In other parts of the world, the railways of Japan had good rolling stock, based in later years on American design concepts but reduced in scale and opulence. South Africa had several excellent trains, with a class system that was less complicated than that of India (first-class for whites, second-class for higher-class Indians, intermediate-class for the so-called poor whites, and third-class for lower-class Indians) but until recently subject to the same type of racial limitations that had been typical of India up to the time of its independence in 1947.

The weights of carriages and cars have differed considerably over the history of railroads, depending on the power of the locomotives available and the track gauge of the particular operator, among other factors. Even with the advent of greater standardization, however, there was still a considerable variation in weights. For standard-gauge operation in 1914, for example, the American Pullman in its full glory turned the scales at 80 tons or even more, while the D-Wagen and a typical

LEFT: *Canadian Pacific's famous* Canadian *passenger train. 'Dome' cars permitted superb views of the scenic route.*

BELOW: *Interior of Amtrak's* Broadway Limited, *showing a bedroom in day use in the late 1970s.*

OPPOSITE
LEFT: *Amtrak's double-deck coaches on the* Southwest Limited *enabled more passengers to be carried in the 1970s.*

RIGHT: *Passengers preparing to board Amtrak's Seattle–Los Angeles–Seattle* Coast Starlight *in the late 1970s.*

BELOW: *A Rohr turboliner carries passengers alongside the Hudson river on Amtrak's* Empire *service in the late 1970s.*

European dining carriage of the period was about 40 tons, and relics of an older generation might be only 8 tons.

Apart from classics of what soon became established as the 'traditional' national carriage and car types as discussed above with relation mainly to Europe and North America, there were also large numbers of carriages and cars to be found in other parts of the world as combinations of features from two or more of the above with any quantity of local variations. Thus in Central and South America there were North American cars completed with the type of accommodation typical of Indian third-class practices, or British-built carriages with superb seating completed in first-class oxhide, or British-built carriages completed with the American type of seating.

Given that passenger traffic was one of the two primary *raisons d'être* for the existence of the railroad and its locomotives, it is interesting at this stage to look at just a few of the greatest engines from the heyday of the steam locomotive between the start of the 20th century and the outbreak of World War II in 1939.

The French were among the first to appreciate the conceptual advantages of compound expansion for steam engines used in express passenger work, and in no other country was compounding pursued with greater diligence or indeed success. Even so, occasional doubts did enter into the minds of French engineers from time to time, resulting in the manufacture of a

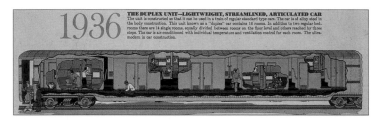

1936 THE DUPLEX UNIT—LIGHTWEIGHT, STREAMLINED, ARTICULATED CAR The unit is constructed so that it can be used in a train of regular standard type cars. The car is of alloy steel in the body construction. This unit known as a "duplex" car contains 16 rooms. In addition to two regular bed-rooms there are 14 single rooms, equally divided between rooms on the floor level and others reached by three steps. The car is air-conditioned with individual temperature and ventilation control for each room. The ultra-modern in car construction.

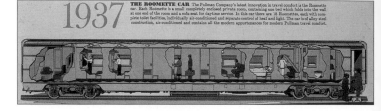

1937 THE ROOMETTE CAR The Pullman Company's latest innovation in travel comfort is the Roomette car. Each Roomette is a small completely enclosed private room, containing one bed which folds into the wall at one end of the room and a sofa-seat for daytime service. In this car there are 18 Roomettes, each with complete toilet facilities, individually air-conditioned and separate control of heat and light. The car is of alloy steel construction, air-conditioned and contains all the modern appurtenances for modern Pullman travel comfort.

group of simple-expansion locomotives, but in overall terms the concept of compound expansion in general thrived and became ever more strong.

This tendency is well illustrated by the 'Pacific'-type locomotives of the Paris, Lyons & Mediterranean railroad. Between 1890 and 1907 the railroad ordered just under 850 locomotives, of which no fewer than 835 were of the compound-expansion type, and in the period between 1905 and 1907 the manufacture of compound-expansion 'Atlantic' type and 4-6-0 locomotives continued unabated. Then in 1907 there appeared the first European Pacific-type locomotive, and in 1909 the railroad produced two prototype locomotives with that type's 4-6-2 wheel layout, one with simple and the other with compound expansion. The availability of these two prototypes allowed the locomotive designers to test and, it was anticipated, reaffirm their belief in the superiority of compound expansion, but at the same time there was another reason for the manufacture of a locomotive of the simple expansion type. It was known that compound expansion made it possible for a

higher proportion of the steam's energy to be converted into work as it expanded, but also that the exploitation of the compound engine's full advantages required a high steam pressure, and that high pressure resulted in increased boiler maintenance requirement and therefore cost. In this second half of the 20th century's first decade, a novel attraction for engineers was the superheater, a system which offered the considerable improvement in the simple-expansion engine's thermal efficiency to the point at which it might once again be a contender for use in high-performance locomotives, which might thus be manufactured and maintained at the reduced overall costs resulting from the use of lower boiler pressures.

The availability of the two otherwise similar Pacific-type locomotives allowed the concept to be evaluated in real operational terms, for the compound-expansion engine used saturated steam whereas the simple-expansion engine had a superheating system. The compound-expansion locomotive had the standard de Glehn layout of cylinders, with the outside high-pressure cylinders located well back

OPPOSITE
ABOVE LEFT: *The 1936 Pullman Duplex unit – a lightweight, streamlined, articulated car.*

ABOVE RIGHT: *The Pullman company's Roomette car, 1937.*

RIGHT: *Pullman's luxuriously-appointed coaches soon transferred to Europe. Here a Pirbright is heading west in England.*

BELOW LEFT and BELOW: *In India, railways were developed by private enterprise under a concessionary system, but locomotives were built to a range of standard designs – the BESA (British Engineering Standards Association). These BESA 2-8-0s were more suitable for freight than passenger work, but all coped well with conditions in India.*

over the rear truck wheels, but the simple engine had an inline arrangement of its four cylinders, as in the railroad's existing Atlantic type and 4-6-0 locomotives. The inline arrangement allowed a much more rigid structure than was possible with the de Glehn arrangement. In other respects the two prototypes were basically similar except for the fact that the compound-expansion engine worked at a higher steam pressure.

The two '231'-class prototype locomotives were used for comparative trials during 1911, and an analysis of the results revealed that the superheated engine developed greater power but also burned 16 per cent less coal than the compound-expansion engine. The next step should perhaps have been the combination of

superheating and compound expansion, but during this period it was impossible to manufacture a superheated compound-expansion locomotive and remain within current weight restrictions. As a result, the Paris, Lyons & Mediterranean railroad ordered 70 simple-expansion locomotives in 1911. In 1912, however, the design problems of the superheated type of compound-expansion engine had been overcome, and 20 such locomotives were manufactured to a pattern that differed from that of the prototype only in its inline arrangement of the four cylinders. For some reason there was still a measure of uncertainty, however, and 20 more simple-expansion locomotives were then made before a 1913 evaluation of the two types of superheated design decided that the

ABOVE: The Columbia *passenger train, hauled by a Royal Hudson-class locomotive No. 2860 in British Columbia, Canada.*

RIGHT: The dining car of the Trans Europ Express.

ABOVE: *The express* Endeavour, *hauled by a Da-class A1A-A1A diesel-electric locomotive. It ran daily between Wellington and Napier in New Zealand's North Island.*

ABOVE RIGHT: *Articulated carriages are used on some New Zealand Railway provincial services. These cars are built from railcars with modernized interiors. The train is headed by a diesel-electric locomotive.*

RIGHT: *The* Canadian, *the legendary express passenger train of the Canadian Pacific Railway taking heavy snow in its stride.*

LEFT: The Northerner *express passenger train, hauled by a 2,051kW Dx-class Co-Co diesel-electric locomotive, running nightly between Wellington and Auckland in New Zealand's North Island.*

BELOW LEFT: A British Great Western Region Saint-class 4-6-0 locomotive heads a passenger train. Though the first locomotive appeared in 1902, 32 were built before being given the name 'Saint'.

BELOW: Southern Railway PS4-class 4-6-2 locomotive number 1401 hauling the crack Crescent Limited *express passenger train between Washington and New Orleans, in the late 1920s.*

RIGHT: *A number of South American railways bought locomotives and cars from the U.S.A. These two passenger carriages in Ecuador are typical.*

BELOW: *The popularity of preserved steam locomotives has encouraged main-line railways to run a number of 'specials'. Here the Didcot–Derby passes Hatton North Junction in England.*

compound-expansion type offered improved performance as well as a 25 per cent reduction in coal consumption. With the issue of simple- and compound-expansion engines finally settled, the Paris, Lyons & Mediterranean railroad ordered no further Pacific-type locomotives of the simple-expansion type, and existing engines of this type were gradually converted to compound-expansion operation.

During 1921 and 1931 the railway contracted for another 230 and 55 Pacific-type locomotives respectively for an overall total of 462. Within these orders, successive batches introduced gradual improvement, mainly to the proportions of the boiler and the exhaust arrangements, without any major alteration of the core layout. Improvements were gradually made, one of the last being based on the Chapelon package of upgrades to the steam passages and boiler proportions. The Chapelon package was evaluated in an engine which was rebuilt with a boiler having still higher pressure, and although a plan was agreed to retrofit this boiler, only 30 of the locomotives were fully modernized in this fashion, the last of them in 1948, after the Paris, Lyons & Mediterranean railroad had been absorbed into the nationalized Société Nationale des Chemins de Fer. Another 284 locomotives were partially modernized.

These Pacific-type locomotives had prolonged and useful careers, but even in improved form they did not achieve the level of overall performance displayed by the Chapelon rebuilds of the Paris-Orléans railway's Pacific-type locomotives. From

1952, the locomotives were replaced in the main routes by electric locomotives, thereafter spending their declining years on other services. The retirement of the class began during the 1950s, but many of the boilers still had considerable life left in them allowing their use as replacements, and as a result the last of the '231C'-class locomotives were not withdrawn until 1969. The details for the 231C class include two 17.3 x 25.6-in (440 x 650-mm) high-pressure cylinders and two 25.6 x 25.6-in (650 x 650-mm) low-pressure cylinders, driving wheels with a diameter of 6ft 6.7in (2.00m), a steam pressure of 228lb/sq in (16 kg/cm²), 11,023lb (5000kg)

of coal, 7,397 U.S. gal (6,159 Imp gal; 28000 litres) of water, total weight of 320,767lb (145500kg), and overall length of 65ft 7in (20.00m).

It was only occasionally that any of the world's great trains was hauled solely by a tank engine, but a notable example of this breed was the *Southern Belle*, which was the Pullman express which ran non-stop several times a day between London's Victoria Station and Brighton. Specially associated with this train was a group of seven 'Baltic'-class 4-6-4 locomotives, the most powerful engines ever operated by the London, Brighton & South Coast Railway.

Express services between London and

ABOVE and OPPOSITE: In poorer countries, such as India and some South American countries, passengers can still look forward to extremely uncomfortable rail journeys.

the south coast of England had previously been hauled mainly by 4-4-0, 4-4-2 and 4-4-2T locomotives. The new 4-6-4 locomotives were to a design that was to some degree a stretched version of the two 4-6-2T locomotives that had supplemented the other locomotives. Created by Colonel L.B. Billinton, the design was specifically created to provide engines able to haul the *Belle* and other fast trains such as the *City Limited* between London and Brighton in 45 to 50 minutes instead of 60 minutes. In fact, the 60-minute timing was never improved upon, even by the successor to the *Southern Belle,* the electric *Brighton Belle,* which replaced the steam train after 1933; but it had to be recognized that the addition of third-class Pullman carriages to the previous arrangement of just first-class carriages made the train an increasingly heavy load.

The design and engineering conventions of the period were generally followed except in the valve gear, which comprised outside Walschaert valve gear that operated inside piston valves between the frames via rocking levers. The primary reasons for this disposition were Billinton's desire for cylinders similar to those of the 4-6-2T locomotives and the need for a well tank under the boiler between the frames, an arrangement which would have been impossible had there been valve motion in the region. There was trouble with the early units of the class, this including a derailment attributable to the combination of the high centre of gravity and the sloshing of water in half-full tanks. This

accident took place soon after the service debut, in April 1914, of the first locomotive, the *Charles C. Macrae.* The solution to this problem was found in making all but the lower 1ft 3in (0.381m) of the side tanks into dummies, an arrangement which lowered the locomotive's centre of gravity so successfully that speeds of up to 75mph (121km/h) were then quite often attained without problem.

The second unit of the class was delivered just before the outbreak of World War I in August 1914, and five further examples were made in 1921–22. Two more received names at that time, these being the *Stephenson* and the *Remembrance,* the latter being named for the railroad company's war dead and also giving its name to the entire class. The class's later units were never fitted with the feed-water heaters and steam-operated feed pumps which, unusually in British practice, were fitted to the earlier ones for a time after their completion.

After the electrification of the line during 1933, the Southern Railway converted the 4-6-4 tank engines into 4-6-0 locomotives known as the 'N15X' class, a guise in which they had a successful second career on the less exacting longer-distance services of the bigger system, lasting well after 1948 into the days after the nationalization of all the separate British railroad companies into the unified British Railways. The fact that this was deemed worth doing demonstrates clearly the high quality of these locomotives, whose last survivor was retired in July 1957. The details of the 'Remembrance' class include a tractive effort of 24,180lb (10968kg), two 22 x 28-in (559 x 711-mm) cylinders, driving wheels with a diameter of 6ft 9in (2.057m), steam pressure of 170lb/sq in (11.9 kg/cm²), 8,000lb (3629kg) of fuel, 3,243 U.S. gal (2,700 Imp gal; 12274 litres) of water, total weight of 222,000lb (100699kg), and overall length of 50ft 4.75in (15.361m).

If there was a single railroad that set the standards which the rest of the world's railroads generally hoped to emulate, it was the Pennsylvania Railroad. To this extent the Pennsylvania Railroad liked to consider itself the 'Standard Railroad of the World', and to this extent the magnificent 'K4' class

OPPOSITE: *A Peruvian steam locomotive hauls a passenger train through the mountains.*

ABOVE RIGHT: *Interior of a French commuter train.*

RIGHT: *Lack of height restrictions in France has permitted the French National Railways to almost double passenger-carrying capacity on some lines with the introduction of double-decker trains.*

of 4-6-2 steam locomotives, introduced in 1914 and soon the core of the railroad's operations until a time well after World War II, could be called the 'Standard Express Locomotive of the World'.

Following a number of other Pacific-type 4-6-2 locomotives, the K4 class eventually totalled 425 engines manufactured over a space of 14 years. In overall terms, the Pennsylvania Railroad was very conservative in the design and construction of its locomotives, preferring to progress by limited steps before committing itself to a major manufacturing effort, and its adoption of the Pacific-type locomotive was prefaced by the evaluation

of one 'K28'-class prototype ordered in 1907 from the American Locomotive Co. By 1910 the Pennsylvania Railroad believed that it knew enough about the Pacific-type locomotive to embark on the construction of such locomotives to its own design, and soon 239 'K2'-class locomotives had been delivered. Superheating was applied to these locomotives only in 1912.

In 1913 the Pennsylvania Railroad contracted with Baldwin of Philadelphia for 30 examples of the improved 'K3' class of 4-6-2 locomotives, whose main novelty was the installation of the earliest type of practical mechanical stoker, known as the 'Crawford' after its inventor, D.F. Crawford,

ABOVE: *Southern Railway PS4-class 4-6-2 locomotive No. 1396 from the glory days of steam trains.*

ABOVE LEFT: *A South Wales Pullman. From the very first, the name 'Pullman' was synonymous with luxurious passenger travel.*

BELOW LEFT: *Great Western Railway's* Cheltenham Flyer, *leaving Swindon station, England, drawn by the locomotive* Tregenna Castle.

OPPOSITE BELOW: *Inter-city Paris–Strasbourg train at Lutzelbourg.*

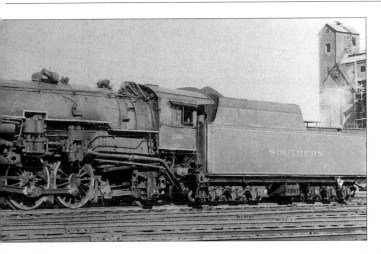

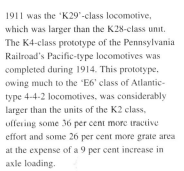

the Superintendent of Motive Power (Lines West). The Pennsylvania Railroad had used such a stoking system since 1905 and nearly 300 such systems were in use by 1914, only 64 of them on Pacific-type locomotives. Later stoker designs used a screw feed, but the principle used in the Crawford system was to push the coal forward with a series of steam-powered paddles that were 'feathered' on the return stroke to avoid pushing the coal back again. The coal was fed into the firebox at grate level in a fashion unlike that which later became common, in which the stoker fed the coal onto a rear-mounted platform for further distribution by jets of steam.

Another Alco prototype supplied in

1911 was the 'K29'-class locomotive, which was larger than the K28-class unit. The K4-class prototype of the Pennsylvania Railroad's Pacific-type locomotives was completed during 1914. This prototype, owing much to the 'E6' class of Atlantic-type 4-4-2 locomotives, was considerably larger than the units of the K2 class, offering some 36 per cent more tractive effort and some 26 per cent more grate area at the expense of a 9 per cent increase in axle loading.

It is worth noting that the Pennsylvania Railroad was atypical among North American railroads in aiming for virtual self-sufficiency in the design and manufacture of its locomotives. A considerable asset in this capacity was the railroad's own locomotive testing facility at Altoona, which was the only North American facility at which a locomotive could be run up to full power on rollers. The facility's extensive instrumentation made it possible for the designers' operating and performance estimates to be checked under controlled conditions, and thus for the right modifications to be effected.

The K4-class prototype was tested at Altoona soon after its completion, the evaluation revealing that few changes were needed for the production version. Sustained operational use did indicate the need for a number of modifications and by 1923, with 200 or more K4-class locomotives completed, the hand-operated reversing gear of the earlier locomotives was replaced by a power-operated reversing arrangement. The earlier locomotives were

also adapted to the improved standard, and during the 1930s most of the K4-class locomotives were retrofitted with an automatic stoking system to overcome the limitation on power output imposed by the limitations of a single man's strength and endurance. Another interesting improvement of the 1930s was the retrofit of a continuous cab signalling system: a receiver picked up a coded current flowing in track circuits, and converted this into the relevant signal on a display in the cab.

Features typical of the Pennsylvania Railroad's conservative approach to technical developments was evident in a number of features including the low ratio of evaporative heating surface to

superheater size, and a boiler pressure only about 75 per cent of that typical in the locomotives of most other contemporary North American railroad operators. This should not be construed as any suggestion that these features were wrong, however, but only that they were different from the norm and geared the particular operating environment of the Pennsylvania Railroad. Limited superheating and a comparatively low boiler pressure, for instance, reduced the amount of maintenance and repair that were necessary, and this suggested that the railroad had decided in overall terms that the benefits of lower maintenance and repair costs more than offset the associated higher fuel consumption, whose cost was in

any case offset by the low prices that the railroad was able to obtain through bulk purchase from local coal mines.

Except for 75 units built by Baldwin, all the K4-class locomotives manufactured during 1924–28 were made by the railroad's Juanita shops at Altoona. There were a few 'special' locomotives among the fleet of K4-class engines. For example, two locomotives with poppet valve gear, thermic syphons in the firebox, and improved draughting were able to develop over 4,000hp rather than the standard 3,000hp in the cylinders, several other locomotives ('K4sa'-subclass units) offered higher cylinder horse power through the combination of the same type of firebox

ABOVE LEFT: *A French National Railways (SNCF) Pacific-class locomotive pulls out of Brussels station heading an express passenger train to Paris.*

ABOVE: *A famous French passenger locomotive type, the Class 231K 4-6-2 Pacific, which originally belonged to the Paris-Lyons & Mediterranean railroad.*

186

and exhaust improvements with piston valves enlarged from a diameter of 12in (0.305m) to 15in (0.381m), one locomotive was fully streamlined for a while, and a number of other locomotives were partly streamlined. Many types of tender were used, including a few which were so big they dwarfed the engine, but held a larger quantity of coal as well as 23,500 U.S. gal (19,568 Imp gal; 88957 litres) of water.

Outside the railroad's area of electrification, the K4-class locomotives were responsible for hauling all of the Pennsylvania Railroad's express passenger services in the period before the introduction of the Duplex locomotives in the aftermath of World War II. The details of the K4-class locomotive include a tractive effort of 44,460lb (20167kg), two 27 x 28-in (686 x 711-mm) cylinders, driving wheels with a diameter of 6ft 10in (2.032m), steam pressure of 205lb/sq in (14.4 kg/cm2), 36,000lb (16330kg) of fuel, 12,000 U.S. gal (9,992 Imp gal; 45425 litres) of water, total weight of 533,000lb (241769kg), and overall length of 83ft 6in (25.451m).

April 1922 was an important month in British railway history, for it marked the arrival of the first of a new class of Pacific-type locomotives whose record can be matched by few others. Some 79 of what were known initially as the 'A1' class of 4-6-2 locomotives were made between 1921 and 1934 for service on the Great Northern Railway. The core notion at the bottom of the design by Nigel Gresley was that a substantial locomotive, with more

than enough power for the task envisaged for it, would be costly to build but economical in operation over a long career. The thinking behind the design also benefited from Gresley's appreciation that the steam locomotive's primary technical asset was simplicity, and that it was essential for the reciprocating forces to be balanced. This latter could be achieved by a minimum of three cylinders. Despite the basic simplicity of these attractive locomotives, however, they suffered from poor detail design.

One of the poorer features of the design was the valve gear, and this was modified during 1926 in a process that cost little to implement yet effected a major reduction in coal consumption. An appreciation of the need for the changes came in 1925, when a smaller 4-6-0 locomotive from the rival Great Western Railway was tried out on the London & North Eastern Railway, which was an amalgamation of the Great Northern, Great Eastern, North Eastern, Great Central, North British and other smaller railway companies. The Pendennis Castle, as the GWR's locomotive was named, managed everything that the A1-class locomotive could achieve, but in the process burned 10 per cent less coal.

The LNER's engineering staff took the opportunity to examine the valve gear of another of the GWR's 'Castle'-class locomotives during the celebrations at Darlington for the centenary of the Stockton & Darlington Railway later in the same year, and then improved the valve

gear of the A1 class to the extent that its coal consumption was reduced by 20 per cent by comparison with its previous figure. The reduction in coal consumption was sufficient for a locomotive of the A1 class to haul an express passenger train from London to Newcastle without the engine change that had previously been required. At much the same time as the valve gear was altered, a boiler type intended for operation at higher pressure was introduced, in some cases combined with a reduction of cylinder diameter. The change added six tons to the locomotive's weight and two tons to its axle loading, but the overall result was worth it and the locomotives fitted with these boilers were designated as the 'A3' class of what was sometimes known as 'Super-Pacific' engines.

From 1928 these locomotives were able to undertake the longest non-stop journey in the world, namely the 393 miles (632km) between London and Edinburgh, with the aid of special corridor tenders so that crews could be changed en route. In 1935 one of the locomotives made a high-speed run from London to Newcastle to test the way for the planned Silver Jubilee express with a 240-minute schedule, and covered the distance of 268 miles (432km) in only 3 hours 50 minutes at an average speed of 69.9mph (112.5km/h). On the return journey, the locomotive reached 108mph (174km/h) on the straight and level stretch at Essendine north of Peterborough, and this speed is still thought to be the world record for an unstreamlined steam

locomotive. The streamlined version of the A1 class entered service to operate on the new high-speed service, and the arrival of the streamlined locomotives allowed the older 4-6-2 locomotives to be displaced from their prime position on the East Coast main line.

The demands of rail transport in World War II resulted in the operation of 24-coach trains on the East Coast main line, and the excellent performance of the A3 and surviving A1-class locomotives was an eloquent testimony to the brilliance of their concept but also, as a result of poorer maintenance, of their poor detail design. After the war, efforts were made to remedy the worst of the poor design features, but progress was slowed by resistance from the design office, which felt that the locomotives were essentially right. The classes were widely used to 1965, and the last was retired only in 1965. The details of the A1-class locomotive included a tractive effort of 29,385lb (13329kg), three 20 x 26-in (508 x 660-mm) cylinders, driving wheels with a diameter of 6ft 10in (2.03m), steam pressure of 180lb/sq in (12.6kg/cm2), 17,920lb (8129kg) of fuel, 6,005 U.S. gal (5,000 Imp gal; 22730 litres) of water, total weight of 332,000lb (150595kg), and overall length of 70ft 5in (21.46m).

After the end of World War I many Prussian locomotives, most especially the 4-6-0 units of the 'P8' class, were delivered to members of the victorious Allied powers as part of Germany's war reparations. Germany started a programme to make good these losses to its own railroad

LEFT: A streamlined 05-class locomotive leaves the Borsig works on its first outing in 1935. These record-breaking locomotives headed Germany's prestige passenger trains.

ABOVE: The famous Flying Hamburger, a two-car diesel express passenger train which, from 1933, ran between Berlin and Hamburg.

system, and in 1919 began work on a 2-8-2 locomotive for secondary passenger traffic in Germany's hillier regions. Work on the 'P10' class of 2-8-2 locomotives was delayed by a number of post-war difficulties, and although it had been designed more specifically for service on the Prussian railroad network, the German state railway had come into existence by the time the first locomotive was completed by Borsig during 1922.

The design in general drew on Prussian locomotive thinking in the previous 20 years, but the single class that had the highest influence on the design was the 'G12' class of three-cylinder 2-10-0 locomotives, built in 1917 to meet the urgent need for a powerful goods engine for lines of medium axle load. To speed the design process, the G12-class locomotive was based on a Henschel design for the Turkish railroad, and it introduced some novel features to a Prussian design, particularly bar frames and a Belpaire firebox with a trapezoidal grate above the driving wheels.

These G12-class design features were translated into the P10-class locomotive, which also had three cylinders. The use of larger driving wheels meant that there was not enough clearance for the firebox to be installed above the driving wheels, so the grate was made in three sections: the parallel front part was located between the rear driving wheels, the intermediate part was outwardly tapered, and the rear part was parallel and the same in width as the widest portion of the intermediate part. The

arrangement set the firebox farther forward, and thus gave a better weight distribution with more weight on the driving wheels, but the resultant complex shape of the firebox walls resulted in maintenance problems and the concept was not repeated.

In the German state railway system the P10-class locomotives were reclassified as '39'-class units, of which some 260 were manufactured between 1922 and 1927. Though classified as secondary passenger engines, the P10-class locomotives were in fact true mixed-traffic engines, and they continued to share their time between passenger and freight work until the disappearance of the last unit during 1967.

After World War II the survivors of the class were split between East and West Germany, 85 of the East German engines being rebuilt with new boilers, round-topped fireboxes and wide grates. In overall terms, the P10 class should be regarded as the apogee of Prussian steam locomotive design, but it was also important as marking the transition to the German state standard locomotives, experience with the P10 class being available before the design of the standard locomotives was finally settled upon.

The American 'Mountain' class locomotives, more formally designated as the '4300' class of 4-8-2 steam locomotives, were very aptly named as they were used on the steep gradients typical of the operations of the Southern Pacific Railroad based in California. Such a route network demanded considerable tractive effort but only modest overall power

output, and this was particularly relevant to the Southern Pacific Railroad, for its eastward-bound trains from Sacramento had to climb over the Sierras, in the process ascending from little above sea level to an altitude of 6,885ft (2100m) in the course of some 80 miles (128km). The Southern Pacific Railroad approached the American Locomotive Co. of Schenectady in 1923 for the manufacture of an initial group of 4-8-2 locomotives to a design that was firmly rooted in standard American design thinking and included a booster engine, driving the rear carrying wheels, to provide an additional 10,000lb (4536kg) of tractive effort.

The 4300-class locomotives burned oil, and the 77 engines of the class (all but a few built by the Southern Pacific Railroad's own plant at Sacramento) were very successful. The details of the 4300-class locomotive included a tractive effort of 57,100lb (25901kg), two 28 x 30-in (711 x 762-mm) cylinders, driving wheels with a diameter of 6ft 1.5in (1,867m), steam pressure of 210lb/sq in (14.8kg/cm^2), 4,700 U.S. gal (3,914 Imp gal; 17791 litres) of fuel, 8,327 Imp gal; 10,000 U.S. gal (37854 litres) of water, total weight of 611,000lb (277150kg), and overall length of 97ft 9in (27.794m).

After the nationalization of the German state railway organizations in 1922, a Central Locomotive Design Section was established under the control of Dr. R.P. Wagner, whose first task was the creation of standard locomotives based on the Prussian concept of the steam locomotive

but taking into account the fact that the type would have to operate in all parts of Germany, and would therefore need the ability to operate effectively on low-grade coal and also to climb gradients steeper than those of Prussia. This demanded the incorporation of larger grates and, in the engines with trailing carrying wheels, a clear space under the firebox for the entry of air and the removal of ashes.

The first of the classes were a pair of Pacific types designated as the '01' and '02' classes, which were basically similar in concept except for the fact that the locomotives of the 01 and 02 classes were of the simple- and compound-expansion type (with two and four cylinders) respectively. Some 10 examples of each class were initially manufactured for trials in several parts of Germany, resulting in the decision to standardize the 01 class as this was cheaper to build and maintain even though the fuel consumption of the 02 class was smaller.

The 01 class was basically simple in concept but comparatively complex in detail, especially as there was a range of auxiliary equipment including a feedwater heater with its heat exchanger in the smokebox ahead of the chimney. The detail design of the 01-class locomotive was the work of the Borsig company of Berlin, and manufacture was initially entrusted to Borsig and AEG. The first engines were completed in 1926, and by 1938 some 231 new engines had been produced, a figure to which must be added the 10 02-class units converted to 01-class standard.

Practical experience with the first engines to be placed in service suggested that later engines have cylinders increased in diameter from 25.6in (650mm) to 26in (660mm), the boiler tubes lengthened in a fashion made possible by the shortening of the smokebox, and as a final step the copper firebox replaced by a steel unit. Other changes included better brakes and larger truck wheels, allowing an increase in the maximum speed from 75mph (120km/h) to 81mph (130km/h).

In the meantime, during 1930, a slightly scaled-down version of the 01 class, designated as the '03' class, had been introduced for lines still limited to a 39,683-lb (18000-kg) axle loading rather than the 44,092-lb (20000-kg) axle loading of the tracks that could be used by the locomotives of the 01 class, and 298 of these smaller engines were built up to 1937.

The speed limit on most German railroad lines was 62mph (100km/h) up to 1937, when it was increased to 75mph (120km/h), so it was not until this date that the 01- and 03-class locomotives were able to reveal their real capabilities. The speed limit was further increased in 1939, and when additional locomotives were manufactured a maximum speed of 93mph (150km/h) was demanded. In the light of the German railroad's experience with the '05' class of 4-6-4 locomotives, the new engines were fully streamlined and given a three-cylinder motive system. These new units were designated as '01-10'- and '03-10'-class locomotives, of which 55 and 60 respectively were completed between 1939

and 1941, only the exigencies of World War II reducing these totals from the originally planned figures of 250 and 140 respectively. These were the last new series-built express steam locomotives built in Germany.

Soon after the end of World War II, 70 and 171 01-class locomotives were in service in East Germany and West Germany respectively. Of these 35 East German and 55 West German engines were rebuilt. The last West German locomotives of this family were retired during 1973, but several of the East German units were operated into the first part of the 1980s,

returned to regular service in an effort to overcome East Germany's shortage of oil. These were the last express steam locomotives in Europe. The details for the 01-class locomotive included a tractive effort of 35,656lb (16174kg), two 23.6 x 26-in (600 x 660-mm) cylinders, driving wheels with a diameter of 6ft 6.7in (2.00m), steam pressure of 228lb/sq in (16kg/cm^2), 22,046lb (10000kg) of fuel, 9,008 U.S. gal (7,501 Imp gal; 34100 litres) of water, total weight of 240,300lb (109000kg) without the tender, and overall length of 78ft 6in (23.94m).

ABOVE: *Modern German Railway (Deutsche Bundesbahn) main-line trains.*

OPPOSITE: *A German Class 01 4-6-2 steam locomotive, which headed the most important German steam trains in its day.*

191

Chapter Four
FREIGHT BY RAIL

FREIGHT BY RAIL

Although the movement of freight, in the widest sense of the word, had been the driving force behind the creation of the first steam railroads, which served mining sites, it was the design and manufacture of the *Royal George* locomotive for the Stockton & Darlington Railway that signalled a new start in the development of the steam locomotive. Designed by Timothy Hackworth in 1827, the *Royal George* was the first 0-6-0 steam locomotive to be built for the mixed-traffic role, and as such the engine inaugurated the emergence of an entirely new type of locomotive that would, early in the 20th century, then evolve into the definitive type of heavy freight locomotive.

During the main period of the Victorian age there were two main types of steam locomotive, optimized for the hauling of passenger and freight trains. In the earlier part of the railroad age, the passenger locomotive was generally of the 0-4-2 or 2-4-0 layout, while the freight locomotive (or, as it was often called at the time, the baggage locomotive) was generally a tank or tender engine of the 0-6-0 configuration. By the 1880s most British and an increasing number of European railway and railroad companies were creating and using larger

0-6-0 freight locomotives and indeed undertaking their first experiments with 0-8-0 locomotives for the hauling of heavy freight trains. In the United States, on the other hand, longer trains were the norm, and the designers and builders of steam locomotives were creating somewhat larger and heavier engines of the 2-6-0 and 2-8-0 layout for the hauling of heavy freight. These locomotives, of the bar-frame construction favoured by the Americans, were well suited to the comparatively rough country and poor track of the early U.S. railroads, and were also manufactured in significant numbers for export to South America, Australia and New Zealand, all of them regions in which conditions similar to those of the U.S.A. prevailed and therefore suggested the adoption of the American rather than European 'solution' to their railroad requirements.

As the 19th century progressed, and the weight of goods carried by freight trains grew steadily but remarkably, many European railways and North American railroads were, by the turn of the century, already starting to consider more effective means of hauling their heavy freight trains, now tasked with the movement not only of

OPPOSITE: *Depot of the Central Railroad, New Jersey, late 1800s.*

RIGHT: *Union Pacific locomotive 934 heads a block fruit train (before refrigerated cars were developed) in Nebraska, circa 1890.*

ever increasing volumes of freight but also considerably heavier bulk loads such as coal and the raw materials required to feed the industries typical of the ever more industrialized Western nations. It was immediately clear that the current types of freight-optimized steam locomotives were inadequate for the task of hauling the longer and heavier trains that were now urgently demanded. In Europe, this led to the production of significantly heavier freight-hauling and switching locomotives, characterized by their 0-8-0, 0-10-0 and 2-10-0 layouts.

In Germany and Austria, very notably, a number of classes of standard locomotives evolved for this specific purpose, and one of the most important of the designers involved in such work was an Austro-Hungarian citizen, Karl Gölsdorf. Within the total of some 45 locomotive designs with which this talented engineer was credited, Gölsdorf created several classes of successful 2-8-0 and 2-10-0 heavy freight locomotives that were not only used within the Austro-Hungarian empire, but also exported in numbers to other countries in Europe, including as a particularly notable example Greece, whose state railroad system operated freight services using a large fleet of 2-8-0 and 2-10-0 locomotives imported from Austria-Hungary.

In Germany, the Royal Prussian state railroad system designed a number of standard classes of heavy freight locomotive based on the extensive use of common but well proven parts for maximum economy of manufacture and maintenance in combination with the highest possible level of reliability. These locomotives included the units of the 'G8' 0-8-0, 'G10' 0-10-0 and '44' classes, which were still in minor production when the various German railways were amalgamated into the nationalized Deutsche Reichsbahn in 1922.

Like their Austro-Hungarian cousins, these German standard designs were also exported in large numbers to other European railroad organizations, including those of Bulgaria, Poland, Romania and Turkey that all had strong economic and/or strategic ties with Germany.

In the initial absence of any significant national industrial and engineering capability, the development of railroads in Russia, from the 1830s, required that locomotives and other equipment of foreign designs, mainly from Germany and the U.K., be imported to provide an initial capability. Operation of these imported engines then provided the initial advantage of the earliest possible development and use of a railroad network, and at the same time the development of the operational experience that then allowed Russian steam locomotive designers to start producing effective engine designs, albeit with a strong British or German influence clearly evident, for domestic manufacture. Plants for the manufacture of all types of railroad equipment, using capital raised at home and also from abroad, were soon established to build all types of railroad equipment including locomotives that were better suited than imported engines to the particular geographic and climatic conditions in which the Russian railroads operated but which, as noted above, often displayed strong British and German design influences and also, to a slightly later and somewhat lesser extent, elements of American practice. The American influence grew as the Russian railroad system

expanded from the core region of western Russia into the less civilized outer reaches of the tsarist empire, where conditions more closely approximated those of the U.S.A. as its railroads expanded across North America. The need to construct large numbers of standard passenger and freight locomotives, together with the ever increasing length and weight of trains required for the movement of larger numbers of passengers and greater quantities of freight, heralded the production of the 'O' class of standard 0-8-0 locomotives. This locomotive, designed in the tsarist period, was so successful that, with only minor modifications, it was built by Russian locomotive manufacturing plants right into the first two decades of the 20th century.

It should not be imagined that the development of an indigenous Russian locomotive designing and manufacturing capability meant that the various private and state-owned railroad organizations came to rely wholly on locomotives of Russian origin. Right up to the revolution of November 1917, which resulted in the establishment of the U.S.S.R. under a communist leadership with wholly different political, economic and social agendas, Russian railroad organizations were at various times buying and receiving large numbers of 0-8-0, 0-10-0 and, shortly before the outbreak of World War I in 1914,

2-10-0 steam locomotives from Germany and the U.S.A. By the 1920s the Soviet government had designed and manufactured several standard classes of locomotive for heavy freight use. These included the 'E' and 'FD' classes of 0-10-0 and 2-10-2 locomotives, to supplement the American-built Baldwin and Alco 2-10-0 locomotives supplied to Russia during World War I.

The relationship of the FD class with other Soviet locomotives of the period is an interesting aspect of how the U.S.S.R. was generally content, having found an acceptable industrial solution to a perceived economic requirement, to keep the resulting artefact in production and service without consideration of any real concept of

OPPOSITE: *Freight being transferred from a Missouri river steamer to a Northern Pacific locomotive, North Dakota, 1880.*

ABOVE LEFT: *A snow-clearing gang and equipment near Stampede, 1886.*

ABOVE: *Railroads played a key role in the industrial and agricultural development of the United States. This picture, from the late 19th century, shows freight cars loaded with cotton in St. Louis, Missouri railroad yards.*

'modernization': if a locomotive was technically successful in meeting state needs and was cheap both to build and to operate, it was kept in production and service in its original form and also in any variants that could readily be derived from it. Thus, when by 1930 it had created the very effective 'S' class of passenger locomotives, of which some 3,000 were built for long-term service without any 'consumer' pressure for radical improvement, the Soviet authorities could take their time in assessing the longer-term needs of a growing requirement for passenger transport, which up to this time had been secondary in Soviet thinking to the demands for the freight transport on which the much-desired industrialization of the Soviet state was heavily dependent. It was now appreciated that higher speeds and

more comfortable (thus weightier) trains would eventually be needed.

The first prototype of the new generation of locomotive appeared during 1932 as what was really little more than an expansion of the 2-6-2 S-class design into a 2-8-4 layout with an additional coupled axle for more tractive effort, and also an additional carrying axle at the rear to allow the incorporation of a larger firebox so that the engine could generate more power for the use of the improved motive system. The design was designated as the 'IS' class in honour of the Soviet leader, Iosef Stalin, and some 640 such locomotives were manufacturing in the period between 1934 and the time of the German invasion of the U.S.S.R. in 1941. The type has disappeared from service in its original passenger train version, but a derived freight version (with

ABOVE LEFT: The Italian locomotive Le Rubican *on the Porrettana mountain line, 1863.*

ABOVE: The Breda works with employees and locomotives, Italy 1892. By the end of the 19th century in Europe, the weight of goods carried had grown significantly, requiring more powerful locomotives.

the same boiler, cab, cylinders, tender and other parts) is the FD class of 2-10-2 locomotive, of which substantial numbers are in use throughout southern China, after being adapted to standard gauge from the Russian 5ft 0in (1.524m) gauge.

The production of closely related passenger and freight locomotives was of course typical of the Soviet authorities' approach, both financially sensible and technically logical, toward the needs of the state railroad system. To this extent, therefore, the Soviet regime differed only marginally from the tsarist system it replaced. Also typical of the Soviet system, however, was the manufacture in 1937 and 1938 of the first three of a planned total of 10 streamlined 4-6-4 locomotives to haul the high-speed *Red Arrow* express between Moscow and Leningrad, a journey of

The production of closely-related passenger and freight locomotives, as shown here, was favoured by Russian authorities, though a large number of steam locomotives were imported from Germany before the war.

slightly more than 401 miles (645km) on which an average speed of 40.5 to 50mph (65 to 80km/h) was planned. The initial pair of locomotives each had driving wheels with a diameter of 6ft 6.75in (2.00m) but the third unit had driving wheels with a diameter of 7ft 2.5in (2.197m). All three of the locomotives were based in design and mechanical detail on the FD class, with which they shared the boilers, cylinders and much else. The German invasion prevented the construction of the last seven of the locomotives, but initial service had revealed the class to have excellent performance including a maximum speed of 106mph (170km/h).

The ever increasing weight and length of passenger and freight trains had made it clear by the end of the 19th century, at least

to the larger and more far-sighted railroad organizations, that the continued success of steam-powered railroad services in all but the flattest and smallest countries demanded the introduction of either larger and more powerful locomotives or of banking, or 'helper', locomotives to ease heavy trains over hilly country. The former was clearly the simpler solution but meant that much of the new locomotives' power would be unnecessary for the more level and less demanding majority of the railroad network, while the latter meant the adoption of new locomotives that could be reserved for use as ancillaries only on the steeper gradients where the standard main-line locomotives actually needed their assistance. For many decades the larger railway companies had been using conventional 4-4-0 and 0-6-0

locomotives for this banking purpose, and had found the concept adequate to their needs. By the late 1880s, however, it had started to become abundantly clear that the demands of banking what had become considerably longer and heavier trains, with further increases inevitable, demanded the use of more powerful (and therefore larger) banking locomotives.

Returning to the subject of banking engines, the British-administered railroads of India also faced problems in the first part of the 20th century similar to those encountered in North America. The need to bank trains over steeper gradients required the design and manufacture of a class of heavy tank locomotive built to the 0-8-4T arrangement. These locomotives, along with some 2-8-4T engines, were used

on the Ghat incline of the Great Indian Peninsula Railway.

South African railways were quick to appreciate the importance of powerful banking locomotives. Shortly before World War I, therefore, they ordered a batch of Mallet-type locomotives from North British of Glasgow. These machines were used on heavy freight and banking duties until the early 1950s, when they were withdrawn. New Zealand railways also needed a solution to the difficulty of moving large passenger and freight trains over difficult terrain. Rather than adopt the banking engine solution, however, the New Zealanders decided to approach the problem from a different angle and opted for the construction of an incline railroad using the Fell system of braking, which required the

OPPOSITE

LEFT: *The Russian S class was a standard-design locomotive used by many independent railways before the Russian Revolution.*

RIGHT: *Russian Su-class 2-6-2 locomotive, of which more than 2,000 were built in 15 years. The 'S' stood for the Soromovo works where the class was built, and the 'u' for* usilennyi, *which means 'strengthened'.*

ABOVE: *The ever-increasing weight of freight carried required more powerful or 'helper' locomotives in all but the flattest terrain.*

RIGHT: *Two examples of Russian steam power.*

manufacture of specially designed 0-4-2 tank locomotives. The Fell braking system worked from a central rail that retarded the locomotive and train working on railroad lines with a steep gradient: this frequently required the use of several locomotives working together, depending on the weight of the train being banked.

Possibly the first North American railroad to appreciate the problem of banking locomotives was the Baltimore & Ohio Railroad. In 1904 this organization felt that it had started to arrive at the right solution to the problem, and therefore manufactured the first American example of the kind of banking locomotive developed by Anatole Mallet as a type with two sets of coupled wheels, of which the first set was

pivoted to become a motor bogie or truck, in the process turning the Mallet type of locomotive into a semi-articulated unit. The Baltimore & Ohio Railroad's Mallet-type locomotive, nicknamed *Old Maud*, was used for experiments in the banking of heavy trains over long and twisting gradients that otherwise required the use of multiple-heading of locomotives. *Old Maud* proved to be eminently useful and, in the years that followed, most of the larger railroad operators in North America either built in their own plants or ordered from specialist locomotive manufacturers Mallet locomotives of the same basic type or alternatively more conventional 2-8-0 or 2-10-0 locomotives to bank heavy trains up steeper gradients.

In the U.K. the Midland Railway constructed a 0-10-0 tender locomotive which also had a nickname, in this instance *Big Emma* or sometimes *Big Bertha*. Manufactured in 1919, just after the end of World War I, this locomotive was used on the Lickey incline at Bromsgrove near Birmingham in the Midlands, where its success as a banking unit meant its retention up to 1956, when it was replaced by a British Railways '9F'-class 2-10-0 locomotive. At much the same time, for the Great Central Railway, John G. Robinson designed some 0-8-4 tank engines for the not altogether unrelated task of heavy hump-shunting in goods yards. These locomotives survived into the later part of the 1940s, in the process lasting long

enough to be taken into the stock of privately owned locomotives inherited by the nationalized British Railways organization. In 1925, the London & North Eastern Railway ordered a Beyer-Garratt locomotive for service on the Worsborough incline near Barnsley in Yorkshire. This 2 8 8 2 locomotive remained in service until the line was electrified in 1955, after which it was tried on the Lickey incline in company with *Big Bertha*, and was withdrawn only in 1956 when it was scrapped. In 1921 the London & South Western Railway ordered three examples of a 4-8-0 tank locomotive designed by Robert Urie, and these engines were employed at the new marshalling yard at Feltham on the edge of London to hump-shunt freight

wagons into formation. All three of the locomotives were withdrawn from service in 1962.

The Mallet type of semi-articulated locomotive had first appeared in the alpine regions of Europe from 1889 but found only a modest level of acceptance. As can be deduced from the above, however, the Americans were more chary even of evaluating the type and thus it was only in 1904 that J.E. Muhlfeld, Chief of Motive Power on the Baltimore & Ohio Railroad, thought that the type would also be useful for the hauling of very heavy coal trains and designed a huge double 0-6-0 (C-C) steam locomotive. This engine was immediately a great success, and the U.S. railroads soon adopted the Mallet type of

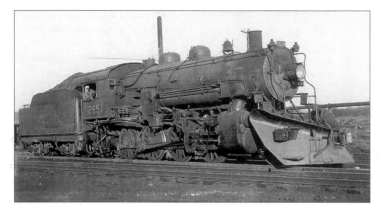

ABOVE: *K-class locomotive K-8-c 2-8-0 (No. 2651) fitted with pilot snow plough at Rigby, Maine, 1939.*

ABOVE RIGHT: *A London & North Eastern Railway Garratt, hauling passenger coaches. Garratt, an Englishman who lived in Australia, invented this famous type of articulated locomotive.*

RIGHT: *Baltimore & Ohio Railroad's EM-1-class Mallet 2-8-8-4 No. 7600, newly arrived from Baldwin and ready to start work on the Cumberland Division, 1944.*

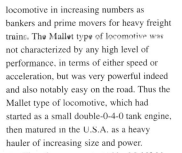

locomotive in increasing numbers as
bankers and prime movers for heavy freight
trains. The Mallet type of locomotive was
not characterized by any high level of
performance, in terms of either speed or
acceleration, but was very powerful indeed
and also notably easy on the road. Thus the
Mallet type of locomotive, which had
started as a small double-0-4-0 tank engine,
then matured in the U.S.A. as a heavy
hauler of increasing size and power.

Thus the process started by Muhlfeld
soon developed into a series of truly
monstrous engines, of which perhaps the
finest example was the *Matt H. Shay* of the
Erie Railroad before World War I, which
had two sets of coupled wheels, in each
case comprising four axles, and a third
essentially identical set under the tender to
provide an overall 2-8-8-8-2 layout for what
became known as the 'Triplex'
configuration. There was nothing new in the

concept of the steam-powered tender, which
had been manufactured and used by both
the Ouest railroad in France and the Great
Northern Railway in the U.K. during the
middle part of the previous century, in both
cases for additional traction during difficult
moments such as starting and continued
motion up steep gradients. The concept of
the powered tender, in all of its forms, had
a major problem, however, namely the
relative shortage of steam for all the
cylinders that had to be operated.

Another problem with the type of long
locomotives that were introduced to provide
greater tractive effort in the particular low-
performance environment typical of freight
operations was the very length of the
boiler's barrel length that was now possible
from the metallurgical and firing points of
view, but which presented difficulties on
railroad tracks with all but the gentlest of
curves. As a result, there were many

attempts to create an effective type of articulated boiler, with two sections connected in the centre by a bellows arrangement, but the technical problems of such an arrangement were beyond effective solution. Among the railroads that sought to develop such a boiler was the Atchison, Topeka and Santa Fe, which produced a locomotive with six coupled axles in two sets, giving the unit a 2-6-6-2 layout at an overall weight of 689,920lb (312948kg), increased by a further 262,080lb (118879kg) by the 12-wheel tender. Fortunately for the crew, this monster was oil- rather than coal-fired!

The Mallet type of locomotive also made an appearance in several other parts of the world, although not on such a gigantic scale as in the United States, and also in generally smaller numbers. British locomotive manufacturing companies built such engines for operators in Burma, China and South Africa; several French railroad companies built and used the type on the railroad network of France; and in Germany the Maffei company produced Mallet-type locomotives for service with the Royal Bavarian state railroad, with the Royal Hungarian state railroad and also, in broad-gauge forms, with the Central Aragon and Zafra-Huelva railroads in Spain.

The U.K. was responsible for the creation of another classic type of articulated locomotive, which was so extensively and successfully operated in many parts of the world at a later date that the Americans, who in fact never adopted the type, came to call it the 'British

Mallet', even though its real name was the Beyer-Garratt, so named for its designer, Herbert Garratt who was an Englishman who lived in Australia and created the first such articulated locomotive in 1909, and Beyer, Peacock and Company that was based in Manchester and later bought Garratt's patents.

In basic terms the Beyer-Garratt consisted of two separate locomotive units that supported, by means of pivots and bearings, the proportionally large boiler carried on a girder frame between them. Garratt's original idea had been that this arrangement would allow the creation of a

large and powerful, yet flexible, passenger engine in which the dimensions of the boiler would not be limited by the height of the large-diameter driving wheels, as was the case with more conventional steam locomotives. Such a passenger locomotive, with a 2-4-0+0-4-2 wheel arrangement, was in fact manufactured for the São Paulo Railway of Brazil during 1915, but the very first of the type were a few small double 0-4-0 locomotives for very narrow gauges, typified by the singular 2ft 0in (0.61m) gauge of the Tasmanian Government Railway (1909) and for the Darjeeling Himalayan Railway in India (1911). The

OPPOSITE: *The magnificent Beyer-Garratt locomotive, favourite for hauling freight in many parts of the world, particularly in Africa and Australia.*

ABOVE LEFT: *The basic Beyer-Garratt locomotive consists of two separate locomotive units which share a large common boiler.*

ABOVE: *Known to Americans as the 'British Mallet', the Beyer-Garratt locomotive had excellent riding and traction qualities.*

Garratt locomotive therefore started life as an engine used almost exclusively on narrow-gauge railroads in mountainous regions, but soon developed into a massive type whose basic features generally included outside cylinders with Walschaert valve gear and, with the exception of the Tasmanian unit, simple rather than compound expansion.

The Beyer-Garratt was not the only type of articulated locomotive that saw service in the first quarter of the 20th century. There was also the Meyer type that first appeared in Belgium during 1873 with origins stretching to an earlier time: the Meyer type of locomotive had two motor bogies or trucks, with the leading unit on a spherical pivot and the trailing unit on transverse members to carry one large boiler. The main frames were those of the two motor units, which therefore carried the couplers, and the boiler supported the tanks. It was only in the 1890s that the Meyer type of locomotive began to gain any real acceptance after the type was recommended to Kitson & Co. in the U.K. by Robert Stirling of the Anglo-Chilean Nitrate Company's railroad. In this British-developed model the boiler, tanks and bunker were installed on a pair of parallel girders whose ends rested on the bogies or trucks. Used for the movement of nitrates to the Chilean coast, the locomotives coped well with a 1/25 gradient of the 17-mile (27-km) route, of which a fair measure was also typified by curves of a moderately small radius. The same type of locomotive was used with considerable success on the

Argentine and Chilean narrow-gauge railroads across the Andes mountains and also, in a considerably broader gauge, on the ore-carrying routes of southern Spain.

Other articulated steam locomotives of the period included not only the original type of Fairlie but also the so-called Modified Fairlie and the Maffei-built Garratt Union, both owing much to the Garratt, and the Hagans which had two sets of coupled wheels and included drive to the rear set. The Hagans was manufactured for

the Royal Prussian state railroad in 1893, and also for the Tasmanian Government.

Despite the success of articulated steam locomotives (of which the Mallet type predominated in North America, the Garratt in Africa, the Meyer in South America, and the older Fairlie in Mexico) for the heavy freight role, the only one to secure additional success in the passenger locomotive role was the Garratt. And not even the levels of technical and commercial success attained by several of these

ABOVE: No. 5505 of the East African Railway, built by Beyer-Peacock in 1945 for Tanganyika Railway.

OPPOSITE: GMA Garratt No. 4165 shunts in factory sidings at Pietermaritzburg, South Africa. These locomotives were favourites for hauling freight in Africa.

articulateds could convince all the world's railroad operators that there was real merit in the apparent complexity of these powerful locomotives. Thus many railroads placed their entire faith in the original type of steam locomotive with a rigid framework carried on the track by wheels on several axles and itself supporting the rest of the locomotive's apparatus. As noted above, the 0-10-0 locomotive was most favoured in central and eastern Europe in countries such as

Austria-Hungary, Germany (most notably Prussia and Bavaria), Italy, Sweden and, most significantly of all, Russia. In this last nation, an excellent design was introduced just before the outbreak of World War I, and this was eventually to be manufactured in numbers running into several thousands, especially as an all-purpose type in the immensely troubled period after the revolution of November 1917 had turned tsarist Russia into the communist U.S.S.R.: many of the locomotives were also

manufactured in Sweden by Nydqvist and Helm, and in Germany by companies such as Vulkan and Humboldt. Such was the basic simplicity and reliability of the design that few changes were ever needed, and the type served the U.S.S.R. long and faithfully.

In North America, the locomotive of 0-10-0 layout was used only as a heavy switcher in the great freight yards. For main-line freight-hauling operations, the Americans preferred the locomotive of the 2-10-2 type, whose bogies or trucks

provided a better ride on the road than any locomotive of the wholly rigid type. The locomotive of 2-10-0 layout was much appreciated in Europe, especially in Austria-Hungary and in the Balkans, where the type's success led to additional use for express passenger services, initially on routes such as the Semmering, Tauern and Arlberg railways in Austria before their electrification, and then in Greece. In this latter, engines of a patently Austro-Hungarian design origin, but manufactured by Skoda in Czechoslovakia after the break-up of the Habsburg empire, were even used on this section of the *Orient Express* route.

Though it did see a measure of passenger service, however, the locomotive of the 2-10-0 type was best suited to freight operations such as the hauling of heavy coal trains, and it was in this role that classic locomotives, such as the 2-10-0 type designed by J.D. Flamme for the Belgian state railroad in the 1920s, made their names. Other 2-10-0 locomotives were produced in Austria-Hungary (in many ways the archetypal parent of the large steam locomotive in Europe), but expansions of this core type included 2-12-0 locomotives produced in limited numbers in both Austria-Hungary and Württemberg, and then at a somewhat later date by France, where the 'A1' class of 2-12-0 locomotives was built for the nationalized railroad system from 1948.

For the purposes of hauling heavy freight trains, however, the locomotive with a long rigid wheelbase was in general inferior to the locomotive with articulated groupings of wheels, such as the Mallet and Garratt types. In overall terms, therefore, the very long coupled wheelbase did not survive long, even though the death throes of the type were extended by final experiments such as the classically huge 4-14-4 locomotive produced in the U.S.S.R. during 1934 for evaluation against an even more substantial Beyer-Garratt 4-8-2+2-8-4 locomotive obtained from the U.K. in the previous year. The fact that neither

was repeated in a sure indication that both the types were unsuccessful.

By the start of the 20th century, the development of the heavy freight locomotive in its basic but specialized role had reached an advanced stage. Quite apart from the use of 0-6-0, 0-8-0 and 2-8-0 engines as their primary locomotives for this task, many main-line railway companies were looking at alternative methods to overcome their operating problems. In the years up to 1914, the majority of British main-line companies had ordered or constructed some 2-8-0 freight locomotives. These included the Great Western Railway, which had a sizeable fleet of '2800'-class locomotives and nine '4700'-class large-wheeled 2-8-0 locomotives. The Great Northern Railway, under the technical supervision of Nigel Gresley, designed some successful standard 2-8-0 locomotives for heavy coal and freight traffic from the north-east of England to London. Perhaps the best known type of British heavy freight locomotive of the Edwardian era was the Robinson ROD (Railway Operating Division) 2-8-0 locomotive, many of which were constructed for use by the British army in World War I.

After the establishment of the London & North Eastern Railway in 1923 through the amalgamation of several smaller railway companies, Gresley designed the 'P1' class of 2-8-2 Mikado-type locomotives to undertake heavy freight work from London on what had recently been the Great Northern Railway's main line. These

locomotives were, paradoxically, too successful in technical terms as their considerable power meant that especial care had to be taken to avoid breaking the couplings of the small two-axle coal and goods wagons then in use. Arguably the best, and certainly the most successful type of locomotive ever designed in the U.K. for the heavy freight role, was Sir William Stanier's '8F'-class 2-8-0 unit, which was manufactured for the London, Midland & Scottish Railway in the period between 1937 and 1944. So successful was the type that the War Office also ordered many batches for its own purposes, which included operations in many parts of the world, especially in the Middle East and Persia (now Iran), where trains hauled by 8F-class locomotives were importantly operated to deliver allied war materiel to the forces and industries of the U.S.S.R. across Persia's northern frontier after the goods had reached the region by ship.

As noted above, in the more developed countries of the British empire, the problem of operating heavy freight was overcome by the use of both conventional and articulated locomotives. The development and adoption of the Beyer-Garratt locomotive after 1907 was particularly important for railroad operations in Africa, where the type proved to be a highly effective solution for some of the worst problems encountered by railway engineers and administrators. In South Africa, most notably, the Beyer-Garratt locomotives of the 'GL' and 'GMAM' classes were outstandingly effective in terms of performance and reliability, and their

OPPPOSITE

LEFT: American-style water columns can be turned off from the top of the tender.

RIGHT: EM-1 locomotive No. 7611 carrying coal at the highest point of the Baltimore & Ohio main-line system. At this point, near Altamont, Maryland, the trains come off the Deer Park grade and immediately drop down onto the Seventeen-Mile grade.

availability in significant numbers successfully overcame many of the difficulties that had previously afflicted railroad operations in this important exporter of raw materials and precious metals.

By the 1880s, the main railroad operators in all parts of continental Europe, eastern, central and western, were heavily involved in the development, manufacture and large-scale introduction of locomotives of steadily increasing size and capability for the operation of heavy freight services and, to a somewhat lesser extent, mixed traffic operations. Among the first to come to a full appreciation of the benefits offered by such locomotives were several of the larger state railroad organizations of the German empire. When, in the aftermath of Germany's defeat in World War I, the new German republic decided to create a national railroad system by amalgamating the various private and state-owned railroads into the Deutsche Reichsbahn during 1922, the already existing process of developing and manufacturing standard classes, generally based on Prussian designs with a measure of input from the railroad practices of Bavaria and Württemberg, was expanded to include 2-8-0, 2-10-0 and 2-10-2T types of locomotives in large numbers. The French railroad operators had drawn major benefit from locomotive construction during World War I, and

also from the import of '140C'-class 2-8-0 and American-built 'Pershing'-type 2-8-0 locomotives. This process was repeated after World War II, when the Société Nationale des Chemins de Fer further benefited from the acquisition of '141R'-class 2-8-2 locomotives as part of the Marshall Plan designed by General George C. Marshall to help Europe recover its economic feet.

By a time early in the 20th century, the American railroad companies had developed a large network of services

operating, among other things, an increasing volume of the freight that represented, on the one hand, the raw materials needed for the rapidly continuing development of American industrialization and, on the other hand, finished goods for domestic consumption or for export from the country's large numbers of major sea ports. In this situation, the design, manufacture and deployment of the latest generation of efficient heavy locomotives to haul these freight trains was of huge importance. A number of the larger railroad companies themselves developed

locomotives to meet the need. The Union Pacific Railroad in particular produced two classes of locomotives of outstanding design. These were the 'Challenger' and the 'Big Boy'. Both types were developed from the late 1930s and construction continued until the late 1940s. The Big Boy, designed by Alco and built to the extent of 25 '4000'-class locomotives, can be regarded as one of the last, and therefore definitive types of huge steam locomotive for heavy freight haulage purposes. The details for these magnificent superheated locomotives included a 4-8-8-4

LEFT: *British Black 8 2-8-0 with a mixed freight near Chippenham, Wiltshire.*

BELOW LEFT: *Type 11/12 locomotive used to haul freight on the Portuguese narrow-gauge lines.*

BELOW RIGHT *Portuguese state railway 2-2-2 locomotive. By the 1880s in Europe it was found that 0-6-0 and 0-8-0 locomotives were more suitable for freight operations.*

ABOVE LEFT: *This early Portuguese state railway series 2-4-0 locomotive was more likely to have been used for mixed passenger-freight traffic.*

ABOVE: *Portuguese state railway 204 locomotive. Increasingly, heavy freight loads demanded larger locomotives.*

LEFT: *Garratt 742 No. 19, en route to Bulawayo, Zimbabwe.*

layout, four 23.75 x 32-in (603 x 813-mm) cylinders, steam pressure of 300lb/sq in (21.1kg/cm^2), and a weight of 772,000lb (350179kg) excluding the tender, which turned the scales at 348,000lb (157853kg) at two-thirds maximum load.

They were the last heavy freight locomotives in service on the Union Pacific Railroad, and the locomotives were not withdrawn until 1959. The Norfolk & Western Railroad, which hauled heavy coal trains in Virginia, had a large fleet of 'Y6B'- and 'A'- class articulated locomotives of the Mallet type, and these too were notable for the superb service they provided from the early 1930s to 1960, when they were finally retired from service as the last steam locomotives used in the U.S.A. for the hauling of heavy freight trains.

Before turning to the introduction of the new motive technologies represented by diesel and electric power, of which the former was applied equally to passenger and freight trains, it is instructive to look at the types of specialized steam locomotives that were adopted for and are often still used for a number of secondary freight transport purposes. The aspect that comes most readily to mind is the movement of coal, which is a material that was at once the reason that steam railways and railroads could initially be created and at the same time one of the prime materials that required mass transport as the onset of the Industrial Revolution and urbanization created increasing demands for coal in areas both close to and distant from the coal fields. At the smallest level of coal movement, by the

mid-1800s the colliery railroad had become an intrinsic part of the industrial landscape, and a notable feature in the creation and operation of these individually small but collectively large networks was the constricted layout imposed on the colliery railroad by the nature of the coal mine it served, and this fact often made it impossible to use the type of medium- and large-sized locomotive typical of main-line service at the time, the type of locomotive most frequently encountered in the colliery railroad operations of the period being the 0-6-0T configuration.

A classic example of the definitive sort of colliery railroad was that located at Ashington in the north-east of England, which started work during 1850. Although initially restricted to services within the area of the coal mine, the colliery railroad was soon expanded to include a connection with the North Eastern Railway's main line at Blyth, which allowed the bulk movement of coal to local ports for export to countries such as Germany, Poland and Sweden. It is also worth noting that Ashington was also a main source for the so-called 'steam coal' that was moved by railroad to locomotive sheds all over the U.K. By the mid-1930s, the company possessed some 15 miles (24km) of track together with about 9 miles (14.5km) of sidings that provided storage for up to 35,000 tons of coal in wagons. The colliery railroad operated some 750 wagons that were hauled by a force of 17 small steam locomotives. Some of the bigger collieries in the U.K. also ran passenger trains to coincide with the

OPPOSITE
ABOVE: *The eastbound* Grand Canyon
Limited *out of Los Angeles, headed by a
4-8-4 Santa Fe 3765-class locomotive,
runs round a freight train in Cajan Pass,
California, in the1940s.*

BELOW: *An ROD locomotive hauls a
train-load of British troops on freight
wagons towards the Western Front, 29
August 1917.*

ABOVE: *Union Pacific's articulated Big
Boy-class 4-8-8-4, hauling a string of
freight cars through Echo Canyon, Utah in
the early 1950s. Lcomotives of this type
were developed from the 1930s.*

beginnings and ends of various shifts,
thereby facilitating the movement of the
miners between the pit head and the
neighbouring villages in which most of
them lived. These services generally made
use of obsolete rolling stock bought from
main-line operators, and as a result some of
the trains were fascinating for their
combination of miscellaneous coaches (of
all classes) from main-line companies
operating in all parts of the U.K. By the
early part of the 20th century, there were
some hundreds of collieries operating in the
U.K., and many of these had their own
railroads, but passenger services ended
many years ago.

Although the U.K. had by far the most
collieries, specialized railroad operations of
this type were just as significant in the
pattern of European coal and railroad
development, especially in the Ruhr region
of Germany, in Poland and in Russia,
where the location and exploitation of large
coal reserves were seen as an important
milestone in the industrialization and
economic development of the countries in
question. As in the U.K., the geographical
constraints on the coal-mining areas that
were thus developed often imposed an
upper limit on the size of the locomotives
that could be employed, but in other parts
of the world, most notably regions such as
South Africa, where an effectively fresh
start could be made and longer distances
had to be covered before the colliery
railroad could link with a main line, it was
possible to use engines larger than those
typical of European practice, generally up

to the 4-8-2 types that provided an effective
haulage capability on colliery
railroad/main-line railroad connecting
tracks which were more like branch lines in
their own right. This concept was as true of
Australia as South Africa, for the vast size
of the country and the dispersed nature of
its coal fields meant that the connections
between the colliery railroad and main-line
railroad were often worked by tender
engines that had originally been operated
for main-line services. In highly congested
countries such as India, however, the most
common gauge used for the coal fields in
Assam and other areas was 2ft 0in (0.61m),
and on this gauge there operated very small
engines, generally of the saddle-tank type
with an 0-4-0 or 0-1-2 layout. This was
not exclusively the case, moreover, as
attested by the use of a 5ft 6in (1.68m)
gauge and main-line engines for the huge
complex of mines around Asansol.

In the United States, the railroad lines
serving coal-mining areas have been
important right from the start of the
industrial revolution in America, and at the
industry's peak there were very many lines,
mostly of the narrow-gauge type, extending
below the surface of the ground to lift the
coal to the surface from the underground
galleries in which it was mined. Such
operations were entirely typical of the coal-
mining industry in key areas such as
Colorado, Pennsylvania, Utah and West
Virginia, whose vast coal deposits
(combined with similarly huge deposits of
iron ore and other essential minerals) were
wholly instrumental in the development of

LEFT: *A Merry-go-round coal train at Didcot station, England.*

BELOW LEFT: *Norfolk & Western class Y6B articulated locomotive 2185 being assembled at the Roanoke yard, 21 May 1949.*

BELOW: *Burlington Northern coal train loading in the mid-1970s.*

OPPOSITE: *An American Big Boy, perhaps the definitive locomotive for heavy freight haulage.*

the U.S.A. as a major industrial nation. As the technology to do so became available, many of these little railroad lines were electrified, but most of the purely coal-mine railroads have faded from existence as other technologies have become available to extract the coal and lift it to the surface. Even so, coal is still a very important freight item for the main-line railroad operators.

China is another geographically vast country in which the availability of significant coal and mineral deposits has played a major part in the industrialization and general modernization of the country, especially in the years following the communist assumption of power in 1949. Thus the experience of the Chinese had mirrored that of the Americans, albeit a century or more later and in a country that was not almost empty but rather filled virtually to the limit with people. The railroads associated with the huge Chinese coal fields have for many years been the province mostly of tender locomotives from their earliest stages and then more recently by the 'SY' class of 2-8-2 standard locomotives built at Tangshan. The scale of the Chinese operation combines with the ability of the communist government to dictate that economic and political considerations should prevail over all else to generate a situation completely different from those that existed in the early days of British and European coal-field exploitation. As a result, the scale of the Chinese operation is larger on every level, and this provides no more fascinating a fact

219

ABOVE: Locomotives of the Canadian National Railway were serviced and assigned to trains from 'roundhouses', like this one in Montreal.

than that the Chinese can therefore operate genuinely larger main-line type locomotives in the coal exploitation industry rather than the genuinely small 0-6-0 and similar colliery locomotives that were typical of British and European practices. Another very striking contrast is that while the steam locomotive has long since disappeared from the British, European and U.S. coal-mining industries, where the smaller numbers of current types are of the diesel-powered variety, it is still very much alive in China and is likely to remain so until well into the 21st century.

As suggested above, railroads for the exploitation of coal and mineral ores are twins within the context of the Industrial Revolution, not only in being wholly

necessary for the sparking of this movement and then its subsequent growth, but also in the vast volume and weight of the two commodities that must be transported. Thus there are many parallels between the railroad systems, together with their associated locomotives and rolling stock, involved in the coal and mineral ore exploitation industries. The first locomotive for use on a railroad transporting iron ore is thought to have been the unit that started work at Irthlingborough in Northamptonshire in 1867, but the British iron-ore industry is now dead, partially as a result of the high cost of transporting the ore between points in the U.K. but more as a consequence of the availability of superior imported ores, such as that from Sweden that typically contains 55 per cent iron rather than the 23 per cent iron that was the maximum contained in British ore.

Among the most interesting of the railways connected with the British iron-ore industry was that in and around the steel town of Corby in the English Midlands' county of Northamptonshire. Here the steel works operated their own railway that extended in a series of extensive branch lines reaching out into the country round the town to deliver a constant supply of iron ore from the various pits. In its heyday during the 1950s, as the U.K. was rebuilding its industrial base after World War II, the steel industry at Corby operated a large fleet of tank engines for its mines division and another large fleet for its steel works. This railroad system was not limited only to

Corby and its environs, moreover, for the Northamptonshire ironstone fields were extensive enough to be used to feed ore to other great steel-making areas, and as a result the Corby railroad system was closely interconnected with the main-line network so that iron-ore trains, sometimes as many as ten per day, could be hauled to other steel-making centres in Nottinghamshire and Yorkshire.

In continental Europe, one of the most fascinating iron-ore railroads using steam locomotives was the Erzberg, or 'iron mountain', railroad of Austria-Hungary. Inaugurated in 1891 and based on a standard-gauge railroad track, this line was used to transport iron ore from the mining site on the mountain (though large hill might be a more apt description) to the steel works at Donawitz, a distance of 121 miles (195km). One of the most interesting features of this railroad, which is still operational and has a ruling gradient of 1/14 over much of its length, is the use of both rack traction for the steeper gradients and adhesion traction for the flat and less steeply inclined sections of the route. The standard locomotive for the route was the type of 0-6-2T four-cylinder rack and traction engine built between 1890 and 1908 by Wiener Lokomotivfabrik, and this could haul a train of up to 110 tons. Similar arrangements were used in other European countries where iron-ore deposits were found at some distance, vertically as well as horizontally, from the industrial regions at which the ore was processed. Another notable iron-ore railroad was that inaugurated in Australia in 1932 to

coincide with the establishment of an Australian steel works at Port Kembla in New South Wales. A railroad was driven up the steep mountainsides of the region to connect the rapidly-growing industrial area with Moss Vale junction with the main line. Some 43-miles (69-km) long, the line was in its time one of the world's lengthiest, purely industrial railroad lines.

With iron ore just as much as with coal, China has one of the most elaborate and extensive specialized railroad systems in the world. In this instance, the centre of this huge undertaking is the Anshan region of northern China, where there are huge deposits of iron ore as well as of coal. The quarries from which the iron ore is extracted are linked to the city and its industrial areas by a circular railroad over which trains move passengers as well as iron ore. In this fashion, the industrial areas of Anshan are fully supplied with both raw materials and a workforce. Oddly enough, this railroad is operated with electrical power, the locomotives being of design and manufacturing dates somewhat earlier than the equivalent dates for the steam locomotives still extensively used on China's main-line services. The Anshan complex comprises 12 control areas, including 15 main lines from which a host of branch lines diverge, and at any time there are over 100 locomotives in use.

While the railroad system employed to move iron ore to American steel-manufacturing centres is not in any way radically different from that of any other similar system in the industrialized world,

ABOVE: *Baltimore & Ohio Railroad coal train.*

LEFT: *A heavy iron-ore train on the Québec Cartier Mining Company Railway, Canada.*

ABOVE: *A double-headed steam train hauls mixed freight on the Jingpeng line. China has one of the most elaborate and specialized railroad systems in the world.*

LEFT: *Three Krauss-Maffei diesel-hydraulic power units haul a Denver & Rio Grande mixed freight train over the Rockies.*

OPPOSITE: *A Chinese coal train on the Nanking bridge. Coal and iron ore are hauled extensively by rail in China.*

the very size of many American steel mills means that they usually possess large railroad networks in and around their plants. The plant lines are often of the standard-gauge type, and this offers the very useful capability for the simple interchange of freight cars between the main line and the plant line. The locomotives used on the plant lines have in more recent times generally been of the diesel-powered type, but an odd exception up to 1980 was North Western Steel & Wire of Sterling, Illinois, which up to that date still operated steam locomotives. With the decline of the steel industry in the U.S.A. as a result of declining demand and the availability of cheaper imported steel, many mills have closed, thereby removing virtually all demand for these specialized railroads; yet in the late 1990s a few steel-mill railroad lines are still operational.

The close relationship between coal and iron ore in terms of railroad requirement is mirrored, with obvious changes, by the interrelationship between any industrialized nation's railroad network and sea ports, which still provide the essential interface between domestic and international transport of the vast majority of bulky and weighty imports and exports. For this reason many main-line tracks are continued right into the dock area, but there are also many ports in which there is a separate railroad system for the docks, thus providing a mobile 'bridge' between the land and the sea so that goods can be transferred between cargo vessels and main-line railroads. As with coal mine and ore

LEFT: Two Chinese QJ-class locomotives haul freight in the Gobi desert of inner Mongolia. 'QJ' stands for Qiang Jing *or 'March Forward'.*

OPPOSITE
ABOVE: Three J's thrash out of Banking station on the Chengde steelworks branch in China.

BELOW: Narrow-gauge iron-ore train in Koolanooka Hills, Western Australia.

railroad systems, the type of railroad needed for effective use in the confines typical of most ports involved small-radius curves and other restrictions on size, and as a result the typical port railroad system relies on small engines, most typically of the tank-locomotive type when such railroads were operated by steam-powered engines. Even so, the need for considerable power for the movement of heavy loads often required the juxtaposition of small and large engines, and a typical system of this type was that of the Bombay Port Trust, which had large 2-10-2 tank engines for hump-shunting and also somewhat smaller 2-6-0 tank engines for the movement of smaller loads.

should be noted that in the complex of the Brooklyn Eastern District steam-powered locomotives were still in comparatively large-scale service right into the 1960s, which was considerably later than the survival of similar locomotives in other large American ports.

Connected to the port conceptually and often physically, the shipbuilding yard has generally relied on the receipt of its basic raw materials, both steel sheet and in later years prefabricated sections, by railroad. The raw materials are then usually distributed within the yard by the shipbuilder's own railroad system. Typical of such a system, which is not as prevalent as it used to be as a result of the more extensive use of trucks and travelling cranes, was the Doxford shipyard at Sunderland in the north-east of England. This yard was revised during the early part of the 20th century with an internal railroad system amounting to 13 miles (21km) of track and based essentially on the use of steam-crane locomotives. The first of these, built by Hawthorn, Leslie of neighbouring Newcastle upon Tyne and providing a 9,000-lb (4082-kg) lift capability, was operating by 1904 and remained in service up to 1971, not because the locomotive was deemed obsolete for its purpose but rather for a number of unrelated factors such as shortages of spare parts and the introduction locally of a smokeless zone policy. The whole of the Doxford railroad system was then abandoned, roads being laid over the tracks and the crane-tank engine concept being abandoned in favour

The larger sea ports of the U.S.A., typified by New York on the east coast and San Francisco on the west were and, to a more limited extent, still are characterized by complex networks of quayside railroad tracks and car-float operations. These lines were usually of the standard-gauge type for maximum interchangeability of traffic between the port network and the main-line system. Another notable feature of the port railroad networks was the fact that they included a high proportion of street running, resulting in the setting of the tracks in the roadway, the general use of small-radius curves and trim clearances, and the general use of light switch engines for motive power. These port railroad systems were among the first to be served by diesel-electric locomotives, although it of the combination of fork-lift trucks and mobile road cranes.

The construction of large ships took place in only a comparatively small number of places in global terms, and the single most important area for shipbuilding in the later half of the 19th century and the first quarter of the 20th century was Clydeside in the Scottish city of Glasgow: it is estimated that during this period as many as four out of every five of the worlds' merchant ships were launched from Glaswegian yards, where the 'maid-of-all-work' locomotive was the Scottish 0-4-0 saddle-tank, or 'pug', engine. There were, of course, a number of other major shipbuilding centres in other parts of the world, especially in Europe and the U.S.A., and those which included a significant railroad system numbered among their total Belfast, Gdansk, Hamburg, Kiel, Malmö and Rostock.

Another type of railroad operation that has existed virtually from the beginning of rail transport has been that associated with logging or, more specifically, the extraction of the felled timber from logging areas. Under circumstances ideal for the railroad operator, of course, logging operations should take place near an existing railroad track, but life is never as conveniently arranged as that, so there has always to be a means of shifting the timber from the site of its felling to the nearest practical railroad. This originally meant the use of expedients such as the use of gravity to roll logs down mountainsides, or dragging them, or floating them down a nearby river. By the

1920s trucks were increasingly used for the task of delivering felled timber to the railroad, but the increasing capability of trucks to carry very heavy loads and move across rough terrain has meant a considerable erosion of the railroad's responsibilities in this task.

For some time the north-west region of the U.S.A.'s and Canada's western seaboard on the Pacific Ocean, in the states of Oregon and Washington and the province of British Columbia respectively, has been one of the world's most important and technically advanced logging areas. Here

U.S. timber companies used logging railroads to deliver timber from the location being worked to the processing area where the saw mills were located, but as the area where trees were being felled altered on a steady basis, the railroads were generally built as lightly as possible with curves and

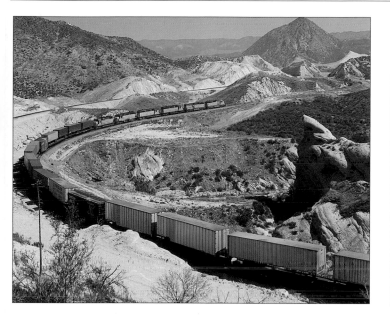

gradients that would not have been considered for more permanent railroads. During the period when steam was the driving force, specially designed geared locomotives were used for effective movement along these steep and winding routes. The type of locomotive most widely used for the task was the Shay, made by Lima, and using a row of vertical cylinders to drive a cranked shaft. Logging railroads made use of a variety of specialized cars to move raw timber, this role-specific equipment including free-wheel sets without frames that could be attached to large logs for movement over the rails.

It is worth noting that major logging railroads were once located in the northern part of the New England states, the central part of the Appalachian region including the states of Kentucky, Pennsylvania and West Virginia, the Sierra mountain region of the state of California, and the Cascade region of the Pacific North-West. Only a very small number of these specialized railroads still remain in operation.

As noted above, the particular nature of logging railroads led to the development of a number of special equipment items, and these included articulated locomotives, of which certainly the most celebrated was the

Shay. Pioneered in 1880 after development by Ephraim Shay, a Michigan logging engineer, the concept of the Shay locomotive was adopted by the Lima locomotive manufacturing company of Ohio. The Shay was built largely for the domestic American market, and most of the locomotives were of the standard-gauge type although modest numbers were also completed in a narrow-gauge format for export markets in Australia, eastern Asia and South America. Typical of the operators of Shay locomotives in eastern Asia was the Insular Lumber Company on Negros Island in the Philippines, which had a railroad of 3ft 6in (1.067m) gauge to deliver teak logs from the island's mountainous interior to the saw mills located near the coast: the logging trains halted on a ledge and a mechanical system then pushed sideways off the cars to fall a long distance into an artificial lake beside the saw mills.

On the other side of the world, not insignificant numbers of Feldbahn (field railway) locomotives built for the German

army in World War I ended their days in the logging role that was, after all, little different in its overall nature from the military railway for which the locomotives had been manufactured. The last Feldbahn locomotives were used at Czarna Bialystoka, a 75-mile (120-km) forestry system close to Bialystok in Poland on the main line from Warsaw to St. Petersburg (then Leningrad), and these steam locomotives were replaced by diesel locomotives built in Karl Marx Stadt in what was then East Germany but which has returned to its original name of Chemnitz in a unified Germany.

As with so many other features of its accelerated emergence into the 20th century from the time of the communists' 1949 victory in the civil war, China was a comparatively late entrant into the field of logging operations that are, in common with many other elements of the Chinese push towards modern industrialization and economic development, centred in the northern part of the country. Large numbers of 2ft 6in (0.76m) gauge railroads are here

employed on the movement of semi-trimmed logs from the felling sites to main-line junctions for further transport through Manchuria to all other parts of China.

The production of sugar is a major industry in several parts of the world, and the growth in the number and/or extent of sugar plantations to satisfy the cravings of an increasingly sweet-toothed world coincided with the industrialization that made sugar refining more efficient and also more exploitable as the finished product could then be moved in bulk by railroad to a port for export. As with many other industries, there also developed the concept of using narrow-gauge railroads within the manufacturing (in this instance growing and refining) site to expedite the whole process. This was especially important for sugar cane, which is grown in hot regions and can lose much of its important moisture (and with it much of the sugar) if there is any delay between cutting and processing. As a result, the spread of sugar-plantation railroads was rapid, and this type of operation was soon to be found in

ABOVE FAR LEFT: *A mixed train of privately-owned and Freightliner containers.*

SECOND LEFT: *Loading piggy-back trailers onto Baltimore & Ohio flatcars.*

THIRD LEFT: *Containers enable goods to be transferred easily from rail to ship and road.*

ABOVE: *Loading logs onto the narrow-gauge Chai He logging railway, China.*

OPPOSITE
ABOVE: *Transporting molten metal from the Krupp blast furnaces to a steel plant in a special torpedo wagon.*

BELOW: *Automatic track-lifting and ballast-tamping machine on a Baltimore & Ohio line keeps the wheels rolling.*

Australia, Brazil, Cuba, Fiji, India, Java, Mauritius and the Philippines.

Java is typical of the regions economically reliant, at least in part, on the production of sugar. This Indonesian (originally Dutch) island in south-east Asia has more than 50 sugar refineries, many of them interconnected by a railroad system that is without doubt one of the most fascinating steam networks of the present day. The 2ft 3.5in (0.70m) gauge

predominates, but some factories have railroads of 1ft 11.5in (0.60m) gauge, and the basic concept is based on a spoke-like arrangement of some 50 miles (80km) of track radiating from the refinery. One of the most attractive features of this apparently anachronistic system of steam railroads, which is also typical of Indian and Filipino operations, is its self-sufficiency in terms of fuel, for the locomotives use bagasse, which is compacted and baled sugar-cane fibres

created as a by-product of the sugar-refining process, as their essentially free fuel. The fuel provides little, though adequate, thermal energy for its volume, and as a result sugar-plantation railroads generally use tender-tank engines.

Sugar is not solely a product of sugar-cane plantations in the tropics, for a chemically identical sugar is produced from the sugar beet that is extensively grown in more temperate regions of the world. The

229

ABOVE: *Logs being loaded onto a train of the Finnish state railway. Timber has been transported by rail almost since the beginning of the railroads.*

LEFT: *A log train being hauled by an 0-8-0 heading towards Chai He, China.*

OPPOSITE: *A Baldwin 2-8-0 locomotive of 1914 is still in active service and is here passing through La Vega in Cuba with a loaded cane train .*

refining of sugar from pulped beet was introduced as early as 1747, and the system was established on a commercial basis during 1801 in the German state of Silesia. Since that time the production of sugar from beet has become an important industry in countries seeing the commercial advantage of not having to import their sugar, these including most northern European nations as well as the U.S.A., where the primary beet-growing states are those of California and Oregon, where the beets are moved to large processing mills by railroad in specially designed cars. As in the tropical regions that have their own railroad systems, major sugar-beet centres in temperate climes often have an internal railroad system.

Despite the emergence of alternative technologies, much of the world's electricity is still produced with the aid of steam, even if the steam that powers the electricity-generating turbine equipment is now generated by nuclear reactors, gas and other heat sources rather than coal. But for nearly 100 years it was the coal-fired power station that was the core of any modern country's electricity generating system, and this demanded the delivery to the power stations of very large quantities of coal, a task that could be achieved only by railroad. Thus the steam locomotive was a vital link in the chain between the coal mine and the power station, and until the 1950s and the large-scale introduction of diesel-powered equipment was the only effective means to

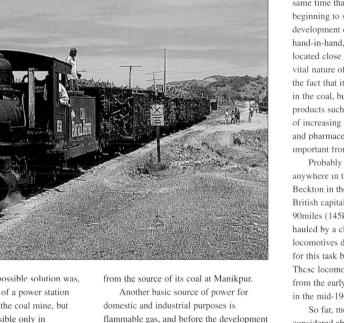

derived from coal at special gasworks
established in towns providing a ready
market for the gas. The production of gas
was therefore reliant on the steady delivery
of large quantities of coal, a fact which
could be assured only by the railroad
network. The production of gas from coal
became viable in the 1830s, at much the
same time that the railroad concept was
beginning to spread its wings, and the
development of the two went very much
hand-in-hand, with the gas works often
located close to the railroad station. The
vital nature of the railroad is suggested by
the fact that it was needed not only to bring
in the coal, but also to take away by-
products such as coke and coal tar, the latter
of increasing importance to the chemical
and pharmaceutical industries that grew so
important from the middle of the century.

Probably the largest complex of its time
anywhere in the world was the gas works at
Beckton in the eastern part of London, the
British capital. Here there were some
90 miles (145km) of track, whose traffic was
hauled by a class of small 0-4-0 side tank
locomotives designed and built specifically
for this task by Neilson Reid of Glasgow.
These locomotives ran in everyday service
from the early 1880s until their retirement
in the mid-1960s.

So far, most of the freight-hauling roles
considered above have been of the heavy
industrial type, even though logging and
sugar obviously do not fall directly into this
category; but it should not be forgotten that
the railroad also found ready niches outside
the industrial scene, most notably for the

deliver coal in the required quantities. In
basic terms, high-quality coal (otherwise
known as 'steam' coal) was generally
delivered by main-line railroad to the
railhead and reception yard as close to the
power station as possible, and then shifted
from this to the power stations in cars
hauled by side- and saddle-tank
locomotives, generally of the 0-4-0 and

0-6-0 types. The best possible solution was,
of course, the location of a power station
as close as possible to the coal mine, but
this was generally possible only in
countries that came late to industrialization.
Typical of these was India, which was
able to create in the state of Madhya
Pradesh a huge electricity generating
complex at Korba, only 10 miles (16km)

from the source of its coal at Manikpur.

Another basic source of power for
domestic and industrial purposes is
flammable gas, and before the development
of the natural gas industry, which relies on
vast networks of pipelines and special ships
to move adequate quantities of this fuel
from the regions in which it is extracted
from oil or other natural deposits, this was

movement of large loads of rural commodities. Some of the more interesting of these that have become associated with railroad transport include fibres such as cotton and jute (and by extension wool in countries such as Australia), palm oil, potatoes, peanuts or ground nuts, grains, and even peat.

As far as cotton is concerned, the world's most extensive railroad operation is that of the Gezira Project in Sudan. This radiates from Wad el Shatie, and comprises very many miles of 1ft 11.5in (0.60m) gauge track over which the cotton-carrying cars are hauled by Hunslet 0-8-0 diesel locomotives. Railways for carrying jute have been built, most notably in India and Bangladesh. As in munitions plants and paper mills, the category of locomotive chosen for this task, at least within the processing works, is of the fireless steam type which draws its working supply of steam from a static source to avoid the danger, almost inevitable with a conventional steam locomotive, that sparks from the firebox or smokestack could set fire to the load in the towed cars or in the fields beside the track.

On the Indonesian island of Sumatra, one of the main industries is the extraction of palm oil, a commodity that is used in the manufacture of soap and margarine. Enormous quantities of the fruit have to be delivered from the plantations to the mills, a task achieved by the use of steam locomotives on several narrow-gauge railroad systems radiating from the factories into the plantations and operated by 0-4-4-0T Mallet-type locomotives manufactured in the Netherlands, while the Indonesian archipelago was still the Dutch East Indies, by Ducroo & Brauns. A natural waste product of the palm-oil process, namely the hard shell of the kernel, is burned as fuel in the locomotives, thereby reducing the direct operating costs of the system, and an advantage of this fuel by comparison with the bagasse used on sugar plantations, is its high thermal value.

Reflecting the vast tonnage of foodstuffs delivered from the hinterland of Argentina to the nation's ports for export, as befitting the former position of this South American country as the 'larder of the world' and one of the world's leading economies, the potato railroads were once a part of the Buenos Aires & Great Southern Railway. These railroads comprised a large system of tracks, in 2ft 0in (0.61m) gauge, for the movement of trains, carrying loads as diverse as potatoes, wheat and beef, hauled initially by Hunslet 4-6-0 locomotives which had been rendered surplus to British army requirement in

the aftermath of World War I, but were later supplanted by Simplex petrol and diesel locomotives.

One of the most remarkable and extensive industrial railway operations in the world operates in the southern part of Ireland. The island lacks an indigenous supply of coal, but peat was found to be a cheap and efficient alternative as a primary fuel. As well as a fuel for domestic hearths, the peat can also be used in a number of industrial applications including service as a fuel for power stations. After the peat has been drained and cut, it is piled beside the 3ft (0.918m) gauge railroad lines laid across the bogs, from which the cut turves are

hauled by diesel locomotives to the plants at which it is milled and compressed into briquettes for use in domestic fires or as the power source for electricity generating stations, where it is blown into the furnaces in the same way as other pulverized fuels.

There are several types of agricultural railroad in North America. Perhaps the best known, and also probably the most important, are the railroads that service the grain elevators that are so characteristic of the mid-western regions of the U.S.A. Often of very large size, these grain elevators are used for the storage of longer-life harvest products, usually wheat and corn, and most of the more substantial complexes are accessed by railroads operated by industrial switch engines, which shunt the main-line freight cars as they are loaded from the elevators.

In large parts of the world the development of the railroads and the discovery of new large-scale sources of important minerals coincided from the middle of the 19th century, and in many respects it is hard to see that either could have developed in its particular way without the other. One of the world's largest suppliers of gold, South Africa saw the coincident development of its railroad network and its gold-mining industry, the first reliant on the wealth brought in by the latter for its large-scale development, and the latter needing the former for the delivery of heavy equipment and the movement of large quantities of the ore from which the pure gold was then smelted. Among South Africa's most significant gold mines was City Deep in the extraordinarily rich gold reef region around Johannesburg, and this operation was perhaps typical of its period in its completion with its railroad system that operated right through the day and night with the aid of six 4-8-4T locomotives manufactured by the North British Locomotive Company. This system allowed for the gold ore to be transported from the head of the two primary mineshafts to the mill, after which the crumbled ore was again moved by railroad to the Jupiter Station junction with the main line, from which the ore proceeded to the smelting facility. At least two other South African gold-mining operations had

their own railroad systems, in each case with the same type of North British 0-8-0T tank engines.

South Africa has and still does generate a large measure of its wealth from the country's extensive diamond deposits, and another rich source of diamonds was the neighbouring country of South-West Africa, which was originally a colony of Germany, which was initially responsible for the discovery and exploitation of the country's diamond wealth. The South-West Africa (now Namibia) diamond industry came into existence during the 1890s, and the modest railroads associated with the industry were remarkable in their use of first-generation electric locomotives, most of these being 0-4-0 and Bo-Bo types built in Germany by Siemens. The trains hauled by these

locomotives were used for the disposal of the rock and other waste materials from the diamond mines, whose management was assumed by the De Beers company after South African forces had taken South-West Africa from the Germans in World War I.

Farther to the north, but still on the western side of southern Africa, lies Angola that was a Portuguese colony but is now independent. In this country lies the Benguela railroad, which extends some 838 miles (1348km) between the port of Lobito and Luau on the border with the Congo, via Benguela itself. This railroad was created in the period between 1904 and 1929 as what was and still is the single most important outlet for the precious minerals mined in Central Africa. Until the Angolan Civil War in 1975, the Caminho Ferro de Benguela

ABOVE: Dv 12- (formerly Sv 12-) class diesel-hydraulic locomotives haul a coal train past a loading point on the Finnish state railway.

was one of the most efficient railroads in Africa, and was owned by Tanganyika Concessions, a subsidiary of the Belgian firm of Union Minier. Angola is a troubled country still, and the reconstruction of the Benguela railroad is a prerequisite of a revived national economy.

A mineral that came to rival iron in the economy of the 20th century was aluminium, the metal extracted from bauxite ore of the type mined in countries such as Jamaica. The bauxite is found in the interior of the island, and both American and British financial resources were used to create the railroad by means of which the ore could be shifted from the mines to a junction with the Jamaica National Railway network for onward movement to the coast for export. The Jamaican railroad system was closed down in the middle of the 1980s, and the bauxite system is now the sole railroad operation in Jamaica. In the later part of the 1960s the original generation of steam locomotives was replaced by a more modern generation of American-built diesel-powered Bo-Bo and Co-Co locomotives. Large quantities of bauxite are also mined in India, where the major operation is that near Renukut. The aluminium smelting plant in this city is served by its own railroad system of 5ft 6in (1.683m) gauge, the primary task for this railroad being the delivery not of bauxite but of the very substantial amount of coal needed for the smelting operation. The most important of the locomotives used in this task are ex-main-line banking locomotives, whose great power makes them very

effective in the slow but steady delivery of massive loads of coal. Another country that is a major exporter of bauxite is Ghana on the west coast of Africa, and here narrow-gauge industrial railroads are used for the delivery of ore from the inland mining regions to junctions with the country's main-line network for onward transmission to the coast.

Another area of the world blessed, if that is the right word, with very important deposits of strategically important and therefore valuable minerals is the island of Tasmania off the south-eastern corner of the Australian continental land mass. Despite its comparatively small size, the island had been revealed to possess huge ore deposits from which tin, lead, silver, gold, copper and iron can be extracted. The terrain of this mountainous and highly forested island is too difficult for the cost-effective construction of major roads, so movement to and from the mineral deposits was generally achieved by tramways or railways. One of the earliest tramways, worked by horse power, was that built at the Mount Bischoff tin mine in 1878, but this was soon converted to a 3ft 6in (1.071m) gauge railroad with steam locomotives. The Mount Lyell operation constructed a 21-mile (34-km) switchback railroad line connecting its copper mine with the coast. Much of the railroad was cut through heavy forest, but it also included two 4.5-mile (7-km) long sections with gradients of 1/16 and 1/20, where the Abt rack and pinion system had to be used by the 0-4-2T locomotives, of which the first was

delivered for service from 1896.

Another important but massive commodity requiring movement in large quantities, mainly for use in the building industry, is stone in its many forms, ranging in size from the upper limit represented by large boulders to the smallest and most compact loads in the forms of gravel and sand. It is worth noting that some of the earliest railroad lines constructed in North America were intended for the movement of stone, typical of this being the opening, in 1826, of the 3-mile (4.8-km) Granite Railway at Quincy, Massachusetts for the animal-drawn transport of stone to the site of the Bunker Hill monument. The Chester & Becket operation, also in Massachusetts, hauled stone from quarries to Chester, where there were stone-cutting facilities and a connection with the main line. Other quarry lines were isolated from all other rail connections, and were used to move stones solely within the quarry facilities.

Interesting as they were, the stone railroads of New England, and indeed of many other parts of the U.S.A. as they were opened up for development, were relatively insignificant in relation to the Dutch (now Indonesian) railroad at Gunung Kataren on the island of Sumatra. This 1ft 3.75in (0.40m) gauge line was built to transport smooth, flat stones manually extracted from the bed of a fast river. From the river, the stones were hauled up to a primitive crusher located beside the state railroad's main line. Part of this line, employed for the generation of crushed stone for use as ballast, was an incline up which the wagons

had to be hauled individually by cable.

Even within the compass of a small and very crowded island nation such as England, there was ample scope for the development and extensive use of small company railroads, not only of the types mentioned above in connection with heavy industries such as coal mining, but also of more immediately consumer-oriented industries. Of these latter, those which could make most extensive use of company railway systems were the giants of the drink and food industries.

The most notable example of a railway owned and operated by a brewer was that of Bass, which operated a system involving private locomotives travelling over a 16-mile (25.5-km) track network connected with the main line at Burton-on-Trent. Of these 16 miles (25.5km), some 8 miles (13km) were located at Shobnall where there were maltings, a cask-washing plant, experimental bottling stores and beer-loading stations as well as sidings with the capacity for 400 wagons. Another 5 miles (8km) of track were used by the connections and sidings between the three main breweries, and the final 3 miles (5km) comprised the Dixie Exchange Sidings and Stores. The system was launched in 1862 and the expansion of the brewery was matched by that of its company railway: the existence of the railway in the middle of Burton-on-Trent meant that there were many crossings of public roads, and for reasons of safety Bass had to build signal boxes at the crossings. Such was the growth of Bass in the later part of the 19th century and the

An Argentine narrow-gauge steam locomotive hauls a mixed load. In South America, the introduction of diesel power was sometimes limited because of the cost of imported diesel fuel relative to locally-mined coal.

early part of the 20th that by the 1920s the company's railway was undertaking the daily movement of more than 1,000 wagons, about one-third of them empty units returning from the main line and the other two-thirds involved in the transport within the brewery of materials such as malt, barley and coal.

Another brewing company with its own railway was Guinness, which had an extensive system in both 5ft 3in (1.596m) and 1ft 10in (0.56m) gauges at its Dublin brewery. This system, operated in parallel with barges on the River Liffey and the Irish main-line railway system, was the starting point for the delivery of Guinness stout to points all over Ireland and also for export trade.

Another type of British company railway was the 2-mile (3.2-km) system

associated with the Port Sunlight refinery and commissioned during 1910 to link the refinery and margarine works with Bromborough Dock and the main-line station at Port Sunlight. In 1913 the operator bought from the North London Railway nine passenger coaches, and these were employed in the transport of workers to and from the main-line station. The Port Sunlight operation used 0-6-0T locomotives built especially for it by Andrew Barclay of Kilmarnock in Scotland. In the early part of the 20th century Cadbury, another economically shrewd but also philanthropic company, built a wide-ranging railway to serve its expanding chocolate factory at Bournville, near Birmingham. The railway was employed to bring in raw materials such as cocoa beans and the coal required to power the chocolate-making process, and

also to delivery the finished products to the local main-line station for onward transport to all parts of the U.K. and indeed to very many other parts of the word.

As has been noted above, some of these small company railroads made use of diesel-powered locomotives, which in the first part of the 20th century had started the process of replacing the steam locomotive as the most important prime mover for heavy freight railroad services. In fact the first appearance of a diesel-engined locomotive as a main-line unit in North America took place in 1928, when the type entered service with the Rock Island Railroad. From this time onward, the position, once apparently unassailable, of the large steam locomotive for the hauling of heavy freight trains was first eroded and then over a period of some 40 years

ultimately destroyed by the diesel-engined locomotive. The diesel-engined locomotive was first adopted in significant numbers for main-line service during the mid- to late 1930s, when General Motors and General Electric, both giants of the American industrial scene, started to market and mass-produce suitable power units. The operators of main-line service in the U.S.A. were at first dubious about the viability of the new type of powerplant, but by the middle of World War II most of the companies had come round to the position in which they saw the diesel engine as the future of power for railroad purposes.

By the mid-1950s the diesel had become effectively paramount in North America, and as a result many classes of steam locomotive, many of them with only a few years of service under their belts,

were withdrawn from service and scrapped. They were replaced by the units of the new 'E' and 'F' classes of standard locomotives, the former intended for express passenger work and the latter for mixed-traffic operations. For switching purposes and trip working the manufacturers produced a whole series of Bo-Bo and Co-Co single-cab hood types. With such motive power on the market, sold at reasonable terms and offering the attractions of reduced manning requirements, easier bunkering, greater fuel efficiency and reduced running costs, most railroads found it very attractive to 'dieselize' as soon and as rapidly as possible. The American manufacturers, which had attained a pre-eminent position as a result of their larger uninterrupted and therefore massive production of heavy transport equipment in World War II, were

also in the prime position to market their wares on the world stage, securing major success in Africa, Asia, Australia, New Zealand and South America. Some European countries, such as Spain and Portugal, also bought diesel locomotives from the U.S.A.

Diesel engines did not have matters all their own way, it should be noted, but they did come to predominate. An alternative to the diesel engine was the gas turbine of the type that had begun to mature for aircraft use in World War II and was extensively and rapidly refined after the war, and in the mid-1960s the Union Pacific Railroad decided to try an experiment with gas turbine traction. This was successfully achieved with a fleet of gas turbine units that were used primarily for heavy freight work on the Union Pacific Railroad's main

lines, and remained in operation until the late 1970s.

Diesel locomotives first appeared on the main-line services of the U.K. in the mid-1930s, when the Great Western Railway introduced streamlined diesel-powered railcars and parcel vans. Together with some later additions built in the 1940s, these remained in service up to the early 1960s. At the same time, the London, Midland & Scottish Railway also ordered diesel locomotives. At first these were just shunting locomotives, but later the railway constructed a three-car diesel multiple unit and, in 1947, ordered two diesel-powered main-line locomotives. In the same year the Southern Railway ordered three main-line diesel locomotives, but these were delivered only after the formation of the nationalized British Railways in 1948. These three

ABOVE LEFT: *A South American 2-10-2 locomotive steams past another freight train at Rio Gallegos.*

ABOVE: *Another 2-10-2 South American locomotive. Many South American countries, lacking an indigenous manufacturing industry, relied on imports, particularly from America.*

237

ABOVE LEFT: *An early Canadian Northern Railway freight train passing a typical western grain elevator, circa 1915.*

ABOVE: *Baltimore & Ohio Railroad workshops at Piedmont, West Virginia at the foot of the 'Seventeen-Mile' grade from Piedmont to Altamont, Maryland, circa 1875.*

FAR LEFT: *Excavating for a 'Y' on the Orange & Alexandria Railroad. Brigadier-General Hermann Haupt, Chief of the U.S. Military Railroads, is standing on the bank supervising the work, the locomotive* General Haupt *heading the work train. From the early days, railways have carried men and materiel to battle.*

LEFT: *Track maintenance is crucial for safety.*

The development of diesel traction in Germany began during 1932 with the introduction of the famous and nicely streamlined *Flying Hamburger* three-car diesel units, which later led to the construction of several experimental main-line locomotives, both before and during the first part of World War II. The result of this process was the introduction, in the period after the end of World War II, of a fleet of modern locomotives of the diesel-hydraulic and diesel-electric types, and these supplanted steam locomotives for all main-line purposes from the late 1950s.

The Soviet state railway benefited greatly from the delivery of Lend-Lease equipment, mainly from the U.S.A. and including numbers of steam locomotives, in the course of World War II. In the period immediately after the war's end and before the dropping of the 'iron curtain', substantial numbers of diesel locomotives were also shipped to the U.S.S.R. from the U.S.A. Experience with these units persuaded the Soviet state railway organization in the 1950s that the time was ripe for these American units to be supplemented and then supplanted by diesel engined locomotives of Soviet design

and manufacture, but nonetheless based strongly on the technology of the American locomotives. The Soviet engines were not as good as their U.S. counterparts, however, and it was not until the 1980s, when other elements of outside technology were more readily tapped, that the Soviets were at last able to make significant strides and start the introduction of modern, efficient designs.

While the appearance of the diesel-engined locomotive was not greeted with the same level of approval as had generally been the case when the steam-powered locomotive made its initial appearance, this was probably the result of a certain blasé element in the perception of a public that had grown up with the railroad as part of its earliest memories, but also in part because early diesel-engined locomotives were both technically crude and, as a result of their limited power, poor in performance. The basic concept of the internal combustion engine had been established as early as 1794, but it was not until 1883 that Daimler patented the high-speed petrol engine, closely followed by the appearance of Rudolf Diesel's 'oil engine' in 1892. Two years later, the first locomotive to use this new form of power was built by Priestman

ABOVE: Santa Fe's diesel locomotive No. 5708 carrying eastbound freight through Crozier Canyon in Arizona.

locomotives were the precursors of the '40' class of main-line locomotives used extensively during the 1960s. As a result of the technical success of these and other early experimental diesel-powered locomotives, British Railways was led to formulate the 1955 modernization plan that led, somewhat prematurely, to the elimination of steam locomotives from British main line routes by 1968.

RIGHT: The famous Union Pacific Centennial-class locomotive hauls its load of piggy-back containers. The commissioning of this class was how Union Pacific chose to celebrate its 100 years of railway operation.

Brothers of Hull: this was a 12-hp (8.9-kW) dockyard shunter with a diesel engine and mechanical transmission. In 1896, another diesel-engined locomotive was constructed for the Woolwich Arsenal in London: manufactured by Hornsby & Son of Grantham, this 9-hp (6.7-kW) single-cylinder machine was somewhat underpowered, but it was generally successful and its quickly proved capabilities were enough to persuade the War Office to order a further four.

The year 1912 was the time for the next breakthrough for the diesel-engined locomotive, for it was in this year that there appeared the world's first diesel-powered railcar. Built by the Sodermanland Midland Railway of Sweden, the railcar was an adapted coach, fitted with a diesel engine and generator. Further examples were made for other Swedish railways by Allmanna Svenska Aktiebolaget.

The ghastly years of World War I restricted the development of diesel motive power in the short term, so it was not until the 1920s that significant progress was once more achieved. It is worth noting, though, that petrol-engined railcars had been produced in the U.S.A. during this period when, in 1917, the General Electric Company built a railcar with electric transmission for the Delaware & Hudson Railroad. Moderately large numbers of similar petrol-engined railcars were soon operational on several railroad lines in the more rural regions of the U.S.A. The first really successful diesel-engined locomotive was a 300hp (224kW) shunter constructed

in 1924 by Alco, General Electric and Ingersoll Rand for the Jersey Central Lines, and some 26 basically similar locomotives were made in the next two years for various railways and industrial companies.

It was during the 1930s that the diesel-engined locomotive finally began to emerge as a major force in the American railroad system. Significant improvements in the technology of diesel engines, including a major boost in locomotive power/weight ratios through a reduction in weight and an increase in power, at last started to make diesel-engined locomotives an attractive commercial proposition to main-line railroads. Much of this new technology was used in the streamlined express trains such as the Burlington Railroad's *Pioneer Zephyr* that was introduced in 1934. The Union Pacific Railroad inaugurated its own streamlined diesel locomotives to service in the same year, and a measure of the importance of the new 1,200-hp (895-kW) locomotives was the fact that they allowed an 18-hour reduction of the scheduled time for the 2,270-mile (3653-km) journey between Chicago, Illinois and Portland, Oregon from October 1934.

The success of the diesel-powered locomotive in the U.S.A. can be seen as the single factor that was most important in opening the floodgates for this type of traction in other parts of the world, where diesel-engined streamlined locomotives began to appear in ever larger numbers to haul prestige express trains: the celebrated *Flying Hamburger*, built for the Deutsche Reichsbahn, was a glamorous propaganda

ABOVE: *Chicago & North Western-type C 624 locomotive, No. 6707 heads a mixed freight in Wisconsin.*

OPPOSITE
ABOVE LEFT: *Denver & Rio Grande diesel-hydraulic locomotive No. 4003. Built by Krauss-Maffei in Germany, these locomotives caused a stir when first introduced because American railroads had not imported locomotives since their earliest days.*

ABOVE RIGHT: *A Chicago & North Western RS-32 locomotive No. 4249-3, hauling scrap at Green Bay, Wisconsin.*

BELOW LEFT: *A British Petroleum company train consisting of 100-ton bogie tankers hauled by a diesel-electric British Rail locomotive.*

BELOW RIGHT: *A switcher at Joliet, Illinois with covered hoppers loaded with phosphate.*

tool for Nazi Germany, and there were
similar streamlined units used on Austrian
and French railways well before the
outbreak of World War II in 1939.

However, this situation did not prevail
in the U.K., where the 'big four' railway
companies were still unconvinced of the
merits of diesel power for the hauling of
high-speed, main-line services and therefore
restricted themselves to experiments with
less powerful railcars on secondary or
branch lines. In 1934 the Great Western
Railway introduced a new diesel-engined
railcar, developed in conjunction with the
bus manufacturer AEC. This was
sufficiently successful for the company to
order a further 17 such engines before
building another 20 units of its own design
at Swindon.

As noted above, it was in the U.S.A.
that there appeared the main impetus for the
replacement of the steam locomotive with
the diesel locomotive. General Motors
began this process in 1937 with the
construction of its first 'E1'-class 1,800-hp
(1342-kW) passenger locomotive, which
was doubly significant as it was also the
first standardized design. Customers could
choose single-cab or cabless power units,
setting a trend in U.S. railroading as
operators could now 'mix and match'
power units. Less than two years later the
'E6'-class diesel locomotive, a more
powerful 2,000-hp (1491-kW) version of
the E1, was manufactured and this was
followed in 1939 by the 'FT' class, which
was a freight-hauling version of the E6-
class locomotive.

ABOVE: Heavy-duty freight sometimes required the support of 'helper' locomotives, particularly up steep inclines.

BELOW: The celebrated Flying Hamburger, *the glamorous German streamlined diesel express of the 1930s. The process of adoption of diesel power in the U.S.A. spread to Europe in a more diffuse, less dramatic way.*

RIGHT: The legendary Union Pacific Big Boy-class 4-8-8-4 locomotive, in its day the most powerful locomotive in the world.

In the next 10 years the speed with which dieselization overtook the steam locomotive in the U.S.A. was remarkable. The rate of this process is indicated by the fact that while there were a mere 314 diesel-engined locomotives on American railroads during 1938, the total had increased to nearly 12,000 by 1950. Looked at the other way round, the total of 40,000 or more steam-powered locomotives in service during 1939 had declined to only just over 15,000 such locomotives by 1950.

This development in the success and popularity of the diesel-engined locomotive was not merely an increase represented in terms of numbers or horse power, but also an improvement in the basic qualities of the diesel-powered locomotive. In the period after the end of World War II, for instance, the 'road switcher' or 'hood' type of locomotive made its appearance as a development of the basic locomotive with a full-width cab and the engine contained within a narrow hood, allowing the

provision of an external walkway on each side. The locomotives of this type were certainly less attractive in visual terms than their predecessors, but offered better fields of vision to the front and rapidly became a typical aspect of North American railroad operations. Evidence of this fact is provided by the delivery by General Motors' Electro-Motive Division of considerably more than 10,500 'GP' type of road switcher engines to American railroads between 1949 and 1975: the early 1,500-hp (1118-kW) 'GP7'

class was superseded by ever more powerful variations, so that power ratings of 3,600hp (2684kW) were available in the 1960s

In 1969 there made its appearance the world's largest and most powerful type of single-unit diesel locomotive. This 'Centennial' class was built for the Union Pacific Railroad by General Motors, and its class name celebrated the centenary of the driving in of the gold-plated 'last spike' of the transcontinental railroad. Production totalled 47 locomotives, each with a 6,600-

hp (4921-kW) engine. The Union Pacific Railroad was not typical of most North American railroad operators, most of which were content to operate with lower-powered locomotives that could be boosted by the addition of 'slave' units coupled to the main locomotive according to the weight of the load being moved.

By the 1960s, only two main manufacturers dominated the scene in the U.S.A., namely General Motors and General Electric, while the celebrated names of the previous generations, such as Alco, Baldwin, Fairbanks-Morse and Lima that had dominated the age of steam, had effectively disappeared.

In Europe the introduction of the diesel-engined locomotive was more diffuse and less dramatic than the equivalent process in the U.S.A. A number of countries opted to make their beginnings on the basis of American expertise, and therefore contracted with American companies such as General Motors to build and equip their railways with diesel-powered locomotives. This was the case in Sweden, although by the 1960s the state railroad system was operated by almost equal numbers of diesel-engined and electrically powered locomotives. General Motors also had considerable success in Denmark where, as recently as 1981, units of the 3,240-hp (2416-kW) 'ME' class were ordered for passenger and goods traffic. In Spain, locomotives from another American company, Alco, were also purchased.

Elsewhere in Europe the situation was

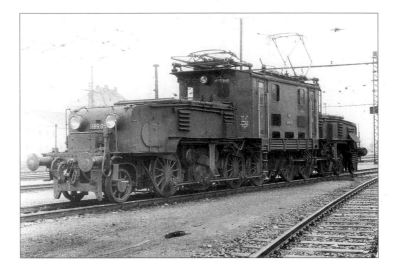

much more varied. In France and Italy the railroads produced their own diesel-powered locomotives. The most individualistic approach was that of West Germany. After World War II, German manufacturers and the Deutsche Bundesbahn placed their faith in the locomotive with diesel-hydraulic motive power as they believed that the combination of a high-speed engine and hydraulic transmission would result in locomotives that were both powerful and reliable. Krauss-Maffei built five prototype locomotives of this type in 1953, each of these prototypes being fitted with a pair of 1,100-hp (820-kW) Maybach engines. The trials of these prototypes were successful, so the Deutsche Bundesbahn ordered 100 examples of the generally similar 'V220' class, which was the inspiration for the 'D800'-class diesel-hydraulic locomotives manufactured for British Railways' Western Region at Swindon in 1960. However, the maintenance of this type of motive system proved to be expensive, so little use was made of its concept outside these two countries.

On the first day of 1948 the Labour government's plan for the nationalization of the British railway system was implemented and British Railways came into existence. Initially the new organization was not radical in its planning, so there was no large-scale move toward dieselization. However, this changed drastically with the publication of the 1955 modernization plan, which called for the replacement, in as short a time as possible,

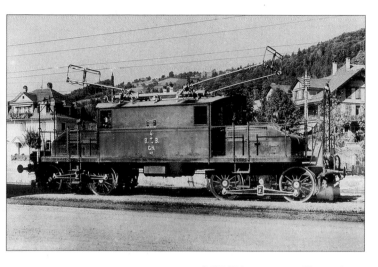

ABOVE: *An early locomotive on the Emmenthal-Burgdorf Thun mountain railway. Not only did these locomotives head passenger trains, they also delivered freight and mail to isolated mountain communities.*

ABOVE RIGHT: *Steam engine on the rack-and-pinion Schafbergbahn, mid-1970s.*

RIGHT: *An electric engine hauling freight at the beginning of the 20th century.*

OPPOSITE
ABOVE: *Class 1189 Crocodile electric locomotive of the Austrian state railway, mid-1970s.*

BELOW: *Great Northern Railway early electric locomotives with a freight train.*

of all British steam-powered locomotives with modern tractive equipment characterized by diesel or electric power. In other parts of Europe, in particular France and Germany, a much more strategic approach was taken, and as a result steam locomotives were retired over a number of years as they approached the ends of their useful lives: so while steam disappeared from British tracks by 1968, in Germany it was 1975 before it finally bowed out.

Despite its attempt to emulate the American railroads' rapid transition from steam to diesel power, the British did not want to use American technology and therefore turned to British companies for the design and manufacture of the new fleet of diesel-engined locomotives. The results were highly mixed. In 1955, for example,

ABOVE: *A Baltimore & Ohio F-series all-purpose diesel-electric locomotive at east St. Louis, Illinois. The 'A' units had a driver's cab, the 'B' or 'Booster' units did not.*

LEFT: *The Baltimore & Ohio at Pittsburg, Pennsylvania. Unfortunately the glory days are over for this venerable locomotive.*

the first of the 'Deltic' class was built by English Electric and later 22 more units were manufactured for service on the East Coast main line. Three years after the appearance of the Deltic, British Railways' Western Region opted for diesel-hydraulic rather than diesel-electric power, and the North British Locomotive Company was therefore contracted to produce the first diesel-hydraulic locomotive for British Railways. The resulting 'D600' class was unreliable and underpowered (and therefore soon retired), and was followed by the more powerful 'D800' class. In overall terms, the Swindon plant created six classes of diesel-hydraulic locomotives built to the

extent of more than 300 units. All of these had been retired by 1977 as their maintenance requirements were too heavy. Some of the diesel-electric designs introduced by British Railways, such as the '47' class which first appeared in 1962 and was built to the extent of more than 500 units, are still in service.

The concept of the diesel-powered locomotive took hold in the U.S.S.R. only in World War II, when the country received American-built locomotives of this type. The Soviets then dissected the technical concepts embodied in Alco and Baldwin locomotives and launched themselves on a course of evolutionary development. The Soviets' first type of diesel-electric locomotive was the 'TE1' class that appeared in 1945, and was succeeded from 1953 by an altogether larger 4,000-hp (2982-kW) locomotive class. This latter

ABOVE LEFT: *The Burlington* Pioneer Zephyr *route three-car train set from the 1930s. Diesel-electrics for passenger use fell into decline after World War II when they became increasingly used for freight traffic.*

LEFT: *Union Pacific's 4-4-0 locomotive* City of Salina, *1934. The 1970s saw the return of diesel-electric and particularly electric traction following its decline after*

was a double unit, and production exceeded 2,000 units in related passenger and freight versions.

In the rest of the world, especially Africa and South America, the ready acceptance of diesel power has been limited, resulting in part from a measure of technological backwardness and in part from the cost of possibly imported diesel fuel relative to locally mined coal. In a race to modernize their countries, many Third World nations bought diesel locomotives, but found that spares, skilled labour and other factors meant that such locomotives were not the bargain these countries thought they should have been. Nevertheless, many countries without their own locomotive manufacturing capability relied heavily on the import of engines, largely from the United States and the former communist block. In countries such as China and South Africa, however, the growth of diesel traction was limited by the availability of rich reserves of coal and other natural resources, which meant that steam locomotives lingered on much longer than in other places. Important though the introduction of diesel locomotives has been in many countries, it has been the onset of electrification that has had the most dramatic effect on railway operation.

The modern rival to the diesel-powered locomotive for the movement of heavy freight trains, especially in smaller countries such as the U.K. in which it was a relatively straightforward task to adapt the whole of the network within a reasonable time and at not too exorbitant a cost, is the

LEFT: *A Canadian Pacific freight train leaves the Connaught tunnel in the Canadian Rockies. The building above the portal is the ventilation fan house.*

ABOVE: *Seattle & North Coast F9-type locomotive at Port Angeles, Washington. The F series was an all-purpose diesel-electric locomotive, built from 1939.*

OPPOSITE
ABOVE LEFT: *Pitts & Shawmut type 6P-7 H357 freight locomotive.*

ABOVE RIGHT: *Seattle & North Coast SW-1200-type H56 road switcher locomotive at Port Townsend, Washington.*

BELOW LEFT: *Bangor & Aroostook type F3 which operated from Bangor in Maine to Aroostook in New Brunswick, Canada.*

BELOW RIGHT: *Norfolk & Southern diesel-electric No. 6634 at Hammond, Maryland.*

OPPOSITE

LEFT: *Type FA locomotive No. 0437 in the snow at Hartford, Connecticut.*

RIGHT ABOVE: *Norfolk & Western SD-40S freight train in Bluefield West, Virginia.*

RIGHT BELOW: *A Union Pacific class D D 40AX Centennial at Council Bluffs, built for heavy freight duty.*

THIS PAGE

ABOVE: *An electric locomotive in a Belgian station. Smaller countries such as Belgium were able to adapt networks for electric running at reasonable costs.*

RIGHT: *Prototype Belgian diesel locomotive No. 5001. The success of diesel power in America came to influence Europe.*

electrically powered locomotive, which had a higher power/weight ratio and as such may justly be claimed to be a prime example of how the exploitation of modern technology has led to major improvements. The result, as far as railroads are concerned, is the current availability of lightweight locomotives with power outputs far greater than those offered by the giant engines of previous generations. The nature of these locomotives, in the period before the practice of working locomotives in multiple had been developed, meant that the hauling of increasingly heavy trains demanded more traction motors in one machine. This not only increased the locomotive's length and weight, which had to be distributed over several axles, but raised problems of flexibility so that the locomotive could negotiate curves of all but the largest radii.

The locomotives of the so-called 'Frontier Railway', extending from Lulea to Riksgransen in Sweden, provide a good example of the early type of European electric locomotive. The railroad's *raison d'être* is the high-grade iron ore mined near Kiruna, some 1,670ft (510m) above sea level. Rail was and indeed remains the simplest and most effective way to get the ore to the coast at the port of Narvik in Norway. In 1914 ASEA/Siemens delivered 1-C+C-1 type locomotives each offering 1,800hp (1342kW), but in 1960 the line was using the 'DM3'-class locomotive, a 1+D+D+D-1 giant of 270 tons rated at 9,750hp (7270kW) with an overall length of 82ft 4in (25.0m).

In Switzerland and Austria, the celebrated 'Crocodile' electric locomotives were created specifically to cope with the steep gradients and tight curves of the region's mountainous railroad lines. These 1-C+C-1 type locomotives were so called because the centre cab windows ('eyes') and the sloping machinery compartment ('jaws') suggested that decidedly non-alpine reptile. Switzerland also produced a variety of experimental multi-axle locomotives for the Gotthard route, including a 1-A+A-1-A+A-1+1-A+A-1-A+A-1 that was a remarkable 111ft 6in (34.0m) in length and weighed 604,800lb (274337kg).

The first main-line electrification in North America was on the Camden to Waverley stretch of the Baltimore & Ohio Railroad's system, and it was here that the railroad introduced 1,440-hp (1074-kW) locomotives turning the scales at 215,040lb (97542kg) and able to haul a 1,870-ton train. The Pennsylvania Railroad, the largest electric operator among the main operators, used the renowned sleek and powerful dual-voltage 'GG1'-class units, which ran passenger services between New York and Washington D.C. These 2-Co+Co-2 machines weighed 515,200lb (233694kg), were 79ft 6in (24.23m) long and had a continuous rating of 4,260hp (3176kW). The Virginia Railroad introduced 30 'Triplex' 1-B-B-1+1-B-1+1-BB-1 locomotives 152ft (46m) long and capable of handling trains of 5,350 tons on 1/50 gradients between Mullens and Roanoke.

Japan had some powerful Bo-Bo+Bo-Bo machines on its Tokaido line, but one of the high points of electric locomotive capability in the 3ft 6in (1.067m) gauge fell to South Africa, where three '3E' 1,200-hp (895-kW) locomotives, working in multiple, hauled 1,500-ton trains from 2,210ft (675m) to 4,980ft (1520m) on the line linking Pietermaritzburg and Glencoe. Such was the pace of development, though, that by the 1980s three '9E' class 5,070-hp (3780-kW) locomotives built by GEC of England and working in multiple, were handling 20,000-ton coal trains on 1/250 gradients.

The 200 miles (322km) of electrified route eastward out of the Indian port of Bombay is notable for some very steep gradients in the Ghats on the route to Igatpuri. In 1925 the railroad received C+C locomotives weighing 268,800lb (121928kg) and producing 2,100hp (1566kW) together with 2-Co-1 and 2-Co-2 passenger machines with a tractive effort of 33,600lb (15241kg), but in 1951 it was able to start replacing these earlier locomotives as it took delivery of its first Co+Co machines each weighing 275,520lb (124976kg) and providing a tractive effort of 75,000lb (34020kg).

In the U.S.S.R. (now Commonwealth of Independent States), the Siberian part of Russia east of the Ural mountains can boast the largest locomotive in the Asian continent. This 'WL-86' class double Bo+Bo+Bo unit is 147ft 6in (45.0m) long and weighs 671,958lb (304800kg), and is operated on the section of the Trans-Siberian Railway connecting Lake Baikal and the Amur river. Built at Novocherkassk in 1985/6, this unit develops 15,287hp (11398kW) and is capable of 100mph (161km/h).

Switzerland has often pioneered the effective use of modern railroad technology. This fact is as true today as it ever was, as indicated by the '465' class of Bo-Bo locomotives each weighing a mere 180,776lb (82000kg) but providing a one-hour power rating of nearly 9,400hp (7009kW). In July 1996 two similar '460' and two '465'-class engines, positioned in a 3,212-ton freight train, lifted it over the 1/37 gradient of the Lötschberg at speeds on the climb ranging from 31 to 43mph (50 to 70km/h) – all in all, a truly prodigious performance.

OPPOSITE

ABOVE: *An English Electric Type 3 trundles under a bridge with a train of empty hoppers heading south towards London.*

BELOW: *Modern freight trains can deliver raw materials to the very heart of industry.*

THIS PAGE

ABOVE: *China's coal-train network is highly developed. Here a double-headed train wends its way to Gantang.*

RIGHT: *Union Pacific locomotive No. 6936 B with mixed freight and passenger trains.*

Chapter Five
FAMOUS TRAINS OF THE 20TH CENTURY

PAGES 254-255: The east-bound San Francisco Zephyr *climbs Echo Canyon, Utah, behind F40PH locomotives 319 and 354.*

RIGHT: Eurostar *3015/3016 of the London–Paris service passing the old Folkestone Racecourse, England.*

PAGE 257: Castle-class 4-6-0 7001 *Sir James Milne near Westerleigh, England with the* Cornishman.

257

Famous Trains of the 20th Century

Although much, indeed the majority of the work undertaken by railroads and railways is of the workaday type, in tasks as humdrum as the movement of freight and commuter passengers, there have always been a number of passenger services that have nonetheless managed to capture the imagination. This is possibly due to the great expanses of terrain these services occasionally cover, the romantic nature (real or supposed) of the cities they link, or simply because of the phenomenal beauty or ruggedness of the country through which they pass. These services came into existence and became famous comparatively soon after the introduction of the steam locomotive and the longer journeys that were made possible for larger numbers of passengers, and the fact that they caught the attention was signalled by the romance of the names which were given them. Some of these named services have disappeared for compelling political or economic reasons, the latter generally involving the emergence, during the last quarter of a century, of air transport as the primary means of mass transportation over longer distances; but others have adapted and survived to become listed as some of the most famous services of the 20th century.

In North America, only one transcontinental train journey for passengers is still operating across Canada, over a distance of 2,776 miles (4467km). This route connects Toronto toward the eastern side of the country with Vancouver on its western seaboard, and is the so-called Canadian National Route operated by the VIA Rail Corporation. The service operates three times per week as the *Canadian*, a name taken over from Canadian Pacific, the operator which inaugurated the route during 1954 using the first streamlined sleeper train to run in Canada. The *Canadian* takes three days and nights to cover the route, which is a combination of touring and point-to-point transport. Thus the *Canadian* includes cheaper accommodation for the passengers using the service for point-to-point transport, and that which is more expensive for the passengers taking the train for its touring aspect and therefore prepared to pay a premium for more comfort and superbly refurbished public cars, which include club, dining and observation units.

Although the railroad services across Canada once started in Montreal, today's starting point is Toronto, and the route proceeds via Capreol (near Sudbury, Ontario), Sioux Lookout, the Manitoba lake district and Winnipeg, which lies 1,217 miles (1958km) distant from Toronto. At Winnipeg the *Canadian* halts for one hour, and then continues west across the rolling grain-farming plain of central Canada to Saskatoon, Saskatchewan and Edmonton in Alberta. Leaving the plains, the *Canadian* then climbs into the Rocky Mountains. The first stop in the mountains is Jasper, where the *Canadian* rests for 70 minutes while some of the cars are diverted to the *Skeena*, another classic Canadian service that connects Edmonton with the western seaboard at Prince Rupert. Now smaller, the *Canadian* pushes on through the Rockies, traversing the Yellow Head Pass before dropping down to Kamloops. From here it embarks on the final stage of its route, travelling alongside the Fraser river, which carried the tracks of the Canadian Pacific Railway on its other bank, down to the terminus at Vancouver on the third morning from the departure of the service from Toronto. The essentially non-stop nature of the service means, inevitably, that some of the finest scenery is passed unseen in the night, but the scheduling of the service ensures that the best views in the Rocky Mountains are seen in daylight.

It is worth noting that Canada could

once offer three transcontinental routes, but experience soon revealed that there was inadequate traffic to support all three. One of the routes closed, leaving just two after the establishment of Canadian National out of the previous Grand Trunk, Canadian Northern and Grand Trunk Western privately owned systems. Up to 1967 there were four transcontinental services every day from the eastern terminus at Montreal. Competition from jet-powered aircraft was certainly a major factor in the scaling-down of these services, but another and indeed more damaging factor was the inauguration of the Trans-Canada Highway in 1968. The loss of traffic meant that the service was very soon scaled down to one train three times per week, but this schedule now seems secure through the combination of steady point-to-point traffic and its inclusion in the plans of a growing number of tourists, especially from Germany, the U.K. and the U.S.A.

Farther to the south, in the United States, James J. Hill was appreciated then as now to be a giant of the railroad business. By 1901 Hill controlled three American railroads serving what was then little more than the wilderness of the Pacific North-West region. These railroads

were the Great Northern, the Northern Pacific and the Burlington, which were collectively known as the 'Hill Railroads'. Hill's single most celebrated train was the *Oriental Limited*, which connected Chicago, Illinois and the Twin Cities of Minneapolis and St. Paul, Minnesota with Seattle, Washington, where connection could be made with steam ships also run by Hill to link the Pacific North-West with

OPPOSITE: The majestic mountains of Canada create scenery of phenomenal ruggedness and beauty to delight the eye of the railroad passengers.

BELOW: Royal Hudson-class 4-6-4 locomotive 2860 British Columbia, *running on British Columbia Railway's North Vancouver to Squamish excursion, above the strait of Georgia, in the late 1970s.*

Japan and China. During 1929, after the trans-Pacific route had faded from importance, the railroad created a magnificent transcontinental service that it named in honour of Hill as the *Empire Builder*.

Although the Great Northern and Northern Pacific, which also served Seattle from the Twin Cities, operated separately from each other, the creation during 1971 of the semi-nationalized Amtrak as a federal corporation resulted in the decision that only the Great Northern route, closer to the U.S. border with Canada, should carry a prestigious passenger train while the more southerly Northern Pacific concentrated on freight services. The prestige service is still called *Empire Builder*, and is probably the best transcontinental railroad service in the U.S.A. and, since 1980, has been able to boast an operation with most modern 'superliner' equipment including day cars, a dining car, a sightseeing lounge car and sleeping cars, all 17ft (5.2m) above track level for the best possible fields of view consonant with safe operation.

The first 427 miles (687km) of the route, from Chicago to St. Paul, are over the Burlington Railroad's tracks, but from St. Paul over the distance of 1,795 miles (2888km) to Seattle, the Great Northern's tracks are used, and the whole journey is 2,222 miles (3575km). The eastern terminus is the Union Station in Chicago, and from here the route proceeds basically west via Milwaukee, along the Mississippi river virtually to the Twin Cities, and then the open plains west of Minneapolis. During its

OPPOSITE: *From the comfort of the domed observation cars, passengers could enjoy the spectacular scenery of the Rockies, clearly visible from the* Canadian.

ABOVE: *Special carriages on Canadian trans-continental trains enabled passengers to enjoy to the full the superb panorama.*

ABOVE RIGHT: *The staff of the Canadian National Railways' ticket office, Vancouver, British Columbia.*

RIGHT: *A telegraphy operator at his job, 1942.*

first night on the tracks, the service halts at Fargo, the town where the Wells Fargo (and precursor of the current American Express) was established, and during the morning of the following day passes Rugby, where an obelisk outside the depot indicates the geographical centre of North America. The *Empire Builder* continues through the plains, in the process passing Glasgow and Havre, to reach Browning, Montana and the start of the climb to and passage over the Rocky Mountains. As the train ascends the eastern side of the mountains, passengers can see to their right the 8,000-ft (2440-m) Triple Peak Divide mountain, whose melting snows in the spring supply water for streams and then a river that finally end in three oceans, namely the Atlantic, Pacific and Arctic. The *Empire Builder* advances

majestically through the magnificent Glacier National Park before crossing the Continental Divide at Marias Pass at an altitude of 5,236ft (1596m), the lowest pass of any railroad route through the Rocky Mountains. From here the *Empire Builder* travels through a country of massed mountains and rivers to Spokane, Washington, and here the portion of the train destined for Portland, Oregon is separated before the rump of the service continues over the final stretch of its journey toward Seattle by means of the Cascade Tunnel, which is 7.75 miles (12.5km) in length and was opened in 1929 as the longest tunnel of the Western hemisphere.

On the other side of the U.S.A., the state of Vermont is regarded as possibly one of the prettiest regions of the country, bordered on its east and west by the states of New Hampshire and New York respectively, and celebrated for its dairy farms, maple syrup and skiing. After the 1995 cancellation of the *Montrealer* as the night service connecting Washington D.C. and Montreal, Canada, Amtrak started a daylight service between Washington and St. Albans, Vermont. Appropriately named the *Vermonter*, the train is operated with the aid of state resources, and is one of the most popular operations in the north-eastern part of the U.S.A. The service includes a distinctive baggage car carrying the name of the train, and the *Vermonter*

also stops at rural towns in Massachusetts, New Hampshire and Vermont which, in the absence of the *Vermonter*, would lack any form of public transport.

Between St. Albans and Palmer, Massachusetts, the *Vermonter* runs over the tracks of the New England Central, a short railroad run by RailTex, a major Texas-based operator of short railroad routes. The New England Central began services during February 1995, only a few months before the inauguration of the *Vermonter*, on tracks once controlled by the Canadian National by means of its Central Vermont subsidiary. South of Palmer, the *Vermonter* reaches Springfield over the tracks of Conrail's Boston Line, and covers the stretch between

Springfield and New Haven on the tracks of the Springfield branch of the North-East Corridor, and then follows the main route of Amtrak's most busy Corridor route the rest of the way to Washington. There can be little doubt, however, that the most interesting section of the entire journey is the portion over the New England Central section, and here the *Vermonter* serves Amherst in Massachusetts and the towns of Brattleboro, Bellows Falls, Windsor, White River Junction, Randolph, Montpelier, Waterbury, Essex Junction and St. Albans in Vermont. During the summer and early autumn, the *Vermonter* shares Bellows Falls depot with the privately operated Green Mountain passenger service carrying tourists on a round trip to Chester, Vermont.

The northbound service departs Washington early in the morning and reaches St. Albans during the evening, while the southbound service reverses this schedule, reaching Washington at about the time its counterpart arrives in St. Albans.

The Western Railroad of Massachusetts was established as a pioneering mountain railroad, and in its original form as completed in the early 1840s departed from Boston, Massachusetts to pass over the Berkshire Hills before connecting with the Erie Canal at Albany, New York. The nature of the route, with a number of fairly long and steep gradients, required the use of powerful steam locomotives. During 1867 the Western Railroad merged with the Boston & Worcester Railroad to form the Boston & Albany Railroad, and in 1900 the New York Central Railroad leased the

OPPOSITE: *Amtraks's Chicago-Pacific Coast* North Coast Hiawatha.

ABOVE: *Chicago, Milwaukee, St. Paul & Pacific 4-4-2, on train No. 21, Chippewa, near Deerfield, Illinois, with five cars going at top speed of 80mph (129km/h), 18 September 1939.*

ABOVE RIGHT: *Chicago, Milwaukee, St. Paul & Pacific 4-6-4, leaving Milwaukee, Wisconsin with train No.101, Afternoon Hiawatha, with 13 cars and a top speed of 61mph (100km/h). The Hiawatha expresses were the fastest scheduled steam trains ever to run.*

RIGHT: *Amtrak's express North Coast Hiawatha, with vista-dome cars in evidence, rolls through the Minnesota countryside en route between Chicago and Seattle.*

LEFT: Milwaukee Road's (Chicago, Milwaukee, St. Paul & Pacific Railroad) Hiawatha at Columbus, Wisconsin.

BELOW: Amtrak passenger express train with 'double-decker' cars.

route. Since that time, the ownership of the route has changed hands on a number of occasions, but the line is still generally known in New England as the 'B&A'. This section now constitutes the single most attractive element of the route travelled by the Boston segment of Amtrak's *Lake Shore Limited* service. This runs on a daily basis over the distance of 1,017 miles (1636km) connecting Chicago's Union Station and South Station in Boston, and in the segment between Chicago and Rensselaer, New York the *Lake Shore Limited* shares with the New York service.

The eastbound *Lake Shore Limited* departs Rensselaer in the middle of the day for a gentle cruise over the Berkshires, climbing out of the valley of the Hudson river by means of a section of track to the Post Road junction abandoned in the early 1970s after the Penn Central Railroad, which then owned the Boston & Albany, ended the passenger service on the grounds that as all freight traffic made use of the Castleton Cutoff west of Post Road to Selkirk, the passenger line to Albany was no longer required. After Amtrak had revised the passenger service, however, the old track was put back into operation. East of Chatham, New York, the track passes over the New York State Thruway, and soon after this traverses the State Line tunnel, thus named as it is located near the New York and Massachusetts state line. The State Line tunnel has a parallel pair of tunnels, but the northern tunnel was closed down in the latter part of the 1980s. East of Pittsfield, Massachusetts the track begins

LEFT: Rolling effortlessly over the Continental Divide at Marias Pass, in the Montana Rockies, Great Northern Railway's famous Empire Builder *speeds westwards toward Seattle and Portland.*

The Empire Builder's *four great domes provide views like these as the streamliner skirts the southern boundary of Glacier National Park for 60 scenic miles.*

BELOW: The eastbound Empire Builder *leaves Belton depot at West Glacier, Montana, heading towards the Rockies and Glacier National Park.*

the climb up to Washington Summit at an altitude of 1,459ft (445m), the highest point on the old B&A. Near Middlefield, on the slope to the east of the track, there are several of the classic stone bridges built by George Washington Whistler, who originally surveyed and built the line, but which was abandoned in 1912 after the track had been revised onto a line of reduced gradient. The westward service from Boston is generally less attractive to the touring traveller because, except during the longest days of summer, the service passes through the most attractive regions at night.

Covering the 2,000 miles (3219km) between Chicago and Oakland, California, the *California Zephyr* is one of the most popular of the western services now operated by Amtrak, for its progress takes the service through some of the most magnificent scenery in the west between the huge Colorado Front Range and the coast of California. The service also covers the 'big ten' curves west of Denver, Colorado, crosses the Continental Divide by means of the celebrated Moffat Tunnel, passes through the deep Gore and Glenwood Canyons, traverses the Utah Desert and climbs over Soldier Summit to reach Salt Lake City, Utah. The service then moves through the deserts of Nevada, climbs over the Donner Pass in California, and finally travels across the Central valley and along the Carquinez Straits to Oakland.

In overall terms, therefore, the *California Zephyr* can be characterized by the splendour of the country through which

ABOVE LEFT: Interior view of Amtrak coach No. 34100 on the Desert Wind *express in Union Station, Ogden, Utah.*

ABOVE: Amtrak's eastbound California Zephyr *loads up in Sacramento, California.*

LEFT: Amtrak's westbound California Zephyr *leaving Glenwood Springs, Colorado, hauled by an F40PH locomotive.*

BELOW: *Amtrak's eastbound* California Zephyr *leaving Green river, Utah behind a F40PH locomotive.*

RIGHT: *Amtrak's westbound* California Zephyr *travelling through Glenwood Canyon, Colorado.*

LEFT: Amtrak's eastbound California Zephyr *heads away from Green river, Utah, with the Roan cliffs in the background. It has three F40PH locomotives, two baggage cars and 12 coaches.*

OPPOSITE: An Amtrak three-powered unit hauls double-decker cars on an express train.

it passes for most of its distance, whereas most other classically beautiful routes have only isolated sections of excellence. Among the other highlights of the route covered by the *California Zephyr* are those of the climb from the Great Plains to the heights of the Front Range, where there are apparently endless horizons, and the west slope of Donner Pass as the service crosses the Smart Ridge dividing the Yuba and American river valleys and aligns itself with the American river canton: as the river disappears into this deep split in the earth, the railroad track continues high on the northern side of the ravine along the route laid out in the 1860s by the Central Pacific Railroad. At American, just to the east of Alta, California

the track adheres to the very lip of the canyon some 2,000ft (610m) above the river's swirling waters.

The original *California Zephyr* service was launched in 1949 but was terminated during 1970. The current service covers basically the same route except for the use of the Donner Pass rather than the original Feather river canyon. Amtrak's revived *California Zephyr* service was started in the middle of the 1970s, but it was 1983 before it began to use the Denver & Rio Grande Western Railroad's line over the Front Range.

The 1,389-mile (2235-km) *Coast Starlight* route, which links Seattle and Los Angeles, California, is Amtrak's most

prestigious service on the western seaboard of the U.S.A. The *Coast Starlight* provides first-class accommodation as well as superb country along the full length of the route: as the advertising material has it, the *Coast Starlight* is the 'hottest train with the coolest scenery'. The service crosses several ranges of mountains, including the Cascade and Coast Ranges in Oregon and California respectively, and to the south of San Luis Obispo, California, travelling along the Pacific coast for some distance. At Oakridge to the south of Eugene, Oregon, the *Coast Starlight* starts its climb into the Oregon Cascades. The Southern Pacific Railroad built the Cascade Route during the mid-1920s, when it inaugurated the Natron

Cutoff between Black Butte and Eugene, and this is among the most phenomenal tracks in the west of the U.S.A. A short distance from Oakridge, the tracks pass across a tall trestle structure at Heather among towering evergreen trees, and then climb their twisting way up the mountain through a series of long snowsheds and tunnels. In the region of Cruzatte, the tracks pass from a tunnel into a snowshed, then traverse a tall curved trestle over the Noisy Creek into another snowshed, then enter a long curved tunnel.

The view from the *Coast Starlight* is splendid in the summer, but truly superb in the winter when the trees around the tracks are burdened with pristine white and the snowsheds really fulfil their task of

protecting the tracks from the snowy avalanches. Unfortunately for the traveller, the southbound *Coast Starlight* generally passes over the Cascades at night during the winter months, although the northbound service does not suffer from this disadvantage.

Amtrak does not serve San Francisco directly, but passengers for this metropolis can alight and board a bus service at Emeryville station, or alternatively transfer to a Cal Train commuter service at San

Jose. In Oakland, the *Coast Starlight* runs down the Embarcedero through Jack London Square, where the service halts at Oakland depot. Between the agricultural region of the Salinas valley and San Luis Obispo, the *Coast Starlight* advances over the 14 miles (22.5km) of the steep Cuesta Grade, a section of the railroad that winds through some of the most attractive scenery in California. Further progress takes the *Coast Starlight* through Vandenberg Air Force Base, and to the north of Santa

Barbara the tracks pass over a huge trestle at Gaviota before paralleling several popular beaches. The southern terminus of the service is Los Angeles' Union passenger terminal, one of the United State's last great passenger stations, which was completed only in 1939.

The country to the south of the U.S.A. is Mexico, and here the 1961 inauguration of North America's newest transcontinental railroad opened the way for travellers to see canyons both deeper and longer than

the Grand Canyon in Colorado. Connecting the cities of Los Mochis, on Mexico's western coast, and Chihuahua, the 407-mile (655-km) Chihuahua Pacifico Railway is very successful, and provides the only surface transportation across the Sierra Madre mountains with the aid of 87 tunnels and 36 bridges as well as a triple loop at one stage, so that the tracks do not have too steep a gradient as they gain altitude. The summit of the tracks is 8,209ft (2502m) near the Divisadero halt,

the point at which the Barranca (copper) Canyon splits off from the almost equally incredible Ulrique Canyon.

Schemed toward the end of the 19th century as a freight route linking Texas and Central America with the deep-water ports of Mexico's western coast, the railroad progressed only with extreme difficulty and therefore took some 60 years to complete. There is now a schedule of two daily passenger services in each direction, resulting in what is generally believed to be among the five greatest scenic railroad services in the world, and there are also two daily freight services, one in each direction. The passenger services make an early-morning start to ensure that the best possible views are obtained by the passengers, whose numbers are swelled on one day a week by the attachment, at Sufragio, of the cars of the *Sierra Madre Express*, which are hauled to the junction from Nogales.

Altogether different, and redolent of another railway age, is the 234-mile (376-km) passenger journey by the Ferrocaril Presidente Carlos Antonio Lopez of the Paraguayan system between Asunción and Encarnación. This is the only part of the country's railroad system that carries passengers, and the trains are pulled by steam locomotives burning wood in their fireboxes. It was in 1861 that the first part of the route, linking Asunción and Paruguar, opened for business, and in 1889 the railroad was bought by a British-controlled operation, the Paraguay Central Railway. The line reached Encarnación in

ABOVE: Amtrak's Coast Starlight *leaves Seattle for Los Angeles and runs past the cargo yard, hauled by Nos. 547 and 568 locomotives with two baggage cars and ten coaches.*

LEFT: The Rio Grande Zephyr *runs into Glenwood Springs, Colorado on its westbound run to Salt Lake City in Utah, behind EMD E9 locomotives Nos. 5771, 5763 and 5762.*

OPPOSITE: Amtrak's eastbound San Francisco Zephyr *emerges from a tunnel and crosses the Weber river in Weber Canyon, Utah.*

1911, and was nationalized in 1961. The line was originally built in the 5ft 6in (1.67m) gauge, but in 1911 was narrowed for full interchangeability with the Argentine national railroad system.

The journey between Asunción and Encarnación takes between 14 and 18 hours, and from Asunción moves south-east through rolling country to Villarica, and from this point the rest of the trip is undertaken through a mixture of flat pampas grassland and marshy areas. At Encarnación the traveller can change onto a service for Argentina, the cars being hauled along the city's main street before being lowered into a ferry for movement, six cars at a time, to Posadas on the Argentine side of the Paraná river. The service between Asunción and Encarnación is operated

twice each week, and is hauled by old British locomotives, generally manufactured by North British of Glasgow or Yorkshire Engineering of Sheffield. There are only nine somewhat primitive passenger cars, the single sleeping car having been withdrawn in 1972 and the single dining car disappeared from service shortly after this.

On the other side of the Atlantic Ocean, and created on altogether smaller geographical and engineering scales, one of the most beautiful railway journeys in the U.K. is the 42-mile (67.5-km) service operated since 1901 between Fort William and Mallaig on the West Highland Line along the rugged west coast of Scotland. Departing from Fort William, virtually in the shadow of Ben Nevis, Britain's highest mountain, the service crosses the River Lochy and then the swing bridge over the Caledonian Canal. The line passes round the northern shore of Loch Eil to reach Locheilside at the western end of the loch. The line then proceeds a short distance

ABOVE: Amtrak's Coast Starlight *hauled by locomotives Nos. 642 and 555 passes the ARGO freight yards as it leaves Seattle for Los Angeles.*

RIGHT: Amtrak's Coast Starlight *to Oakland, Portland and Seattle leaving Los Angeles hauled by locomotives Nos. 569 and 567.*

OPPOSITE: Amtrak's Seattle–Los Angeles Coast Starlight *as it travels alongside the Pacific Ocean.*

along a narrow glen to reach the 21 arches of the celebrated Glenfinnan viaduct and, via this, Glenfinnan. Further progress takes the service to the edge of Loch Eilt. From Lochailort station, a sequence of short tunnels and then another viaduct carries the service across Glen Mamie to reach the Atlantic coast at Loch nan Uamh, and then another sequence of short tunnels ducts the line to Arisaig. Here the line turns north, and at Morar it crosses the River Morar before a final 3-mile (5-km) run to the station at Mallaig, a small port dedicated mainly to fishing.

The enjoyment that could be derived from the journey by the passenger was considerably enhanced by the availability of an observation saloon in which there was a running commentary on the interesting features of the route. These Gresley observation carriages were the last of their type in the U.K. and were also very popular with passengers, despite the fact that their use required additional payment, but they had to be withdrawn when the turntable at Mallaig was dismantled, thereby making it impossible for the railway staff to turn them. During the summer, some of the trains are hauled by steam locomotives.

The name *Flying Scotsman* began to impinge on the consciousness of Britain on the very first day of 1923, for it was on this date that the express service of this name was inaugurated, covering the 404 miles (650km) of the route connecting London and Edinburgh, the capital of Scotland. Express services on this route began in

1862, with a journey time of 10 hours 30 minutes, a figure that has been steadily reduced to a current figure in the order of 4 hours 30 minutes. In the period up to 1935, the *Flying Scotsman* was generally hauled by an 'Atlantic'-type locomotive in the section between King's Cross Station in London and Leeds, where the task was taken over by an 'A3'-class locomotive of the 'Pacific' type as far as Newcastle, where another Pacific-type locomotive took over for the final section to Edinburgh's Waverley Station.

After leaving King's Cross Station, the *Flying Scotsman* passed through nine tunnels and then across the Welwyn viaduct of 40 brick-built arches before steaming via Stevenage, Hitchin, Huntingdon, Peterborough, Grantham and Retford to Doncaster. Further northward progress was by means of Wakefield and Leeds. Here, after the engine had been changed, the train was reversed out of the station before turning north once more to reach Newcastle and another engine change before passage into the border regions around Berwick-on-Tweed. Crossing into Scotland, the line generally parallels the coast for the rest of the distance to Edinburgh.

Throughout its course, the *Flying Scotsman*, later hauled by diesel-engine locomotives and now by electric locomotives, passes through some of the most attractive scenery in the eastern part of England, and also traverses some excellent pieces of civil engineering of the heyday of the Victorian age. These artefacts include numerous bridges, viaducts and tunnels.

LEFT: Wood, not coal, fuels this Paraguayan locomotive.

OPPOSITE

LEFT: British Rail No. 37405 climbs slowly to County March Summit on the West Highland Fort William–Glasgow line, Scotland.

RIGHT: The Mallaig to Fort William service, headed by a Class 37 diesel, passes a lighthouse on the Caledonian Canal.

The London & North Western Railway, known as the *Irish Mail*, was the first service anywhere in the world to be named. The service, covering the 264-mile (425-km) route between London and Holyhead on the island of Anglesey off the north-western coast of Wales, where the ferry to Ireland is boarded, was originally known unofficially as the *Wild Irishman*, and first ran in August 1848. The service departed from Euston Station in London and began its exit from the British capital via the Primrose Hill tunnel and then, some 17 miles (27km) from Euston Station, the Watford tunnel, that was created so that the railway line did not cross the estate of the Earl of Essex. Some 35 miles (56km) farther along the tracks, the *Irish Mail* crossed over the Wolverton viaduct of six arches and then, 10 miles (16km) still farther on, the Kilsby tunnel that is 7,270ft (2216m) long and, at the time of its completion, the world's longest railway tunnel. Further

progress took the *Irish Mail* through Birmingham, Manchester, Crewe and Chester before it reached the north coast of Wales, where the main towns are Rhyl and Colwyn. Shortly after Colwyn, the line passes underground once more, in this instance to emerge on the other side of the headland known as Penmaen Mawr. In this region there was inadequate space between the mountain and the shore for the line, and in some places, as a result, the stone of the mountain had to be blasted, and in others large sea walls had to be constructed to allow the outward extension of the coastline so that there was room for the tracks to be laid. Covered ways were made to protect the railway line in areas where it was felt that it might be damaged by rocks and smaller stones falling from the steep side of the mountain. The work of pushing the line forward was severely hampered when,

during October 1846, the combination of a gale and a spring tide swept away a considerable part of the progress that had been made on the western side of the headland, and it was at this stage that the engineers decided that the better solution, then adopted, was an open viaduct to take the tracks into Bangor.

A fact worthy of recognition with regard to the line between London and Holyhead was the installation during 1860 of the world's first water troughs: laid between the two rails just to the east of Bangor, these troughs allowed the train to collect water as it proceeded, without the need for a halt on the section between Chester and Holyhead. The *Irish Mail* then reached the Menai Strait between the mainland of Wales and the island of Anglesey. Here a classic railway bridge was built under the supervision of Robert

OPPOSITE: A winter view of the
Glenfinnan viaduct with the ex-LMS Class
5 No. 5305 crossing, heading for Mallaig.

LEFT: A Class 3714 No. 37405 crossing
the Glenfinnan viaduct on the Fort William
to Mallaig line in the Scottish Highlands.

Stephenson with a span of 1,100ft (335m)
over the fast currents of the strait.
Stephenson initially planned for the bridge
to be made of cast iron with intermediate
piers, but this plan was vetoed by the
Admiralty, which demanded that there
should be no obstruction of the strait as a
possible menace to shipping. Stephenson
considered a number of alternative plans
before opting, in March 1845, for the use of
tubular wrought-iron beams to create a
bridge with 460-ft (140-m) openings and
also a roadway, formed of a hollow
wrought-iron beam with a diameter of about
20ft (6m). The resulting Britannia Bridge
has four spans, two of them 460-ft (140-m)
long over the water and the other two 230-ft
(70-m) long over the land. The bridge was
opened for public use in March 1850, doing
away with the previous system in which the
railway passengers had been compelled to
disembark in Bangor and cross the Menai
Strait by coach by means of Telford's
suspension bridge, before re-embarking on a
train for the final stage of the journey to
Holyhead and the ferry to Ireland.

One of the most fascinating railway
journeys in England has for long been that
represented by the 304 miles (490km)
between London and Penzance, the latter

located at the south-western corner of the county of Cornwall. The line was inaugurated in August 1859, and at that time the train service halted at virtually every station and the passengers had also to change at Exeter and Plymouth before they arrived at Truro, where they were conveyed by horse-drawn carriage to Falmouth, where they boarded the West Cornwall narrow-gauge railway for the 33-minute culmination of their journey in Penzance. The fastest possible journey time from London to Penzance was 14 hours 50 minutes.

In 1862 the route saw the introduction of the *Flying Dutchman* service, which covered the route between Paddington Station in London and Churston on the Torquay branch of the South Devon Railway at an average of 56mph (90km/h), making feasible a time of 10 hours 20 minutes between London and Penzance. In 1863 the basic line was extended from Truro to Falmouth, removing the need for the horse-powered relay, and by 1867 the broad-gauge track of the Great Western Railway had been extended to Penzance. In 1890 the Great Western Railway introduced the *Cornishman* express service, which did not halt at as many stations and was therefore able to reach Penzance in only 8 hours 42 minutes. After the Great Western Railway had been forced to comply with the standard gauge of the other British railway companies, completing its conversion of the Penzance line in 1892, the *Flying Dutchman* was able to trim 15 minutes off its time, in the process becoming the world's fastest main-line

railway service. During 1896 the *Cornishman* recorded a time of 3 hours 43 minutes during a non-stop service to Exeter, at that time the world's longest non-stop route with a distance of 194 miles (312km), and trimmed the time to Penzance to 7 hours 52 minutes. During July 1904 the new *Cornish Riviera Limited*, running non-stop to Plymouth, reached Penzance in exactly 7 hours, further reductions in the

ABOVE: Gresley A3-class 4472 Flying Scotsman *at Carnforth. The* Flying Scotsman *service was inaugurated on the first day of 1923, and covered the 404 miles (650km) between London and Edinburgh.*

time coming in May 1914 with a figure of 6 hours 30 minutes and in 1927, after the introduction of the 'King'-class locomotives as the most powerful engines in Britain, to 6 hours 25 minutes.

Leaving Paddington Station, the train passes over the Wharncliffe viaduct, which was built in 1838 with eight 69-ft (21-m) spans, and the next notable feature of the journey is the Sounding Arch Bridge built in 1838 and widened in 1891. This bridge is one of Isambard Kingdom Brunel's masterpieces, and has two large but very flat brick-built arches each spanning 128ft (39m), but with a rise of a mere 24ft 3in (7.4m). Another major achievement in engineering terms is the Sonning Cutting, which is some 4 miles (6.5km) long and 60ft (18m) deep: the cutting was made in 1839 and opened in 1840 after considerable construction problems had been overcome. In its early period, a notable feature of the Great Western Railway's line to the south-west of England was the number of one-sided stations created under Brunel's supervision: both platforms were on the same side, but set a short distance apart, and this removed the need for passengers to cross the line (either over the tracks or by a bridge) to change between the up-train and down-train sides typical of other companies' stations. Such stations were built at Reading, Taunton and Exeter, but none now survives.

Located on the border between the counties of Somerset and Devon, the 3,274ft (998m) of the Whiteball Tunnel paved the way toward the flat, fast run

LEFT and BELOW LEFT: The Irish Mail *crosses the fast currents of the Menai Strait between mainland Wales and the island of Anglesey. The Britannia Bridge was built under the supervision of Robert Stephenson, who used tubular wrought-iron beams to create a bridge with four spans, two of them 460ft (140m) long over the water and two 230ft (70m) long over the land.*

BELOW: Throughout its history, the Flying Scotsman *has been hauled by steam engine, diesel engine and electric motive power. Here a Deltic 7 locomotive heads this famous train.*

279

LEFT: HST (High Speed Train) 43141 and 181 locomotive, on the Paddington to Penzance line in England.

OPPOSITE

LEFT: HST 43 and 43041 locomotive passing Talacre on the Holyhead–Euston line, nicknamed the Irish Mail.

RIGHT: A 47-class locomotive arrives at Penzance with the Cornishman.

along the coast of the English Channel, characterized by the Kennaway, Phillot, Clerk's, Coryton and Parsons tunnels between Dawlish and Teignmouth, and during 1905 the tunnels were widened so that a double-track arrangement could be introduced. Passing through Newton Abbot and proceeding still farther to the south-west, the line crosses from Devon into Cornwall by means of the Royal Albert Bridge, which is 1,109ft (338m) long and spans the River Tamar. The world's only

chain-link suspension bridge with the strength to support express trains, the Royal Albert Bridge should be regarded as Brunel's civil engineering masterpiece: two tubular main spans, each 450ft (137m) long, are supported by three piers that allow a clearance of at least 100ft (30m) from the water. The central pier, whose footings are anchored in rock 79ft (24m) below the river's high-water level, was constructed by masons working in a pressurized diving bell, and this was the first time such

equipment had been used for civil engineering. The construction of the Royal Albert Bridge took seven years, and was opened in May 1859, just four months before Brunel's death.

Over the 53-mile (85-km) section of the route linking Plymouth and Truro, the line passes over 34 viaducts. These were originally timber units designed by Brunel, but were later rebuilt in brick. Created to span the area's large numbers of deep but narrow valleys leading down into the sea,

the viaducts were made in two standard spans, with a length of 66ft (20m) for use on the Cornwall and Tavistock lines, and 50ft (15m) for use in western Cornwall. The line reached Penzance in March 1852, when it opened to standard-gauge trains, but 15 years later the Great Western Railway's broad gauge reached the town.

Despite the fact that the South Eastern & Chatham Railway and its successor, the Southern Railway, had operated services from Victoria Station in London to Paris,

France, it was May 1929 before this service was dignified with a name to indicate its special role. The name of this prestige service was the *Golden Arrow*, and while the first such trains were intended solely for first-class Pullman passengers and hauled by 'Lord Nelson'-class 4-6-0 steam locomotives, the onset of the depression led to the decision of May 1931 to add second-class accommodation to broaden the service's passenger base and thereby ensure its survival through lean times. In

the period following, the tractive effort was switched to rebuilt examples of the 'Merchant Navy' class of 4-6-2 locomotives, and then from 1951 these were in turn succeeded by 'Britannia'-class 4-6-2 locomotives.

The *Golden Arrow* was one of the first British trains to have a public address system for announcements in French as well as English as befitting an international service. Another notable aspect of the service was the inclusion of the so-called

Trianon cocktail bar, in which the more affluent passengers could ease their thirst. Carrying a Union flag and the French tricolour on the front of the locomotive, the *Golden Arrow* left Victoria Station at 11.00 a.m. every morning, and initially made only moderately fast progress as it navigated the gradients at Grosvenor Bridge, before the Penge tunnel and before Bickley Junction. A further limit on speed at this early stage of the journey was the need to steam through the cutting before Orpington, and

then after Tonbridge came two further gradients before the Sevenoaks tunnel. From this point to the British terminal at Dover Marine the line was essentially level, and this permitted a speed of up to 60mph (96km/h). At Dover Marine, 70 miles (113km) from Victoria Station, the train's carriages were loaded onto the rail-fitted ferry *Canterbury*, which covered the sea distance between Dover and Calais in only 1 hour 15 minutes. At Calais, the carriages were unloaded from the ferry and coupled to a French locomotive, a Pacific-type unit of the Nord railway, for the 184-mile (296-km) run to Paris with the translated name *Flèche d'Or*. The train reached Paris at 5.35 p.m.

The service that was later known as the *Orient Express* was launched during 1883 in eight countries by Georges Nagelmackers, a Belgian mining engineer who had established the Compagnie Internationale des Wagons-Lits to operate sleeping cars on the service linking Paris, Munich and Vienna in 1876. Nagelmackers added the suffix 'et des Grands Express Européens' to the name in 1883 at the time that the service was extended to Bucharest in Romania via Budapest in Hungary, the total journey time being 77 hours outbound and 81 inbound. Passengers wanting to travel to Constantinople (now Istanbul), the capital of the Ottoman Empire, had their journey extended to Giurgiu, where they were ferried across the Danube river to Rustchuk in Bulgaria for the seven-hour railroad trip to the Black Sea port of Varna, where they embarked on a steamer of the Austrian Lloyd line for the final stage to Constantinople. The total time from Paris to Constantinople was 82 hours.

It was appreciated that this route was hardly the most effective, so from August 1888 the service was altered from Budapest onward so that the train now travelled via Belgrade and Nis in Serbia (later Yugoslavia) and then the Dragoman Pass into Bulgaria. Here the service passed through Sofia, the capital, and then proceeded via Tatar Pazardjik to Plovdiv,

ABOVE: The Cornish Riviera Limited, *here photographed in 1953, originally began running in July 1904. It ran non-stop from London to Plymouth to reach Penzance in exactly 7 hours, though further reductions in time occurred later.*

LEFT: The Flying Dutchman *service covered the route between Paddington Station in London and, eventually, Penzance in Cornwall. The service was originally introduced in 1862.*

ABOVE: *No. 7029 comes off the Royal Albert Bridge at Saltash on its return trip to Truro, celebrating the first steam train from Devon to Cornwall since 1964.*

ABOVE RIGHT: *An 1859 engraving of the Royal Albert Bridge.*

where it moved onto the track of the Oriental Railway for the last leg into Constantinople. The total distance of this service was 1,996 miles (3212km), and this was covered in a little more than 67 hours.

From 1888 the service was considerably upgraded, and after this time the passengers had very comfortable sleeping cars as well as the other standard features of Wagons-Lits luxury, including a dining car serving the best French cuisine. It was in 1891 that the service finally received the name *Orient Express*, by which it is still known, and among the people who enjoyed its attractions were European diplomats, the nobility and at times even royalty.

The *Orient Express* departs from the Gare de l'Est in Paris, and then proceeds up the valley of the Marne river to the Champagne region toward Épernay and Châlons where, at a later date, provision was made for the addition of extra cars coming south from Calais for connections from the U.K. From Châlons the service steamed to Nancy after crossing the Moselle river and passed into Germany at Deutsch-Avricourt, thereafter travelling though Alsace and the Homarting-Arzwiller railroad tunnel that was paralleled by the tunnel for the Marne-Rhine canal. After passing Strassburg (now Strasbourg), the *Orient Express* crossed the Rhine river at Kehl and advanced into Baden-Württemburg. The route now

proceeded via Stuttgart, Augsburg and Ulm to Munich, the capital of Bavaria, and thence into Austria-Hungary at Simbach, although the crossing point was soon shifted past Lake Prien to Salzburg. The next halt was Vienna, the capital of the Austro-Hungarian Empire, and from 1894 the service here had a connection with the express service from Ostend in Belgium, passing from Austria into Hungary and then Romania via Bratislava, Budapest, Szged and Timisoara to Bucharest. From the Romanian capital the service crossed the Danube river by means of the Peiterwarden bridge and passed into Serbia at Subotica before an easy sector via Nis to Plovdiv, where passengers to Greece

283

ZURICH ARLBERG STAMBUL
STUTTGART BELGRAD STAMBUL

LEFT: The Orient Express *service, the epitome of luxurious and exotic travel, was launched (though not known by that name) in 1883, and continues to this day.*

OPPOSITE: In 1929, the prestigious train service operating from Victoria Station, London to Paris was given the name Golden Arrow, *and the locomotives carried both the Union flag as well as the French tricolour.*

changed. From Plovdiv, the *Orient Express* steamed down the valley of the Maritza river to enter Greece and pass along the coast of the Aegean Sea to Salonika (now Thessaloniki) and thence the Sirkeci station in Constantinople.

In 1900, the Wagons-Lits company launched a service linking Berlin and Constantinople via Breslau (now Wroclaw), thereby avoiding Vienna, but this experimental operation lasted only two years.

The *Orient Express* was abruptly brought to a halt in 1914 by the outbreak of World War I, both sides then adapting their passenger cars for use as railroad ambulance transports. During 1916, in the middle of World War I, the Germans established the Mitropa company to provide a service between Berlin and Constantinople, and employed requisitioned Wagons-Lits cars for this *Balkan Express* service designed to provide a significant link with their Turkish allies. After the Armistice that ended World War I in November 1918 there were moves to re-establish the *Orient Express* service as rapidly as possible, but the severe disruption of the physical infrastructure

during the war combined with political and economical turbulence after it to make the resumption of *Orient Express* services possible only in 1921. (Interestingly enough, this document was signed in the Wagons-Lits Dining Car No. 2419, which was later destroyed at Hitler's insistence by SS troops during 1944.) In 1923, as a result of the Franco-Belgian occupation of the Rheinland after Germany defaulted on the payment of its war reparations, the service was diverted via Zürich in Switzerland and the 6.5-mile (10.5-km) Arlberg tunnel, which had been completed in 1884, and this revision soon became permanent.

Other notable European services of the period included the Swiss *Arlberg-Vienna Express*, renamed the *Arlberg-Orient Express* in 1932, which ran from Vienna to Budapest via Hagyeshalom, and to Bucharest via Sighisoara, a sleeper service between Paris and Athens that ran twice a week, and a service between Paris and Istanbul that ran three times a week.

Disrupted again by World War II, even though there was for a time a more limited alternative operation between Zürich and

ABOVE LEFT: The Swiss main line was electrified in 1906, the same year the Wagons-Lits company started the Simplon Express *service as a major link connecting Paris and Lausanne in Switzerland.*

LEFT: The Brig portal of the Simplon Tunnel which was the longest tunnel in Europe up to 1991.

ABOVE, TOP and OPPOSITE: A pre-production prototype of a TVG (Train Grande Vitesse) at the Gare de Lyon, Paris during trials on existing track in 1979.

Istanbul, the *Orient Express* was resumed in 1947 with ordinary coaches as well as one or two sleepers and occasionally a dining car. The section between Budapest and Belgrade was terminated in 1963 when the *Tauern-Orient* sleeper service was inaugurated from Ostend to Athens, using the Tauern tunnel that had been completed in 1909. The service was withdrawn in 1976.

Today Wagons-Lits Austria still provides the staff for the sleeper service connecting Vienna and Paris, while a dining car of the Hungarian Railways provides *haute cuisine* on the route between Budapest and Salzburg, and Romanian railways operates the sleeper service between Budapest and Bucharest.

In 1906 the Wagons-Lits company started the *Simplon Express* service as a major link connecting Paris and Lausanne in Switzerland. The route used the recently opened Simplon Tunnel, which was the longest such tunnel in Europe up to 1991, and from Lausanne served Milan and Venice in Italy with the port city of Trieste, at that time part of Austria-Hungary, as its south-eastern terminus. The Viennese authorities would not allow any eastward extension of the service, however, and this meant that the *Simplon Express* covered a route shorter than had originally been planned.

After World War I, the Allied governments involved in the creation of the Treaty of Versailles (signalling an end to Germany's involvement in World War I) created the political framework for the *Simplon-Orient Express*. They asked the

Wagons-Lits company to run the route, which was expressly designed to provide a link between Western Europe and Romania and Yugoslavia, both recently liberated from occupation, as well as Greece. The new service avoided Austria and Hungary, now separate countries, as well as Germany, which was also forced to allow the resumption of the *Orient Express* service through its territory.

The start of the *Simplon Express* was later moved farther north to Calais on the southern coast of the English Channel, and the connection between the Calais Maritime station and the Gare de Lyon in Paris was provided by the route that had been opened in 1870. From Paris the *Simplon Express* followed the Seine river valley to the Laroche-Migennes point at which a fresh locomotive replaced the original unit, after which there was an easy gradient up to the Blaizy-Bas summit and then a descent to Dijon, the capital of the Burgundy region. Here the route altered to the east, the line climbing from an altitude of 950ft (290m) at Mouchard to 2,955ft (900m) at the entrance to the Mont d'Or tunnel, which opened in 1915 and passes through the Jura mountains to Vallorbe in Switzerland. Before the completion of the tunnel, the *Simplon-Orient Express* was routed through Pontarlier to Vallorbe.

After crossing the Orbe river, the train joined the Swiss main line, which had been electrified in 1906, on the section between Neuchâtel and Lausanne, and then continued along the shore of Lake Geneva through Montreux before following the

Rhine valley to Brig at the mouth of the Simplon Tunnel. The line emerged from the tunnel at Iselle in northern Italy, and from this point the Swiss-operated line dropped some 1,180ft (360m) over a distance of 17 miles (28km) through the Trasquera tunnel, Iselle station, the Varzo Spiral Tunnel, five smaller tunnels and the larger Preglia tunnel, before joining the Italian railway system at Domodossola. On the Italian section of its route, the *Simplon-*

Orient Express passed Lake Maggiore, and followed the flat line, completed during 1848, from Milan to Venice, passing Lake Garda and Verona. After reversing out from Venice, the train then crossed the causeway to Venice-Mestre, where the line rejoined the coastal main line outside Trieste.

All the passengers had to change at Trieste, but westbound passengers were permitted to sleep in the standing train and catch the connection to Paris during the

following morning. From Trieste, the line climbed from sea level to 985ft (300m) at Poggioreale del Carso on the current frontier between Italy and what is now Slovenia but was then part of the Austro-Hungarian empire. The route of the *Simplon-Orient Express* through Laibach (now Ljubljana) and Agram (now Zagreb) continued to Vinkovci-Belgrade and Nis, where it divided: one part went to Constantinople on a thrice-weekly basis and

the other to Athens twice weekly. The Constantinople train also had connections to Bucharest, reached via the Vinkovci-Subotica branch line that crossed the Romanian frontier over the Danube river near the Iron Gates. The service provided by the *Simplon-Orient Express* for the entire 2,150 miles (3460km) between Calais and Constantinople took three nights and four days in each direction.

The service's celebrated blue-and-gold

OPPOSITE: Eurostar *3016/3015 approaching the Willesborough level-crossing to the east of Ashford in Kent. The crossing is manually operated and the keeper's hut is just out of view in the left foreground. Note the signboard on the right.*

RIGHT: The Eurostar *London–Paris (via the Channel Tunnel) high-speed service moved swiftly from the date of its inception in 1987 to its service debut in 1994. Because of the Channel Tunnel restrictions, it has only two power cars, one at the front of the train and one at the rear.*

sleeping cars, which were of all-steel construction, first appeared in 1926, four years after their debut on the *Train Bleu*, which was the prestige service linking Calais and San Remo via Nice. By 1929 the *Simplon-Orient Express* was able to offer a daily service from Paris to Istanbul, and this service included a dining car and sleeping cars. During 1930 the *Simplon-Orient Express* became the main prop of the Wagons-Lits company's *Taurus Express*, an even longer route that linked London with Cairo, the capital of Egypt.

The *Simplon-Orient Express* was somewhat revised in 1932, when Ostend-Orient, Amsterdam-Orient, Berlin-Orient, Prague-Orient, Vienna-Orient and Paris-Orient or Arlberg-Orient sleeping cars started to join the service at Belgrade on different days. This provided three daily Istanbul sleepers and two services daily (four from Thessaloniki) to Athens. In overall terms, the *Simplon-Orient Express* can be regarded as a highly romantic (or perhaps romanticized) service whose advertising consciously played not only on the luxury of the operation but also on the 'mystery' of what had until the end of World War I been the Ottoman Empire that had long entranced the thoughts of many Europeans. The service was a popular medium for any number of the Balkan nobility, and King Boris liked to drive the engine of the *Simplon-Orient Express* in Bulgaria. The Wagons-Lits company maintained reserves of block ice, coal and rolling stock all along the route, and this permitted the maintenance not only of an

almost notorious level of luxury and elegance on board, but also (and somewhat more prosaically) a considerable reliability of service in regions little noted at the time for their technical skills. Another feature of the service in the summer months was a shower in the baggage car. The Wagons-Lits company also provided daily dining cars for the Lausanne-Trieste-Svilengrad, Nis-Thessaloniki and Amfiklia-Athens sections of the route and it offshoots, and a kitchen van for the Uzunköprü-Istanbul section.

The outbreak of World War II in 1939 did not at first stop the travels of the *Simplon-Orient Express*, which was eventually brought to a temporary halt only in 1942, and individual sleeping cars with neutral Turkish staff served most of the overnight sectors. The *Simplon-Orient Express* resumed services to Istanbul during January 1946, and in 1949 added a branch service to Athens. The service in the period after World War II had lost much of its pre-war glamour, and this was exemplified by the fact that dining cars gradually became a rarity. The *Simplon-Orient Express* came to an end in 1962, and the last sleeping car service between Paris and Istanbul was operated in May 1977.

At the technical level of modern railroad operations, the 626-mile (1008-km) service between London and Berne, the capital of Switzerland, is one of the most fascinating examples that can be found. The service begins in London's St. Pancras Station at the terminal specially built for the so-called *Eurostar* trains, which operate regular services via the Channel Tunnel to

northern European termini at Brussels and Paris. Access to the passenger assembly hall is provided by barriers that automatically scan the service's special tickets: if the ticket is accepted, the barrier's gate opens to allow the passenger through to the security examination area. Every passenger with a first-class ticket is welcomed onto the train by a steward, one of whom waits by the door to each coach, and help can be provided for other passengers.

The design of the *Eurostar* train was undertaken on a collaborative international basis, and the group responsible for the design process based its work on the principles validated in the French TGV (*Trains Grande Vitesse*), but numerous changes were necessary to optimize the design for the new service: factors that had to be borne in mind included the need for the train to operate in the U.K.'s much more restricted loading gauge; the fact that the electrical supply was to come from three different systems, including current collection via a third rail in the U.K.; that there were to be four signalling systems; and that notably demanding safety standards were required for operation through the Channel Tunnel. The design of the train's exterior was British with a central driving position and one window in the front of the cab. The design of the train's interior was a joint Franco-Belgian undertaking, and the success of this team is more than amply suggested by the fact that the *Eurostar* has more usable volume than the TGV despite being smaller in its overall dimensions. At the technical level,

ABOVE and OPPOSITE LEFT: *Food and beverages are served in the TVG dining areas where passenger comfort is of the utmost importance.*

OPPOSITE RIGHT: *First-class passengers on* Eurostar's *service from Waterloo to Paris.*

especially in the mechanical and electrical aspects of the vehicle, the design team had a number of problems to solve and apparent conflicts to resolve. An instance of the type of problem to be overcome can be found in the particular safety requirements imposed on trains using the Channel Tunnel. It is necessary that passengers can be moved from one end of the train to the other, and this fact made it impossible for additional power units to be used in the middle of the 20-vehicle train: the *Eurostar* train therefore has just two power cars, located at the front and rear of the train, with additional powered bogies under the first and last passenger coach to compensate in part for the loss of the power that two equivalent TGV sets would have provided. Other features that had to be borne in mind were the need to reduce the overall size of

the bogies; the need to provide a taller pantograph to touch the high overhead contact line in the Channel Tunnel; the need to create steps that would automatically adjust to the different heights of the platforms in three countries; and the need to provide all the complicated signalling equipment that was required.

Despite the complexity of the project and the inherent difficulty of co-ordinating the efforts of a three-nation design and industrial team, the *Eurostar* was rapidly and successfully taken from the date of its inception in 1987 to the date of its service debut in November 1994.

At the end of the 20th century, the U.K. lacked any dedicated high-speed railroad tracks and, as a result, the *Eurostar* has to operate within the context of the dense and often considerably slower railroad traffic in

the south-east of England. In the south-eastern part of London, where the routes of the capital's railway lines were laid down in the 19th century and are therefore somewhat winding in their disposition, the necessarily slow speed of the *Eurostar* at least allows the passenger to see his surroundings. After it has emerged from the city and the suburbs into the countryside of Kent, the train can accelerate to about 100mph (160km/h), especially on the essentially straight section between Tonbridge and Ashford. A number of *Eurostar* services stop at the specially rebuilt Ashford station, which also caters for local and inter-city trains and thus makes feasible a measure of interchange as well as the boarding of passengers who have arrived by car. Shortly after leaving Ashford, the train switches from the British

Rail track network to that of Eurotunnel and arrives at the Dollands Moor conglomeration of sidings, depots and loading docks for cars and heavy goods vehicles. Here the shoes collecting current from the third rail are lifted and the pantograph is raised.

The beginning of the 21st century saw a vast upgrade on the UK side, with new high-speed tracks laid and a brand new terminal built at London's St. Pancras Station, bringing it up to a similar standard to the European side.

The Channel Tunnel is 31 miles (50km) in length and as such is the second longest railroad tunnel in the world, as well as the tunnel with the longest underwater section. In the Channel Tunnel and on the TGV lines onto which the train emerges on the French side of the tunnel, French cab

signalling is used to pass instructions to the train driver. The maximum speed permitted in the Channel Tunnel is 100mph, and the trip takes only about 20 minutes before the train hurtles out of the tunnel into France near the huge marshalling yards of the Coquelles terminal. The route to Paris lies through the new exchange station at Fréthun, and soon after this the train is travelling on the high-speed tracks through country that is basically level and therefore allowing the creation of a track possessing only gentle, sweeping curves. On this part of the journey it is generally announced on the train's public-address system that the maximum permitted speed of 186mph (300km/h) has been reached.

Facilities for exiting passengers at the Gare du Nord, where the *Eurostar* service from London terminates, are not good, and passengers needing to get to the Gare de Lyon to connect with the Swiss service need to travel by taxi or métro underground link. The TGV used for the service to Switzerland may be Swiss-owned, but is painted in the same livery as the French trains of the same type. Once embarked on the train, the passenger can quickly appreciate the generally superior nature of the *Eurostar* train he has recently quit, despite the greater height and width of the TGV.

The TGV leaves the Gare de Lyon comparatively slowly, for exactly the same reasons as the *Eurostar*'s progress through the southern part of London. However, in the region near the great marshalling yards at Villeneuve St.-Georges, the TGV is

ABOVE and RIGHT: Earlier examples of the French railway's TGV (Trains Grande Vitesse) locomotives which had the enormous advantage of running, right from the start, on specially built high-speed track.

passing into a less congested region and can begin to reveal its true performance, especially when, at Lieusaint, it joins the Ligne à Grande Vitesse, generally newly built and optimized for the TGV to operate at its maximum speed. The track in question is the Sud-Est LGV stretching to Lyons, Valence and, ultimately, Marseilles. The service to Berne and Lausanne uses this line only as far as Passilly, from where there is a short link to the older main line at Aisy. From Aisy to Dijon the track's alignment is good enough to allow the train to maintain a high speed until it is time to decelerate for the approach to Dijon's main station. The fastest services take a mere 99 minutes to complete the 196-mile (315-km) distance from Paris to Dijon.

After departing from Dijon, the TGV

veers from the Salines river valley and starts to climb toward the mountains, initially with good views to the right although, as the train climbs ever higher, the views become more restricted as a result of the defiles through which the train progresses. The train emerges from its climb to reach the plateau town of Frasne, where there is a rail junction. From here the main line runs straight ahead to Vallorbe, a small Swiss town just over the border, and then starts its descent with pleasant views across villages and farmland until its reaches Lake Geneva (Lac Leman) at Lausanne. The other line from Frasne heads off to the left and winds across comparatively flat land until it nears the mountain barrier of the Montagne du Lermont. The track follows a narrow defile through the mountains that is guarded by the

OPPOSITE: TGV No. 23122 (unit 61) at the Gare de Lyon, Paris.

town of Pontarlier, with its impressive castles high on the hillsides above the line of the rail and road tracks as these close on the Swiss frontier.

The first village the train approaches on Swiss soil is Les Verrières, and slightly farther on St.-Sulpice and Fleurier can be seen below and to the right in the Val de Travers. The railroad tracks carry the train past lovely scenery until a dramatic change brings panoramic views across Lake Neuchâtel. The town of Neuchâtel, again guarded by a castle, is old and lies on the important main line of communication between Basle at one end and Lausanne and Geneva at the other. Neuchâtel's station handles the traffic of the Swiss federal railways and, to a more limited extent, that of the Berne-Lötschberg-Simplon Railway, and it is on the tracks of the latter that the TGV now runs across the generally level and fertile broad plateau to Berne, where the service terminates in the curving and rather gloomy station, well situated near the centre of this small capital city after a run of 4 hours 32 minutes. The timing and speed of the combined *Eurostar* and TGV service between London and Berne are such that the passenger can board the train in London at 9.53 a.m., arrive in Paris at 2.08 p.m. (Central European Time), depart from Paris at 3.50 p.m. and arrive in Berne at 8.22 p.m.

In the northern part of Africa, the service on the main line connecting Casablanca and Gabès carries its passengers right along the south-west coast of the Mediterranean through North Africa

between the cities of Casablanca in Morocco and Gabès in Tunisia, a distance of some 1,105 miles (1778km) in all on a line whose construction was started in 1915. A French possession from 1840, Algeria was treated as a *département* of the metropolitan state, and its Société Nationale des Transports Ferroviaires was built and operated to the French standard as an essentially coastal network to provide communication along the coast of the three French possessions in North Africa. Constructed as a standard-gauge operation, the rail service was generally efficient and reliable in the period up to the outbreak of World War II, but then began to decline during this war and the troubled period following it as France sought to restore its position but faced growing demands for

independence from Morocco, Algeria and Tunis, which gained their objectives in 1956, 1962 and 1962 respectively.

Neither the Moroccan nor the Algerian railroads appear to be proud of their operations, and this is reflected in the essentially run-down nature of their services. Across Morocco from Fez to the Algerian border, the compartments are awash with the bodies of passengers seeking to rest on uncomfortable wooden seats. The border is reached at Oujda, which is a dull but not dismal town characterized by wide streets and solid housing of the European pattern. The initial stages of the passage through Algeria offer a number of odd aspects, including the sight of rusted train wrecks alongside the line before Oran, then an almost Moorish-

LEFT: A 4-4-2 locomotive, built in 1926, heads a passenger train in Cairo, Egypt in 1945. Note that the passenger carriages are painted white to reflect the heat.

OPPOSITE

The Union Limited *was a luxury one-class express service linking Cape Town and Pretoria in South Africa from 1910 and was extremely popular. Top left is the dining car; top right the observation car, and bottom left shows a cabin interior.*

OPPOSITE BELOW RIGHT: The Union Express *arriving at Johannesburg, South Africa, circa 1930.*

Spanish style is apparent in Tlemcen, while Sidi-bel-Abbès is wholly redolent of the French Foreign Legion. Even a brief look at Oran reveals the fact that the building of most North African appearance in the city is the railroad station, where it is claimed that the easiest method of securing a corner seat is to board the train and start a rumour that the train for the service in question is in fact just arriving at another platform.

As in many industrial countries, the railway route into the capital, in this instance from Oran to Algiers, is not a pretty sight as the track penetrates a seedy mass of industrial areas on its way toward the station nearer the centre of the city. Between Algiers and Constantine there are genuinely stunning rock formations and a deep ravine crossed by a slender bridge. The next main station is Annaba, and the service that resumes from this city is one of

the most interesting in the world for its awfulness, for it comprises third-class coaches in which a not inconsiderable number of compartments lack both seats and windows. The next major arrival is at Souk Ahras, the border town some 10 miles (16km) from the Tunisian frontier.

In Tunisia things change dramatically and, fortunately for the traveller, for the better. The train is moderately clean and in much better condition than its Algerian counterpart. On the way to Tunis, customs officers check the baggage of passengers by merely turning it upside down. The 118 miles (190km) between the border and the capital are of narrow metre-gauge track, and this explains why the passengers have had to change trains. In the south of the country, at Sfax, the traveller has to change

trains once more. The connection to Gabès is poor, however, and the trains that eventually arrive seem as reluctant as the traveller is eager to reach the end of the line after the trip from Casablanca.

Organized tourism up the River Nile is now more than 125 years old. The Thomas Cook & Son company, in the form of the son John rather than the father Thomas, began to operate tourist river steamers on the Nile from about the middle of the 1870s. The steamer operation was based in Cairo, Egypt's capital city that was linked with the country's main port of Alexandria by the Middle East's first railroad, constructed in 1855. This link included a bridge over the Nile outside Cairo that is also used by the service extending up the Nile to Aswan. Operating from the Cairo Main station, this service was inaugurated as the *Star of Egypt* by the Wagons-Lits company, which marked its silver jubilee in 1898 by expanding simultaneously into Russia and Egypt.

In Egypt, the company's cars were painted white to reflect heat and also had double roofs to help prevent its ingress, and the dining cars, built by Ringhoffer of the Austro-Hungarian empire, featured a type of primitive air-conditioning in which blocks of ice cooled the air circulating between the skins of the roof. The Wagons-Lits company, which was the great rival to Thomas Cook that it managed to buy in 1928 but lost once more during World War II, inaugurated the initial service between Cairo and Luxor in 1898 with a high-class arrangement that

LEFT: The Union Limited, *connecting Cape Town and Pretoria was renamed the* Blue Train *in 1939 and was painted in a blue-and-cream livery. The train was later hauled by an electric-powered locomotive, with blue-and-gold livery, as seen on this* Blue Train *near Fountains, Pretoria in the mid-1970s.*

OPPOSITE: Spectacular scenery and luxurious travel conditions have delighted passengers on South Africa's Blue Train *for many decades.*

included dining and sleeping cars. To a time at least as late as 1908 the lines extending up the Nile to Aswan were of the narrow-gauge type, and in this year the classic night train left Cairo on Mondays, Wednesdays and Saturdays, returning from Luxor on Tuesdays, Thursdays and Sundays. It was in the same year that the Luxor service was extended to Aswan, a 597-mile (960-km) journey. The line leaves Cairo, crosses the Nile on the Alexandria line bridge and then turns south along the Nile's left (west) bank through Asyût. The line recrosses the Nile at Nag 'Hamâdi, and thereafter follows the right (east) bank of the river to Luxor and Aswan.

In 1906, from the estate of the late George Mortimer Pullman, Lord Dalziel bought the British section of the Pullman operation as well as the exclusive right to the name Pullman on railroad cars

throughout Europe and Egypt. During 1907 Dalziel gave up these rights to Wagons-Lits, of which he was a director. Wagons-Lits began using Pullman cars in about 1925, and the new units for service in Egypt were shipped from England to Alexandria. More Pullman cars were shipped in 1929, when the *Sunshine Express*, an all-Pullman day train from Cairo to Luxor, was begun. New sleeping cars now operated in the night train, named the *Star of Egypt*. At Aswan it continued to El Shallal, above the cataracts and the Aswan Dam, connecting with steamers to Wadi Halfa, in the Sudan, where the Sudanese Railways line to Khartoum avoids a huge bend in the river. When the new Aswan Dam was built, the Aswan terminus

was forced to move to El Sadd el All.

The *Sunshine Express* service ended during 1939, but the sleeping cars were revived after World War II, and the *Star of Egypt* continued until about 1958–59, when the Wagons-Lits operation in Egypt was nationalized. The Egyptians then discovered that they could not really manage without the expertise of the original company, which was then permitted (indeed encouraged) to return, so that a joint company could be created to operate the service. The Hungarian sleeping cars that the Egyptian railroad had bought in the interim were then relegated to use on slow trains, and the modern all-sleeper train, with a lounge car, has rolling stock built in the 1980s by a West German

company: the dining car has been replaced by a supply car, and passengers take their meals in their cabins.

At the present, one train suffices on the service between Cairo and Aswan, as most people prefer either to cruise on the Nile or to fly. The railroad journey between Cairo and Aswan, now an all-sleeper service, takes some 16 hours, which is 30 minutes slower than the equivalent service in 1938.

Much farther to the south on the African continent, the major home of prestige railroad services in South Africa exists. The first luxury train to operate on the 3ft 6in (1.07m) gauge track over the 999-mile (1607-km) route between Cape Town and Pretoria, the country's political but not economic capital, was inaugurated

in 1903. This service was run by the Cape Government Railway and the Central South African Railway. Then in 1910, when the Union of South Africa was established, all of the country's independent railroad operators merged to create South African Railways, and the train service between Cape Town and Pretoria was then named the *Union Limited*. Although the train was a luxury one-class express, with a fare somewhat higher than was otherwise standard for the route, it was so popular that in the 1930s more coaches were added for extra capacity, and the smart Pacific-type locomotives hitherto used to haul the train, were replaced by 4-8-2 locomotives.

The twice-weekly train was renamed the *Blue Train* (*Bloutrein* in Afrikaans) during April 1939. This was not, of course, the first time a train service had operated with this name, for the *Train Bleu* service had connected Paris and the Côte d'Azur since the 1920s. This change of name in South Africa coincided with the introduction of new blue-and-cream cars with clerestory roofs, although the locomotives remained unaltered in South African Railways' black livery. The passenger compartments were of the super de-luxe type with dust-proofing and air-conditioning, and the accommodation included blue leather-upholstered seats, loose cushions and writing tables with headed writing paper. At the rear of the train was an observation car. In spite of the railroad track's gauge, the width of these coaches was 10ft (3.05m).

To ensure that there was adequate space

available for all the various on-board services, which included fully equipped bathrooms, the accommodation was limited to a mere 100 passengers on each journey, and this accommodation had to be booked many months in advance. The train is now hauled by electrically-powered locomotives with blue-and-gold livery between Pretoria and Kimberley and again between Beaufort West and Cape Town, and its schedule is three round trips weekly from October to March and one from April to September. The then President Mandela of the new 'multi-racial' South Africa inaugurated this new version of the *Blue Train* in June 1997. Built from the undercarriage of the original *Blue Train* sets, these two new trains feature only two levels of accommodation (luxury

and de-luxe) as opposed to the previous arrangement of four classes.

The luxury suites differ from the de-luxe accommodation in that they are more spacious and offer larger bathrooms, and whereas de-luxe features a private shower or bath, the luxury suites all have a bath. There is 24-hour butler service, laundry service and two lounge cars, and while all the accommodation has televisions and telephones, the luxury suites also feature little 'extras' in the form of CD players and video recorders. Another attractive and popular feature is the imaging provided by the TV camera positioned on the front of the train, and this provides the passengers with a 'driver's eye-view' of their journey.

The extensive nature of the upgrading

inevitably meant that the capacity of the *Blue Train* had to be reduced, in this instance from a maximum of 107 to just 84. The *Blue Train* no longer serves Johannesburg, but is instead routed through Germiston as it travels between Cape Town and Pretoria, which is also the southern terminus of the classic railroad service to the Victoria Falls in Zimbabwe (originally Rhodesia).

Railroads in what was then the Cape Colony started in 1857, when a pioneering 45-mile (72-km) line was opened from Cape Town to Wellington. In 1873 the first trains completed the 644 miles (1036km) on the route from Cape Town to Kimberley across the Karoo, and as the great imperialist and railroad pioneer Cecil

ABOVE LEFT: *Dining car on the* Trans-Karoo Express, *mid-1970s.*

ABOVE: *In contrast with the packed and noisy commuter trains leaving Cape Town, the long-distance express trains, such as the* Pride of Africa, *offer spacious and pleasant facilities.*

OPPOSITE and Page 48: *A Russia Class P36 heads a passenger train. Russian railways, particularly on the Trans-Siberian route, had strategic objectives as well as carrying passengers.*

Rhodes progressed northward through the southern part of Africa, the railroads were rapidly extended to the north: the 146-mile (235-km) section from Kimberley to De Aar was created in the impressively short period of 20 months between March 1884 and November 1885. This section between Cape South and De Aar is the southern part of the route covered by the *Pride of Africa* service from Cape Town to Victoria Falls via Beaufort West, De Aar, Kimberley, Klerksdorp, Johannesburg, Pretoria, Mafikeng (border), Gaborone, Plumtree (border), Bulawayo and Hwange.

The modernity of the flat-roofed station in Cape Town is perhaps an unlikely spot for the traveller to launch himself on one of the most fascinating and enjoyable railroad journeys anywhere in the word, but it is here that he boards the *Pride of Africa*. Impressive in its bottle-green livery, this train offers, right from the beginning, the promise of a truly memorable experience. At the head of the train, two '6E'-class Bo-Bo electric locomotives, in the livery of South African Railways, sit in a double-heading arrangement to haul the cars over the 440 miles (708km) to Beaufort West, in the course of which the train also climbs from the sea-level altitude of Cape Town to a height of more than 4,000ft (1220m) across the Karoo. Another fact that the traveller can hardly miss is that the spacious accommodation and quiet but friendly welcome onto the service contrast most starkly with the packed and noisy accommodation of the commuter trains linking Cape Town with its suburbs. The

nature of the *Pride of Africa* reflects the desire of Rohan Vos, the service's owner and creator, to offer the very highest of standards, and Vos often appears to see the service on its way as one of the world's most romantic travelling idylls. Rovos Rail is Vos's creation, and in 1986 the company started the restoration of old, derelict railroad cars and of the steam locomotives to haul them. Dating originally from 1919, each sleeping car, bar and lounge car as well as observation car, complemented by still older Victorian and Edwardian dining cars, were sympathetically renovated with nothing of the original 'flavour' lost as modern conveniences were incorporated. The accommodation provided in the sleeping cars comprises suites with double or twin beds, together with private showers and lavatories.

Spread beneath the flat-topped Table Mountain, Cape Town has one of the most dramatic locations on earth. As it begins its journey to the north, the *Pride of Africa* soon emerges from the city and rides the track round the edge of Table Bay before heading inland. In the wine-growing region of Paarl and the Hex river valley, there is a feeling of quiet but determined domestic economy, but an indication of the fact that the traveller is in the southern part of Africa is provided by glimpses of strangeness, such as scrub areas with ostriches clearly at home among sheep and horses. In the last glimmers of daylight, the train arrives at Matjiesfontein. Here there is a one-hour halt, allowing the traveller to investigate this small town in which, late in the 19th

century, Laird Logan set up a small refreshment hotel to restore the equilibrium of travellers on the service of the Cape Government Railways.

As the *Pride of Africa* now continues across the Karoo, most of the passengers gravitate to the observation car to watch the fantastic onset of the South African night, and the setting of the observation car, with its seven pairs of carved roof-supporting pillars and arches, is highly conducive to a feeling of time stretching nostalgically backward into the past. Later, the travellers gather for dinner and finally return to their suites for sleep. Despite the narrow gauge of the South African Railways' track, the ride of the *Pride of Africa* is quite smooth.

At Beaufort West the current changes from DC to AC, and two '7E'-class Co-Co locomotives are attached to haul the train to De Aar. There is now a 146-mile (235-km) stretch of non-electrified line from De Aar to Kimberley, and the electric locomotives are replaced by a pair of '34'-class Co-Co diesel-electric locomotives. During the following day the *Pride of Africa* reaches Kimberley's classic Victorian station. Kimberley, the centre of the South African diamond-mining industry, is located deep in the stark extent of the Karoo. Now with two high-speed '12E'-class Bo-Bo electric locomotives undertaking the traction, the *Pride of Africa* speeds from Kimberley toward Pretoria. The following day the service strikes north through groves of fruit trees, past African townships where flocks of children run down to the tracks smiling and waving, and enters the open country

where in the observation and lounge cars the traveller can embark on his railborne wild-life safari with the first sightings of varied herds of grazing animals.

Crossing into Botswana at Mafikeng, the *Pride of Africa* has the first of seven locomotive changes between Pretoria and the Victoria Falls. The train starts to climb the steep mountains that separate the lush, fertile Hex river valley from the elevated, arid Karoo. The climb of 1,750ft (535m) over a distance of 50 miles (80km) is the single most spectacular section of the journey and also has its highest point at a location just south of Johannesburg, at an altitude of 6,017ft (1834m). There is also a series of four completely straight tunnels in the 10.25-mile (16.5-km) Hex river tunnel system, which ranks it as the fourth largest of its type anywhere in the world.

The last complete day on the train is filled with spectacular views of the African bush. After crossing into Zimbabwe at Plumtree, an afternoon visit is made to Bulawayo, which was once the capital of the Matabele nation and later became the centre of mining in the area. Here the traction effort is assumed by a '15'-class Garratt articulated steam locomotive, and this vast machine hauls the *Pride of Africa* through the night along the 72-mile (116-km) stretch between Gwaai and Dete, one of the world's longest straight stretches. At Dete the service is on the eastern edge of the Hwange National Park, and the halt at Victoria Falls marks the end of the magnificent journey after a distance of some 2,000 miles (3218km).

ABOVE: The Japanese railway's Shinkansen below Mount Fuji on the Tokyo–Hakata line.

LEFT: A Shinkansen, typically mounted on a viaduct to avoid urban congestion.

OPPOSITE ABOVE and BELOW: A line-up of four Shinkansen 'bullet trains', while another awaits departure. A Shinkansen service leaves Tokyo every six minutes during peak periods.

It was during 1858, many thousands of miles to the north, that the first plans for a Trans-Siberian Railway linking Moscow and European Russia with the Pacific coast of Siberia were first promulgated. However, as a result of the Crimean War (1853–56), it was 1875 before an official plan was put forward. There followed a number of other schemes before the year 1891 finally saw the granting of official approval by the Russian government. Moreover, with a speed and determination that appeared unusual in the general lethargy of Russian development during the later part of the 19th century, the Tsarevich Nikolai cut the first sod of grass in Vladivostok. The planned railroad was clearly to be one of the world's greatest and most difficult engineering feats, and was seen by the Russian government as a primary aid in the task of consolidating Russia's hold on Siberia and its Far Eastern reaches on the shores of the Pacific Ocean, in the process improving both the Siberian and overall Russian economies as well as realizing the possibility of being able to exert political pressure on China.

Such was the size of the task faced by the Russians in the construction of the Trans-Siberian Railway that though work began in 1891, it was 1903 before the first through service was operated. This original level of service included a train ferry over Lake Baikal, the deepest lake in the world. During the winter, however, the ice covering the lake soon became too thick to be broken by any current ice breaker, so the train ran over the lake on a specially laid winter section of rail. The land link between Moscow in the west and Vladivostok in the east was finally completed in 1905 when the line round the southern edge of Lake Baikal was finished. Blasted out of the solid rock of the lake's shore, in places 4,000ft (1200m) tall, this 42-mile (68-km) link had no fewer than 38 tunnels which had to be bored, and the steepest gradient was located just to the east of Ulan Ude, where an incline of 1/57.5 had to be climbed.

At first, part of the route was laid across Manchuria (this section of the track is now the Chinese Eastern Railway) to create as direct a route as possible from Chita to Vladivostok via Harbin. This section over Chinese soil was deemed sensible at the time as the fairly flat terrain of Manchuria allowed it to be completed more quickly and more cheaply than would otherwise have been the case. After the Russo-Japanese War (1904–05), which had strained the line to capacity if not actually beyond this point as the Russians sought to rush large numbers of troops and vast quantities of supplies and equipment from European Russia to the Far East, the Russians decided that strategic requirements called for a connection to be constructed from Chita to Vladivostok by means of the Amur river valley and Khabarovsk. Although considerably longer than the direct route across Manchuria, it did ensure that the whole route was at last wholly in Russian territory.

The line, beginning in Moscow and connecting with Vladivostok via Omsk,

Irkutsk (on the shores of Lake Baikal) and Khabarovsk, was created as a single-track route, and by 1913 most of it had been converted to double-track layout. However, it was the 1950s before the complete route was of the double-tracked type. Further upgrading of the Trans-Siberian Railway continued, and by the mid-1970s some three-quarters of the line from the European end had been electrified. One of the most interesting aspects of the Trans-Siberian Railway is its vast number of bridges, large and small, as the line traverses the huge number of valleys that are generally aligned north to south. On the line's western section the bridges include eight with a span of 985ft (300m) or more, including those over the Irtysh, Oh and Yenisei rivers, all of them more than 1,985ft (600m) wide, and on the eastern section there is a huge bridge over the Amur river near Khabarovsk.

An English traveller produced a detailed description of the journey as it was in 1913, when the service started from the Yaroslav station in Moscow. The train, hauled by a finely maintained Pacific-type locomotive, comprised long cars in green-and-gold livery. In the passenger part of the train the corridors were fully carpeted, and the dining car had an ivory-white ceiling and panelled walls with large windows. The service also included a bathroom car, a pharmacy, and a car with reading and games rooms. Standards declined in the period between World Wars I and II, after the tsarist regime had been replaced by that of the communists and Russia had become the Union of Soviet Socialist Republics.

LEFT: The Australian XPT eight-car high-speed diesel electric passenger train was developed in 1981 as the Australian version of the British HST 125 (High Speed Train) by New South Wales Railways.

BELOW LEFT: The Sunlander *on the run from Brisbane to Cairns on Queensland Government Railways, Australia.*

OPPOSITE: An Australian W-class locomotive, now preserved. In the 1950s, this class of locomotive hauled the Broken Hill Express, *whose passenger services were eventually taken over by the famous* Indian-Pacific *service.*

The main element of the passenger services along the Trans-Siberian Railway was then provided by the *Trans-Siberian Express*, which had a special sleeping car and dining facilities. There was also the *Blue Express*, which included 'hard' and 'soft' accommodation as well as a sleeping car. These trains, which were relatively light with only eight or nine cars, took just under 10 days to complete the 5,973-mile (9612-km) journey from Moscow to Vladivostok at an average speed of a mere 25mph (40km/h). The situation improved little in the later period of the communist state between the end of World War II and the collapse of the U.S.S.R. into the Commonwealth of Independent States in 1990. In this later period, the service included four-bunk 'soft'-class compartments that were spacious and clean, but there was also a public-address system that spouted a constant stream of communist propaganda. The quality of everything, large and small, was decidedly poor. The electric locomotive and cars were of Czechoslovak and East German manufacture respectively, and it would not be unfair to say that virtually the only 'all-Russian' element of the service was the constant supply of tea from old-fashioned samovars.

Not that far from Vladivostok in global terms lies Japan. Here, just after its defeat in World War II, the Japanese authorities planned the construction of a straight railroad line linking Tokyo and Osaka by means of trains travelling at 125mph (200km/h). Given the massive extent of the reconstruction effort that had to be undertaken in the aftermath of the war, however, this initial plan failed to reach fruition and it was 1958 before an aerial survey of the planned route was made. Then, in the next year and within a week of parliamentary authorization for the plan, work on the line began with a ceremonial ground-breaking event. Only 65 months later, during 1965, the two cities were linked by their first full service.

Given the fact that a high-speed journey was the line's *raison d'être*, the alignment of the track was arranged so that every curve had a radius of at least 1.5miles (2.4km) and, with a view to avoiding urban congestion and minimizing noise, the line was in places supported at a height of 21ft (6.4m) on viaducts with high parapet walls. Other aspects of the line were the lack of level crossings and the traverses of estuaries and river valleys on long viaducts. Some 66 tunnels, 12 of them more than 1.25miles (2km) long, were bored through the rock of mountains that stood in the track's path, and to mitigate the suction effect that can be created by two trains passing each other in opposite directions at high speed, in this instance at a combined velocity of more than 250mph (400km/h), the gap between the nearer rails of the opposing tracks in the tunnels was increased from the standard figure of 6ft 0in (1.8m) to a figure between 9ft 0in (2.74m) and 9ft 6in (2.89m). Because of the train service's high speed, care also had to be taken when building the embankments to ensure that there was an adequate degree of compactness in the heaped earth.

On every day in the time frame between 6.00 a.m. and 9.00 p.m., a Hikari (lightning) train leaves Tokyo every 15 minutes and covers the 322 miles (518km) to Osaka in the time of 3 hours 10 minutes, in the process stopping only at Nagoya and Kyoto, at an average speed of over 100mph (160km/h). Each train consists of 16 cars and carries an average of 1,000 passengers. Because of the tunnels and the cars' high windows, travellers do not get a chance to see much of the beautiful scenery through which the train progresses. It is only when the line crosses river valleys that they can appreciate the Japanese countryside and the distant mountains, including Mount Fuji, of which there are superb views.

Today the Tokyo–Osaka route is the busiest of several Shinkansen (bullet train)

services, with trains departing Tokyo as often as every six minutes at peak travel times. West of Osaka, the Shinkansen network has been extended to Kobe, Okayama, Hiroshima and, by way of an undersea tunnel, to Hakata on the island of Kyushu. North of Tokyo, the Shinkansen system has been expanded to include Niigata, Yamagata, Sendai and Morioka on separate routes. Tokyo is thus the hub of a series of radiating lines, but there are no through trains between the western and eastern Shinkansen lines. However, there are regular express trains from Tokyo all

the way to Hakata on the Osaka line.

Service is provided by three classes of trains: the Kodama local trains that make frequent stops, the Hikari limited-express trains, and the Nozomi extra-fare super-express trains. On the section of the network between Tokyo and Osaka three generations of equipment are now in service, the newest dating from the early 1990s. The latest equipment is used for the Nozomi service, and during March 1997 the Nozomi 500 entered service between Osaka and Hakata. This unmistakable train regularly operates at up to 186mph (300km/h) and is now the

fastest regularly scheduled train in the world. North of Tokyo, there is a mixture of new train types in service, including the double-deck 'Max' trains.

During the 1960s, far to the south of Japan on the island continent of Australia, there were two trains running on entirely different routes but sharing the name *Brisbane Express*. One of these routes, intended mainly for business passengers, generally in a rush and with limited interest in the world outside the train, was that routed over the newer 643-mile (1035-km) coastal track, and much of this trip was run

ABOVE: *South Australian Railway's 3ft 6-inch Class 400 4-8-2 and 2-8-4 No. 407 leaving Port Pirie for Peterborough, originally Petersburg. Though here hauling freight, Garratt locomotives were used on the* Broken Hill Express *passenger service for many years.*

LEFT: *Locomotive No. N457 on the Melbourne– Albury Twin City Express. Albury, historically, was where passengers travelling between Sydney and Melbourne changed trains, swapping the standard gauge of the New South Wales Railway for the broad gauge of Victorian Railways.*

OPPOSITE: *No. R707, a 4-6-4 express passenger locomotive, used to haul broad-gauge (5ft 3in) passenger trains in Australia.*

during the night. This service was actually divided into two, the *Brisbane Limited Express* covering the distance in 15 hours 30 minutes and the slower *Brisbane Express* following in the time of 17 hours 50 minutes.

The other route was intended more for the tourist, and therefore offered considerably greater attractions and, while including a section covered at night, traversed most of the most pleasant country by day. A departure at 1.55 p.m. meant that the descent of the Cowan Bank and the crossing of the Hawkesbury river were made in good light, as was the run along the shores of Brisbane Waters. The passengers also had good views of the well-inhabited country as far as Wyong, and then of hillier and more timbered terrain nearly as far as Broadmeadow, which was the junction for trains to Newcastle. This was an area containing many coal mines, and much coal traffic could be seen on the way to Maitland, where the shorter coastal route branched off to the north. The 'main' route continued westward through a comparatively flat dairy-farming region as far as Singleton, which was passed at about nightfall. The line then began gradually to climb into the foothills of the Great Dividing Range via Murrurundi, the depot town for the banking engines required to assist the heavy traffic crossing the range in both directions, which included 1/40 gradients on both sides of the central Ardglen tunnel.

West of the Great Dividing Range, the line descended easily to Tamworth before ascending once more up the Moonbi Range to reach the Northern Tablelands. Daylight reached the train as it was passing through the undulating countryside before Tenterfield, which was the last major town to be passed before the train crossed into Queensland, where there was a change-of-gauge station at Wallangarra, where the passengers had to transfer themselves and their possessions onto the narrow-gauge express to Brisbane through pleasant hilly country to the Darling Downs, which are some of the finest farming lands in Australia. Some 5 hours 30 minutes after leaving Wallangarra, the train reached the Toowoomba, famous for its magnificent gardens. The descent of the mountains from Toowoomba was beautiful but slow. As a result, the Queensland Government Railways introduced a co-ordinated bus/rail service between Toowoomba and Helidon, the latter located at the bottom of the range: travellers heading for Brisbane could therefore spend more than one hour in Toowoomba, and could then board the bus and rejoin the train at Helidon for the final run into Brisbane. In the reverse direction, inhabitants of Toowoomba could get home an hour ahead of the train by using the bus. The arrival of the *Brisbane Express* in Brisbane was shortly after dusk at 6.25 p.m., some 28 hours 30 minutes after the service's departure from Sydney and after a run of 715 miles (1150km).

This great service no longer operates, however, as it was cancelled after a great length of the line from Glen Innes to the Queensland border had been abandoned.

There can have been few areas more

disheartening to earlier generations of Australians than the region spanning the border of South Australia and New South Wales. By 1876, however, lead sulphide (the ore from which lead and, to a lesser extent, gold are extracted) was found on the New South Wales side of the border, and by 1883 the Silverton area was booming with mines and even smelters. In the same year, lead sulphide was discovered at Broken Hill and the government of South Australia, appreciating the commercial importance of the region, hastily built a narrow-gauge line from Petersburg (now Peterborough) to the border. The line was completed in January 1887, but the government of New South Wales refused to allow the line to be extended across the border. This situation

resulted in the establishment of a private company to create and run the Silverton Tramway Company as a link between the South Australian Railway's line and Broken Hill via Silverton. By this time Silverton, a town with 36 hotels, was already in decline, while Broken Hill was still a boom town and, though now declining, remained so through most of the 20th century.

Although it is geographically in New South Wales, Broken Hill uses the South Australian time zone, and most of its commercial business is undertaken with Adelaide, which is altogether closer than Sydney. To make this connection with Adelaide, a regular train service connected the two cities, the *Broken Hill Express* being one of the few Australian passenger

express services hauled for many years by Garratt locomotives. The service was basically of the overnight type, and the South Australian Railway built up the tonnage with freight wagons. To the east of the border, the Silverton Tramway Company, with its 36 miles (58km) of line, provided the locomotives and a number of the freight cars. The locomotives originally employed to haul the service were of the 'Colonial Mogul' type, followed in 1912 by 'A'-class 4-6-0 locomotives, in 1951 by 'W'-class 4-8-2 semi-streamlined locomotives similar to those used in Western Australia, and from 1960 by Co-Co diesel-electric locomotives up to 1970, when the standard-gauge system bypassed the private line.

Early traffic on the South Australian Railway side was handled by 'Y' or 'X'-class examples of the Colonial Mogul type of locomotive, but the growth of traffic soon required that larger locomotives be adopted and this led to the design of the highly successful 'T' class of 4-8-0 locomotives, of which 78 examples were built from 1903 onward with some units remaining in service right to the end of the steam era. These locomotives hauled the services 140 miles (225km) to Terowie, where there was a change to the broad-gauge system, with an 'S'-class 4-4-0 locomotive taking over for the additional 140 miles (225km) to Adelaide. The 'S'-class units were replaced in the 1920s by larger and more powerful engines. In 1953, the '400'-class Garratt locomotives were introduced and rapidly took over the Broken Hill traffic, and from

1959 the South Australian Railway bought '830'- class Co-Co diesel-electric locomotives that then took over from steam locomotives on this semi-desert route. This standardization rang the death knell for the *Broken Hill Express*, for the *Indian-Pacific* eventually took over the passenger traffic on the line and the broad-gauge services were withdrawn from Terowie.

In the 1950s, the *Broken Hill Express* left Broken Hill at 7.48 p.m. behind a Silverton W-class locomotive, covering what was possibly the most scenic part of this semi-desert journey in darkness to the border, which it reached at 9.21 p.m. Here a 400-class Garratt locomotive took over for the run to Peterborough, where passengers for Port Pirie had to change at 3.58 a.m. The train reversed out of Peterborough, with a new locomotive for the short run to Terowie, where Adelaide passengers changed to the broad-gauge service at 4.50 a.m. After a 20-minute refreshment pause, the broad-gauge service departed for its 9.20 a.m. arrival in Adelaide after a journey of 362 miles (582km).

Although a rapidly escalating level of railroad construction was evident in Australia from the 1850s, it was not until 1917 that a passenger could travel across the continent between the Pacific and Indian Oceans, a railroad distance then reckoned at 2,704 miles (4352km). When this passage finally became possible, Australia still operated a number of different railway gauges, and this made the journey a considerable effort as there were many changes involved and the route, now

fairly direct and by standard-gauge track throughout, at that time meandered by way of Melbourne and Adelaide.

In its early days, the transcontinental service demanded that the traveller boarded the standard-gauge train in Sydney in time for a departure at 7.25 p.m. and a night run to the Victorian border at Albury, where at 7.23 a.m. there was 23 minutes for the passenger to change onto the broad-gauge train that reached Melbourne at 12.51 p.m. Here there was a gap of some 3 hours 30

minutes, allowing the passenger time for a meal and other refreshment before he boarded the broad-gauge train that departed Melbourne at 4.30 p.m. for an overnight passage to Adelaide in South Australia, reached at 9.55 a.m. on the second day. Some 50 minutes later, the passenger was on yet another broad-gauge train north to Terowie, where 30 minutes were available for refreshments and the change to another narrow-gauge train that circumnavigated its way to Port Augusta, reached at 10.05 p.m.

on the second day for yet another change, in this instance to a standard-gauge train for the journey across the Nullarbor Plain.

The crossing of this vast region of semi-desert then took about one and a half days, and this section included the world's longest railroad 'straight' of 297 miles (478km). The first halt on the western side of the Nullarbor Plain was the gold-mining town of Kalgoorlie, reached at 1.38 p.m. on the fourth day of the trip. At Kalgoorlie the passenger had to wait until 5.15 p.m. before

he could leave on the narrow-gauge express service to Perth, which the train reached at 9.47 a.m. on the morning of the fifth day. The whole journey had taken just over four-and-a-half days, allowing for the two-hour time difference between the western and eastern sides of the continent.

It was not until 1969 that the route via Broken Hill to Perth was completely revised to a standard-gauge track arrangement, and in 1970 the *Indian-Pacific* service was inaugurated, cutting the journey of 2,461 miles (3961km) to a time of just over two-and-a-half days. Since then, a standard-gauge line has been laid almost into Adelaide. Unlike European railway systems, which would provide a through-car service, for the section between Melbourne and Port Pirie via Adelaide, the *Indian-Pacific* takes a lengthy and time-consuming side jaunt from near Crystal Brook to Keswick in the Adelaide suburbs and back.

The *Indian-Pacific* now departs Sydney at 2.55 p.m., soon passing through Sydney's inner suburbs, and reaches the open railroad at Blacktown for acceleration to its highest cruising speed. The train crosses the Hawkesbury river beyond Penrith, and then starts the climb into the Blue Mountains: the current route is the third ascent, and provides excellent views of these superb mountains, with similar views possible on the descent along the western sides of the range. At the foot of the mountains the train moves through rolling farming country to Parkes, which is reached after nightfall. From Parkes, the route covers virtually nothing but semi-desert country almost the entire remaining distance to Perth.

On the other side of the Tasman Sea from Australia lies New Zealand. The nation's most important commercial centre is Wellington, on the North Island, and in earlier times this was linked to the city of Christchurch, the seat of provincial government and main gateway to the vast farming hinterland of Canterbury on the South Island, by coastal steamers. The first proposal for a rail line to connect the two cities was suggested as early as 1861, but it

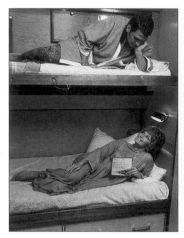

was only 11 years later, in 1872, that work began on a broad-gauge line north from Christchurch, this being altered to the 3ft 6in (1.07m) gauge in 1877. A line south from Picton, the port opposite Wellington on the north-east corner of the South Island, was started in 1875. Progress was then made as and when the political will and economic resources allowed, but by 1916 the northern line had reached Wharanui, only 56 miles (90km) from Picton, while the southern section had reached Parnassus, only 83 miles (133km) from Christchurch. It was to be another 20 years before further real progress was made toward closing the gap through the mountainous terrain around Kaikoura, and the complete 216-mile (348-km) line opened only in December 1945.

In 1954 the introduction of a roll-

RIGHT: The Rotorua-Auckland express, headed by a K-class 4-8-4 locomotive No. 909 at Eureka, between Morrinsville and Hamilton. The Rotorua-bound train in the background is leaving the crossing loop.

BELOW RIGHT: The Endeavour express running daily between Wellington and Napier on New Zealand's North Island. The train is headed by a 1,063kW Da-class A1A-A1A diesel-electric locomotive and comprises day coaches and a licensed buffet-car.

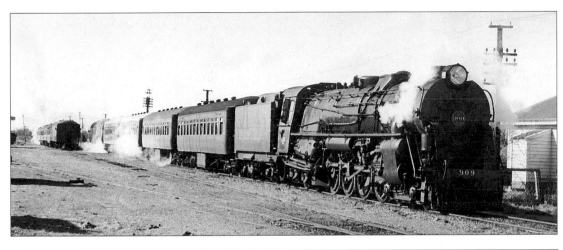

OPPOSITE
ABOVE LEFT: The first Indian-Pacific express leaves Perth, Western Australia, on its trip eastwards across the continent on 30 August 1970.

ABOVE RIGHT: First class honeymoon suite aboard the Australian trans-continental Indian-Pacific express.

BELOW LEFT: The Silver Star express, headed by a 2,051kW Dx-class Co-Co diesel-electric locomotive. It ran overnight, Sunday through Friday, between Auckland and Wellington in New Zealand's North Island.

ABOVE: *The 'Grass Grub', the local nickname for the Picton–Christchurch train, in Kaikoura station with No. DF6064 in charge. The Kaikoura mountains and the Pacific Ocean are in the background.*

LEFT: *Interior of the buffet car of the Southerner.*

OPPOSITE: *The southbound* Southerner *is hauled across Otago Harbour on a causeway. A small country with limited population, New Zealand nevertheless had its share of crack passenger services.*

on/roll-off rail ferry altered the connecting sea crossing from Wellington, and in 1988 the service was further improved with rebuilt rolling stock. The journey from Wellington to Christchurch has several interesting aspects. The 50-mile (80-km) sea crossing can be very memorable, especially in the event of adverse weather in the Cook Strait before the ship reaches the more sheltered waters of Marlborough Sound. Then there is the ride through the hills of Marlborough, followed by the exhilarating passage through the harsher mountains around Kaikoura with the Pacific Ocean as an intimate companion, and finally the gentler landscape leading toward the Canterbury Plains.

The concept of a luxury service for the *Coastal Pacific Express* on the route linking Picton and Christchurch followed the successful introduction of such a service between Christchurch and Greymouth through the alpine scenery of the South Island. Several of the cars were converted with larger windows, separated by narrow pillars for excellent fields of view. The high-backed seats are fitted with sheepskin covers. Other aspects of the accommodation include full carpeting, large ventilators and window curtains. The livery is a combination of interior pink-and-grey and exterior mid-blue with red-and-white bands.

With all the passengers embarked, the train cruises out of Picton (originally known as Waitohi) and completes a steep climb before traversing the Waitohi viaduct. By the time the train has reached Elevation, only 2.5 miles (4km) from Picton, the

mountains have taken on an alpine aspect, with stands of conifers and logging tracks, but the pastures visible below with their scattered trees are more similar in appearance to English parkland. Before Blenheim, the train passes over the Wairau river on a long but low bridge. Blenheim itself serves as the gateway to the increasingly well-known wine-growing regions of Marlborough, and past this town the train starts another long ascent, in this instance toward the bleaker regions around the Dashwood Pass. Another gradient takes the train to the unusual bridge over the Awatere river: this is a combination bridge with the railway carried on an upper deck with the road on the deck below it. After passing over the Blind river, the train then travels along a long causeway to get across the large salt lakes on the approaches to Lake Grasmere. Near Wharanui, the train starts on a long section of coastal running, and here the passengers can enjoy about 90 minutes of magnificent scenery before the stop at Kaikoura. For much of the way, the railway and the road are squeezed into a narrow strip between the mountains on the west and the shore on the east. In about 62 miles (100km) of line to Oaro there are 20 tunnels, several embankments and steep cuttings, sharp curves and isolated bridges.

The line's winding alignment, which follows the ins-and-outs of the coastline, ends on the approach to Kaikoura. This is a fishing port and former whaling station, and lies on a peninsula about mid-way between Picton and Christchurch. The train pauses briefly here before resuming its journey by means of another curving viaduct, then there is another stretch of spectacular coastal running along a section of line marked by nine tunnels. Beyond Oaro, at sea level again, the train climbs steeply and passes through the Amuri Bluff tunnel and then the Okarahia viaduct. Soon the suburbs of Christchurch come into view and the journey is complete as the train pulls into the station.

LEFT: The northbound Southerner *stands in Dunedin station with DJ-class locomotives 3211 and 3050 in charge.*

Chapter Six
RAPID TRANSIT SYSTEMS
AND THE DECLINE OF STEAM

PAGE 316: The Wuppertal monorail, Germany.

RIGHT: A train on London's Docklands Light Railway at Westferry.

RAPID TRANSIT SYSTEMS AND
THE DECLINE OF STEAM

One of the primary criticisms aimed at the steam locomotive right from its beginnings was the fact that as an engine it was manpower-intensive. A driver and fireman were both essential on the footplate for even the shortest trip, and large numbers of other staff were required throughout the entire railroad system to cope with matters such as coaling, watering, oiling and ash disposal. The beginning of the railroad era was a time in which manpower was both relatively abundant and relatively cheap, so these problems were initially not of major significance, but as time progressed and the world's railroad systems increased in extent and complexity, the manpower problem began to become more acute.

Long before the driver and fireman arrived to drive a steam locomotive, the latter's steam had to be raised and then maintained. Lying from cold, the average steam locomotive required at least four hours to reach its working pressure, and as a result burned a considerable (and increasingly expensive) quantity of high-quality coal before it even started to move and thus begin to generate revenue. A 1952 survey found that of the total weight of coal used by a 'Hall'-class 4-6-0 locomotive, designed and manufactured for the Great Western Railway, more than one-fifth was burned in non-productive work including cleaning, the building-up of the fire, standing and manoeuvring.

A feature typical of railroad and railway systems all over the world was the sheer number of the engine sheds that were required right through the entire system, for these sheds were the 'bases' at which steam locomotives had to stand periodically for basic servicing of the types quoted above. A main-line engine would often be in steam for a week or more, but frequent washings of their boilers were essential if these essential parts of the whole locomotive system were not to 'fur up' and thus cease to work as efficiently as they might. The task of washing out the boiler required that the fire be dropped and the boiler emptied of water, for only after these had been completed could the maintenance crew embark on the filthy and incredibly laborious task of using hand tools to scrape away all the deposits that had accumulated in the boiler and the mass of tubes it contained. The task involved the use of rods and high-pressure water jets, inserted into the boiler through inspection holes, for the removal of the lime scale that had grown on the interior surfaces of the boiler and on its

tubes; if left, such lime scale increased the weight of the locomotive to an appreciable extent, reduced the overall efficiency of the boiler system, and as a result seriously degraded the ability of the steam locomotive to operate both well and economically. Another aspect of the servicing procedure was the removal of as much as possible of the dirt that collected in other parts of the workings of the steam locomotive, whose performance and operating economy were also highly dependent on the type of mechanical cleanliness that could be ensured, and then only to a strictly limited degree, by the removal of deposits of ash and clinker from the firebed, ash from the pan, soot from the interior of the boiler tubes, and char from the smokebox: if left, all of these had a major effect for the worse on the ability of the steam locomotive to generate and use its steam economically.

Routine maintenance was also needed on items such as valves and pistons, together with other parts of the steam locomotive's workings requiring lubrication. This somewhat cleaner aspect of maintenance combined with the dirty aspects of the task as mentioned above to make the operation of a steam locomotive

much more manpower-intensive and therefore more expensive than any other type of motive power during the 19th century. The manpower-intensive and time-consuming nature of steam locomotive operations is perhaps encapsulated in the small but significant fact that while modern trains can be driven from either end, trains pulled by steam locomotives are essentially single-ended, so the locomotive had to be uncoupled at the end of a journey and turned round before it could be coupled to the return service: this task required the attentions of several men, and generally took between one and two hours.

The cost in terms of manpower and time was only one aspect of steam locomotive operations that came to militate against their continued use as and when alternatives began to become available. Another aspect of steam locomotive operations that gradually began to assume increasing importance was their essentially anti-social nature, and this fact began to gain significance from the beginning of the 20th century to peak, in the Western world, during the 1950s. In short, increasing national affluence and an expanding awareness of the ideas of better working conditions and the desirability of greater leisure time meant that dirty, manual tasks such as the maintenance and operation of steam locomotives gradually became something to be avoided wherever possible: thus the crews of steam locomotives, who had been among the heroes of the Victorian era and feted in numberless songs, acquired during the 20th century something of the pariah among the working classes as men condemned to dirty and laborious employment that generally took them far from home on long shifts. The effect of this process was to reduce the pool of skilled and industrious manpower from which steam locomotive driving and maintenance crews could be drawn, and as a result the overall standard of these crews became increasingly difficult to maintain. Although this tendency was most readily appreciable in the wealthier countries of the Western world, it also began to appear (albeit later and more slowly) in Latin American countries and also in many Third World nations, where the adherence to the concept of the steam locomotive was seen not as a reflection of the success and economic viability of the existing system when the adoption of 'modern technology' might cost much in both capital and operating terms, but rather as further evidence that

the nations of the Third World were being kept deliberately in the past as a reflection of the First World's belief that they were inferior and therefore incapable of buying and using 'modern technology'. As recently as 1982, a Brazilian report on the continued operation of the Teresa Cristina Railway suggested that steam locomotives should be replaced by more modern diesel or electric locomotives as soon as possible, as the retention of steam power was undesirable for reasons as diverse as the tendency of the steam locomotive's crews to suffer from high levels of stress, high levels of vibration as a result of the workings of the locomotive and the unevenness of track, hearing loss as a result of the high levels of noise, a tendency toward infection as a result of the 'thermal overload' to which the crews were often subjected, a tendency toward back problems later in life as a result of the work, a tendency toward lung disease as a result of the coal dust, and a tendency toward loss of sight as a result of the brightness of the light coming from the firebox.

Many of these factors were obviously unjustified or, where justified, somewhat exaggerated, but the report in general

LEFT: A newcomer in electric train operations in 1906 was this Baldwin-Westinghouse-built locomotive designed to operate on both direct and alternating current (direct current over the New York Central line and alternating current on New Haven's own line). This type of locomotive was capable of handling a 200-ton train in local service at an average speed of 26mph (42km/h). The maximum speed travelled to maintain this average speed was about 45mph (72km/h).

OPPOSITE: Whatever its failings, steam locomotion nevertheless possesses a unique emotional appeal, and even when the country through which the railroad passes has been raped for the construction of tunnels and cuttings, as seen here in the Cumbria region of north-west England, nature is quick to re-establish itself. This is one of the reasons why preserved railroad operations have proved so enduringly popular.

highlighted the increasing unrest felt by the persons who were still maintaining and driving steam locomotives at a time when the operation of diesel or electric locomotives was clearly coming to be seen as a far cleaner and less laborious option, better suited to the dignity and long-term well-being of the modern working man.

In these circumstances, therefore, the change to diesel and electrical locomotives was in general the subject of an enthusiastic welcome by the members of a work force

that had become increasingly disenchanted with the steam locomotive and all the work and discomfort that its operation entailed. Unlike the steam locomotive, which is wholly reliant on the movement of large quantities of coal, first from the reserves in the depot into the tender (often by mechanical means) and then from the tender to the firebox (most generally by shovel), the diesel locomotive uses an easily transportable liquid fuel that is loaded into the locomotive's fuel tanks and from there

to the burners by mechanical means. The diesel fuel also possesses the advantages of being consistent in its qualities, lacking the waste products that would choke the operating system and, most importantly of all for the locomotive's crew, having no need for the disposal of wastes after use. Another point in favour of the diesel locomotive, so far as the operating company as well as the crew are concerned, is that while the steam locomotive needs a full head of steam before reaching its maximum

operating capability, a costly and time-consuming process, as noted above, the diesel locomotive is free from this stricture. The same is also true of the electric locomotive, and as a result neither of these types requires any significant measure of 'warm up' time, with consequent saving in fuel and labour costs, and for the same reason provide greater tractive effort on gradients and during acceleration.

The most cogent argument against the use of steam locomotives was the need for

huge weights of coal to be transported from the various coal-mining regions to strategically placed dumps serving the railroad industry. Sometimes countries and railroad operators were fortunate that deposits of the right grade of coal were located close to major industrial regions, which of course grew up where the raw materials (including coal) for their operations were most readily available, but in others railroad systems were only partially co-located with their fuel supplies, especially where there was already a thriving economic life based on other aspects of transports such as shipping, for instance. What could not be avoided, however, was the fact that large-scale railroad systems required large coal dumps located at about one tender's steaming distance from each other. The primary disadvantages of such dumps were, on the one hand, that they had to be maintained with frequent deliveries of coal and in themselves demanded large numbers of men for the movement of the coal and, on the other hand, needed very large areas of increasingly expensive land. The beautiful irony of this coal situation was, naturally, that the delivery of coal to these dumps demanded an extensive schedule of transport by trains hauled by a coal-burning steam locomotive. The movement of coal in the required tonnages was a major task, but speed of delivery was not vitally important and as a result the coal-delivery trains were among the longest, heaviest but slowest to be encountered on any railroad system. The coal-delivering trains generally operated at night, together with most of the other freight services, to avoid daylight congestion of a system that was most profitably employed during the day for passenger and light freight services.

Not just any type of coal was suitable for use in steam locomotives, which worked to best effect only with the high-quality coal mined only in a limited number of areas. In the United Kingdom, for example, it was the coal from the collieries of South Wales that was thought the best for steam locomotion, and this coal offered a 13 per cent better return, in terms of steam generated per unit of coal, than the coal mined in Yorkshire. It was this factor that required the movement of large tonnages of coal so that the fuel for steam locomotives would be available in areas in which it was not mined. The cost of this movement of coal was just one of the many factors that began to militate against the continued use of coal in the first half of the 20th century, and another was the notably rapid exhaustion of the best reserves of high-quality coal. This meant greater costs as less accessible deposits were exploited, and also reduced operating efficiency as many operators switched to coal of reduced quality in an effort to cut direct costs. Thus it was the combination of the increasing shortage and increased cost of high-quality coal with the availability of oil that was both plentiful and comparatively cheap that led to the demise of the steam locomotive in the Western world. The comparative costs of steam and diesel locomotion in the early

1950s, measured in terms of pence per mile, were about 36 pence for the coal-fired locomotive and 11 pence for the diesel-engined locomotive, which was thus more than three times cheaper to operate than the steam locomotive. Another aspect that was inevitably and correctly factored into the notional equation concerning the cost-effectiveness of the diesel-powered locomotive vis-à-vis the steam locomotive is that the former is generally available for service for about 90 per cent of its life, while the latter has far greater 'down' periods.

As noted above, a major factor that boosted the change from steam to other forms of locomotive power was the anti-social nature, either real or imaginary, of the work associated with the steam locomotive. The driver and firemen of steam locomotives had of necessity to work in conditions that were both dirty and arduous, whereas the drivers (the firemen now being superfluous) of diesel and electric locomotives were favoured with a far more user-friendly environment in cabs that were sealed from the weather and radically cleaner than the cabs of steam locomotives.

Another aspect of the switch from steam to diesel locomotion – and this was an aspect that became increasingly important to the populations of Western nations as the 20th century progressed – was the fact that such locomotives were considerably more friendly to the environment than the steam locomotives they replaced. There was less smoke and no

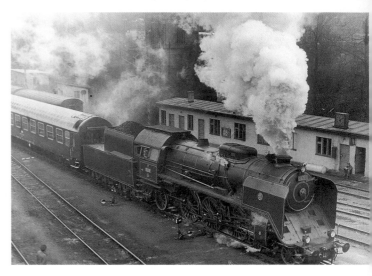

steam to act as pollutants of the air, and as a consequence there were clear advantages in overall terms as well as in smaller specifics such as the cleanliness of buildings and the reduced irritation to the eyes, lungs and skins of people living near the railway, which was in fact an omnipresent feature of urban life by the beginning of the 20th century: the exhaust gases of the steam locomotive contain acids that get into people's lungs and also coat and then etch their way into the stonework of buildings. In this regard it is worth noting that most of the cities and larger towns of the Western world were virtually black with the deposits of steam locomotives by the middle of the 20th century, and it was only after these engines

ABOVE: With their abundant supplies of coal, lack of pressure from environmental and customer lobbies, and unwillingness to invest in new technology when there was still mileage to be had from the existing system, the communist regimes of Europe were slow to abandon steam locomotion, with the result that engines were still being built or, increasingly, rebuilt right into the 1970s as indicated by this photograph taken in Czechoslovakia during 1975.

OPPOSITE: SY1422 with bankers JS 6217 and 6218 on the Chengde Steelworks branch, China.

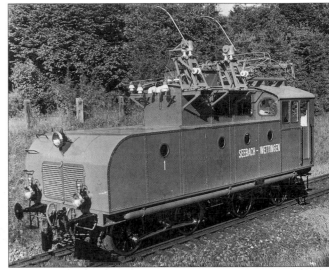

ABOVE: Chicago, Milwaukee & St. Paul Railroad Class 6886-E-12GE100A electric locomotive.

ABOVE RIGHT: Swiss Federal Railways Seebach-Wettingen locomotive Ce 4/41 Eva, 1904.

OPPOSITE: Fast freight train on the Baltimore & Ohio Railroad's Susquehanna river bridge at Havre de Grace, Maryland.

had been replaced by diesel and electric locomotives that it made economic sense to undertake the extensive programmes of cleaning and restoration that have once more revealed the fact that many buildings, once thought to be entirely indifferent, are in fact magnificent bequests from the past.

Electrification is an extremely costly process in the initial stages, when equipment had to be installed and electricity-generating capability built. This is in general a one-off capital cost, however, and is supportable when the result is a system offering the assurance of high-density movement of passengers and/or freight. Where such a 'market' is thought to be available, most notably in the regions surrounding large

conurbations or connecting major cities, it makes sense to proceed with electrification on the basis of a comparatively few electricity-generating stations of high capacity located strategically to feed power to the electric motors of locomotives by means of overhead wires or a conducting rail on the ground. This allows the use of simpler and therefore cheaper locomotives that do not need to generate their own power, but is viable in economic terms only when there is a high level of traffic. In areas offering a lower level of traffic, it makes greater economic sense to reduce the capital outlay required by forsaking the concept of an external power source and instead rely on the slightly greater operating cost associated

with on-board generation of power through the use of either a diesel powerplant or a diesel-electric generating system.

It is worth noting, however, that diesel and electric power have not replaced or indeed largely supplanted steam locomotion in every country. Up to a time within the last ten years, India was still seen as the world's second most important 'steam country' after China, and to a large extent the railroad systems of the two nations reflected two radically different approaches to steam locomotion: in 1990 China was operating some 8,000 steam locomotives, of a mere six classes, while India had considerably smaller numbers of engines but of a far larger variety of classes.

The Indian railroad system was also based on the continued use of steam locomotion on tracks of four different gauges. Then the nature of the Indian railroad system was radically overhauled, and by 1997 India's use of steam locomotion had been radically curtailed. Even as the Indian railways organization was undertaking its long-term programme of progressive modernization, the national feeling against the continuance of steam locomotion, in emotive as well as practical terms, was strengthening. Steam locomotion had now effectively disappeared from the wide-gauge railroad system, leaving for extinction by the beginning of the 21st century only the surviving pockets of steam locomotion on the metre-gauge track system currently represented by the 'YP'- class 'Pacific'-type and 'YG'-class 'Mikado'-type locomotives. On the narrow-gauge track system, 1997 saw the advent of diesel locomotives on the previous steam line from Pulgaon to Arvi, this leaving only the 24-inch (610-mm) gauge Matheran and the famous Darjeeling lines, both of them used mainly for the tourist trade rather than for more practically oriented commercial purposes, with steam locomotion: even so, financial requirements imposed by the government of India mean that even the Darjeeling Himalayan 'toy railroad' is now threatened. Completed in 1889, the railroad climbs its way for some 50 miles (80km) from the flat lands of West Bengal up to Darjeeling in a beautiful location some 7,250ft (2210m) above sea level. The

LEFT: Locomotive No. 797 on the local line from Kurseong to Darjeeling below Sonada, India.

OPPOSITE: Narrow-gauge steam railroads are still of importance in remoter and less accessible parts of the world, for here the amount of traffic makes it very problematical whether or not the financial return will justify the expense of new locomotives, rolling stock and infrastructure.

current situation of the railroad is appalling, with stations in need of repairs, carriages requiring restoration and tracks in need of maintenance lest they subside, and the only real chance for the railroad's survival is the Darjeeling Himalayan Railway Heritage Foundation, which is seeking to save the line by developing it as a major tourist attraction.

Oddly enough, however, the railroad-minded visitor to India will fortunately discover the fact that there have been a number of fascinating survivals on the wide-gauge system, most of these relics being associated with industrial service. These hangovers from the past include a heavy 0-8-4 hump shunter and the last examples of the great 'XE' class of 2-8-2

OPPOSITE: YB 534 goods train from Mottama nearing Tha Ton, Myanmar (Burma).

RIGHT: Despite their technical obsolescence and increasingly evident lack of environmental 'friendliness', surviving main line steam locomotives still possess a considerable majesty with their semi-exposed workings and overwhelming impression of power.

locomotives. These are the only units left in the world of large, classically styled British Mikado-type locomotives and, at 200 tons, are the final examples of the big British steam locomotive left in service anywhere in the world. Toward the other end of the size scale, the most fascinating aspects of steam locomotion to survive in India are employed in the sugar field railroads of the country's northern regions. In one of the paradoxes so beloved by nature, it is here in a country that has now disposed of virtually all of its active steam locomotives that there are the world's two

oldest steam locomotives still in active service. These are the metre-gauge 0-4-0 type locomotives named as the *Mersey* and *Tweed*: the engines were manufactured in 1873 by the Great Bridgewater Street Works of Sharp Stewart.

In Pakistan, India's north-western neighbour, the national railroad organization's core is provided by the 66-inch (1676-mm) track system using British steam locomotives designed at the start of the 20th century, most notably inside-cylinder 0-6-0 and 4-4-0 type locomotives. Bangladesh (East Pakistan up to 1971) is

India's north-eastern neighbour but has little more than the remnants of a railroad system, so it is in Myanmar (formerly Burma), farther to the east, that one can find further railroad remnants of the original British presence in the Indian subcontinent. Virtually closed to foreigners for almost two decades and still difficult to visit, Myanmar has a small but fascinating collection of old British steam locomotives. Despite the fact that there are fewer than 50 examples left in service, these locomotives are of three important British-derived classes, all of them standard designs of the Indian railways

organization during the 1920s: after the retirement of India's last 'YP'-class metre-gauge locomotives, the 'YB'- and 'YC'-class locomotives are the world's last Pacific-type locomotives still in service.

With about 5,000 steam locomotives in active service, despite a fall of 3,000 from the peak figure of 8,000 in 1990 – still a number greater than the rest of the world put together, China is the most important country so far as steam locomotion is concerned. Despite the sheer numbers of steam locomotives in service, however, it is a disappointment to the railroad enthusiast

ABOVE: Locomotive HGS 2306 on Khyber stands at Shahgai Station, the Khyber Pass, on the Afghanistan/Pakistan border.

ABOVE RIGHT: Engine SPS 2976 en route between Mithalak and Malakwal, on the Dorridge Special from Sargodha, Pakistan.

OPPOSITE: YC 630 passing Payagyi station on the double-track main line between Bago and Pyuntaza, Myanmar.

that this total comprises only three types. This is the result of the fact that China, as a communist state, is a firm adherent of the concept of centralized planning without competition from commercial organizations, and this makes extensive standardization both logical and easy. This standardization also derives from the fact that much of China's railroad system was destroyed in World War II and the following Chinese Civil War, so it was only after the establishment of communist rule in 1949 that rebuilding of the system, together with its locomotives and rolling stock, could be undertaken. The absence of much pre-war equipment thus made the communists' centralized planning concept that much more attractive.

In numerical terms the world's most important steam locomotive, the 'QJ'-class locomotive is of the 2-10-2 type, and is partnered on Chinese main-line services by the 'JS' class of lighter Mikado-type locomotive. The most important class of steam locomotive for industrial purposes is the 'SY' class of Mikado-type locomotives to a design basically similar to that of the American 'light Mike' of the period before World War II. In the later part of the 1970s, China achieved considerable international note by the revelation that it was still manufacturing steam locomotives. Such was the pace of this effort, indeed, that there were occasions during the 1980s when the Datong Locomotive Works, located on the border with Inner Mongolia,

was completing one QJ-class locomotive every day.

Construction of steam locomotives has now almost entirely ended, reflecting a radical shift in emphasis within the communist system: the central government's plan that steam locomotives should be the norm was stymied when China's separate railway bureaux achieved a measure of autonomy and stopped their purchase of such locomotives as they opted for major modernizations of their systems. The change reflected partially a desire for greater operational efficiency, and also in part a revulsion, if that is not too strong a word, against steam on environmental and emotional grounds. Thus the Chinese railroad situation in the last years of the

333

20th century is akin to that which held sway in the Western world during the 1950s and 1960s, where there was a wholesale swing away from steam locomotion in favour of diesel and electric power.

Even so, the manufacturing facility at Tangshan is still delivering about one SY-class 2-8-2 locomotive every month, generally for industrial purposes and particularly for the coal-mining industry: by the end of the 20th century nearly 1,750 SY-class locomotives had been delivered. The Chinese are also happy, for the obvious commercial reasons that have become more important to the communists in the 1990s, to manufacture steam locomotives for state railways and also for tourist lines, and as a result Tangshan has already produced a small number of Mikado-type locomotives for Vietnam as well as a few SY-class locomotives for preserved railways in the U.S.A.

The most significant highlight in the Chinese retention of steam locomotives is the network of provincial lines that are not an intrinsic part of the state system. Developed with local financing, these railroads cannot generally run to the purchase and operating costs of diesel locomotives, and certainly not to those of electric locomotives, so they seem likely candidates for the retention of steam power until a time well after the disappearance of steam locomotives from the state system. Together with a declining number of industrial operators such as the coal, iron, stone, forestry and manufacturing industries, these provincial railroads are

ABOVE: China's first electric railway opens to traffic. People gave a warm send-off to the first electric locomotive when it pulled out of the Chengtu station on 1 July 1975.

ABOVE RIGHT: *China's first electric railway running from Paoki in Shensi to Chengtu in Szechwan. A passenger train is travelling through the mountains pulled by an electric locomotive.*

RIGHT: *Although it is declining in importance, steam locomotion is still very important to China for tasks such as logging.*

OPPOSITE: *Majestic 6991 and 6898 locomotives on the Jing Peng line, climbing over a curving viaduct with east-bound goods.*

planning to retain steam power for many years into the future. Indeed, in the case of the narrow-gauge railroad lines used for forestry work with standard 0-8-0 type locomotives of both European and Chinese origin, a not inconsiderable number of new steam locomotives was introduced during the 1980s.

In overall terms, therefore, it seems likely that steam locomotives will remain important to certain elements of the Chinese railroad system to at least 2015. This is a pleasant thought for those fascinated by steam power, for it will mean the use of steam locomotives for more than 200 years before their disappearance as first-line equipment. However, it should not be ignored that steam locomotives had disappeared from China's national railroad network by 1995.

The situation in North Korea, China's eastern neighbour, is basically similar to that in China, and thus a measure of steam locomotion remains for service on non-electrified lines and for shunting duties. The situation with the steam locomotive equipment of the North Korean railroad system is somewhat obscure, as a result largely of the closed nature of this most centralized and introspective member of the world's declining number of communist states; but it is thought that there are still many types of steam locomotive still in existence if not actually in operational service. North Korea is well provided with deposits of high-quality coal but is sorely vexed in overall financial terms, so it is likely that locomotives such as ex-American

'S160'-class 2-8-0 locomotives and 0-6-0T-type units will continue to be seen alongside ex-Chinese 'JF'- and 'JF6'-class Mikado-type locomotives.

The most fascinating exemplar of the countries that still retain steam locomotion is Indonesia (The Dutch East Indies until shortly after World War II), especially the large island of Java. For its size, this island had until the late 1970s one of the most varied but also most aged fleets of steam locomotives anywhere in the world. Although most of the island's main railroad lines are now the home of more modern diesel locomotives, steam locomotives had nonetheless survived in large numbers in association with the island's huge sugar industry, whose great sugar-cane plantations are still dotted with a large assortment of steam locomotives, some of them in working order but others in a state of total disrepair.

The origins of Indonesia as a Dutch colony is reflected, inevitably, in the presence of locomotives mostly of European, particularly Dutch and German, origins. If one had to sum up the relationship between Java and Europe in terms of the former's steam locomotion, the most apposite counterpart elsewhere in the world would be that of Cuba and the United States, the former being the last stronghold of the latter's steam heritage.

The steam locomotives of the Javanese agricultural system may be old and, when broken down, difficult to repair, but in overall commercial terms paid for themselves at a time well into the past and

are now operating at a virtually total profit, especially as their fireboxes burn bagasse, the natural and wholly free waste product of sugar-cane processing. On Sumatra, the large island to the east of Java, an equivalent situation prevails in the palm-oil processing, where the palm-oil plantations used steam locomotives whose boilers are heated by nutshells which are, again, a free by-product of the processing operation.

There is not much of the once extensive steam locomotion effort still evident in the Philippines except on the island of Negros, where there are still a number of sugar-plantation lines operated by small steam locomotives. A notable system of this type is the Hawaiian Philippine Sugar Company's 36-inch (914-mm) network

ABOVE and OPPOSITE: A 700mm-gauge 0-8-0 No.2 of 1913 shunting cane wagons in Java.

which has seven Baldwin locomotives known locally as 'Dragons'. As in Java, the Hawaiian Philippine locomotives burn bagasse through most of the sugar-cane season except the first weeks, when oil is burned until there are sufficient stocks of bagasse to allow a switch to this free fuel.

The other home in South-East Asia of steam locomotion as a significant factor is Vietnam, where steam locomotives survive both on the main lines and for industrial purposes. Although there are only a relatively few steam locomotives in daily service, a number of Mikado-type units operate on the country's metre-gauge and standard-gauge lines. Steam locomotives are most prevalent on the main lines to the south of the capital, Hanoi. In overall terms, the Vietnamese railroad organization is desperately hampered by an overactive bureaucracy, low wages, and lack of foreign exchange for the improvement of the situation with imported equipment. In combination with the lingering effects of the Vietnam War that ended in 1975 after the railway system had been very badly damaged, however, this is a situation that effectively guarantees the survival of steam locomotion for some time into the future.

An ex-French colony, Vietnam is also of significance as one of the last areas in the world with locomotives of the French school of thought, a type that is otherwise virtually extinct. However, the standard-gauge locomotives of the 2-8-2 type are of the Chinese 'JF' class and as such are especially important as some of the last examples of the classic American

Mikado type, which has all but disappeared in China.

The very great majority of African railways was built under European colonial rule, or at least inspired by European thinking and often financed with European capital. Under these circumstances it is hardly surprising that almost all of the steam locomotives and rolling stock used on the continent's railroads were imported, mostly from the United Kingdom as a

direct consequence of the British predominance in colonial and economic affairs during the 19th century.

The importance of industry in South Africa was responsible for elevating this country to the position of the continent's greatest exponent of steam power to the extent that until recent years, and a thorough-going modernization of the South African railroad system, it was one of the most important elements in the worldwide

survival of steam locomotion. What cannot be denied now, however, is that the declining importance of railroads to South Africa and the overhaul of the system have signally reduced the importance of steam locomotion to the extent that its only surviving centres, already under threat, are the gold-mining and coal-mining industries.

Zimbabwe (formerly Rhodesia), South Africa's north-eastern neighbour, was until

very recently the 'Land of the Garratt' as some 90 per cent of the country's steam locomotives were of this type. Since that time, though, steam locomotion has been largely supplanted by diesel locomotion, though a small number of British-manufactured Garratt locomotives survive on shunting and tripping duties around Bulawayo. To the east of Zimbabwe on the coast of Africa to the south of Tanzania, Mozambique also has a small number of

steam locomotives still in service.

On the other side of the African continent Ghana, once a perfect example of the British railway concept translated to a colonial setting, again has no steam locomotion left, a fact that is made all the more poignant by the fact that the move away from a railway capability ignored British pleas for the retention of at least part of the country's steam heritage.

Farther to the north and east, steam locomotion is still evident in two countries, namely Sudan and Eritrea. Despite its ethnic, religious and financial problems as well as the civil war of recent decades, Sudan had tried to maintain its excellent railway system together with at least some of the British-manufactured steam locomotives working on it. In Eritrea, a former Italian colony, there are efforts to recreate the main-line railroad connecting Massawa, Asmara and Agordat, which was closed in 1974 and has suffered years of damage in the war with Ethiopia. If the railroad is in fact brought back into service, it is likely that these services will be hauled by renovated 0-4-4-0 Mallet tank engines built by the Ansaldo company of Italy during the 1930s.

Like Africa, Latin America at one time possessed some of the most exciting and varied steam railroad systems anywhere in the world, but is now falling prey to more modern thinking and a general contraction of railroad capabilities. The most important exception to this general tendency is Paraguay, which operates the last entirely steam-hauled main-line service in the world between Asunción, the national capital, and Encarnación, a town almost on the Argentine border. This classic railroad was slowly recovering a measure of life from 1997, following an earlier cessation of traffic, and one of the features of the line is the continued use of a number of Edwardian wood-burning 'Mogul'-type locomotives, built by North British of Glasgow. The railroad's maintenance works are located in the village of Sapucay and are in effect a working museum with all its equipment steam-driven through belts in classic 19th-century fashion. By contrast with Paraguay, Uruguay has disposed of its fleet of British locomotives, including the world's last 4-4-4T-type locomotives built by the Vulcan Iron Foundry of Newton-le-Willows in 1915, deemed redundant to a railroad system radically scaled down in favour of roads.

In Argentina little remains, although Henschel 2-8-2-type steam locomotives survive on the 29.5-inch (750-mm) gauge Esquel branch. Argentina's other railroad of the same gauge is in the far south, extending from Rio Gallegos to Rio Turbio, and for its coal-carrying services the current force of Mitsubishi 2-10-2 type locomotives are being replaced by diesel locomotives. The industrial railways of Brazil have proved a treasure house of discovery in recent years, but few are now believed to operate steam locomotives. One other limited stronghold of steam locomotion in Latin America is Bolivia, where some former Argentine 2-8-2 and 4-6-0 type locomotives have made an unexpected return to steam working, especially for shunting.

Cuba has a secure niche in railroad history as the final stronghold of U.S. steam power, in this instance of the middle period of American steam locomotion with no locomotives dating from the period before 1878. The primary reason for the survival of steam locomotion in Cuba was the advent to power in 1959 of the regime headed by Fidel Castro, who soon fell out with the U.S.A. in a process that saw the virtual end of trade with any but the communist-bloc countries. For the steam enthusiast this is a blessing, for if the revolution had not occurred, American commercial interests, wholly predominant in Cuban life, would have pressed for rapid dieselization.

Although most of the locomotives operated on Cuba were built specifically for the island, some are ex-American railroad units. As a result, the Cuban register of steam locomotives includes all the great

LEFT: *A massive Beyer-Garratt locomotive No. 4065, built by Henschel in 1954, at Rosmead, South Africa.*

BELOW: *Locomotive No. 4065 climbing from Jagpoort to Lootsberg.*

OPPOSITE: *Paraguayan steam railroad operations may appear decidedly rustic, but retain some of the classics of steam locomotion still serving a useful purpose in the closing stages of the 20th century.*

American steam locomotive manufacturers such as Alco, Baldwin, Davenport, H.K. Porter, Rogers and the Vulcan Iron Foundry, whose designs are represented by a range of engines from 0-4-0 and 0-6-0 type saddle-tank engines to 2-6-0 type 'Mogul', 2-6-2 'Prairie' and 2-8-0 type locomotives. There are also a limited number of 4-6-0 locomotives as well as a few 2-4-2T and 0-4-4T engines.

Cuba has a great variety of gauges, including oddities such as 27-inch (686-mm), 34-inch (864-mm) and 36-inch (914-mm) gauges as well as 24-inch (610-m), 30-in (762-mm) and standard gauges, and as a result there is very little interchange

between the different systems, although an exception is a number of the standard gauge networks which connect with the state railway's main lines. This fact makes it possible for sugar-mill trains to run (often for distances of 15 miles/24km or more) as 'main-line' trains where the distances from the cane fields to the factory requires through running. Another example of extensive working over the state system is the Fructuosa Rodriguez sugar mill, which undertakes round trips of 37 miles (60km).

Even in Cuba steam locomotion is now threatened, for the Soviets delivered a not inconsiderable number of diesel locomotives for both the standard- and

narrow-gauge railroad systems.

In global terms, the steam locomotive was gradually supplemented and then replaced in main-line service by the diesel-engined or electrically-powered locomotive within the context of a process that also saw the gradual but widespread advent of what are currently designated rapid-transit systems. These systems were specifically intended for the rapid delivery of passengers within the great cities of the period, which then became the bases for today's vast conurbations. The first rapid-transit systems were based conceptually on the tramway, whose origins can be traced back to the plateways used in mines and

quarries to ease the passage of horse-drawn wagons. The first street tramway to be introduced in a city was the New York & Harlem line of 1832. This led to the coining of the American term 'street railway', which is still in use. The world's second horse tramway, constructed during 1835 in New Orleans, is still in use today after a continuous history of more than 150 years, a remarkable testimony to the sound basic nature of the concept even though the services are now operated by electric cars. Crowning the efforts of American promoters, the tramway reached Europe in 1853 with the inauguration of the Paris system, and seven years later the first British system of this type was operational in Birkenhead. During 1861 the first section of London's network was opened, and the British capital was followed in 1963 by Copenhagen, the Danish capital.

The boom time for the construction of horse tramways was the 1870s, but even by this time the very real limitations of animal power had become apparent, and advocates of the tramway concept soon turned to the idea of mechanical power. Initial consideration was given to steam power, which was already very successful for railroad use, but though steam trams were developed and put into operation on many suburban and rural light railways, it was clear from the very beginning that steam power was ill-suited to urban applications. Other power sources, such as compressed air, gas and petrol engines were evaluated with little success, and cable tramways enjoyed considerable success for a time.

LEFT: A 2-6-0 1510, manufactured by Alco in 1907, shunting at the Boris Luis Santa Coloma Mill, Cuba.

OPPOSITE LEFT: BLW 2-6-0 1531 on FCC tracks from José Smith Comas Mill, Cuba.

OPPOSITE RIGHT: The standard-gauge side of Osvaldo Sanchez Mill with a 2-4-2T 1204 (Rogers 1894) and a 4107 Whitcombe 40053-class 25DM18 gasoline-electric, photographed in Cuba.

The most successful of the latter was that in San Francisco, where it is still used. All of these tractive methods were either mechanically unreliable or economically unrealistic, and rapidly became secondary after electric traction had become feasible.

The first electric vehicles were battery-powered, but in 1879 a German, Werner von Siemens, demonstrated his new type of practical dynamo. This was clearly the way ahead for electric traction using electricity generated at a fixed station and transmitted to its user by a conducting rail or overhead wire. The first electric tramway for public use was opened in Berlin during 1881 by

Siemens & Halske, and used a 180-volt current fed through the running rails. The first lines of this type in the U.K. were the Portrush & Bushmills (later Giant's Causeway) Tramway in Northern Ireland and Volk's Railway at Brighton in 1883, of which the latter is still operational.

Electrified running rails were not suitable for street use as a result of their safety considerations, so a change was made to overhead wires of the type first used on the Bessbrook & Newry line in Ireland in 1885. A slotted overhead tube was trialled in Paris during 1881, and other European cities with street railways included Frankfurt, which opened in 1884 and now possesses the lengthiest period of non-stop electric street tramway operation anywhere in the world: Frankfurt also used the slotted overhead tube system initially, but in 1906 switched to the more conventional overhead wire.

As they did not need poles and overhead wires, underground conduits were sometimes preferred as an alternative to overhead current collection where aesthetic considerations were thought to predominate over the practical aspects of tramway operation: such a system was used in London until the end of tramway operations

in 1952, and in Washington, D.C. until 1962. The U.K.'s oldest street tramway is that along the front at Blackpool, and has operated on an overhead system since 1899 although it made use of the conduit system when it was inaugurated during 1885.

Experience soon revealed that the overhead wire with trolley pole collection was without doubt the most practical solution to the problem of delivering electric power to a tramway car, and the first city tramway system of this type was created in

Richmond, Virginia, during 1887. By 1900, almost all of the original American horse tramways had been adapted for electric traction, and Europe was not far behind the U.S.A. in this respect. In another striking piece of evidence to his technical expertise, Siemens developed the bow collector as an alternative to the trolley pole and this in turn led to the pantograph which is today the most frequently-used method of collecting electrical power from an overhead line. Before the end of the 19th century, electric

tramways were common in many parts of the world including the Australian city of Melbourne, the Japanese city of Kyoto and the Siamese city of Bangkok. British tramways in the U.K., and also in those parts of the world in which the British influence was strongest, generally opted for double-decked trams as a means of maximizing capacity without creating a larger footprint. On the mainland of Europe, a single-deck tram towing a trailer was more common, and in the U.S.A. larger trams mounted on

two bogies soon became the norm.

The golden age of the tramway is generally regarded to have been the first quarter of the 20th century: virtually every major city operated such a system, most of the systems under municipal control rather than private ownership. As well as offering cheap and reliable transport for the masses, the tramway also played a major part in the relevant city's economic development and in the growth of its suburban belt.

Technical developments in mechanical

OPPOSITE: A Norwegian State Railways Class El 16 electric locomotive heading a passenger train.

RIGHT. A Class 20 electric locomotive alongside a Class 800 EMU (electric motor unit) of Belgian State Railways, late 1970s.

BELOW RIGHT: A Sprinter EMU of the Netherlands State Railways.

as well as electrical engineering also permitted the design and introduction of larger and more powerful cars, and the fusion of the tramway and railroad concepts allowed the introduction of high-speed intra-urban lines, which became typical of urban areas all over the world but especially in North America, where over 15,000 miles (24140km) of such line covered the continent.

By the 1920s the tramway situation was decidedly less rosy than it had been at the beginning of the century. Labour and materials were rising rapidly in cost and, as might have been expected, local and national politicians, voted into office by those who might suffer the economic consequences of fare increases, were unwilling to authorize the costlier tickets required to allow tramway managers to match expenditure with income. The problem here was that the systems resulting from the initial capital investment were reaching the ends of their useful lives, and

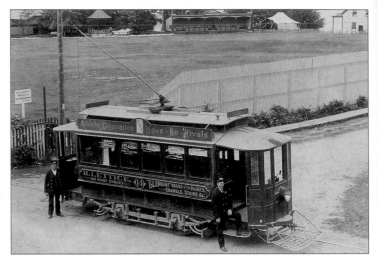

that the profits from the good years had not been retained by the city authorities for the renewal that would be the inevitable requirement of considerable use. Thus the maintenance of tramway systems was becoming increasingly expensive, there was insufficient capital for the large-scale renovations that were needed and, perhaps most threateningly of all, there was the prospect of declining markets as a result of the start of mass-production of motor cars and motor buses. The overall consequence of this concatenation of events was real competition for the tramway at a time when it was more viable in economic terms to introduce feeder bus services than to extend the existing tramway systems to cater for the cities' continued growth.

Then came the great financial depression, which started in the U.S.A. during 1929 and soon spread to Europe. This effectively decimated the economies of most Western countries, in the process resulting in the swift collapse not only of many small-town tramways but also of the majority of intra-urban networks. Both of these were systems that operated at small profit margins, and were thus prone to the effects of competition. The motor bus effectively took over from the tramway, and from the early 1930s the trolley bus was in effect a way of killing off the tramway without wasting the electrical supply infrastructure which had been developed to supply its power. There is some evidence that in the United States where municipal

ownership was less common than in Europe, bus and oil companies tried to take over failing tramways so that the companies could replace them and so increase the profitability of both. It is perhaps ironic that this type of sharp business practice got its comeuppance within a little more than ten years as bus profitability disappeared in the face or the surge of private car ownership. Many municipalities had to intervene to ensure that at least the basic elements of a public transportation system remained.

Tramway managers did not give in without a considerable struggle, however. In the U.S.A. the President's Congress Committee of Streetcar Companies, generally known as the PCC, undertook the research and sponsored the production of a

ABOVE LEFT: *An early British Columbia Electric Railway trolley in Vancouver, 1900. This open-air, double-truck car is on Westminster Avenue (now Main Street at 9th Avenue).*

ABOVE: *One of Victoria, British Columbia's first trolleys under the B.C.E.R. The photograph was taken in 1898 near Esquimalt Naval Station.*

ABOVE: B.C.E.R. Street Car 105 on a run from Harris (East Georgia) along Victoria Drive, via Georgia to Kitsilano Beach where the photograph was taken.

RIGHT: These B.C.E.R. electrically-powered units of decidedly strange appearance were created for the important task of track cleaning to ensure maximum traction without the interference of snow, leaves and other litter.

new design of tram that would offer levels of comfort and performance equal to those of the private motor car. The result was the so-called PCC car, which staved off the closure of many tramway systems, and also saved many others, to form the basis of a revival of the tramway concept. Some of these are still operational, and indeed have become something of a grail for those fascinated by tramway heritage as an aspect of urban renewal. The PCC arrived in Europe late in the 1940s, and one of the first lines modified was the U.K.'s pioneering Blackpool Tramway: this was modernized with large numbers of trams built to the PCC concept, and so ensured the system's survival up to the present.

Before this, the stringencies of World

War II had hastened the decline of tramways in the U.K. and France, but at the same time created the opportunity for large-scale reconstruction in Belgium, the Netherlands, Germany and eastern Europe. In the U.K. the nationalization of municipal electrical supplies was another reason for the replacement of tramways by cheaper motor buses in much of the country, although some tramways, such as those of Glasgow and Liverpool, enjoyed a revival after World War II with new trams and reserved-track extensions, but never enough to ensure they became a dominant part of the network. The last city system to close in the U.K. was that of Glasgow, which shut during 1962.

The 1960s constituted a decade of

despair for the concept of public transport in many parts of the world. Most of those involved in industry and all types of traffic planning came to the belief that the motor car would become the standard form of transport for the majority of people, with buses only for those who could not afford cars, and that cities could somehow be adapted to cater for the increased levels of motor traffic that would result. By 1962, the only tramway system left in the U.K. was that of Blackpool, which had a reserved track along the sea front. A few tramway systems survived in North American cities, though the general belief was that it was only a matter of time before these last vestiges of an earlier age fell to the apparently unstoppable surge of the motor

ABOVE: Trams running along Des Voeux Road, Hong Kong.

LEFT: A brightly painted tram in Hong Kong.

OPPOSITE: Trams arriving and departing from Glasgow Central Station, Scotland.

car. In other parts of the world, planned or anticipated modernization of tramway systems came rapidly to a halt as costs rose in the aftermath of the disappearance from the tramway supply market of all types of mass-production economy.

The one stronghold of the tramway in this period was the mainland of the European continent. Here, in general, there was continued investment in the tramway, the largest commitments to the concept being those of the countries in the northern and eastern parts of the continent. Thus nations such as France, Italy and Spain proceeded toward the abandonment of the tramway, while West Germany emerged as the main force in tramway development, in

which the German manufacturer Düwag came to prominence as a designer of tramcars in general, and of articulated tramcars in particular. These latter could be operated by just one person, with most fares collected off the car by season ticket sales or ticket machines at stops.

This increase in the passenger/crew ratio was just one of the ways in which the operating economics of the tramcar were improved to the point at which the tramcar once again emerged and was financially superior to the bus. Moreover, despite an increase in car ownership, large-scale modernization of tramcar fleets and the infrastructure over which they operated encouraged patronage, especially as

passengers came to appreciate the advantages of travelling on a tramcar operating over reserved tracks. This was at a time when urban motor car transport was becoming increasingly slow as cities filled with cars all travelling in and out of the centre at the same basic times, and all needing somewhere to park in urban areas never designed for this type of congestion. In many city centres, most especially in Austria, Belgium and Germany, the tram was liberated from the worst effects of traffic congestion by the construction of shallow subway systems under busy crossroads and crowded streets.

Belgium, the Netherlands and the countries of eastern Europe became the

home of the Europeanized PCC car, which attracted traffic by its high performance and frequent service. As the communist regimes of eastern Europe allowed little in the way of private car ownership, the availability of high-capacity public transport was of key importance. Full metro systems (known in the U.K. as underground railways) were unaffordable outside the major conurbations, so for many cities the tramway was the most important aspect of municipally-controlled urban transport. Centralized planning inevitably meant that the U.S.S.R. rapidly came to the position of the world's largest tramway operator, with Leningrad (once more known as St. Petersburg, as it had also been called up to

OPPOSITE LEFT: *A City of Birmingham tram at Pype Hayes Terminus, England.*

OPPOSITE RIGHT: *Streamlined double- and single-decker trams on the seafront at Blackpool, England.*

LEFT: *Trams operating in Johnston Road, Wanchai, in busy Hong Kong.*

1914) possessing the largest tramway network. In the 1960s, the world's most prolific tramcar manufacturer was the Czechoslovak firm CKD Tatra of Prague. As communist-bloc economic agreement made it the supplier for most of Eastern Europe as well as the U.S.S.R., the company expanded its production facilities to the extent that it was delivering 1,000 cars per year, or almost three every day.

By the late 1960s, farther-sighted Western planners had begun to appreciate the disadvantages of massive reliance on the motor car and, as a result, a steady reduction in public transport. In some major cities peak-time traffic congestion was reaching virtually 'gridlock' proportions, and this had resulted in an attempt to cater

for the ever-increasing demands of motor car ownership by the creation of new mega-highways in urban areas: these could be created only by the destruction of vast construction paths through the cities in question, a process that divided communities both physically and economically and, as soon became apparent, resulted in major economic and social decline. This tendency was especially notable in the U.S.A. and, to a lesser extent, Canada. Many cities therefore saw a swift economic decline in their city centres as new shopping malls, reliant almost entirely on motor car transport, were created to fulfil the requirements of populations moving steadily from high-density housing in the city centre to low-density housing in the suburbs.

The social and economic ramifications of this process were not all that had now begun to worry the planners, however, for there were also increasing concerns about the environmental pollution inherent in the system. Therefore the planners and politicians decided to turn their eyes east across the Atlantic Ocean to see how the planners of Europe had overcome the problems to keep and indeed strengthen the flourishing nature of their city centres. An early appreciation of the European success was a need for an effective policy for low-cost public transport that could offer a very real alternative to the motor car by the high average speed it could maintain along reserved-track tramways.

The consequent revival of the fortunes

of the streetcar (otherwise the tram), usually within the context of a light rail vehicle, has been just as extraordinary in North America as it has been in Europe, and reflects the signal fact that while the Americans may not yet have overcome their fascination with the motor car, they have finally come to an appreciation that it is not feasible, either economically or socially, to rebuild their cities to allow unfettered use of the motor car. This appreciation has surfaced in many parts of the country, but is perhaps strongest in California with its sturdy if perhaps idiosyncratic approach to environmental matters.

As noted above, American planners started to look to Europe in the 1970s for concepts of the means they could employ to rescue their cities from outward-spreading decay and resultant economic decline. With urban transportation now owned by public bodies, the development of improved public transport could be undertaken with a combination of city, state and national resources. This situation arrived at much the same time as the end of the American involvement in the Vietnam War, which meant that the military manufacturers were beginning to look for different markets to keep their production capabilities working at maximum profitability after the curtailment of military equipment spending, and decided that public transport would rapidly become the scene of considerable growth. An initial consequence of this situation was that Boston and San Francisco, two cities still operating tramway systems, contracted with Boeing-Vertol for

OPPOSITE ABOVE: *Trams safely share the streets with pedestrians in Russia.*

OPPOSITE BELOW: *Copenhagen's suburban S-Bahn.*

THIS PAGE
RIGHT: *Amtrak AEM7 No. 905 at Harrison Station, New Jersey with the Metroliner services from New York and Washington, D.C.*

BELOW LEFT and RIGHT: *Amtrak Metroliners used in the North East Corridor between Boston and Washington, D.C.*

LEFT: In small and densely populated countries such as Belgium, an efficient network of commuter and rapid transport systems is rightly appreciated as a vital tool in the easing of road traffic congestion and the timely movement of passengers in urban environments.

BELOW: As one of the hub nations of continental Europe and, just as importantly, of the European Union, Belgium has sensibly made its main-line railroad network an intrinsic element of the northern European system so that its services can travel into neighbouring countries as well as the services of other countries passing into Belgium or even through it.

the production of new LRVs (light rail vehicles) of the articulated type. These were based on a design schemed as the basis for an LRV which the company hoped would emulate the PCC of some 40 years earlier in becoming standard throughout the U.S.A. and also offering considerable export potential. The company's hopes were sound but its product was not, and the LRV was a disaster at the technical level as the company sought to 'reinvent the wheel' rather than learning from the wealth of experience available from practical operations elsewhere.

Thus it was in Canada that the first successful development of the new type of LRV emerged in North America, for it was here the city Edmonton decided that rather than create a wholly new concept it would draw on the experience of current European success and therefore opt for the alternative approach of adapting European technology to the North American situation. The city thus constructed a new light rail line, partly on redundant railroad alignment and partly in city subways, and from 1978 used this for the operation of Siemens-Düwag trams imported from West Germany. The system was immediately successful, and as such was rapidly adopted as the model for San Diego in the U.S.A. and Calgary in Canada. In these two cities, it was decided that the creation of subways would be too expensive, so pedestrian and transit precincts were established in the city centres, it being rightly appreciated that trams, being guided pollution-free vehicles, could be operated successfully and safely in

LEFT: A suburban electric trainset built by Soreframe under a Budd licence for the Portuguese State Railways, seen here on the Cascais line.

BELOW: A Class 4020 EMU of the Austrian State Railways, late 1970s.

areas otherwise reserved for pedestrians.

The success of these systems in attracting back to the use of public transit large numbers of motor car owners, who would never have considered the use of a bus, led to a considerable expansion in both the development and construction of light rail systems, and this has continued right up to the present. Major cities such as Baltimore, Buffalo, Dallas, Denver, Los Angeles, Portland, Sacramento and St. Louis have built new light rail lines, many of them as part of systems that are still expanding geographically, and is scheduling to meet the demand engendered by their success. More recent examples of new and emerging systems are to be found in Jersey City and Salt Lake City, and progress toward similar systems has been made in other cities such as New York and Seattle. Moreover, the success of the concept persuaded cities such as Cleveland, Pittsburgh and Philadelphia, which operated systems based on the earlier streetcar concept, to invest in the new type of rolling stock and begin a programme of expansion.

The example of Los Angeles is notably important, for this was an urban area that discarded its trams and intra-urbans during the 1960s in the belief that the city could live and breathe with the motor car. The dense pollution that has become a characteristic feature of Los Angeles finally proved to the city fathers that their predecessors were wholly wrong, and the city has inaugurated two new light rail lines, with a third already under construction.

ABOVE: *The Metro maintenance depot in Rio de Janeiro, Brazil.*

RIGHT: *A suburban EMU in Rio de Janeiro on the approach to Don Pedro Station.*

OPPOSITE: *Four different-style EMUs on the approach to Don Pedro Station in Rio de Janeiro, Brazil.*

Farther to the south, Mexico is a country in which the blight of the motor car has in places reached a situation even more acute than that of the worst of the American cities, and a similar approach has been belatedly adopted. As a result there are new light rail lines in Guadalajara, Monterey and, most significantly of all, the huge conurbation of Mexico City. Tramways had virtually disappeared from South America by the end of the 1960s, but the first new light rail lines have now appeared in Buenos Aires and Rio de Janeiro.

Light rail first came into existence on the mainland of Europe in the form of new rolling stock and track segregated from public roadways to ensure that the services could maintain a high average speed. The pioneering concept of the European light rail system was derived largely from the planning which took place in the Swedish city of Gothenburg where, during a period of some 15 years, an ordinary city street tramway was extended through the suburbs, both new and existing, on high-speed reserved track, and every possible incentive was used to persuade the public to make extensive use of public transport. The existing rolling stock gave way to high-performance trams, and traffic restrictions were imposed to give priority to trams in the central area. This Swedish system was created without the cost of building tunnels, in the process not only minimizing cost but at the same time keeping public transport on the surface as an attractive and readily accessible system.

Many other cities in other parts of the

world have adopted the same concept since 1980: just in Europe, for example, in Austria there are Graz and Linz, in Belgium there is Ghent, in the Netherlands there is Amsterdam, and in Switzerland there are Basle and Zürich. These fine examples are matched slightly differently in other Austrian, Belgian and German cities, where in general it was thought that the best way of improving the average speed of public transport in city streets was to provide a segregated path in subways: examples of this approach are to be found in cities such as Antwerp, Brussels, Hanover, Köln, Stuttgart and Vienna. However, the growing capital cost of underground work has begun to make this type of operation prohibitively expensive, and as a result there has emerged a swing back to the concept of road traffic restrictions to provide public transport with priority.

LEFT and OPPOSITE: A Class 1042 electric locomotive heading an Austrian State Railways express train on the Semmering Line.

The creation of these new and upgraded systems has led to the establishment of a novel terminology to help differentiate such systems from ordinary tramways, and Supertram, Light Rail, Metro, Sneltrom (express tram) and Stadtbahn (town rail) are just some of the names now used, and a number of upgraded subway tramways in Germany are marketed in the same way as underground metros by using the term U-Bahn (underground railroad). It is worth noting that a feature which did much to enhance the popularity of the subway during the 1970s and 1980s was that it offered the possibility of level boarding of high-floor cars in the city suburbs. On surface lines in the suburbs, there was often space available to install platforms level with the vehicle floor, which made the vehicles readily accessible for passengers in wheelchairs or those with prams and buggies; in other parts of the system the vehicles use fold-down steps.

Apart from the public desire for the creation or revitalization of light rail systems as a means of cutting down the pollution and increasingly slow speed of private motor car transport in city centres, the primary driving force for the urban transport revolution was the mass of legislation enacted during the 1960s to lay the groundwork for progress towards the new era in public transport. As a result of this legislation, local authorities were allocated the task of developing plans for integrated transport systems, and in the major conurbations, PTEs (Passenger Transport Executives) were established to assume responsibility for the development and operation of public transport in their areas.

One of the first PTEs to make progress was the Tyne & Wear PTE, located in the heavily industrialized and heavily populated north-west of England, which launched its public transport plan in 1973. This proposed the establishment of a light rail system to take over the alignment of 26 miles (42km) of run-down local railway track that were to be connected into 8.5 miles (13.5km) of new infrastructure to create a network of electrified suburban lines as the heart of an integrated passenger transport system. The initial route was opened in stages between 1980 and 1984 and, as the U.K.'s first modern light rail system, with a capacity of more than 40 million passengers per year, was largely successful in one of its primary tasks of assisting in the regeneration of Tyneside.

In London, a key issue in the planned regeneration of the docklands area east of the city was public transport. The light rail concept was deemed appropriate and affordable in this context, and was adopted during 1982. The initial 7-mile (12-km) system was then extended to 13 miles (21km), and is now being further extended to the region south of the Thames river. The network has proved very popular, and more than 22 million passengers per year are carried. Many of the U.K.'s major cities are planning to use a range of systems, from segregated and automated operation (on former rail alignments) to conventional street tramways.

LEFT: *An intermediate-level compartment at the end of a TATOA double-deck commuter coach on Toronto's GO Rapid Transit System.*

BELOW : *Exterior of Toronto's GO Rapid Transit System.*

During the 1990s new technology has been developed to provide low-floor trams with step-free entrances only 13.75in (0.35m) above rail level. Surface systems achieved exactly the same effect just by building up kerbs slightly to create a matching height. This is now the favoured solution for improving the accessibility of trams, and over 2,000 low-floor cars have been delivered or ordered for European systems. In the U.K. all new systems are required to offer step-free access to trams, resulting in new rolling stock which will be supplied from manufacturers in Belgium, Germany and Italy.

In countries such as France, Italy and Spain which, like the U.K., had abandoned their tramway heritage, there has also been a resurgence of interest in the tram. France has introduced new systems in cities such as Grenoble, Nantes, Paris and Rouen, and comparable systems are in the offing for Bordeaux, Montpellier, Orléans and Toulon. The Spanish city of Valencia has similarly built a new tramway and other cities are developing plans for improved public transport. In Italy, Genoa has a new segregated light rail line and many cities are planning tramway systems with the support of companies.

The tram as used in Australia and New Zealand was based closely on its British counterpart, although double-deck vehicles were less frequent as a reflection of the less cramped conditions typical of antipodean cities. There was a rapid decline of the tram concept in the 1950s and 1960s as small-town systems were terminated for economic

have been constructed and two local rail lines have been converted to light rail operation and linked by street operation with the city centre.

The return of trams to Sydney, Melbourne's great Australian rival, occurred in 1997 with the opening of a short line built and operated by the private sector. This was designed as the basis of an expanded network, including operation in city streets, to be largely completed by the time the Olympic Games are held in the city in the year 2000. Elsewhere, Brisbane is considering the introduction of trams and the surviving route in Adelaide is scheduled for modernization. This line was due for extension in the 1980s, but a change of political power saw the introduction of the German type of O-Bahn guided bus way system.

Trams had disappeared from the city streets of New Zealand's major cities by the 1960s. The year 1995 saw their return to

ABOVE: *Bombardier's LRC (Light, Rapid and Comfortable) train operated by VIA Rail, Canada.*

RIGHT: *Netherlands State Railways three-car train set, in the late 1970s.*

reasons, while at the same time cities such as Adelaide, Brisbane and Sydney sacrificed their trams for industrial and political reasons. However, the southern hemisphere's largest system, some 137 miles (220km) long, is that of Melbourne, which survived intact thanks to good management and political support. The system's first new trams for 20 years arrived in 1975, and since that year the arrival of more than 350 more new cars has transformed the system from a very traditional and conservative operation to one that is much more customer-orientated. Several new extensions

OPPOSITE: *The Docklands Light Railway, serving the East End of London.*

THIS PAGE
RIGHT: *A tram in Nicholson Street, Melbourne, Australia.*

BELOW: *Docklands 42 and 57 arriving at Poplar, bound for Stratford, East London.*

Christchurch in the form of a heritage loop through the city centre using museum cars to provide a service aimed mainly at tourists. The construction of light rail systems are also being planned for Auckland and Wellington.

Japan has in general suffered even more than the U.S.A. and Europe from the effects of massed private cars, so local conditions were not good for the short-term survival of the street tramway. However, many surviving tramways have now been upgraded to run on segregated track. These form the basis of a substantial network of light railways that are an important part of

the well-used public transport network. Ironically, some small-town street tramway operations have survived and are currently being modernized, and the first low-floor tram, based on a German design, was introduced in 1997. Elsewhere in Asia, rail-based urban public transport is less common. Located in Calcutta, India's only surviving tramway is a substantial network, but years of poor investment have left services in a precarious state. By contrast Manila, the capital of the Philippines, opened a new segregated light rail line across the city in 1984, and the success of this system has encouraged the construction of two more lines using private capital. The North Korean capital of Pyongyang has built a new tramway system and in Malaysia a new light metro system opened in 1996.

China had little tramway operation. In 1997, however, it regained the ex-British colony of Hong Kong, where British-style double-deck trams have run since 1904, and these continue to compete successfully with intensive bus operation on the streets of Hong Kong island. A complete contrast is the 20-mile (32-km) long light rail system, built since 1988, in the suburban township of Tuen Mun. This is one of the most heavily patronized rail systems in the world and carries over 112 million passengers every year.

In Africa the light rail concept is limited to Tunisia and Egypt. Tunis has created a 20-mile (32-km) system since 1985 with German-built articulated cars operating on four surface lines that carry 90 million passengers a year. Alexandria has a street tramway and a suburban light rail line, while Cairo, Heliopolis and Helwan operate modernized light rail lines.

The concept of the light rail system is not of rigid definition, but in effect was conceived to accommodate all types of tracked transport in the gap between the bus and the heavy metro, or conventional railway, and can be operated like any of them. A light rail system is costlier to make than any bus system on city streets, but for a given capacity can be cheaper to operate, has lower whole-life costs, offers a higher average speed, produces less pollution, and

in general is more successful in attracting motorists to public transport. In comparison with a metro or urban railway, a light rail system is cheaper to build and operate but operates at a lower speed. Among its other advantages, however, are the fact that it offers a visible example of successful public transport, provides better penetration of urban areas, is typified by better security, and generates less noise. Light rail can cater economically and effectively for passenger

flows between 2,000 and 20,000 passengers an hour, and as a result is usually to be found in cities with populations between 200,000 and 1 million.

The light rail concept is usually based on the use of steel-wheeled vehicles running on steel rails and collecting electrical power from an overhead wire. Diesel light rail is a concept that has been evaluated to only a limited extent, and may prove to be useful for low-cost starter lines

ABOVE: A key element in the success of rapid transit systems in busy urban areas is the use of double-decked cars which can carry more passengers on a given number of axles.

OPPOSITE: Another vital aspect of systems such as the Metrolink, is the layout of stations with extensive car parking facilities and platforms which optimize the rapid movement of passengers.

that can then be adapted to the full light rail concept. The steel rails can be grooved so that they lie flush with a street surface, or may be ballasted like normal railroad track, and this capability makes light rail the only system that can operate on both city streets and jointly with conventional rail services. It also offers the possibility of extending regional railroad services to the city centre by way of transfer points from rail to street track. This notion, adopted with very considerable success in the German city of Karlsruhe with dual-voltage light rail vehicles, is now extending to other cities.

Light rail is also very flexible in its applications, and can thus operate in a wide range of built-up environments. It can serve as a tramway in the street, though maximization of its advantages over the bus requires the minimization of unsegregated street track. Within public streets the track can be segregated by any of several means. The track can be laid in tarmac, concrete, ballast or even grass according to the operational and environmental needs of the whole system. Light rail can be built on previous railroad alignments, or indeed share track with the railroad in the form of little-used freight lines or those with limited passenger services, and technical progress means that the required safety arrangements are readily available for mixed services.

A topic closely related to the light rail revolution is the re-emergence of commuter trains, sometimes called heavy rail to differentiate it from light rail, as an important aspect of urban regeneration, for while the light rail system is dedicated to

OPPOSITE: The Tokyo-Kawasaki City
Monorail, Japan,

*LEFT: A surburban double-deck EMU
runs into Milsons Point Station after
crossing the Sydney Harbour Bridge,
Australia.*

*BELOW: A double-deck EMU on
surburban service halts at Central Station,
Sydney.*

the rapid movement of people between
various points in the urban environment, the
commuter rail system has been re-
established as the most cost-effective means
of moving the work force into the urban
environment at the beginning of the
working day and then returning the same
people to their homes outside the city at the
end of the day. The commuter train never
wholly died in the U. S.A., but was severely
strained by the rivalry of the private motor

car between the 1950s and 1980s and
declined to a very low technical and
commercial level.

In recent years, however, there has been
a considerable renaissance in commuter
operations in the U.S.A.'s major cities, and
in a growing number of these conurbations
the regional authorities have taken to
operating what may be termed 'heavy rail'
commuter services with their own trains
running on track either acquired or leased

from the railroad companies; in a number
of other conurbations the regional
authorities have contracted with the local
railroad company for the operation of heavy
rail services.

In the area covered by the Connecticut
Department of Transportation, for instance,
a contract has been signed with Amtrak for
the operation of a 50.6-mile (81.4-km)
Shoreline East commuter service between
New London and New Haven via six

367

intermediate stations. The service was launched in 1990 with two EMD 'F7M'-class locomotives and Pullman Standard cars dating from the 1950s and bought from the Port Authority of Allegheny County, Pittsburgh, following the latter's termination of its own commuter services. The Connecticut Department of Transportation has since expanded the operation by leasing from Guildford two 'GP38'- and one 'GP7W'-class power cars to haul 10 Bombardier Comet cars, supplemented by 11 existing Budd 8SPV200 railcars remodelled by Amtrak's Wilmington facility as standard cars.

At the start of 1996 the service was organized on the basis of peak-time schedules during the working week with two reciprocal runnings to ensure that the trains were positioned correctly for peak times. During 1996 the traffic carried increased by 6.5 per cent and, in anticipation of the high track speeds expected from Amtrak's forthcoming electrification of the line, an order was placed for six 3,000-hp (2237-kW) diesel locomotives to be manufactured by AMF Technotransport. The Connecticut Department of Transportation also controls (and with the New York Department of Transportation jointly subsidizes to the extent of 60 per cent of the operating deficit and 63 per cent of the capital cost) the commuter services operated by Metro-North between the city of New York and New Haven. The Connecticut Department of Transportation has also pressed the case for bus shuttles to its stations, thereby

ABOVE: A stainless-steel Rock Island Railroad coach No.150 on commuter services out of La Salle Street Station, Chicago to Vermont Street.

ABOVE RIGHT: Southern Pacific double-deck suburban coach in San Francisco Station.

OPPOSITE: The Alweg Monorail leaves the Convention Center for downtown Seattle.

promoting reverse commuting, and such services now operate in Greenwich, New Haven, Norwalk and Stamford.

The Long Island Rail Road Company, which is a wholly-owned subsidiary of the Metropolitan Transportation Authority, an agency of the State of New York, operates commuter services between the city of New York and destinations on Long Island, and operates within the limits of a budget allocated by the Metropolitan Transit Authority and including a sizeable element of capital investment in new rolling stock, station improvements and general infrastructure maintenance.

The extent and nature of the system's operations is revealed by the fact that in 1996 it carried 73.6 million passengers, and this was the fourth year in succession that the number of passengers had increased. However, in the first part of 1996 a reverse trend became evident, probably as a result of a fare increase of almost 10 per cent.

The Long Island Rail Road's services reach out into the Long Island counties of Nassau and Suffolk as well as to certain parts of the eastern Queens part of the New York conurbation. The services had nine

branch lines that converge onto three main stations in New York, namely Penn Station, Flatbush Avenue in Brooklyn and Hunters Point Avenue that is open only at peak hours and served only by diesel trains: the bulk of the daily traffic is handled by Penn Station, in the form of 208,000 passengers, the other two stations handling 40,000 passengers between them. It is worth noting that the Long Island Rail Road also handles a large quantity of freight services.

By the middle of the 1990s the Long Island Rail Road's programme to improve Penn Station was well under way, the $190 million programme being designed to better the access to and the movement within the station, as well as to improve the station's facilities in terms of the level of comfort and information for the passengers. This effort is reflected in the fact that the average passenger now has 20 per cent more space and a 40 per cent increase in access points, the latter including five stairways, three escalators, five elevators to Long Island Rail Road platforms, and even a new entrance. The importance attached to the attraction of commuter travellers back to the train (there are now 42 rather than the original 36 train movements per hour) is also revealed by general enhancements such as improvements of the signs and master destination board, a new public address system, more effective lighting, and a traveller concourse with seats and washroom facilities.

The Long Island Rail Road started to receive new rolling stock in 1997–98, but up to that time operated a fleet of

locomotives comprising 28 2,000-hp (1491-kW) 'GP36-2' class, 23 1,500-hp (1119-kW) 'MP15AC' class and three 'FL9AC'-class units as primary haulers, and also eight 1,000-hp (746-kW) 'SW1001' units for shunting operations. Passengers are carried in a fleet of 1,125 cars including 760 'M1'-class multiple-unit cars on the electrified inner suburban lines of the city of New York and in Nassau and Suffolk counties, and 174 examples of the 'M3'-class car obtained in the mid-1980s. Operations to other parts of the network are handled by trains hauled by diesel-electric locomotives, which are scheduled for early replacement in the railroad's major reinvestment programme. The Long Island Rail Road also has an eye open to the use of more flexible technology in the future, and is therefore evaluating dual-mode (diesel and third-rail electric) traction. The operator runs a single train in each direction during the peak-hour period between Penn Station and Port Jefferson on a non-electrified line using some of its 10 prototype double-deck cars obtained from Mitsui in Japan and powered by two FL9AC-class locomotives rebuilt to their current configuration by Adtranz, or ABB Traction as it then was.

It was in March 1995 that the Long Island Rail Road signed contracts worth some $250 million for new locomotives and passenger cars. The bulk of the contracts' value went to General Electric for 23 examples of its 'DE30AC'-class diesel-electric locomotives for push/pull operations, as well as options for another 23

OPPOSITE: A Chicago & North Western Railroad suburban train with double-deck coaches leaving Chicago.

OPPOSITE: A Chicago & North Western Railroad suburban train with double-deck coaches leaving Chicago.

RIGHT: Class F40PH locomotives 236, 355 and 353 on the eastbound California Zephyr *coming down the Denver & Rio Grande tracks through Price River Canyon just above Helper, Utah.*

units that could be all of the same type or alternatively eight of the same type and 15 of a revised dual-mode type. The contracts also covered the manufacture and delivery of 48 new passenger cars. By this time research had revealed that passengers had a decided preference for 2+2 seating rather than the 2+3 arrangement typical of the 10 prototype cars that had been initially evaluated over a two-year period with maximum accommodation for 180 passengers. The order therefore comprises cars with provision for a maximum of 145 passengers, reduced to 139 passengers in cab cars.

Farther to the south along the eastern seaboard of the U.S.A. is the area covered by the Maryland Mass Transit Administration's Maryland Rail Commuter Service. This provides services over the 75.6-mile (121.6-km) route linking Washington, D.C. and Perryville via Baltimore on electrified track within the context of Amtrak's 'North-East Corridor' operation, a 37.9-mile (61-km) route linking Washington, D.C. and Baltimore on

non-electrified track, and a 72.6-mile (116.8-km) route linking Washington, D.C. and Martinsburg on non-electrified track. The service between Washington and Perryville is the responsibility of four electric locomotives hauling Japanese-built passenger cars, while the services on the other two routes are operated with older stock using diesel locomotives.

During 1994 the Maryland Rail

Commuter Service posted a total annual passenger figure of some 5 millions which, at 6 per cent over the previous year, seemed to indicate a levelling off of growth from the 20 per cent figure evident in previous years. Operating within the context of the Maryland Mass Transit Authority, the Maryland Rail Commuter Service is able to offer tickets and passes valid throughout the system and this is clearly a decided

inducement to passengers to use all aspects of Maryland Mass Transit, which include the bus, light rail and metro services of Baltimore and, it is hoped for the near future, Washington, D.C. The Maryland Rail Commuter Service is growing slightly with the aid of a federal financial package that is allowing a 13.4-mile (21.6-km) extension to Frederick with the aid of new track, signalling equipment, rolling stock, etc.

Further evidence of the integrated nature of the Maryland Mass Transit Authority's nature is provided by the Maryland Rail Commuter Service's completion of a new station at Dorsey, which has a major parking capability at its own links to the Maryland state highway system.

The Maryland Rail Commuter Service's train equipment comprises four 'AEM7'-class electric locomotives and 25 3,000-hp (2238-kW) 'GP40WH-2'-class locomotives, together with more than 100 passenger cars in the form of 43 refurbished New Jersey Transit Authority and 63 new Sumitomo cars, complemented in due course by 50 double-deck cars ordered in 1995 from Kawasaki.

Located farther to the north, around Boston, the Massachusetts Bay Transportation Authority provides commuter rail services on 11 routes into Boston on a network comprising 308.1 miles (495.9 km) of track originally owned up to the 1970s by Penn Central and Boston & Maine. From 1988 the Massachusetts Bay Transportation Authority's sphere of influence was extended by the inauguration of a service to Providence, Rhode Island, on Amtrak tracks. All of the Massachusetts Bay Transportation Authority's services are operated under contract by Amtrak.

The Massachusetts Bay Transportation Authority controls an integrated and comprehensive local and regional transportation system based on four metro lines, five light rail lines, four trolley bus and 155 bus routes, all operating within the same basic fare system to encourage

ABOVE: Illinois Central Railroad double-deck set No. 218 runs through Grant Park, Chicago, and dives down the incline into the underground station by Waker Drive, Randolph Street Station at Chicago South Shore.

ABOVE RIGHT: Chicago elevated railroad train about to cross the bridge over the platform ends of the Chicago & North Western Railroad Station. F unit No. 424 waits on the right.

OPPOSITE: Milwaukee Road Railroad Push-Pull arrives at Union Station by the Chicago river.

interconnection between various elements of the overall system, which also includes the 'heavy rail' commuter system. In 1995 the Massachusetts Bay Transportation Authority recorded a passenger total of 23 million, and further expansion of the commuter service is imminent from the inauguration of a 22.9-mile (36.8-km) extension from Framingham to Worcester on the western side of the network south of the line to Fitchburg, and from the start in the later 1990s of 'Old Colony Railroad' services along three routes to Kingston, Middleboro and Scituate to the south-east of Boston and including 21 new stations. These latter extensions of the network are estimated to result in the delivery of up to 15,000 more passengers per day to the

South Station in Boston. The success of the Massachusetts Bay Transportation Authority in schedule-keeping, fare management and general efficiency has led to the local decision to consider other extensions to the route network to both the north and south of Boston, including coastal destinations such as Newburyport and Greenbush.

The Massachusetts Bay Transportation Authority operates its services with 58 diesel locomotives and 420 passenger cars. The diesel locomotives include 25 'F40PH-2C' bought from General Motors, and 18 'F40PH' and 12 'F40PH-2M'-class units rebuilt to an improved standard by Morrison Knudsen. Further capability is being provided, largely for the Worcester

and Old Colony services, by the delivery of 25 more locomotives remanufactured to an upgraded standard by AMF Technotransport. The passenger cars are of mixed origins and include 67 units made by Messerschmitt-Bölkow-Blohm in West Germany, 147 units fabricated by Bombardier in Canada, 92 double-deck units constructed by Kawasaki in Japan, and 58 Pullman Standard units originally made in the U.S.A. and now upgraded.

Much farther to the east, Metra is the name of the commuter branch of the Chicago Regional Transportation Authority under the overall supervision of North-East Illinois Regional Commuter Railroad Corporation's Chicago Commuter Rail Service Board, this mass of nomenclature finally revealing that Metra is in fact the organization that operates commuter rail services to and from the Chicago conurbation. The Metra system covers the six north-eastern counties of Illinois, and its extent of some 500 miles (805km) of route (including 1,200 miles/1930km of track) includes elements operated under contract by the Burlington Northern Santa Fe Railroad (originally the Burlington Northern Railroad, one route) and the Union Pacific Railroad (formerly the Chicago & North Western Railroad, three routes) on their own track but with Metra-owned equipment. Owned and operated by Metra itself are the track and equipment of the former Illinois Central, Milwaukee Road and Rock Island Railroads, and Metra has also leased the Norfolk Southern line to Orland Park for its South-West Service. Metra additionally operates two *Central Heritage Corridor* services in each direction between Chicago and Joliet.

During August 1998 Metra introduced a commuter service to the 52.8-mile (85-km) Wisconsin Central route linking Franklin Park (on Metra's own route between Chicago and Elgin) and Antioch via nine intermediate stations. Further extensions of the system are under active consideration.

Metra's rolling stock in the closing stages of 1995 included 137 diesel locomotives, 165 electric railcars and 700 passenger cars. The most important of the diesel locomotives were 28 3,200-hp (2386-kW) F40PH class, 86 3,200-hp (2386-kW) 'F40PH-2' class, 15 3,200-hp (2386-kW) 'F40C' class and 30 3,200-hp (2386-kW)

'F40PHM-2'-class units, while the most important types of electric railcar were the 150-passenger 'MA3A' class of which 130 were in service and the 150-passenger 'MA3B' class of which 35 were in service. Entering service since 1994 have been a number of 'highliner' electric multiple-unit cars after their reconstruction with full accessibility to physically handicapped passengers by Morrison Knudsen and later by Amerail.

Back on the east coast between Massachusetts and Maryland is the state of New Jersey, and this is the area of commuter train responsibility exercised by the organization known as New Jersey Transit Rail Operations Inc., which carries an annual total of some 42.7 million passengers over a system that comprises nine routes into Hoboken, Newark and the city of New York, and is operated with an integrated fare system to facilitate interchange within the various elements of the whole complex. Within this complex, New Jersey Transit Rail Operations owns much of the infrastructure (the other parts being in the hands of Amtrak and Conrail), all its own rolling stock and 145 stations.

The system operates some 600 services on every day of the working week, and these services fall into several distinct sectors. On the Jersey Coast line between Penn Station in New York and Bay Head there are *Jersey Arrow* services operated by electric multiple-units as far south as Long Branch, and also diesel-hauled services as far as Bay Head. On the North-East Corridor from Penn Station to Trenton (and

including the branch line to Princeton) there is another *Arrow* service also operated by electric multiple-units. From Newark extends the line into the Raritan Valley as far as Hackettstown operated by General Motors electric units, while the Morris and Essex lines are generally operated by electric multiple-units together with a number of diesel-hauled trains. Diesel services are standard on the services to Boonton, the Pascack Valley and Port Jervis, and the link to Atlantic City via Philadelphia is served by a fleet of five diesel locomotives and 18 passenger cars.

At the end of 1995 New Jersey Transit Rail Operations had 78 diesel-electric and 28 electric locomotives together with 300 electric multiple-units and 389 passenger

OPPOSITE ABOVE: *A New Jersey Transit Authority EMU No. 1521 crosses the Passaic River into Newark Station on service from Penn Central Station, New York.*

OPPOSITE BELOW: *Another New Jersey Transit Authority EMU bound for Penn Central Station, runs through Harrison, New Jersey.*

RIGHT: *A classic Pennsylvania GG1 locomotive runs through Harrison, New Jersey with a New Jersey Transit train bound for Penn Central Station, New York.*

cars. The most numerous of the diesel-electric units were 13 3,000-hp (2238-kW) 'GP40PH-2'-class and 40 3,000-hp (2238-kW) 'F40PH-2'-class locomotives: the electric locomotives were 20 5,795-hp (4320-kW) 'ALP44'- and eight 6,000-hp (4475-kW) 'E60CP'-class units, and the primary electric multiple-units were 68 'MA1G'-class units in married pairs, 182 'MA1J'-class units in married pairs and 29 MA1J-class units in single cars. Recent additions have included another 17 ALP44-class electric locomotives to replace E60CP units, and the first Bombardier cars to replace older MA1G-class electric multiple-units.

On the other side of the U.S.A., operating in the extreme south of California on the west coast, is the North San Diego County Transit Development Board, which in 1995 started the *Coaster* service operated under contract by Amtrak over the 41.75-mile (67.2-km) route linking San Diego and Oceanside. This service runs over part of the 83.3 miles (134km) of route that the North San Diego County Transit authority bought from the Burlington Northern Santa Fe Railroad and includes the branch line between Oceanside and Escondido which is under consideration for a light rail service. The North San Diego County Transit Development Board has upgraded the route of the *Coaster* service in a number of ways, including six new stations and two upgraded stations, and for its service (comprising five trains to/from San Diego and one train to/from Oceanside in the

morning and evening of each day of the working week) five 'F40PHM-2C'-class diesel-electric locomotives and 16 double-deck coaches (eight cab cars and eight passenger cars) supplied by Bombardier and being supplemented by another five coaches.

Farther to the north along the Californian coast is the region in which there operates the Southern California Regional Rail Authority in and around the

Los Angeles conurbation. It is planned that this system will eventually cover some 400 miles (645km), and the first three lines came into service during October 1992 after the Southern California Regional Rail Authority had purchased 338 miles (544km) of route from the Burlington Northern Santa Fe Railroad as the beginning of a programme designed to bring effective commuter services to five counties in the Los Angeles region. The

services introduced in 1992 operated under the designation 'Metrolink', and comprised the routes linking the Union Station in Los Angeles with Moorpark (the Ventura Line), Montclair (the San Bernardino Line), and Santa Clarita (the Santa Clarita Line), and two services added in 1995 were the Riverside Line on Union Pacific track and the Orange County Line, the latter extending to Oceanside and a link with service to San Diego. Further expansion came in October 1995 when the Metrolink network was extended to include the route between Irvine and Riverside via Santa Ana and Anaheim, so by the beginning of 1996 the Metrolink network comprised 338 miles (544km) of route with 42 stations, and during its first three years of service carried steadily increasing numbers of passengers, peaking in the year up to October 1995 at

OPPOSITE: A PATH (Port Authority Trans-Hudson) train from Newark, New Jersey to the World Trade Center, New York, halts at Harrison to pick up passengers.

4.4 million, a 33 per cent increase over the previous 12-month period.

The Metrolink services are operated by Amtrak, as noted above, using 23 'F59PH'-class and eight 'F59PHI' class locomotives optimized for the type of low emissions now considered absolutely vital for all traffic operating in the heavily polluted Los Angeles basin, and 94 double-deck

passenger cars delivered by Bombardier. The operator was also to have received 26 special 'California Cars' ordered from Morrison Knudsen, but the order for these commuter cars was later cancelled because of manufacturing problems, and Metrolink instead leased more Bombardier cars from GO Transit of Canada.

There are several other commuter or

'heavy rail' operators in the U.S.A. filling the specialized niche between the 'light rail' systems of the city centres and the main-line services still running passenger and freight services between the U.S.A.'s main centres of population, but the above pen picture provides an encapsulated view of the overall nature of such services in the U.S.A.

RIGHT: A PATH train on service from the World Trade Center comes over the Passaic river into Newark, New Jersey.

Chapter Seven
HIGH-SPEED TRAINS

PAGES 378-379: British Rail diesel-electric HST (High Speed Train).

RIGHT: *SNCF (Société Nationale des Chemins de Fer Français) electric-powered train.*

HIGH-SPEED TRAINS

As the year 2000 approached, one of the most far-sighted railroad concepts to be entertained for many years, initiated in 1996, was coming to fruition in Europe as a collaborative venture by Belgium, France, Germany, the Netherlands and the United Kingdom. Based in Belgium, the 10-year plan was conceived to create high-speed rail links connecting Paris, Brussels, Köln (Cologne), Amsterdam and London. This PBKAL project is making good progress, and it was anticipated that all the proposed links would by fully operational by 2005, although some parts, such as the links between Brussels and Antwerp and between Brussels and Liège, should be established by 2002, and the tunnel connecting the northern and southern railroad stations in Antwerp should be ready for traffic by 2003.

However, though many of the most fascinating railway developments are those taking shape in the western part of Europe, the development of the 'railroad culture' is not restricted to the more affluent countries of the northern hemisphere. In the developing countries of the southern hemisphere there have developed a number of railroads reflecting the desire of such countries to exploit their natural resources,

OPPOSITE: *A Rail Europe TVG (Train Grande Vitesse) Duplex.*

RIGHT: *The* Eurostar *high-speed trains run between London and Paris and Brussels through the Channel Tunnel.*

and typical of these nations is Brazil, where new railroad lines have been developed into the rain forests of the Amazon basin. The creation of this type of infrastructure should be (but in some cases has not been) balanced by efforts to counter the adverse environmental consequences of such developments. Railroad development in Africa has been spasmodic and singularly poorly planned in overall terms, and although the continent's nations that have gained independence in the last 35 years have indeed invested in railroads, in overall terms the development of the continent's railroad network has been hampered by the devil's brew of general political instability, frequent civil war and constant lack of resources.

The development of the railroad system in China has been greater than that of anywhere else in the world: since 1949 and the end of the civil war that saw the defeat of the ruling nationalist party by the communists, the country's network has been extended by more than 30,000 miles (48280km). This development is not to the main-line network, for other elements of modern railroad thinking have entered the Chinese transport equation in the form of a growing number of 'light rail' and

underground railroad projects. Typical of the latter, for instance, is the plan for the system in the southern city of Shenzhen, a 9.5-mile (15-km) network extending under the city proper to the outlying suburb of Futian, linking Lowu and Lok Ma Chau. This advanced system will make it possible for passengers to travel from Hong Kong into the centre of the city in only some 20 minutes. In Hong Kong itself, construction began late in 1998 on the first element of the region's new West Rail Project and, on completion, this double-track electrified system will cover some 21 miles (34km) from Yen Chow Street in Kowloon to Tuen Mun: a notable aspect of the system, designed to provide no interference with the already overcrowded road system of this ex-British colony, is the fact that while 8.5 miles (13.7km) will be underground some 5.5 miles (8.8km) of the rest of the network will be elevated. It is planned that the system will possess nine stations, including two providing the possibility of interchange with the main-line railroad between Kowloon and Beijing. Hong Kong is also the recipient of a new 21.1-mile (34-km) 'light rail' system, in this instance connecting the new Chek Lap Kok airport on Lantau island with Kowloon and

providing, as a world 'first', check-in
facilities at its various stations.

As the world's railroad systems
continue to grow in importance from the
decline evident in the middle 50 years of
the 20th century, the revival of rail transport
is now seen in a somewhat different light,
especially among the nations of the Western
world. The desirability of railroad transport
is not regarded exclusively as a factor of
economic importance, but also as an
element of the social and ecological
significance increasingly attached to the
curtailment of the importance that has until
very recently been attached to the motor
vehicle as the pre-eminent means of moving
people and goods both within and between
urban centres. There is now far greater
emphasis on the creation of integrated road
and rail transport systems that will lessen
pollution by reducing the numbers of
private cars and trucks gridlocking urban
streets, and ease national levels of
congestion and social irritability by
trimming the numbers of private cars and
trucks using the road network. In short, the
concept that has developed is that neither
the motor vehicle nor the train should
exercise a dominant influence on transport
policy as they once did in successive
periods, but that the railroad should become
a major partner to the motor vehicle within
the context of an integrated approach to the
creation of a transport system that serves
the needs of the population.

Rising traffic congestion and its
attendant pollution have placed emphasis on
the establishment of a viable alternative to

ABOVE: Hong Kong has one of the best suburban railroad systems in the world, this being part of the line connecting Kowloon with Hong Kong proper.

OPPOSITE: As this photograph nicely reveals, the Chinese railroad system is comprehensively integrated into the everyday lives of the Chinese workers who have to use it.

the vital qualities of life for urban populations, much work has still to be done in improving matters and, perhaps just as importantly, persuading potential railroad travellers that the train has much to offer as an alternative to the car.

Though the perception of the significance of railroad use as a social and ecological tool to reduce the reliance of the Western world on the motor vehicle is most generally seen in terms of relevance to ownership and use of the private motor car, it is in fact of equal importance in terms of reducing the extent to which trucks and other heavy road vehicles are needed. In its capacity as the means of moving large loads, the railroad has seen something of a renaissance, albeit a limited one, with a number of important changes evident in its operations. From the 1960s the method of sending freight by railroad in individual wagons, the standard concept since the dawn of the railroad age, has become considerably less popular as obsolescent ways of handling freight, in which the railroads concentrated on the running of bulk movements of one particular type of load, whether a unitary mass such as coal or a fragmented mass such as a mixture of goods, allowed road competition to steal away business. The carrying of bulk loads is among the most cogent arguments for railroad development, for every railroad load trims the number of trucks on the world's roads. The delivery of bulk loads of coal, stone and other mass items such as mineral ores is still one of the railroad's most important economic offerings, and has

road transport by railroads that can operate services that provide the right blend of cleanliness, convenience, affordability and efficiency. It is only if they can provide this combination of attributes that the railroads stand any realistic chance of persuading motorists to switch to railroad transport. The growth and importance of 'light rail' and metro tram systems in the world's largest conurbations have indicated that although railways can make a difference to

become financially more attractive as railroad technology enhancements have made it possible to operate longer and heavier trains.

In the U.S.A. and other parts of the world such as Australia, China and the southern part of Africa, the movement of bulk loads by railroad is far more significant than it is in Europe. In the U.S.A., the Burlington Northern Railroad (now the Burlington Northern Santa Fe Railroad) introduced a train that delivered a load weighing more than 11,000 tons in 100 wagons. In South Africa, trains of up to some 20,000 tons are hauled some 550 miles (885km) from the Sishen iron-ore mines to the port of Saldanha: a fascinating aspect of these trains is that a motorcycle is carried on each of the five locomotives, allowing the crew to make regular inspections of the train, which can be more than 1.5 miles (2.4km) long.

In their attempts to boost the freight business, railroad operators have considered a number of unorthodox concepts. The idea of the TOFC ('Trailer On Flat Car') started in the U.S.A., permits truck trailer units to be carried on flatcars, and during the 1970s American and Canadian railroads were dealing with slightly less than 2 million TOFC loads each year. Problems with loading gauges precluded the use of such innovations in the U.K. and continental Europe until recent times, but in 1996 proposals were put forward for 'piggyback' trains of the North American pattern to become operational by 1999.

Another chance helping to transform

the nature and extent of freight transport by railroad has been the spread of containerization. The widespread use of containers for the movement of freight all over the world, and the adaptability of the container for movement by ship, railroad and truck has constituted a genuine revolution in the way freight is handled. In the U.S.A. extremely long trains of flatcars are used to deliver vast numbers of containers between the east and west coasts, and between the Great Lakes and the Gulf of Mexico, for it makes better economic

ABOVE: Unloading passengers' cars from a Finnish State Railways car-carrying train.

LEFT: A truck being loaded onto a German Deutsche Bundesbahn 'piggyback' train.

OPPOSITE
ABOVE LEFT: A special car-carrying unit on a passenger train of the Finnish State Railways.

ABOVE RIGHT: DB piggyback wagons permit the long-distance, high-speed transport of goods while still aboard these truck trailers.

BELOW RIGHT: Imported cars being loaded onto a Santa Fe Autoveyor at Long Beach, California for shipment east.

sense to do this than ship the containers via the Panama Canal or via the St. Lawrence Seaway. The monumental size of this effort can be ascertained from the fact that each of these trains is generally more than 1 mile (1.6km) long, and is hauled by no fewer than six locomotives. The extent and importance of container traffic in the U.K. has also grown enormously, and was originally given the brand name 'Freightliner' by British Railways in a very real perception of the business's essential nature, and today is just as important to the British railway business, especially since the opening of the Channel Tunnel and the consequent facilitation of rapid rail transport to and from the European mainland, where container freight has also become increasingly the norm for bulk delivery.

The concept of genuinely integrated transport links is also highly relevant to the modern freight transport business, and as a result there have appeared ever increasing numbers of regional 'intermodal' freight depots, and still more are planned: such intermodal depots greater improve the interchangeability of freight between the road and railroad networks, and are located strategically in regions where nodes of the two types of freight movement exist comfortably close to each other.

Despite the resurgence in the use of the railroad for the movement of freight, it is the railroad's capability in terms of high-speed passenger transport that has caught the eye of the public to a far greater extent. This is largely the result of the advanced, even futuristic, lines of the special trains developed for the task, the gaudy liveries in which such trains operate, and the very high speeds at which such trains run on services that are considerably faster than those of the private motor car. The high-speed railroad services are admittedly slower than those offered by the regional passenger aircraft that are their main rivals, but the railroad services have the advantage of

ABOVE LEFT: *Potash train east of Lytton, British Columbia.*

ABOVE: *A Canadian Pacific freight train on the Notch Hill Loop, British Columbia.*

LEFT: *Another Candian Pacific freight train crossing the Lethbridge viaduct over the Oldman river in Alberta.*

OPPOSITE

LEFT: *Configuration of tracks at the west end of Santa Fe's computerized classification yard at Barstow, east of Los Angeles, California, showing simultaneous arrivals and departures without interference.*

RIGHT: *A heavy freight train of the Canadian Pacific Railway wends its way through the Rocky Mountains, the beauty of the scenery unseen by all except the crews of the locomotives.*

operating at a high average speed from city centre to city centre, whereas the regional aircraft operators have to contend with the fact that their passengers must first travel out of the city centre to book into their service, then often have to wait before take-off, and then reverse the whole process at the other end of the service. The operators of high-speed railroad services can therefore offer point-to-point services between city centres cheaper but not notably slower than those of the airlines.

The best known of these high-speed services anywhere in the world are those provided by the Train Grande Vitesse (TGV), a French train which travels so fast that special lines had to be laid with greater than normal spacing between the tracks to

reduce the buffeting which ensues when the trains pass each other. Another feature of the line is that they conform closely to the terrain contours and thus avoid the need in most cases for tunnels. The tracks are also built with a special camber that permits curves to be negotiated safely at very high speed. Movement on the TGV, between Paris and southern France and Switzerland, is so smooth that not only is the impression of the high speed hard to judge, but there is also little chance to study the local scenery. This journey takes a breathtaking 4 hours 32 minutes. Combining *Eurostar* and TGV services, the passenger can depart London at 9.53 a.m., reach Paris at 2.08 p.m. via the Channel Tunnel, leave at 3.50 p.m. and arrive in Berne by 8.22 p.m. In 1990, a

TGV achieved a world train speed record travelling at 320.2mph (515.3km/h).

A feature of the early TGV trains was their long nose section, although more recent examples have a less angular front, the change improving the aerodynamic lines of the train within the context of a programme to improve overall efficiency that also witnessed the partial change from steel to aluminium alloy for the superstructure of the cars. Another key feature of the TGV is an electronic device that continuously monitors the line: whenever it senses a change, it adjusts the power input to the traction motors to maintain the speed set by the driver. First-class travellers on the TGV have all the benefits of luxurious semi-compartment

seating, but second-class passengers also enjoy high-quality accommodation, and there are two areas of seating bays optimized for family groups as well as a play area and a nursery. In addition, there is special accommodation for the disabled.

Although the international design and manufacturing group responsible for the design of the *Eurostar* train used the same basic principles as found in the TGV, it also introduced a number of changes. The main difference between the *Eurostar* and the TGV is that the former, operating in several countries, had to be able to employ the electrical supply of three different systems, including current collection from a third rail in the U.K. and from overhead lines elsewhere. The resulting *Eurostar* design

ABOVE, FAR LEFT: Preparing to unload a Sea-Land container from a flat wagon onto a truck at a Netherlands State Railways container depot.

ABOVE CENTRE LEFT: Southern Pacific's triple-unit, double-stack railroad cars being loaded with containers. The articulated cars, built in three units over four sets of bogies, reduce the weight of rail equipment needed to carry containers by nearly one-half, compared with traditional single-level flatcars.

ABOVE CENTRE RIGHT: Trailers on Kangourou wagons of an SNCF specialist freight train, in the late 1970s.

ABOVE: Santa Fe Railroad's Ten-Pack unit awaiting loading of road trailers for its TOFC (Trailer On Flat Car) traffic at Hobart Yard, Los Angeles.

LEFT: Part of the display on the inaugural day of Channel Tunnel traffic from the Willesden Euroterminal, London.

ABOVE: A Santa Fe Railroad Six-Pack unit being loaded with truck trailers.

ABOVE RIGHT: Another scene on the inaugural day of Channel Tunnel traffic from Willesden Euroterminal, with a Railfreight Class 47 locomotive.

RIGHT: Engine 47375 about to leave with the second inaugural train from Euroterminal.

has an exterior that was designed in the U.K. and an interior that was a collaborative Belgian and French undertaking. There were many mechanical and electrical problems that had to be solved in the design and manufacturing processes. The safety requirements of the Channel Tunnel, for example, require that passengers can be shifted from one end of the train to the other, and this fact made it impossible for the train to be designed as two sub-units merely connected in the middle. The *Eurostar* has two motor cars, these being located at the front and back of the 20-car set, and to offset to a limited extent the advantage in power enjoyed by two equivalent TGV sets, motorized bogies are used under the first and last passenger cars. Two other notable aspects of the design were the need for the overall size of the bogies to be reduced, and for a higher-extending pantograph to make contact with the higher overhead electric power lines installed in the Channel Tunnel. The need for the *Eurostar* to be fully compatible with the railroad arrangements of the three countries in which it was designed to operate dictated the creation of footsteps that automatically matched themselves to different platform heights, and the solution of problems associated with the various complex signalling systems used in Belgium, France, Germany and the U.K.

These and other aspects and problems were successfully negotiated and, to the great credit of the international design and manufacturing teams, the programme was fully completed between 1987 and 1994,

when regular scheduled services were inaugurated during November.

Lying 377ft (115m) under mean sea level, the Channel Tunnel is a prodigious engineering feat and, at an overall length of 31.03 miles (49.93km), is the lengthiest underwater tunnel anywhere in the world. Passage through the Channel Tunnel by *Eurostar* takes about 20 minutes, and on emerging on the French side of the tunnel the *Eurostar* can accelerate to its highest permitted speed on the part of

the route connecting Calais with Paris.

The completion of the Tokaido section of Japan's Shinkansen railroad system in 1960 heralded a new era in rail transportation. For the previous 21 years the world record for the highest scheduled train speed had been held by Italy, which during July 1939 operated a three-car articulated set over the 195.8-mile (315.1-km) route linking Florence and Milan at an average speed of 102mph (164km/h). Japan's new railroad was designed for operations at

130mph (209km/h). Specially designed and constructed to permit operations at very high sustained speeds, this railroad features curves with a radius of no less than 2,185 yards (2000m), and though designed in an era before the concept of 'environmental friendliness' became so common as to become a truism, the line was conceived on the basis of carriage some 21ft (6.4m) above towns on viaducts with high side walls to avoid urban congestion and minimize noise. There are no level

crossings on the track, valleys and river estuaries are crossed on long viaducts, and wherever mountains blocked the intended way no less than 66 tunnels, of which 12 are more than 1.5miles (2.4km), were driven through the barrier.

As is the case with the TGV, the need to cater for the aerodynamic effect of two trains passing in opposite directions at a combined speed of more than 250mph (400km/h) had to be factored into the operational equation. As a result, the

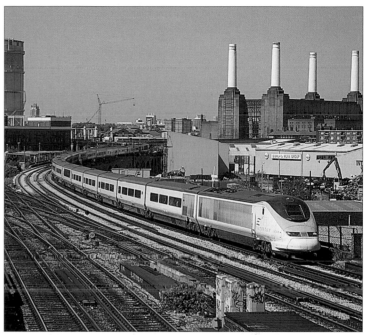

distance between the nearest rails of opposing tracks in the tunnels was increased from the standard 6ft (1.8m) to a figure of between 9ft (2.7m) and 9ft 6in (2.89m).

During the later 1990s, a Hikari (lightning) train of the Shinkansen system departs Tokyo for Osaka every 15 minutes in the time period between 6.00 a.m. and 9 p.m., and the service covers the 322-mile (518-km) route in a mere 3 hours 10 minutes. Making only two halts, at Nagoya

and Kyoto, each 16-car train, carrying 1,000 passengers on average, travels at an average speed of over 100mph (160km/h). Despite the age of its design, reflecting the railroad technology of the 1960s rather than the 1990s, the Hikari is still an impressive train, but is now being replaced by the altogether more capable Nozomi 500, which entered revenue-earning service during March 1997. This unmistakable train makes one round trip between Osaka and Hakata daily as the fastest regularly

ABOVE: The 18.52 Waterloo to Paris Eurostar service, standing at Ashford station in Kent before diving into the Channel Tunnel.

ABOVE RIGHT: Power-cars 3005 and 3006 head west past Queen Street, east of Paddock Wood, Kent, operating the 12.31 Brussels to Waterloo train.

OPPOSITE: A British Rail HST 125 diesel-electric train.

scheduled train service in the world, and in the course of its journey travels at speeds of up to 186mph (300km/h).

In Russia, the core element of the Commonwealth of Independent States that emerged from the collapse of the U.S.S.R. in 1991, a publicly quoted company, High-Speed Railways, has undertaken with the Ministry of Railways of the Russian Federation the collaborative development of the Sokol as an electrically-powered high-speed train for the movement of passengers. Under consideration since 1987 as an alternative to the ER 200 concept of Soviet

times, and designed by the Central Construction Bureau of Marine Engineering, the train is built by Transmash at Tikhvin. Designed for ecologically-friendly operation, the Sokol is designed to carry more than 800 passengers, in both tourist and business classes, with speeds of between 155 and 217mph (250 and 350km/h). The train is 1,059ft (322.8m) long and has 12 cars, and was created to use two types of traction power in the form of 3,000-volt direct current and 25,000-volt alternating current delivered to 16 three-phase induction motors each rated at 905hp

(675kW) for a combined power of 14,485hp (10800kW). A refreshment car is standard, and other features of the Sokol are an international telephone capability and special accommodation for physically-handicapped passengers.

Intended primarily for service on the new specialized high-speed main line linking Moscow and St. Petersburg, the Sokol can also run at speeds up to 125mph (200km/h) on more conventional railroad lines. It is planned that 150 Sokol trains should be in full service by 2010, but of course the parlous state of the CIS's

OPPOSITE: A Soviet ER 200 high-speed 14-coach electric passenger train.

LEFT: A suburban diesel multiple unit with a main-line electric locomotive in Moscow.

economy makes it difficult to predict real progress. As work on the Sokol continues, special stations are being constructed to handle the trains: during July 1997, work started on the new terminal next to the Moscow Station in St. Petersburg and, at the other end of the line, the Riga Station in Moscow is also being remodelled.

Although trials with the operation of very-high-speed trains had been undertaken since 1903, it was to be more than 60 years before the potential of very-high-speed railroad transport for full public services, with services averaging more than 100mph (160km/h) start-to-stop but possessing a maximum operating speed of at least 130mph (209km/h), finally started to become a reality. The first of the new breed appeared in Japan in 1965 with the inauguration of the Japanese National Railways' almost futuristic Shinkansen line from Tokyo westwards to Osaka. The line had been opened in 1964, but a preliminary period of operation at more normal speeds had been deemed prudent before full-speed services were introduced. Despite the impression they gave with their rocket-like lines for minimum drag, the Shinkansen ('new line') trains are in essence orthodox in their basic concept. The very high speed of these trains is attributable, therefore, not to any radical revision of train concepts but rather to the use of very high power: the standard 16-car Shinkansen has available to it for continuous running no less than 15,870hp (11840kW), and the train's notably high acceleration (a feature of vital importance in very fast start-to-stop speeds) is derived from the fact that every axle is powered.

The very high performance and the resultant extent of the great international fame gained by Japan with its Shinkansen trains thus served to disguise, if that is the right word, the capability that the Japanese engineers had extracted from existing railroad technology by the exercise of ingenuity in the creation of a 'clean sheet of paper' design. Up to 1964 the Japanese National Railways had used only the 42-in (1067-mm) gauge, but despite the additional cost involved, the organization secured authorization for the creation of a new line system that was wholly separate from the existing system, even to the extent of its gauge. The capital investment required for the construction of a completely new standard-gauge (56.5-in/1435-mm) track system to link some of Japan's most

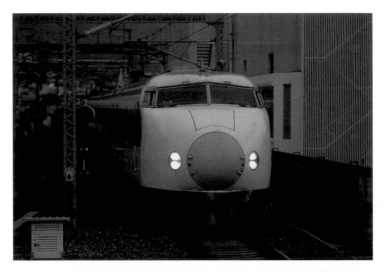

LEFT: The Shinkansen Kordanna *arriving at Kyoto, Japan in July 1995.*

BELOW: A Shinkansen (Nozomi) R-500 high-speed train set.

OPPOSITE: The Hokuriku Shinkansen express.

important cities was enormous, but the enthusiasm and far sightedness of the men urging the undertaking was fully justified, not just in terms of the kudos gained for Japan, but also by the tripling of passenger ticket sales on the Shinkansen routes between 1966 and 1973.

The financial price of high-speed railroad operations to the Japanese was very large. For a start, land had to be bought at the escalating costs of the period for the construction of new railroad tracks into and out of the major urban centres, and at the same time the need to create track with the radius of any curve no less than 2,735 yards (2500m), to ensure the trains' safe negotiation of such curves, also required the purchase of rural land. In addition to the

purchase of the necessary land there was also the high cost of construction for track in a new gauge and to improved standards of accuracy, and also the inordinately high expense of boring tunnels through major obstacles to avoid bypassing these obstacles, which in the short term would have required additional land purchase and in the long term have reduced average speed by increasing the track length. However, one advantage that accrued from the powerful nature of the trains themselves was that comparatively steep gradients, up to 1/65, could be allowed.

So far as the trains themselves were concerned, the primary innovation was the self-signalling system that was introduced. Both acceleration and deceleration are

therefore not only automatic but in fact started automatically when required, on the final deceleration to a halt being wholly under the control of the driver. The Shinkansen system has no line-side signals, and all the important data concerning state-of-the-line are transmitted to the driver's cab by coded impulses sent along the main overhead power lines and passed onto the train by the pantograph. The automatic nature of the system is also reflected in the fact that the trains themselves transmit the signals required to set the route ahead of them wherever there is something to be selected. Another feature of the system, made necessary by the fact that Japan lies on a major fault line on the earth's crust and is therefore prone to volcanic activity, is the location of seismographs in the primary control centres, and these are linked into the system to generate automatic stop signals to all trains in the event that an earthquake is detected.

As the system was originally completed, there were 480 cars disposed in 40 sets each of 12 cars, each 12-car set being divided in electrical terms into six two-car units, one of which containing the buffet car, and with the highly streamlined ends and driving cabs (leading to the popular nickname 'bullet train' for the Shinkansen train) located at the front and back of the train. By 1970, however, the level of traffic and the fact that demand for the services was still increasing led to the decision to lengthen each train to 16 cars including two buffet cars. At much the same time, the frequency of the services operated

over the Shinkansen service was boosted from 120 to more than 200 per day in each direction, and this intensification of the service was made possible by the fact that there were now some 1,400 cars in service, these being used to constitute some 87 16-car sets.

In 1970, as soon as the technical and commercial success of the original system had become evident, the Japanese developed a plan to extend the Shinkansen network from the 320 miles (515km) of the original line to some 6,400 miles (10300km) to tie most of Japan's major cities into the system. The first stage of this process involved the 1,188 miles (1912km) of new track for the links between Tokyo and Okayama, Tokyo and Hakata, Oomiya (Tokyo) and Niigata, and Oomiya (Tokyo) and Morioka. The sheer volume of the work involved, especially in the mountain regions that the lines had to penetrate and in the 11.6-mile (18.6-km) undersea tunnel between two islands meant an enormous quantity of civil engineering work needed. The extent of this work is indicated by the fact that on the 247-mile (398-km) route between Okayama and Hakata, some 55 per cent of the track was laid in tunnels and 31 per cent on bridges or viaducts, meaning that only 14 per cent was laid as conventional railway on the ground. It should be borne in mind, however, that while much of the civil engineering task's size was attributable to the nature of the Japanese home islands with their masses of mountains and deep river valleys, part of it was the result of the decision that was taken

at this time to reduce gradients to a maximum of 1/65 and increase the maximum radius of curves to 4,375 yards (4000km) so that the maximum speed could be increased from 130mph (210km/h) to 162mph (260km/h). This maximum speed has not been fully realized in service, but even so the trains, operating on an hourly schedule, cover the 735-mile (1182-km) distance between Tokyo and Hakata at an average speed of 110mph (176.5km/h) in a time of 6 hours 40 minutes.

Considered in a different perspective, the Shinkansen type of service would cover the comparable distance in the United States, typically between New York and Chicago, in just half the current scheduled running time of 18 hours 30 minutes.

It is worth noting that the train sets

built for service on the Hakata extension have provision for operation at a higher speed in the future: the power available was increased by some 48 per cent to 23,600hp (17595kW) and the additional weight of the relevant electrical equipment was offset by the construction of the car superstructures in light alloy rather than steel. The data for the 16-car sets operated on the Shinkansen routes for high-speed passenger service include propulsion by alternating 25,000-volt 50-Hz electrical current fed via overhead catenary and step-down transformers and rectifiers to 64 248-hp (185-kW) motors each driving an axle by means of gearing and flexible drive, total weight of 2,031,200lb (921352kg), overall length of 1,318ft 6in (401.880m) and maximum speed of 130mph (210km/h).

The excellence of the train sets operated on the Shinkansen services may be judged from the performance and overall capabilities of contemporary American and European counterparts. In the United States, for example, there appeared during 1967 the Pennsylvania Railroad's Metroliner Two-Car Trainset. The origins of this type can be found in the generally low level of service provided to American passengers by the railroad companies during the 1960s. This reflected the fact that most railroads were operating passenger services only at a considerable financial deficit, and at the same time losing passengers to the airlines over long- and medium-distance routes, on which the airliner could offer an average speed perhaps 10 times higher than that of the train, and to the private motor car for

ABOVE LEFT: The Seikan tunnel with main bore on the right, and works tunnel to the left. The tunnel provides a rail link between Honshu and the northern island of Hokkaido.

ABOVE: Japanese National Railways 130-mph (210-km/h) Shinkansen high-speed train.

OPPOSITE: One of Amtrak's Metroliners carrying passengers between major cities in the New York-Washington North-East Corridor.

short-distance routes, in which potential passengers seemed increasingly to prefer the advantages of door-to-door transport even though there was no or, at best, only modest time advantage. Faced with this situation, which seemed likely to end with the cessation of virtually all passenger services, the American railroad operators decided that they could in fact compete with the motor car if they disposed of their fleets of wholly obsolescent passengers cars and adopted not only new cars but also a new 'go get 'em' marketing image.

One route that seemed eminently suitable for the treatment was the Pennsylvania Railroad's electrified main line between New York and Washington, D.C. via Philadelphia on what is now known as the North-East Corridor, and it was for this that there was designed and developed the Metroliner Two-Car Trainset. The Pennsylvania Railroad had bought the 'MP 85'-class prototypes of possible locomotive types from the Budd Company of Philadelphia as early as 1958, and during 1963 the city of Philadelphia purchased on behalf of the railroad some Budd Silverliner passenger cars. Later in the decade the railroad received a measure of U.S. federal government aid toward a $22 million scheme for the creation of new high-speed self-propelled trains, as well as $33 million toward the improvements required for the permanent way if operations at the planned maximum speed of 160mph (257km/h) were to become a reality.

Orders were placed in 1966 with Budd for 50 (later increased to 61) stainless steel

Metroliner cars. These were powered on all of their wheels, could attain considerably more than the specified speed and had the truly impressive short-term power/weight ratio of 34hp (25.35kW)/tonne. They also had a system for dynamic braking down to 30mph (48km/h), and also provision for automatic speed control, acceleration and

deceleration in the basis of new concepts, and other modern features of the cars were air-conditioning, airline-type catering, electrically-controlled doors, and even a public radio telephone service. The order included parlour cars and snack-bar coaches as well as ordinary day coaches. Each of the cars had a driving cab at one end, but

there was provision for access between adjacent cars when the cab was not in use. The cars were arranged on a semi-permanent basis in pairs as two-car units.

Reflecting enthusiasm rather than practical consideration and the step-by-step approach typical of the Pennsylvania Railroad during its heyday, however, the

decision was taken to order the type straight 'off the drawing board'. The result was the discovery of a catalogue of faults whose rectification several times delayed the new cars' entry into revenue-earning service. Pennsylvania Central took over the programme in 1958, and it was only in 1969 that the first limited services began, revealing the need for a modification programme (costing no less than 50 per cent of the original purchase price) before full public service could be considered.

In May 1971 the new Amtrak organization took over from Pennsylvania Central, and by the middle of 1972 the Metroliner was being used for some 14 daily services operated at a start-to-stop speed scheduled for a speed as high as 95mph (153km/h). Even so, speeds as high as the announced 150mph (241km/h) could not be achieved in public service, for the work that had been completed on the track was sufficient for a maximum speed of only 110mph (177km/h). A programme of track work was later implemented for the North-East Corridor: at a cost of $2.5 billion   (75 times the originally estimated cost!) this included the track between New York and the Boston line. Only after the completion of this work was the originally envisaged speed feasible, but the Metroliners were now beginning to show their age and were replaced on the primary section of the route between New York and Washington by 'AEM7'-type locomotives hauling trains of Amfleet cars that are in effect unpowered Metroliners. This change meant the relegation of the Metroliners to

the route linking New York with Harrisburg via Philadelphia.

The original schedule of 2 hours 30 minutes for the service between New York and Washington was never managed, but the hourly services did manage the trip in 3 hours with four intermediate halts at an average speed of 75mph (120km/h). The data for the Metroliner Two-Car Trainset included propulsion by 11,000-volt 25-Hz alternating electrical current fed via overhead catenary, step-down transformer and rectifiers to eight 300-hp (224-kW) motors of which one was geared to each pair of wheels, total weight 328,400lb (148962kg), overall length of 170ft 0in (51.82m) and maximum theoretical speed of 160mph (257km/h).

Altogether greater success attended a number of pioneering European high-speed trains, of which perhaps the most successful of all was the British High Speed Train 125 introduced to service in 1978 as the fastest diesel-electric train anywhere in the world. The HST 125 was a considerable if belated step forward in British express passenger train history and, in the process, marked the first genuine success for the U.K.'s nationalized railway industry in the field of passenger transport. The key to this success was the decision, taken right at the beginning of the programme, not to attempt too much and therefore to limit the design team to well-established technology and thus minimize the risks associated with the use of novel technologies.

The HST 125 should therefore be regarded as a development, perhaps of a

ABOVE. *British Rail's High Speed Train was designed to produce significant decreases in journey times on non-electrified InterCity routes. The prototype train comprised two power coaches each containing a 2250-hp (1678-kW) diesel engine, five Mk III passenger coaches and two catering vehicles.*

ABOVE RIGHT: *A British Rail HST 125. The 125mph (200km/h) High Speed Train is an important technical advance based on the stretching of existing technology.*

OPPOSITE: *An Amtrak Metroliner in the North-East Corridor between Washington, D.C. and Boston.*

fairly extensive nature, of current thinking and even equipment with the possible exception of the bogie suspension. The most radical change in the HST 125 was associated with the type's operation, for instead of being an entirely separate unit that could be detached for the hauling of other types of train or for the type of frequent maintenance that was required with older generations of locomotive, the HST 125 locomotive was schemed within the context of a self-propelled and therefore fully integrated train of the fixed-formation type. This opened the realistic possibilities of speeds in the order of 125mph (201km/h) without problem and, as there was no need for provision for alternative use, of a much simplified locomotive (without vacuum-brake equipment, slow-running equipment and the like) that would be lighter, cheaper to build and operate, and also require less maintenance.

It has to be admitted that self-propelled trains do possess a number of disadvantages, but also advantages such as the ability to reach a terminus and exit on the return service in a time as little as 20 minutes and, as a result of their lower weight and reduced complexity, the ability to cover up to 250,000 miles (402325km) per year with little likelihood of mechanical problems. Moreover, an important fact in the decision to adopt the HST 125 was that the shorter journey times for long-distance routes would have spin-off advantages such as a reduced demand for sleeper carriages, which were costly to purchase and operate but generated little in the way of revenue.

It was originally decided that a fleet of 132 HST 125 trains would be built to allow British Railways to provide high-speed services over its primary non-electrified routes, most notably those linking London's Paddington and King's Cross stations with destinations in the west of England, southern Wales, Yorkshire, north-east England, and Scottish cities such as Edinburgh and Aberdeen; and also north-east to south-west diagonal services in England via Sheffield, Derby and Birmingham. The plan was then to reduce the number of HST 125 trains to 95 as a means of generating a comprehensive schedule of high-speed services unmatched elsewhere in the world at the time.

The shortening of the scheduled service time made possible by the use of the HST

LEFT: *An HST 125 with a rake of nine coaches in a winter setting.*

OPPOSITE
ABOVE LEFT: *The arrangement of the power car for the HST 125.*

ABOVE RIGHT: *An InterCity 125 crossing the world-famous Forth Bridge during its journey from King's Cross, London to Aberdeen, Scotland.*

BELOW: *An InterCity 125, setting out from the 'Granite City', Aberdeen, at the start of its run to London.*

125 on routes allowing the maximum speed to be maintained for some time was considerable, which translated into a 20 per cent reduction in the time required for many services: for example, the route between King's Cross and Newcastle could be covered in as little as 2 hours 54 minutes by comparison with the 3 hours 35 minutes required for services hauled by 'Deltic'-class diesel locomotives. The advent of the HST 125 was clearly approved by the travelling public, which appreciated not only the reduction in journey times but also the improvement in the level of comfort provided by the HST 125's specially designed cars.

In mechanical terms, the design of the

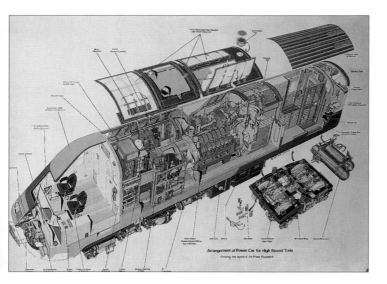

HST 125's locomotive was based on the use of one 2,260-hp (1685-kW) Paxman Valenta lightweight diesel engine installed in each of the motor/baggage carriages at each end of the train. The specific power of the engines was about double that of the standard diesel engines used in others of British Railways' classes of locomotive, and the engines were also notably compact. These two aspects of the powerplant meant that the motor/baggage car could be designed within a weight limit of 154,000lb (69854kg), and that it was also possible to allocate volume in the rear of each unit's overall length of 58ft 4in (17.792m) for baggage and the guard's accommodation. It was also appreciated from the beginning of

the programme that the low axle-loads of the HST 125 trains would have a beneficial effect on the longevity of the tracks over which they operated.

The HST 125's Mk III carriages resulted from 10 years of development from the Mk I type that had been standard since the 1950s and, despite the addition of features such as air-conditioning, sound-proofing, advanced bogies, automatic corridor doors and a level of comfort hitherto unprecedented for second-class passengers, there was a 40 per cent reduction in weight per seat, this being partially attributable to the adoption of open-plan rather than compartmented accommodation, and partially to an increase

OPPOSITE: An HST 125 on the East Coast Main Line. By the mid-1990s these locomotives were being transferred to the other express lines.

RIGHT: The prototype 125-mph (200-km/h) HST of British Rail during trials on the East Coast Main Line. The world speed record of diesel traction was achieved during these trials when the HST reached 141mph (227km/h) on 11 June 1973.

BELOW RIGHT: The interior of the second class saloon coach of British Rail's HST 125.

in length from some 64ft (19.51m) to 75ft 6in (23.01m) for an extra two seating bays. A feature of the HST 125's operation that especially appealed to passengers was the very smooth ride afforded at high speed even over indifferent track. This was the result of the use of some aspects of the air suspension developed for the APT. Including refreshment vehicles, the HST 125 trains generally had seven or eight passenger cars for nine- or 10-carriage sets with a power/baggage carriage at each end.

The avowed object of the HST 125 was the provision of a superior service on existing track without the additional cost of what would have been involved in electrification or even the most limited of reconstruction and modification efforts. This concept meant that the HST 125, despite its higher speed, had to be able to halt when required at signals within the warning distances inherent in the current generation of signalling equipment: for this reason the braking system included disc brakes on all the wheels and an advanced wheel-slip correction capability.

British Railways proceeded via the construction and evaluation of a complete HST 125 train set. This, on occasion, reached speeds as high as 143mph (230km/h), which represented a world record for diesel traction. Even though the performance of the HST 125 was impressive, however, there was a number of

ABOVE LEFT: *Germany's ICE (InterCity Express) railroad service is one of the three types of train operating on Germany's extensive railroad network for long-distance services between distant termini with few intermediate halts, and offers an attractive combination of comfort and speed of 174mph (280km/h).*

ABOVE: *The IR (InterRegio) is the slowest of the three elements constituting that operated by the German railroad network, and was designed for the creation of quick connections between cities and country areas at speeds of 124mph (200km/h).*

LEFT: *Britain's HST 125.*

OPPOSITE: *The LRC (Light, Rapid and Comfortable) train prototype during tests in Canada in 1978. The LRC incorporates automatic body-tilting.*

individually small but cumulatively annoying minor problems as the first production trains entered service. These problems were quickly solved, however, and a factor that particularly endeared the HST 125 to passengers at this time was the fact that the failure of one power/baggage carriage did not immobilize the whole train and the power/baggage car at the other end was sufficient to move the train, albeit at a slower but still useful speed. The data for the HST 125 in its 10-carriage set included the powerplant of two 2,250-hp (1678-kW) Paxman Valenta 12RP200L diesel engines, each possessing an integral alternator delivering electrical current to the four motors in the bogie frames, total weight of 844,132lb (382898kg), overall length of 720ft 5in (219.58m) and maximum speed of 125mph (200km/h).

A slightly later contemporary of British Railways' HST 125 was the Deutsche Bundesbahn's '120' class of Bo-Bo electric

locomotives intended for more flexible operation at moderately high speeds on mixed-traffic routes. There are three types of electric motor (direct current, one-phase alternating current and three phase alternating current), and the characteristics of each type were already well understood by the beginning of the 20th century. Despite the availability and nature of the three types of electric motor, the choice between them was generally governed by the preferred method of power supply and control rather than any specific motor quality. The direct current and one-phase alternating current commutator motors proved to be the most adaptable of the types to the control equipment then available, and as a consequence three-phase alternating current motors were little used. In more modern times, however, technical developments have made the three-phase alternating current motor a more practical item: the two types of three-phase electric

motor are the synchronous type, in which the frequency is connected directly to the supply frequency, and asynchronous or induction type. The latter has first-class traction features, and after a number of European experimental installations of induction motors during the 1960s and 1970s for both diesel-electric and electric locomotives, the Henschel company of West Germany built during 1971 three private-venture diesel locomotives with 2,500-hp (1864-kW) engines powering induction motors, using an electrical system produced by Brown Boveri. The Deutsche Bundesbahn bought these locomotives, which were tested exhaustively and then placed in full service. During 1974 one of the locomotives was stripped of its diesel engine, ballast being added to keep the locomotive's weight unaltered, and the locomotive was coupled permanently to a pantograph-equipped electric test coach.

The evaluation of this all-electric

conversion persuaded the Deutsche Bundesbahn to place a contract for five eight-wheel locomotives based dynamically on the experimental conversion, and these units appeared in 1979. The specification called for the locomotives to haul passenger trains of 700 tonnes at 99mph (160km/h), fast freight trains of 1,500 tonnes at 62mph (100km/h), and heavy freight trains of 2,700 tonnes at 50mph (80km/h): despite its weight of 185,185lb (84000kg), the locomotives achieved these tasks without problem. Full advantage was taken of the good adhesion of the induction motors, with a continuous rating of 7,510hp (5600kW), making the units the most powerful four-axle locomotives anywhere in the world.

Initial evaluation discovered several problems as well as revealing the overall capabilities of the locomotives, but once these difficulties had been not so much cured as brought under control, the locomotives were tested on a number of types and weights of train, and one of them was also subjected to high-speed trials hauling one test coach. This combination touched 143.5mph (231km/h), thus beating the previous world record for traction by induction motor, established in 1903 in the Zossen-Marienfelde trials in Germany with high-speed motor coaches. Another impressive achievement was an acceleration from stationary to 124mph (200km/h) in just 30 seconds. One of the locomotives was later evaluated on the Lötschberg route in Switzerland where, in severe weather conditions, it proved almost as effective on a 1/37 gradient as a lower-speed locomotive

designed specifically for such tasks.

These results and later were decidedly encouraging, but the Deutsche Bundesbahn has yet to decide whether or not to exploit the manifest capabilities of such three-phase traction, which is notably expensive. What cannot be denied, however, is that the induction motor is the most promising new development in electric traction, and could well become less expensive if it enters production to the stage at which economies of scale become significant The data for the 120-class locomotive include propulsion by 15,000-volt 16.67-Hz alternating current from overhead wires rectified by thyristors and then inverted by thyristors to variable-frequency three-phase alternating current for supply to four 1,878-hp (1400-kW) induction traction motors with spring drive, tractive effort 76,435lb (34670kg), total weight 185,185lb (84000kg), overall length 63ft 0in (19.200m) and maximum speed of 99km/h (160km/h).

Given the bi-lingual official nature of Canada, the LRC Bo-Bo locomotive uses as its designation an acronym that was specially selected to be the same in both English and French: LRC stands for Light, Rapid and Comfortable in English and Lèger, Rapide et Confortable in French. What is also evident, however, is that the L could also stand for Lourd (heavy), for the LRC passenger car turns the scales at some 57 per cent more than the same-capacity equivalent hauled by the British HST 125 motor/baggage carriage, which is itself 20 per cent lighter than the LRC's locomotive. These weight factors aside, the LRC is a significant offering in the high-speed train stakes, its capabilities tarnished only moderately by the number of failures it had encountered during a number of early efforts to get the type into full service before all its teething problems had been eliminated.

The LRC entered service in 1981 on the route linking Toronto and Montreal, a 337-mile (542-km) journey for which a time of 3 hours 40 minutes was initially scheduled for a 45-minute saving over the schedule of the 'Turbo-train' used on the route since the late 1970s. By July 1982 the schedule timed had been extended to 4 hours 25 minutes, the same as that of the Turbo-train, with the caveat that the schedule was also subject to alterations that might result in a delay of almost one hour. This was a reflection of the fact that during the previous winter there had been major problems with powdery snow getting into the locomotives' advanced internal equipment and causing havoc.

Despite these and other problems, there is no doubt that the LRC is essentially of capable concept that was not pushed into service until a 14-year development period had been completed. The most interesting feature incorporated in the LRC is provision for a tilt of up to 8.5° to improve safety and passenger comfort as the train passes round curves at high speed. This tilting capability is restricted to the passengers cars as it was thought unnecessary and also expensive for incorporation in the locomotive, which carries a large diesel engine providing power for traction and also for the

ABOVE and OPPOSITE: The LRC type of train was designed and built to provide moderately fast and comfortable passenger railroad services in Canada's more heavily populated areas. However, in service, it was soon found to be compromised by the weight of the locomotives and passenger cars, resulting in trains whose poor power/weight ratio adversely affected the *type's operating economics and, as a result of the need to cruise at high power settings in an effort to maintain an adequately fast schedule, mechanical reliability that was far inferior to that originally specified. Another problem was the fact that development and introduction of the equipment was also inordinately protracted.*

considerable demands of the air-conditioning and heating systems necessary for passenger comfort in the excesses of the Canadian summer and winter. The initial order covered 22 locomotives and 50 passenger cars for service with VIA Rail Canada, but problems with the passenger cars' most advanced feature, the tilting system, meant that in the short term there were too many locomotives for the number of carriages available, and the surplus was used to haul other trains, for example the *International Limited* between Toronto and Chicago in the northern U.S.A.

The data for the LRC locomotive include propulsion by one 3,900-hp (2908-kW) Alco Type 251 diesel engine powering an alternator feeding (via rectifiers) four direct-current traction motors geared to the axles, total weight of 185,185lb (84000kg), overall length of 66ft 5in (20.24m) and maximum theoretical speed of 125mph (201km/h) limited by general track conditions to 80mph (129km/h).

Such was the success of the British HST 125 that there were major hopes that other railroad operators might adopt it. As events turned out, the only country to evince any significant interest was Australia, in the form of the railway administration of the New South Wales Public Transport Administration. However, the version adopted in New South Wales as the XPT (Express Passenger Train) has a number of differences from the British original to reflect the somewhat different operating conditions of this Australian state.

Most notably, the XPT is an eight-car train and therefore shorter than its British counterpart with two motor/baggage cars and between seven and nine passenger cars. Although the Paxman diesel engines of the XPT are rated at something like 10 per cent less than those in the British motor/baggage car, increasing their life and improving fuel economy to marked extents, the lower weight of the shorter train gives the XPT a higher power/weight ratio, and in combination with lower gearing (itself a reflection of the fact that Australian track alignments are incapable of supporting speeds in the order of 125mph/200km/h)

this produces significantly higher acceleration, and this improves the overall performance of the train on services with numerous stops and slow sections. Another change was effected in the bogies, for early evaluation of the HST 125 revealed that the original British pattern was not ideally suited to the tracks typical of Australian operations. Less obvious modifications were made to the ventilation system so that it could cope more effectively with the greater heat and dustiness of Australian service, and the passenger cars were manufactured from stainless steel to provide a commonality with other modern elements

of the rolling stock operated by the Australian railways, and in particular that of the *Indian-Pacific* service operating across the continent between Sydney and Perth.

The XPT entered full service in 1982, having first put paid to the criticisms of a not inconsiderable number of detractors by recording an Australian rail speed record of 144mph (231km/h) near Wagga-Wagga during August 1981. The XPT's first scheduled services were three daily routes operated out of Sydney, and a reflection of the capabilities of the new type was provided by a time saving of 1 hour 46 minutes for the 315-mile (506-km) route

linking Sydney and Kempsey. The original Australian order was for 10 motor/baggage cars and 20 passengers cars, enough for four seven-car trains and a reserve of two motor/baggage cars, but the success of the new type was such that in April 1982 there followed an additional order for four motor/baggage cars and 16 passenger cars to create six eight-car trains reflecting the increased traffic on the routes operated by the XPT. Further proof of the success of the XPT had already been provided in February 1982 by the decision of the Victorian Railways to contract for sufficient rolling stock to create three trains for the service

RIGHT: *A pre-production TGV running on existing track in Alsace, France during trials in 1979.*

RIGHT: *A pre-production TGV running on existing track in Alsace, France during trials in 1979.*

OPPOSITE: *The introduction of the TGV on France's railroad network was preceded by a considerable quantity of infrastructure work to provide the right type of tracks and routes for these high-speed trains, and the subsequent extension of the TGV network meant additional work. That the French had planned correctly, however, is indicated by the fact that the TGV network operates at a profit.*

linking Melbourne and Sydney.

The data for the XPT high-speed diesel-electric passenger train include propulsion by one 2,000-hp (1491-kW) Paxman Valenta diesel engine and alternator supplying direct current via solid-state rectifiers to four traction motors geared to the axles with hollow-axle flexible drive, a total weight of 826,500lb (374900kg), overall length of 590ft 2in (179.88m) and maximum speed of 100mph (161km/h).

The Soviet counterpart to the HST 125 was created as the ER 200, and this was planned as a 14-car train whose greater size reflected the generally larger passenger loads carried by Soviet train services in a country in which private car ownership and air travel were both severely restricted. The ER 200 was the Soviet railroad organization's first high-speed electric train of the self-propelled type, and was first built in 1975 at the Riga Carriage Works in

what is now the independent country of Latvia in the centre of the three Baltic states. The authorities' plan was to create a train capable of offering a genuinely high-speed service on the 406-mile (650-km) route connecting Moscow and Leningrad, the two most important cities of the U.S.S.R. The route is essentially straight, so the new train needed nothing like a tilting mechanism to ensure safety and comfort on curves of comparatively short radius, but only the power output needed to accelerate the train to a high cruising speed and then maintain it at that basic level, and the brakes to decelerate the train safely. The power output selected for the task was some 13,840hp (10320kW), and the chosen braking system combined electro-mechanical disc brakes for speeds below 22mph (35mph) and rheostatic brakes for speeds above 22mph; an electromagnetic rail brake was added for emergency use.

In electrical terms the train's 14 cars comprised six two-car powered units, each with 128 seats, and at each end an unpowered cab/passenger/baggage car with seating for 24 passengers, a small buffet section and baggage accommodation. A number of modern systems were designed for the new train, these systems including an 'autodriver' to respond automatically to transponder units located at track level to set the speed desired between particular points. It was reported that the ER 200 completed the journey between Moscow and Leningrad in 3 hours 5 minutes at an average speed of 106mph (170km/h) during a 1980 test run, but entry into public service

at anything like these speeds has not yet taken place. The data for the ER 200 high-speed electric train included propulsion by 3,000-volt direct current delivered via an overhead catenary to 48 288-hp (215-kW) traction motors driving the axles of the 12 intermediate cars by means of gearing and flexible drives, total weight of 1,829,806lb (830000kg), overall length of 1,220ft 6in (372.00m) and maximum speed of 124mph (200km/h).

There can be little doubt that the most impressive high-speed train in large-scale service anywhere in the world at the end of the 20th century is the TGV (Train Grande Vitesse, or high-speed train) operated by the French national railways, more properly known as the Société Nationale des Chemins de Fer. The origins of this type can be discerned as far back as 1955, when two French electric locomotives separately established a world train speed record of 205.7mph (331km/h) while undertaking tests designed to provide data on the design of the locomotive and the track that was required for very high-speed running. At the time, this might have been regarded as little more than experimental work, and as such not in any way bearing a practical relationship to the everyday world of railroad operations, which was currently limited in France to a maximum speed of only 87mph (140km/h). The lie was put to this impression by the fact that just 21 years later two prototype examples of a new French train intended for full service and not just trial work had on almost 225 times recorded a speed in exceed of

ABOVE LEFT and RIGHT: *Work in progress on the Digoin railway project in France, in 1978. This was part of the very considerable effort that the French had to make to ensure that the system had the right combination of tracks and routes for the TGV.*

RIGHT: *A track inspection coach, capable of measuring the quality of track at 125mph, running behind the power car of a High Speed Train in the mid-1970s.*

OPPOSITE: *A prototype of an SNCF TGV during trials in the late 1970s. From the beginning of the prototype trials, it was clear that at the mechanical level, the TGV was clearly on the verge of considerable success.*

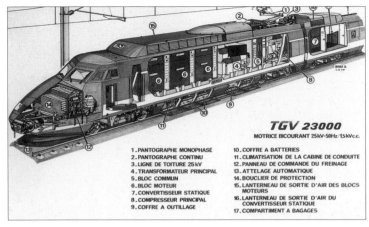

TGV 23000
MOTRICE BICOURANT 25kV-50Hz/1,5kVc.c.

1. PANTOGRAPHE MONOPHASE
2. PANTOGRAPHE CONTINU
3. LIGNE DE TOITURE 25 kV
4. TRANSFORMATEUR PRINCIPAL
5. BLOC COMMUN
6. BLOC MOTEUR
7. CONVERTISSEUR STATIQUE
8. COMPRESSEUR PRINCIPAL
9. COFFRE A OUTILLAGE
10. COFFRE A BATTERIES
11. CLIMATISATION DE LA CABINE DE CONDUITE
12. PANNEAU DE COMMANDE DU FREINAGE
13. ATTELAGE AUTOMATIQUE
14. BOUCLIER DE PROTECTION
15. LANTERNEAU DE SORTIE D'AIR DES BLOCS MOTEURS
16. LANTERNEAU DE SORTIE D'AIR DU CONVERTISSEUR STATIQUE
17. COMPARTIMENT A BAGAGES

LEFT: This cutaway illustration reveals the interior of the first generation of TGV power cars with their powerful electric motors and, below a pantograph assembly, the associated transformers and converters.

BELOW: The trials of the TGV in the 1970s and early 1980s were marked by the establishment of a series of world speed records.

requirement of fast passenger trains and considerably slower freight trains operating over the same tracks, which made the creation of scheduling that was both safe and efficient very difficult. As a result, the flow of traffic along the route was arranged in so-called 'flights', with passenger trains and freight trains scheduled in batches for movement at different times of the day. This system was at best a palliative, and there was thus a very strong argument for the creation of additional capacity. The start of work on the evaluation of the various ways in which this extra capacity could be provided started in 1966, and by this time it had already been decided that the new track

186mph (300km/h).

Just as significantly, the French railway organization had already started work on 236miles (380km) of new track designed to allow trains to run at these speeds on the route linking Paris and Lyons, the latter the central station in the route between Paris and Marseilles that had been the primary route of the old Paris, Lyons & Marseilles railroad company as it linked France's three most populous cities. As a result, the route was the location of the railroad company's heaviest traffic in the period leading up to World War II, and this factor increased after the end of the war as France was rebuilt. Electrification of the line in the period after the war improved the quality and reliability of the service, but also added additional passenger traffic, and by the 1960s the route was decidedly congested.

The main problem was the conflicting

would serve not only to reduce the pressure on the existing track, but also to allow the operation of more advanced trains at very much higher speeds than had hitherto been possible, in the process drawing passengers from the parallel road and air services, relieving pressure on these already overtaxed routes.

One fact that was evident from the beginning of the study was that the dedication of the new line to passengers rather than mixed traffic would offer significant construction and speed advantages as it would remove the need for the cambering of curves at the compromise (and therefore not optimized) angle required to cope with all speeds and weights of traffic. The new track was therefore conceived for the very much higher speeds that would be typical of the new trains operating only with passengers. The axle loads of freight vehicles can reach 44,092lb (20000kg) and those of electric locomotives 50,705lb (23000kg), but it was soon seen that if the axle loading of trains operating on the new line could be limited to a figure in the order of 37,478lb (17000kg) this would facilitate the maintenance of the track in a condition fully suitable for the operation of trains running at very high speed.

Drawing on the experience of the 1955 high-speed test operations, the French railway organization was able in 1967 to begin limited operations at speeds of up to 124mph (200km/h) on the route connecting Paris and Bordeaux on the south-west region of the country's railroad network. The same region was also used for further

LEFT and BELOW: Though not as advanced in purely aerodynamic terms as some of the high-speed trains that followed its pioneering lead, the TGV is still notably 'clean' in its exterior lines, and the avoidance of complex two- and three-dimensional curvatures also helped to keep manufacturing costs under control. This last fact was important as the creation of the required infrastructure was so expensive.

LEFT: Trolley service aboard Eurostar, *Rail Europe.*

OPPOSITE
ABOVE LEFT: First-class dining aboard Thalys, *Rail Europe.*

ABOVE RIGHT: A first-class meal aboard Eurostar.

BELOW LEFT: The upper-storey bar of a TGV Duplex double-decker.

BELOW RIGHT: The bar aboard Thalys, *Rail Europe.*

evaluation of high-speed running by special sets of railcars: the first experimental set with gas turbine power was run at speeds up to 147mph (236km/h), and one of the production sets with the same type of powerplant completed 10 runs at speeds of more than 155mph (250km/h). It was the initial experimental set with gas turbine propulsion for very high speeds that indicated the way forward, however, and this TGV001 (later redesignated as the TGS

so that the TGV appellation could be used for the parallel version with electric propulsion) became the first French train to be designed for running at a speed of 186mph (300km/h): the TVG001/TGS completed 175 runs in which it exceeded a speed of 186mph and also recorded a maximum speed of 197mph (317km/h). There was also built a special high-speed electric motor coach that reached a maximum speed of 192mph (309km/h),

clearly indicating that the French railroad organization was pushing forward the frontier of train performance right across the board of available technologies.

It was originally planned that the new track between Paris and Lyons should be used for high-speed passenger services based on trains using the technology pioneered and proved in the TVG001/TGS experimental set. The cost of buying the land and then undertaking the considerable

task of demolishing existing buildings and then building the new track within the built-up area of Paris was deemed too great for serious contemplation, so the new track was based on the use of the first 18.6 miles (30km) of existing track south from the Gare de Lyon, and therefore only a limited running speed, to the point at which the new track diverged from the existing network for the main length of the run to Lyons at very much higher speed. The new

RIGHT: A TGV Duplex of Rail Europe.

BELOW LEFT: The Thalys 2 service on the important route linking Paris and Amsterdam in the Netherlands.

BELOW RIGHT: The Thalys 2 service operates with the latest generation of locomotives, the Eurostar type.

OPPOSITE: A unit of the latest generation of TGV trains, the TGV-R, cruises through northern France in the region of Lens.

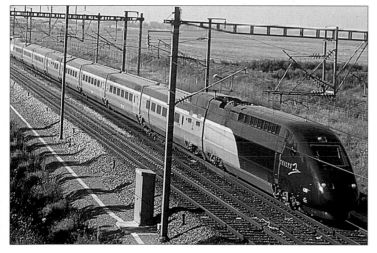

ABOVE: A Pendolino train of the Italian State Railways reveals its tilting upper element, the main attribute possessed by this type of train for the fast negotiation of curves designed for slower trains.

ABOVE RIGHT: An Italian State Railways Settobello.

OPPOSITE: A Rail Europe TGV at speed.

track was linked with the existing network at two other places to provide a link for services to Dijon and to the Swiss cities of Lausanne and Geneva. The whole task required a very considerable injection of money from the French government for the capital investment in the new infrastructure, but the current financial strength of the services between Paris and Lyons meant that those planning the new service were not being fanciful when they predicted a considerable and comparatively rapid return on the capital investment.

Planning was well under way and final government approval of the new system was imminent when a radical change was

imposed by the financial problems that started to affect the Western world late in 1973 after the Arab nations that were the world's main sources of oil decided to raise their prices dramatically in an effort to use the 'oil weapon' as a means of reducing Western support for Israel, which had just achieved a major military success against Egypt and Syria in the Yom Kippur War of October 1973. Gas turbine propulsion for the TGV was therefore abandoned in favour of electric propulsion using overhead lines delivering 25,000 volts at 50Hz. Final planning for the route, and the revision of the TGV for electric propulsion was being undertaken, taking into account the fact that

only very fast passenger trains would be using the new route, which meant that gradients of hitherto impossible steepness could be used as the trains would have the kinetic energy to climb such gradients without major loss of speed: it was felt that so great would be this kinetic energy, which is the product of the train's mass and the square of its velocity, that gradients of 1/28.5, four times steeper than those of the current tracks, could be employed. The reduction in the amount of diversion and levelling required to establish the current type of flatter route meant a saving of about 30 per cent in construction cost and also reduced the time required to build the new

423

ABOVE: *The Italian railroad system's Fiat Ferroviaria ETR 450 trains offer considerable air-conditioned comfort.*

LEFT: *The network covered by the ETR 450 service extends from Salerno, just below Naples, in the south via Rome and Florence to Bologna in the north, where the network bifurcates north-east to Padua and Venice, and north-west to Milan and Turin.*

OPPOSITE: *Like most other high-speed trains of the present generation, the ETR 401 or Pendolino train is electrically powered by current delivered from an overhead line by a pantograph arrangement.*

tracks. The longest gradient on the new line is such that the speed of the TGV is reduced from 162mph (260km/h) at the bottom to 137mph (220km/h) at the top, this 25-mph (40 km/h) loss of speed being quickly recovered once the train has reached level ground once more.

The initial order for the all-electric TGV was made in 1976, and delivery began in 1978. The basic structural and aerodynamic design of the TGS was carried over to the TGV but the propulsion arrangement was, of course, entirely different and for obvious cost and reliability reasons made use of existing components wherever possible. Each of the TGV trains is a 10-car set in the form of two motor cars and an articulated assembly of eight passenger cars with the adjacent ends of two cars carried by a common bogie. The available power is 8,450hp (6300kW), and this is transmitted to 12 motorized axles in the form of the four axles of each of the two motor cars and the two adjacent axles of the end bogies of the passenger cars at each end of the articulated set of cars. A useful feature of the electric propulsion arrangement is the fact that it can also be operated on the 1,500-volt direct current system used on the previously electrified elements of the French railroad system, while six of the train sets are also equipped to operate on the 15,000-volt 16.67-Hz power of the Swiss railroad system. For alternating current operation there is a transformer in each motor car.

The TGV train sets are based on a development of the type of bogie developed initially for the TGV001/TGS, and as the new lines are restricted in terms of their use to only the TGVs, the camber of the tracks on the curves is optimized for these train sets, which therefore require no tilting mechanism. The electric traction motors are mounted on the body of the motor car, and a flexible drive arrangement is used to transfer the motive power to the axles. By this means, the unsprung mass of the bogie is very low, and this is one of the reasons that the forces imposed on the track at 186mph (300km/h) are less than those of a standard electric locomotive moving at 124mph (200km/h).

The new TGV lines have no trackside signalling arrangements, for the driver receives signal indications in the cab. The maximum speed permitted on any section of the track is shown on a display in front of the driver, who thus sets the controller to the speed indicated, the control system then maintaining this speed on an automatic basis. The TGV has three braking systems, all of them controlled by the single driver's brake valve. These systems are of the dynamic, disc and wheel tread types. The dynamic system makes use of the electric traction motors as generators, feeding energy into resistances, and in the course of braking the motors are excited from a battery, so that failure of the overhead supply does not affect the braking: the dynamic braking system is effective from maximum speed to 1.9mph (3km/h). In normal service, the disc brakes are applied to half their maximum braking capacity and wheel tread brakes are used only lightly to

clean the wheel treads, but under emergency conditions all three systems are used fully for maximum deceleration effect, and the braking distance from 162mph (260km/h) is 3,825 yards (3500m).

Most of the 87 TGV train sets were completed with both first- and second-class accommodation, but six were delivered with only first-class accommodation and another three for the carriage of mail rather than passengers. The train sets were built by the Alsthom company, which undertook the manufacture of the motor cars and the passenger cars at Belfort and La Rochelle respectively. The vital initial testing and evaluation of the TGV in its production form was undertaken on the existing route between Strasbourg and Belfort, which is sufficiently straight that a sustained speed of 162mph (260km/h) was feasible, but as soon as the first part of the new line had been completed the rest of the test and evaluation effort was transferred to this location, and one of the train sets was modified with enlarged wheels to allow tests above the normal maximum speed: in February 1981 this train set established a new world train speed record of 236mph (380km/h).

Scheduled passenger services on the southern section of the new line were inaugurated during the course of September 1981, and the success of the new service's speed and comfort was soon attested by a 70 per cent increase in passenger loads. The northern section of the route between Paris and Lyons opened for service late in 1983, allowing the inauguration of a scheduled

service in the time of 2 hours for the 266-mile (428-km) route at the average speed of 134mph (215km/h), although the 1983 raising of the maximum permissible speed from 162 to 168mph (260 to 270km/h) allowed a slight reduction in time and thus a modest increase in average speed. Apart from a small number of teething problems, including modest damage to the overhead power lines at maximum speed, the TGV has operated with commendable efficiency and reliability from the start of its operational career. The ride on the new lines is excellent, although a degradation of comfort is evident when the TGV operates on older lines.

The success of the TGV led to a comparatively modest but steady expansion of its route network, and the data for the TGV high-speed articulated multiple-unit electric train includes propulsion by 1,500-, 15,000- or 25,000-volt direct current delivered from overhead wires and passed via rectifiers and/or chopper control to six 704-hp (525-kW) traction motors at each end of the train set and powers the axles by means of spring drives, total weight 841,711lb (381800kg), overall length 656ft 9.5in (200.19m) and maximum speed 162mph (260km/h) as the type entered service but later increased to 186mph (300km/h).

The Italian counterpart of the TGV, although to a smaller size and of slightly lower performance, is the ETR 401 Pendolino four-car train, which was the world's second class of tilting trains to enter service after the much slower Japanese

ABOVE: *The ETR 401 Pendolino express at Orvieto station on the line between Rome and Florence.*

'381'-class train that entered service in the mid-1970s. The ETR 401 resulted from a project financed by the Italian industrial giant Fiat, and the type is able to provide high speed by the combination of moderately good streamlining and the high power/weight ratio resulting from the use of an abundance of power in a comparatively light train. Adequate stopping power is offered by the incorporation of three separate braking systems: the standard system is dynamic braking, using the motors as dynamos, for low-speed use there is a system of conventional electro-pneumatic air brakes, and finally there is an electro-magnetic rail brake that, by its very nature, is wholly independent of the wheels and their adhesion to the track. Unlike the TGV, the ETR 401 was designed for use on existing track and was therefore designed

OPPOSITE: *The ETR 401 Pendolino express leaves a tunnel on its way from Florence and Rome.*

with the very small axle load of 23,148lb (10500kg), and this ensures that the operation of the train has minimal adverse effect on the track.

The most interesting feature of the train at the technical level is, of course, the tilting system designed to maximize safety and the comfort of the 170 passengers as the train rounds curves at speeds higher than those for which the track was originally created. The maximum tilt angle is 9°, and the tilt is produced actively, under the control of a system of accelerometers and gyroscopes, rather than merely passively in response to the curve and the g forces exerted on the train as it passes round the curve. The propulsion arrangement of the ETR 401 is of the electric type, and draws current from overhead lines by means of a

pantograph current collector installed on a frame mounted on one of the bogie bolsters so that it is not affected in its task by the tilting.

There have been a few accidents with the ETR 401, but in general the operation of this type of train has been moderately successful. The train first entered service on the 185-mile (298-km) route between Rome and Ancona across the Appennine mountains. The nature of this route allows the ETR 401 to develop its maximum speed of 156mph (250km/h) for only a relatively short time, but provides ample scope for the tilting system to reveal its advantages on the short-radius curves typical of any railroad system operating across a mountain range. The ETR 401's high speed offered the possibility of a reduction of 45 minutes by comparison

with the standard scheduled time of 3 hours, a saving of some 25 per cent, but the operator sensibly opted not to press the matter to the limit and therefore scheduled the service for a time saving of some 20 minutes. The acceptance of the ETR 401 has gradually extended to other routes in Italy, but the type's somewhat chequered operational record has meant that there are still doubts about the system, which had been exported to Spain in the form of the so-called 'Basculante' trains.

The data for the ETR 401 Pendolino high-speed electric train with a body-tilting system include electric propulsion by 3,000-volt direct current from an overhead catenary to eight 335-hp (250-kW) motors (two to each car), each driving a single axle by means of cardan shafts and gearing, total weight of 354,938lb (161000kg), overall length of 340ft 2.5in (103.70m) and maximum speed of 156mph (250km/h).

An extremely ambitious concept that was ultimately cancelled as a failure because of its complex tilting system, the '370' class or 'APT' (Advanced Passenger Train) was intended to provide British Railways with an extremely capable train for service well into the 21st century. The origins of the APT-P can be found in the 1960s when British Railways entrusted its much-enlarged Research Department at Derby with the task of undertaking a complete study of one of the railroad's most basic problems, namely the rising of a flanged wheel over a railed track. From the results of this study there appeared the technical feasibility for the design of a

train, albeit still with flanged wheels, offering the possibility of very smooth running at higher speeds than was currently practical or even permissible with the current generation of trains running over British Railways' tracks with their comparatively tight curves and imperfect vertical as well as lateral alignments.

The key to this capability was seen as the incorporation of a high-quality tilting system that would operate entirely automatically to keep the train dynamically stable and the passengers comfortable as the whole assembly travelled round tight curves. This concept was not unique, and was under active consideration or development at much the same time by railroads in countries such as Canada, Italy and Japan. However, it was only the Canadian LRC train that was conceived in terms as ambitious as those of the ATP as in the other schemes the body was designed to tilt passively in response to the forces imposed on it rather than actively to match the tilt to the curve as the train entered it. In the APT the body-tilting system was therefore planned as a positive element of the train's control system, each of the coaches modifying its angle of tilt in relation to the camber of the track and the forces imposed on the train on the basis of sensors reporting the movement of the coach in front of it. The maximum tilt angle was 9°, and at this angle the outer side of the coach was 1ft 4in (0.406m) higher than the inner side. The premise on which the whole system was based in financial terms was that on journeys of more than 200

miles (322km), the APT would be able to operate at much the same speed as the French TGV but without the enormously expensive process of creating a wholly new track system. It was conservatively estimated that the development and production of the APT-P to run on existing tracks would be only about one-fifth of the cost of the TGV and its special track system.

At the conceptual level, therefore, the APT appeared to be a winner, and this fact

ABOVE: British Rail's 155mph (250km/h) experimental APT (Advanced Passenger Train) began secret trials on a 4-mile (6-km) length of disused track near Derby in 1973, carrying a British Rail research team. The trial provided data for the building of two prototypes, the start of a fleet that was to cover inter-city routes.

ABOVE and LEFT: *The APT-P (P for Prototype) offered British Rail considerable capabilities, but was beset by technical problems that led to the type's cancellation. Before this happened, however, the prototype APT-P trains had revealed that their overall level of performance was genuinely excellent.*

seemed to be emphasized in that the tilting body system was only part of the complete package, whose other element was a radically improved suspension system incorporating a self-steering feature in the bogies.

British Railways requested the necessary financial package from the British government in December 1967, and in 1973 permission was given for the construction of the first experimental four-car set with gas turbine propulsion. This

OPPOSITE: British Rail's APT on a run between Carlisle and Carnforth at about 130mph (209km/h).

RIGHT: Though it suffered from a few technical difficulties, the APT-P was perhaps cancelled too promptly, for the type could have provided British Rail with an excellent high-speed passenger capability for its longer-distance services within the U.K.

was secretly tested by British Railways, which revealed the experimental rig in 1975. This prototype was the APT-E (Advanced Passenger Train Experimental) that successfully operated at a maximum speed of 151mph (243km/h) on the section of the main-line track west of London between Reading and Swindon and, perhaps more importantly, averaged slightly more than 100mph (161km/h) between London and Leicester.

The success of these early trials led to the granting of permission for the

manufacture of three 14-car production prototype trains, each comprising two central and non-tilting power cars in which 8,000hp (5965kW) would be generated, and 12 tilting cars for use as six-car forward and rear sections each incorporating a buffet car as well as carrying 72 first- and 195 second-class passengers. Although gas turbine propulsion had originally been planned, this was now considered too expensive in terms of its fuel consumption and, in the absence of diesel engines offering adequate

power at the modest power/weight ratio that was clearly required for maximum speed and the highest possible acceleration, the decision went to electrical power. This decision was reinforced by the fact that the main routes on which the new train was designed to operate, most notably those linking London with Glasgow and Liverpool were already electrified.

The other side of the coin from a rapid acceleration and a high maximum speed is the ability to halt quickly and securely, and for this reason the APT was planned with a

hydro-kinetic braking system and disc brakes to provide deceleration to a halt from a speed of 155mph (250km/h) in a standard distance of 2,500 yards (2285m) and a maximum-effort distance of only 2,000 yards (1830m).

The first of the 14-car APT-P (Advanced Passenger Train – Prototype) trains was delivered in 1978. The performance of the train was highly impressive, but before the type could enter service there was a catalogue of small problems to be overcome, and the type

ABOVE: Pre-production model of the electric-powered Advanced Passenger Train (APT), 1980.

ABOVE RIGHT: Technical trials of the APT-E (Advanced Passenger Train – Experimental) near the M1 motorway, north of London, in 1974.

completed only one return service between London and Glasgow before the appearance of other problems, combined with the threat of industrial action, persuaded British Railways to take the type out of service and the government to postpone and finally to cancel the planned APT-S (Advanced Passenger Train – Series) full-production version. The data for the APT-P high-speed electric passenger train with advanced tilting capability included propulsion by 25,000-volt alternating current delivered via overhead catenary, step-down transformer and thyristor-based control system to four body-mounted 1,000-hp (746-kW) motors

in two power cars and driving wheels by means of shafts and gearing, total weight of 1,014,942lb (460378kg), overall length of 963ft 6in (293.67m) and maximum speed of 150mph (241km/h).

Many railroads have operated within the context of automatic signalling systems since the early part of the 20th century. With many rapid transport systems now based on computer-aided operations, automatic route setting has been combined with other functions to produce operating systems that are fully automatic. Though such systems can be very advanced, most trains still need a human operator to ensure

that the train is ready to depart and to give the starting signal. The world's first totally unmanned train was the VAL (Véhicule Automatique Léger), a 'light rail' rapid transit system which was opened in April 1983 in the French city of Lille. The VAL is a fully automatic system of which parts are elevated, on the surface and under the ground. Moreover, the stations on this system, pointing at least one possible way to the future, are also unstaffed. For reasons of passenger safety, the platforms have glass panelling along the edge, and this incorporates automatic sliding doors which open in concert with the doors of the VAL

train only when the latter has come to a complete halt. The rubber-tyred two-car trains are driven automatically on concrete runways located 5ft 3in (1.6m) apart. There are times, however, when the cars have to be manually driven, and for such an eventuality there is a small control panel at each end, allowing staff the ability to manoeuvre the vehicles in areas such as maintenance depots.

In Canada, a fully automated Skytrain was built to provide a link between Vancouver's two 'Expo 86' sites. Opened in December 1985, the Skytrain was thus called because much of the original

ABOVE: Pre-production model of the APT-P electric-powered Advanced Passenger Train during a commissioning run at Beattock, Scotland, 1980.

LEFT: Advanced Passenger Train – Experimental (APT-E) demonstrating its body-tilting during the first series of track trials in 1973.

ABOVE: *The passenger cars of the APT-P train ushered in a new generation of accommodation for British Railways passengers, the interior of each car being ergonomically designed for the carriage of the maximum number of passengers with adequate legroom, comparatively wide aisles, and features such as adequate tables and fold-down trays on the backs of seats. The accommodation was also, of course, heated and air-conditioned, and access and* egress were achieved by doors at the ends of each car.

RIGHT: *This prototype of the ATP, seemed to offer British Rail the opportunity, then lost, to take the lead in the provision of advanced passenger transport capability.*

ABOVE: The APT-P would have provided British Rail's market-leading InterCity longer-distance rail services with an attractive and cost-effective inducement for passengers to travel by rail rather than car or aircraft.

6.5-mile (10.4-km) route was carried on viaducts. Like those of the VAL system in Lille, the Skytrains are designed for unmanned operation, although a number of personnel have a roving brief on the system to discourage vandalism and offer assistance to members of the travelling public. The cars, made of aluminium alloy, each turn the scales at some 31,360lb (14225kg) and have provision for 108 passengers of whom 40 are seated. Evidence of the safety

consciousness of this 'light rail' system's operator is provided by the fact that the first service of the morning is operated in the standard automatic fashion but also carried a member of the staff at the front of the forward car to watch for any obstruction that may have blocked the line during the night.

Like the French and Canadian systems, the Docklands Light Railway opened in London during 1987, is fully automatic. However, unlike the other two systems, the

trains of the Docklands Light Railway each carry a 'train captain' with the task of checking tickets and assisting the travelling public. The train captain also gives the starting signal to the control computer and, in an emergency, drives the train from a set of controls at the front of the vehicle.

In the current age, in which the computer is becoming increasingly paramount for control functions that would previously have offered employment to people, the more advanced railroads of the world are being steadily revolutionized by the installation in their vehicles of microprocessors to detect faults and failures, and thus to reduce the possibility of accidents resulting from these defects and going undetected and therefore unreported. Locomotives are equipped with onboard computers allowing operational and status data to be read directly or transferred to the maintenance depot for action.

ABOVE LEFT: The driver's position of the APT-P, revealing a clean and uncluttered look designed to maximize driver concentration.

ABOVE: A trial run of British Rail's APT-P on the West Coast Main Line. This line will probably see the first regular tilting train service in Britain, but not with the APT, with their introduction to Virgin Rail in the new millennium.

OPPOSITE: A British Rail InterCity 125 at Teignmouth in the late 1970s.

INDEX

A

439

Picture Acknowledgements

Mechanical, Archive & Research Services, London, England: pages 20 left, 24 top right, 26 bottom, 27 both, 28 below, 47 below, 52 below right
Military Archive & Research Services, Lincolnshire, England: pages 8, 14 left, 18 top right, 24 bottom left, 29 top right, 31 below right, 32, 37, 38 below left and right, 43 top right, 44, 46 top left and right, 51 top left, 51 top right, 53 below, 55 top left, 63 top right, 64 top right (above and below), 64 below right, below left (above and below), 65 below left, 65 below right, 73 below, bottom left and bottom right, 74–75 all, 76 above left, 79 above, below 1st, 3rd and 4th from the left, 80 all, 81, 83 both, 84 both, 88, 94 both, 95 below right, 97 below right, 101 above left, 105 above right, 106 top left, 107 top, 112 above left, 112 below right, 113 top left, 136 left, 137 top right, 142, 147 left, 149, 150 below left, 151 right, 154 left and right, 155 all, 163 top, 165 right, 166 top, 167 below, 170 top and below right, 174 top both, 176 right, 206 top left, 213 left, 216 below, 227 top left, 238 top left, 238 below left and right, 240

above, 241 top left and right, 242 below, 245 below, 246 both, 247 top, 248 right, 249 all, 250 all, 251 both, 252 both, 263, above left and right, 284, 302 both, 303 both, 395 right, 397, 400 both
*Amtrak: pages 171 left, 172 right, 173 all, 262, 263 below, 273, 353 below left and right, 401, 402
Ann Ronan Picture Library, London: pages 69, 72, 76 above right, 78 above, 85 below right
Ann Ronan at Image Select, London: pages 9, 10, 11 all, 12 below left and top right, 13, 14 right, 15 all, 17 all, 18 top left and bottom right, 20 centre and right, 21, 24 bottom right, 33 top right, 42 both, 45 top right and below, 50, 53 top left and right, 56 left, 62 below, 63 below
*Association of American Railroads, U.S.A.: pages 23 below, 30 below, 52 top, 55 top right, 61 top, 82 all, 242 top
*Atchison, Topeka & Santa Fe Railway: pages 161 top right and below left, 169 top left, 216 top, 387 below, 389 left, 390 above far right, 391 above left
*Austrian State Railways: pages 244 top, 245 top right, 355 below, 358, 359
*B.C. Provincial Archives: pages 35 right, 40
*Baltimore & Ohio Railroad: pages 18 below left, 22 right, 25

both, 26 top left, 29 below, 36 top left, 38 top, 43 below, 49 left centre and below, 52 below left, 89 below, 134, 143 left, 159 top, 163 below left, 206 below, 213 right, 221 top, 228 second left, 229 below, 238 top right, 326
BBC Hulton Picture Library, London: page 203 left
Bek, Prague: page 324
*Belgian Railways: pages 146 top left, 345 above, 354 both
*Berne-Lötschberg-Simplon Railway: page 286 above left
*Bombardier Inc.: page 409
*British Columbia Railways: pages 259, 260
*British Rail: pages 241 below left, 304 above, 378–379, 403 both, 405 all, 406, 407 both, 408 below, 415 below, 428, 429 right, 431, 432 both, 433 both, 434 both, 435, 436 both, 437
British Transport Films, London: page 218 top
*Bundesarchiv: page 188 both
*Burlington Northern Railroad: pages 54, 97 above left, 161 below right, 167 top, 218 below right, 227 top right
*Canadian National Railway: pages 34, 61 below, 85 above right, 152, 153, 169 top right, 220, 261 all, 388 above left, 389 right
*Canadian Pacific Corporate Archives: pages 31 left, 35 right, 36 top right, 39 top, 41 both, 59 top left and right,

spanning top of pages 62–603, 172 left, 177 below, 248 left, 260, 388 above right and below
C.F.C.L./Image Select: pages 323, 366
*Chicago & North Western Railroad: page 57 below
*Chicago, Burlington & Quincy Railroad: pages 39 below right, 48 top right, 92
*C&O Historical Society: page 106 above right
Colin Garratt/Milepost: pages 116 below, 117 both, 118 right, 119, 121, 174 below, 175 below
*Danish State Railways: page 352 below
*Delaware & Hudson Railroad: page 22 left
* © Denver Public Library, Western History Department: page 23 below
*Denver & Rio Grande Railroad: page 222 below
*Deutsche Bundesbahn: pages 122 below, 191, 233 all, 386 below, 387 above right, 408 above left and right
*Deutsches Museum, Munich: pages 86 above right and below (both), 87 all
*EBT Bahn, Burgdorf: page 245 above right
Fiat Ferroviaria: pages 426, 427
*Finnish state railways: pages 136 right, 137 top left, 146 below, 230 right, 234, 386 above, 387 above left

Freightliner Ltd.: pages 228 far left, 228 third left
*Friedrich Krupp GmbH, Duisburg, Germany: page 229 top
*General Electric Company: pages 244 below, 327 right
*Great Northern Railway: pages 47 top right, 95 below left, 102, 265 above
*Gulf Oil Company: page 30 top
*Hawker Siddeley, Canada: page 360 both
*Holloway College: page 60
Hsinhua News Agency: page 335 above left and right
*Illinois Central Railroad: page 241 below right
Image Select, London, © Andrew Rapacz: page 231
Image Select: page 91
*Indian National Railways, Delhi: page 65 above
*Italian State Railways: pages 33 top left and bottom left and right, 64 top left, 103 below, 200 both, 423 both
*J. Dunn: page 396
J.M. Jarvis: page 108 above and below left
Japanese National Tourist Office: pages 398 below, 399
*Krauss-Maffei AG: pages 122 above, 124 right, 128 both
*Library of Congress: pages 29 top left, 49 top right
*London Transport: page 57 above

*Mack Trucks Inc.: page 166 below left
Milepost: pages 90, 126 below
*Milwaukee Road: pages 56 right, 264 above
*Missouri Pacific Railroad: pages 112 above right, 199 right
*National Gallery of Art, Washington, D.C.: pages 6–7
*National Library of Australia: pages 66 both, 156 left
*National Railway Museum, York, England: page 24 top left
*Nelson Gallery, Atkins Museum: page 28 top
*Netherlands State Railways: pages 345 below, 361 below, 390 above far left
*New York, New Haven & Hartford Railroad: page 322
*New Zealand Railway and Locomotive Society: pages 104–105 below, 105 above left, 106 below, 107 below, 177 top right, 178 top, 310 below, 311 both
*Norfolk & Western Railway Co., Virginia: page 218 below left
*Northern Pacific Railroad: pages 47 top left, 48 below, 51 below, 89 above right, 93 below, 137 below, 138 left, 158, 159 below, 198, 199 left
*Norwegian State Railways, Oslo: page 344
*Novosti: pages 125 left, 126 above

*Österreichische Galerie: page 58
©P.B. Whitehouse: pages 201 all, 202 both, 203 right, above and below, 204 right, 205 both, 236
Pilatus Railway, Lucerne: prints from JG Moore Collection, London: page 62 top left and centre
*Portuguese State Railways: pages 214 below left and right, 215 top left and right, 355 above
Québec Cartier Mining Co: transparency from the J.G. Moore Collection: page 221 below
*Queensland Government Railways: page 304 below
©Railfotos, Millbrook House Limited, Oldbury, W. Midlands, England: pages 68, 70–71, 77, 78 below, 79 below (2nd from left), 85 below left, 95 above, 96, 97 above right, below left, 98 all, 99 above, 100 both, 101 above right and below, 103 above, 104 above, 105 below right, 108 below right, 109, 113 below, 114 both, 115 both, 116 above, 118 left, 120, 124 left, 125 right, 127 both, 129 both, 130, 131, 132–133 (P. Harris), 135, 138 right, 139, 140 all, 141, 143 right, 144, 145, 146 top right, 147 right, 148, 150 top, 156 right, 160, 161 top left, 164, 165 left, 169 below, 170 below left, 175 top, 178 below left, 179

both, 180, 181, 182, 184 top left and below, 190, 192–193, 204 left, 206 top right, 207 both, 208, 209 both, 210, 211, 214 top, 215 below, 219, 222 top, 223, 224, 225 top, 226, 228 above, 230 left, 232, 237 both, 253 both, 254–255, 256, 257, 264 below, 265 below, 266 all, 267 both, 268, 269, 270, 271 both, 272 both, 274, 275 both, 276, 277, 278, 279 all, 280, 281 both, 282 both, 283 both, 285, 288, 289, 291 right, 292, 294, 299, 300, 305, 306 both, 307, 308, 309, 312, 313 both, 314–315, 348 below, 349, 350 left, 352 above, 353 above, 368, 369 both. H. Ballantine: pages 318–319, 325, 328, 330, 332, 333 both, 334, 336, 337, 338, 339, 340 both, 342, 343 both, 348 top, 351, 362, 363 both. P.J. Howard: pages 356, 357 both, 367 both, 371, 372, 373 both, 374 both, 375, 376, 377. G.W. Morrison: pages 321, 329, 331, 335 below, 341, 350 right, 364, 365. J.B. Snell: page 370, 384, 385, 390 below, 391 right above and below, 393 right, 394, 395 left (P. J. Howard), 397 above (E. Talbot), 404 (P. J. Robinson), 428–429, 430
*Santa Fe Railway: pages 36 below, 48 top left, 49 top left, 99 below, 111 both, 112 below left, 113 top right, 168, 171 right, 176 left

Santa Fe Railway: print from the J.G. Moore Collection: page 239 top
*Science Museum, London: page 16
*SNCF: pages 123, 163 below right, 183 both, 185 below, 186 both, 286 above and below right, 287, 290, 291 left, 293 both, 380–381, 382, 383, 390 above centre right, 392, 393 left, 412, 413, 414, 415 above left and right, 416 both, 417 both, 418, 419 all, 420, 421 all, 422
*South African Railways: pages 295 all, 296, 297, 298 both
*Southern Pacific Transportation Co.: page 43 top left
*Southern Pacific Railroad: pages 86 above left, 89 above left, 390 above centre left
*Southern Railway: pages 178 below right, top of 184–185
*Swiss Federal Railways: pages 286 above left, 327 left
*Swiss National Tourist Office, Zürich: page 31 top right
*Union Pacific Railroad Museum: pages 39 bottom left, 45 top left, 46 below, 55 below, 73 below, 93 top, 110, 150 below right, 151 left, 162, 166 below right, 217 below, 239 below, 243, 247 below
Union Pacific Railroad: print from the J.G. Moore Collection, London: pages 194–195, 197

*U.S. Library of Congress: page 196
*Vancouver Rapid Transport: pages 346 and 347 all
*VIA Rail, Canada: page 361 above, 410, 411 both
*Victorian Railways: page 67
*Western Australia Government Railways: page 310 above left and right
*Westrail, Perth: page 225 below
*Wuppertaler Stadtwerke: page 316
*York County Historical Society: page 26 top right
York Trailer: page 227 below

* Prints/transparencies through Military Archive & Research Services, Lincolnshire, England.